Hometown Memories . . .

School Days
and
Farm Chores

Tales from the Good Old Days in Northwestern Minnesota

A TREASURY OF 20TH CENTURY MEMORIES

OTHER BOOKS FROM HOMETOWN MEMORIES

Claremont Tales	**Taylorsville Tales**	**Burke County Tales**
Catawba County Tales	**Cleveland County Tales**	**Blue Ridge Tales**
Foothills-Piedmont Tales	**Memorable Tales of the Smokies and Blue Ridge Mountains**	
Caldwell County Tales	**Albemarle Tales**	**Lincolnton Tales**
Montgomery Tales	**Lee County Tales**	**Rowan County Tales**

Cold Biscuits and Fatback and other Richmond County Tales
Skinnydipping in the Mule Trough and Other Rockingham County Tales
Lunch in a Lard Bucket and Other Cabarrus County Tales
Rooster in a Milkwell and other Moore County Tales
It Always Rains When Old Folks Die and other Tales from Davidson and Randolph County
A Prayer for a Baby Goat and other Tales from Alamance County
The Mill Village and the Miracle Bicycle and other Tales from Gaston County
Wilmington Tales
Guilford County Tales
Asheville Tales
The Class of '47 Was Me and other Tales along the North Carolina Coast
The Elegant Tarpaper Shack and other Tales from the Heartland of North Carolina
Outhouse Spiders and Tin Tub Baths—Tales from the Blue Ridge Mountains
Wringer Washers and Ration Stamps—Tales from Forsyth County
Front Porch Stories, Back Porch Bathrooms —Tales from Alexander, Davie, Iredell, Rowan, and Yadkin Counties
Crank Victrolas and Wood Cook Stoves —Tales from Green, Lenoir, Pitt, and Wayne Counties
Mules, Mud and Homemade Soap —Tales from Anson, Stanly and Union Counties
Life in the Good Old Days in Alamance, Caswell, and Rockingham Counties
Life in the Good Old Days in Catawba, Lincoln, and Gaston Counties
Life in the Good Old Days in Buncombe and Henderson Counties
Moonshine and Blind Mules and other Western North Carolina Tales
Ain't No Bears Out Tonight and other Cabarrus County Tales
Two Holers and Model T Fords and other Randolph County Tales
Ham Biscuits and Baked Sweet Potatoes and other Montgomery, Richmond , and Scotland County Tales
Possum Hunters, Moonshine and Corn Shuck Dolls and other Tales from Wilkes County
Chasing the Ice Truck and other Tales from New Hanover County and Wilmington
Steam Whistles and Party Line Phones and other Tales from in and around Roanoke
Squirrel Gravy and Feed Sack Underwear—Tales from the Tennessee Mountains
Miners' Lamps and Cold Mountain Winters—Tales from Southwest Virginia
Cold Outhouses and Kerosene Lamps—Tales from Southeastern Ohio
Coal Camps and Castor Oil—Tales from Southern West Virginia
Brush Brooms and Straw Ticks—Tales from Northwest Georgia
Dust Storms and Half Dugouts—Tales from the Upper Panhandle of Texas
Lessons by Lamplight—Tales from Southeastern Kentucky
Frozen Laundry and Depression Soup—Tales from Upstate New York
Paper Dolls and Homemade Comforts—Tales from Northwestern Virginia
One-Room Schoolin'—Tales from Central West Virginia
Cow Chips in the Cook Stove—Tales from the Lower Panhandle of Texas
Moonshine and Mountaintops—Tales from Northeast Tennessee
When We Got Electric…—Tales from Northwest West Virginia
Outside Privies and Dinner Pails—Tales from Southwest Iowa
Milking the Kickers—Tales from Southwest Oklahoma
Rolling Stores and Country Cures—Tales from Northeast Alabama
Penny Candy and Grandma's Porch Swing—Tales from North Central Pennsylvania
Rumble Seats and Lumber Camps—Tales from Northern Michigan
Lye Soap and Sad Irons—Tales from Northwest Missouri

Almost Heaven—Tales from Western West Virginia
Hobos and Swimming Holes—Tales from Northern Wisconsin
Saturday Night Baths and Sunday Dinners—Tales from Northwest Iowa
Sod Houses and The Dirty Thirties—Tales from Northwest and North Central Kansas
Coal Oil Lamps and Cattle in the Crops— Tales from Northern and Mountain West Idaho
Morning Chores and Soda Fountains—Tales from The Texas Hill Country
County Schools and Classic Cars—Tales from Northeast Iowa
Dust Storm Days and Two-Holers—Tales from Southwest and South Central Kansas
Wood Fire Saunas and Iron Mines—Tales from Michigan's Upper Peninsula
Kerosene Lamps and Grandma's Washboard—Tales from Northeastern Missouri
Picture Shows and Five Cent Moon Pies—Tales from North Carolina's Blue Ridge Mountains and Foothills
Corncob Fuel and Cold Prairie Winters—Tales from Eastern and Northeastern South Dakota
Filling Stations, Shine, and Sorghum Molasses—Tales from The Tennessee West Highland Rim
Down in the Holler—Tales from Southwestern Virginia
Monday Washdays and Outhouse Roosters—Tales from West Virginia's Eastern Panhandle and also Northwestern Maryland
Party Line "Rubberneckers"—Tales from Southwest and South Central Wisconsin
Tumbleweed Feed and Gopher Trapping for Pocket Money—Tales from Southeast and South Central North Dakota
Willow Whistles and Barefoot Summer Days—Tales from Southeast Kansas
Hitch Up the Horses We're Going to Town—Tales from North Central Michigan
Pie Suppers and Wind Up Record Players—Tales from Southwest Missouri
Victory Gardens and Long Handled Dippers—Tales from Southwest Minnesota
Wind Chargers and Syrup Dinner Pails—Tales from Southern South Dakota
Swimming Pits and Tire Tube Sledding—Tales from Southeastern Ohio
Iron Wash Kettles and Peddling Wagons—Tales from Southwest Kentucky
Company Script Cards and Battery Radios—Tales from Southern West Virginia
Threshing Rings and Chalkboard Lessons—Tales from Central Wisconsin
Rabbit Tobacco and Mountain Farms—Tales from The Tennessee Mountains
Field Mules and Buttermilk Cornbread—Tales from Northeast Georgia
Harvest Recess and Picker Shacks—Tales from Northern and Downeast Maine
Green Stamps and The Wringer Washer—Tales from Northwestern Illinois
Drive-In Movies and General Stores—Tales from Northeastern Kansas
Soddies and Outdoor Tillies—Tales from Central Nebraska
Coal Miners and Mountaineers—Tales from Central West Virginia
Silo-Filling Feasts and Sunday Chicken—Tales from Northwestern Pennsylvania
Flour Sack Dresses and Victory Stamps—Tales from Roanoke and The New River Valley of Virginia
Keep the Hoe Sharp and The Shotgun Loaded—Tales from The Texas Upper Panhandle
Blizzard Banks and Buggy Trips—Tales from Southwestern and South Central New York

At Hometown Memories, our mission is to save and share the memories of days gone by... before they are lost forever. As of this publication, we have created 102 books of memories, and saved and shared over 25,000 stories and 13,000 pictures. We hope you enjoy them!

Hometown Memories . . .

School Days and Farm Chores
Tales from the Good Old Days in Northwestern Minnesota

A TREASURY OF 20TH CENTURY MEMORIES
Compiled and edited by Todd Blair and Karen Garvey

HOMETOWN MEMORIES, LLC
Hickory, North Carolina

School Days and Farm Chores

Publisher: Todd Blair
Lead Editor: Karen Garvey
Design and Graphic Arts Editor: Karen Garvey and Laura Montgomery
Marketing Research Director: Laura Montgomery
Office Services Assistants: Laura Montgomery and Tim Bekemeier
Warehouse Manager: Tim Bekemeier
Assistant Editors: Monica Black, Lisa Hollar, Danis Allison, Amanda Jenkins, Aubrey Rogers, Reashea Montgomery, and Tiffany Canaday

ISBN 978-1-940376-39-4
Copyright © 2016

All rights reserved by Hometown Memories, LLC and by the individuals who contributed articles to this work. No part of this work may be reproduced in any form, or by any means, without the written permission of the publisher or the individual contributor. Exceptions are made for brief excerpts to be used in published reviews.

Published by

Hometown Memories, LLC
2359 Highway 70 SE, Suite 112
Hickory, N. C. 28602
(877) 491-8802

Printed in the United States of America

Acknowledgements

To those Northwestern Minnesota folks (and to those few who "ain't from around here") who took the trouble to write down your memories and send them to us, we offer our heartfelt thanks. And we're sure you're grateful to each other because, together, you have created a wonderful book.

To encourage participation, the publisher offered cash awards to the contributors of the most appealing stories. These awards were not based upon writing ability or historical knowledge, but rather upon subject matter and interest. The winners were: Cecilia M. Plante of Crookston, MN; Lloyd Gran of Erskine, MN; and Connie S. of Bagley, MN. We would also like to give honorable mention to the contributions from Michael Holst of Crosslake, MN and Rose N. Taylor of Minneapolis, MN. The cash prizewinner for the book's cover photo goes to Jean Koppes of Staples, MN (you'll find their names and page numbers in the table of contents). Congratulations! It was extremely difficult to choose these winners because every story and picture in this book had its own special appeal.

Associate Editors

Carl Dahlquist
Cindy (Pesola) Fox
Mary Jean Gust
Dorothy Hartel
Marlyss Rivard Hernandez
Jill J. Holm
Fern Jackson
Joan Johnson
Jean Koppes
Richard E. Koppes
Alexander G. Kovach
Helen Goldthorpe LeClaire
Darlene Leonard
Virginia (Wilcowski) Long
Roger H. Majesk
Lorraine D. Niemea
Marie Schildt
Norma Sims
Marilyn Kern (Robert) Swanson
Melinda K. Taylor
Rubelle Towne
Irene Twist
Tom Twist
Howard Tyrrell
Lana Violette
Robert Weiland

INTRODUCTION

We know that most folks don't bother to read introductions. But we do hope you (at least eventually) get around to reading this one. Here's why:

First, the creation of these books is in its seventh generation after we took over the responsibilities of Hometown Memories Publishing from its founders, Bob Lasley and Sallie Holt. After forty nine books, they said goodbye to enjoy retirement, and each other. Bob and Sallie had a passion for saving these wonderful old tales from the good old days that we can only hope to match. We would love to hear your thoughts on how we are doing.

Second—and far more important—is the who, what, where, when, why and how of this book. Until you're aware of these, you won't fully enjoy and appreciate it.

This is a very unusual kind of history book. It was actually written by 217 Minnesota old-timers and not-so-old-timers who remember what life was really like back in the earlier years of the 20th century in Northwestern Minnesota. These folks come from all walks of life, and by voluntarily sharing their memories (which often include their emotions, as well), they have captured the spirit and character of a time that will never be seen again.

Unlike most history books, this one was written from the viewpoint of people who actually experienced history. They're familiar with the tribulations of the Great Depression; the horrible taste of castor oil; "outdoor" plumbing; party line phones; and countless other experiences unknown to today's generation.

We advertised all over Northwestern Minnesota to obtain these stories. We sought everyday folks, not experienced authors, and we asked them to simply jot down their memories. Our intention was by no means literary perfection. Most of these folks wrote the way they spoke, and that's exactly what we wanted. To preserve story authenticity, we tried to make only minimal changes to written contributions. We believe that an attempt at correction would damage the book's integrity.

We need to include a few disclaimers: first, we asked for names because we think names make stories better. However, important names are missing in some stories. Several folks revealed the names of their teachers, neighbors, friends—even their pets and livestock—but left out the names of some important characters. Second, many contributors did not identify dates or names in pictures or make corrections to their first draft copies. We're sure this resulted in many errors, but we did the best we could. Third, each contributor accepts full responsibility for his or her submission and for our interpretation of requested changes. Fourth, because some of the submitted photographs were photocopied or "computer printed," their quality may be very poor. And finally, because there was never a charge, "fee," or any other obligation to contributors to have their material included in this book, we do not accept responsibility for any story or other material that was left out, either intentionally or accidentally.

We hope you enjoy this unique book as much as we enjoyed putting it together.

The Hometown Memories Team
August 2016

TABLE OF CONTENTS

The Table of Contents is listed in alphabetical order by the story contributor's last name.

To search for stories by the contributor's hometown and year of birth, see Index A and B beginning on page 277.

James B. Allen	99	Jacob Efta	26
Kathleen Anderson	252	Maynard Embretson	183
Janyce Bakken	30	Marie Engen	64
Martha Wilkowski Barclay	205	Donna M. Erickson	96
Dan Bartsch	76	James Evans	202
S. James Berg	69	Janice Knight Evensen	60
Alice Bergeron	175	Dave Fastenow	168
Michelle Bickford	43	Catherine Fieldseth	223
Carol Birkeland	95	Joyce Flermoen	108
Gary Bjorstrom	269	Betty Flora	203
Andy Boessel	98	Jinny Foldoe	83
Debbie (Bahr) Braaten	245	Cindy (Pesola) Fox	192
Arlis Bresnahan	56	Harold Freyholtz, Jr.	97
Carolee Bruder	80	Jim Frick	38
Richard Bullock	97	June E. Gartner	118
Jack Burt	131	Shirley Gillan	163
Marvelyn M. Burtwick	129	Thomas H. Gilmore	157
Mic and Deborah "Blanche" Buschette	180	Chris Wahlberg Goodson	72
Scott Cameron	161	Dennis Gordon	47
Sandra Carlson	128	Lloyd Gran	17
Sarah Carson	126	A. Beth Grandstrand	213
Hazel Cartier	42	Peter Donald Gravdahl	67
Heidi Lamb Castle	112	Darlene Greendahl	77
Donald W. Coil	250	Gordon Greniger	156
Marilyn Dahl	136	Sister Mary Jean Gust	116
Harvey Dahline	148	Tim Gust	186
Darlene Davidson	155	Allan R. Gustafson	50
Ginny Davis	261	Carole Hagen	247
LoAnn DelGrande	255	Violet Hagen	53
Donovan Diekow	158	LaVerne Halverson	99
Patrick T. Doll	117	Marilyn Hansel	242
Peggy Rattei Donahe	54	Bertina Hanson	53
Judy Drewes	199	Joyce E. Hanson	248
Karen Ann Rhen Duczeminskyj	144	Patricia Berg Hanson	130
Ethelmae Duenow	265	Nancy Dahlquist Harris	102
Mark Edman	242	Dorthy Hartel	160

Name	Page	Name	Page
Gary D. Hartel	260	Elizabeth Anderson Lindsay	57
Jacob Harvala	125	Virginia Wilcowski Long	103
Sandy Henrickson	137	Lisa A. Lundquist	128
Andrea Hepola	82	Duane Lysne	167
Marlyss Rivard Hernandez	104	Elmer Maciejewski	195
J. Sharon Hertle	138	Andrea Mackey	107
Constance Hinnenkamp	235	Roger H. Majesk	179
Josiah Hoagland, Sr.	133	Doug Maki	101
Betty Holm	25	Alta Mandt	228
Jill J. Holm	189	Marie Marte	185
David G. Holmbeck	80	David McKeever	184
Michael Holst	22	Evelyn A. McKeever	71
Clarence Horsager	110	Glennys Medenwaldt	127
Jerry Huebsch	46	Clifton Melby	158
Thomas Huebsch	164	Ethel Mindermann	110
Fern Jackson	98	Kathryn Goligowski Motl	248
Sharon Jackson	153	LaDelle Neal	135
Lynn M. Jeffers	60	Pat Nelson	213
Arlene Jenkins	134	Helen Nemzek	97
Elden Johnson	246	George Newton	126
Joan Johnson	45	Lorraine D. Niemela	129
LaRayne Johnson	196	Dennis E. Nordstrom	64
Ruth Johnson	102	Dennis O'Gorman	114
Richard Allen Julseth	176	Barbara Olson	66
Delores Kading	267	Eileen Olson	85
Kay Keller	198	Shelia R. L. Olson	156
Betty (Laznicka) Kelly	257	Audrey J. Orlando	253
Cynthia L. King	93	Edward Pavek	253
Nancy Pepin Kjeldahl	89	Cindy Pazdernik	74
Carol M. Kofstad	66	Marlene Pedersen	212
Jean Koppes	24	Bette Peterson	226
Richard Koppes	45	Patricia Peterson	224
Darlene Koropatnicki	211	Cecilia Merschman Plante	15
Alexander Kovach	184	Frances Paul Prussner	166
Tom R. Kovach	200	Kenneth Raap	219
Violet Kramer	216	Janice (Olson) Ramsey	215
Karl Kuebelbeck	63	Sandra Renollette	107
Helen Kuester	43	Tim Renollette	111
Theresa Kunze	71	Delores M. Richter	170
Helen Goldthorpe LeClaire	249	Connie (Strandlien) Riewer	20
Gerald Lenk	215	Jeanne Roberts	63
Darlene Leonard	171	Robert Ronning	231
Ardell Nyhus Lewis	59	Vergene L. Routhe	263
Bernard Lewis	61	Nancy (George) Rudd	91
Elsie Olson Lindgren	132	Thomas Salomonsen	76

Angeline Sande	183
Carol J. Sayres	264
Marie Schildt	155
Mary Lou Meers Schwagerl	150
Andrea Searancke	122
Francis Seifert	207
Connie Sell	86
Doris Selzler	184
Joan Sethre	69
Tom Shaughnessy	98
John Sherack	251
Tina Siems	182
Norma Sims	222
Clarence Sindelir	54
Delores D. Smith	127
Lavonne Smith	242
Gaylord H. Solem	236
Grace Sonstegard	70
Jeffrey D. Sorenson	44
David Steinhorst	79
Mary Lu Stephanie	49
Marlene Mattila Stoehr	40
Ronald D. Stork	272
James L. Swanson	142
Marilyn Kern (Robert) Swanson	225
Melinda K. Taylor	44
Merlaine Taylor	254
Rose Niemela Taylor	24
Mabel Tesch	197
James R. Thompson, M.D.	157
Daniel Thonn	33
Jill A. Torgerson	220
Lawrence Torske	63
RuBelle Towne	239
Irene Bromenshenkel Trisko	29
Lorraine Trout	234
Irene Twist	208
Pat Twist	259
Paul Twist	218
Tom Twist	216
Howard Tyrrell	35
Mary Ann Uselman	123
Daniel R. Vandergon	224
Lana Violette	188
Leonard Vonasek	120
Helen Wagner	214
Robert Weiland	174
Henry Wieland	243
Pauline Wilcowski	190
Joanne Williams	100
Keith H. Winger	169
Mavis Winger	233
Gaylan Witt	131
Shirley Worth	143
Nancy Zondlo	204
Index A (Hometown)	277
Index B (Year of Birth)	283

The Tales...

True stories intentionally left just as the contributor wrote them.

Living in Minnesota
By Cecilia Merschman Plante of Crookson, Minnesota
Born 1931

Cissy was the fourth child born to a Minnesota family. Born in 1931, her parents were not very excited about having a new baby. It was the Depression years. The stock market crashed in 1929. From 1930 to 1933, industrial stocks lost 80% of their value. From 1929 to 1932, about 11,000 U.S. banks failed. Statistics scarcely convey the distress of millions of people who lost jobs, savings, and homes. Agriculture distress was intense—farm prices fell by 53% from 1929 to 1932.

Living on a small farm the Merschman family was able to provide the most of their food with cattle, pigs, chickens, and ducks. In the summer, gardening provided food for canning and preservation for long winter months. There wasn't much money for other staples and clothing. Cissy's mother Gina sewed and remade clothing from used clothing for the children. She also did some sewing for neighbors who were not as handy with a sewing machine. The family had to ration the wear of their shoes. The children ran barefoot all summer, only wearing shoes for church and when the weather got cold.

To brighten the event of a fourth child was the fact that she was a girl, the first girl in the family. Babies were then born at home with the assistance of a doctor from a nearby small Minnesota town. It was February, but an early thaw, so the roads were muddy. They were concerned as to whether the doctor would be able to get there without too much difficulty. The doctor made it, but Gina had a difficult delivery. The little girl had trouble taking her first breath. The spank on the bottom did not make her gasp for that first breath. Seeing the baby starting to turn blue, Doctor Larson decided to shock her into breathing by dipping her from warm water into cold water. That brought results.

There were a lot of chores to do on a farm in the '30s and '40s. In the country, modern conveniences were not yet available. Wood and water had to be hauled in. In the summer, water was collected in a rain barrel so they would have soft water for washing their hair and final rinse of laundry. Sometimes they would have to go to the pond for water if there had not been enough rainfall. In the winter, they collected snow and put it in a boiler on a stove to melt for washing clothes or taking baths. It took lots and lots of snow. The clothes were washed in a gas-powered washing machine that had an agitator for swishing the clothes around inside the machine to cleanse them and a wringer that Gina had to push the clothes through to squeeze out the water.

Cissy and her brothers

Cissy's brother, Leroy

There were two rinse tubs. The last rinse tub had bluing in it so the white clothes would look whiter.

Writing these memoirs bring back a lot of memories. Writing about the collecting rain in the rain barrel reminds Cissy of the song they learned in the elementary grades. It went like this:

*Playmate, come out and play with me
and bring your dollies three.
Climb up my apple tree.
Shout down the rain barrel.
Slide down the cellar door,
and we'll be jolly friends forever more.
I'm sorry playmate, I cannot play with you.
My dolly's got the flu. Boo-hoo-hoo-hoo-hoo-hoo!
Ain't got no rain barrel! Ain't got no cellar door.
but we'll be jolly friends forever more.*

It wasn't all work and no play. The Merschman brothers built a playhouse over a pond south of the garden. They built a boardwalk out to the house they built on stilts. Many summer days were spent out in the playhouse. The playhouse was located near some berry trees: chokecherry, pin cherry, June berry, as well as wild raspberry and wild strawberry. Therefore, they had those edibles to eat in their playhouse. They were never bored. They always found something to do.

In the summer months, the children played in the dirt by the house making roads with their little toy cars and trucks. Some days they took old tires and ran pushing them up and down the driveway. In the evening after dark, they would chase and catch fireflies. They would rub the fireflies onto their clothing to see their clothing glimmer. When the neighbor kids came over they would play kick-the-tin-can, anti-I-over, hide-and-seek, or softball. As the children grew older, they played board games, checkers, and Chinese checkers. They played card games—rummy, 7-up, hearts and whist to name a few. Marbles was another activity.

It was ripe plum time and as usual Cissy was traipsing along with her brothers and a couple of neighbor boys. The boys were picking plums and putting what they didn't eat into their pockets. Cissy was dressed in a sleeveless summer dress with no pockets. She didn't know where to put her extra plums. She asked, "Where can I put my plums?" Her brothers said, "Put them in your bloomers." Well, Cissy's bloomers had elastic around the legs, so that's a pretty good idea thought the little almost four-year-old Cissy. Into her bloomers they went. They stayed there okay, but when she fell on her butt, she squished them. OOOOOOPS! She was upset that she had squished all of her plums. She went crying to her mother about what happened. Gina hugged her, laughed, and consoled the crying Cissy:

*I love you little!
I love you big!*

Cissy and her bantam chicken

I love you like a little pig!

The Merschman children were repeating little love jingles. Cissy tells her mother, "I love you with all my heart." Then she turns to her dad and says, "I love you with all my gizzard!" Everyone laughs, but Cissy didn't know what was so funny. She didn't know that people didn't have gizzards. (She had seen the gizzards when they butchered chickens.)

The children were growing up when the U.S. became involved in the war. By 1959, Hitler had ignited World War II and initiated his policy of exterminating Jews from Germany and other European countries. About six million Jews were killed under Hitler's policy. Roughly, 45 million people, civilians and combatants, had been killed by the time hostilities ceased in 1945, the price the United States and its Allies paid for halting German and Japanese aggression.

Because of the war effort the United States, citizens had to put up with rationing of certain staples, such as gas, sugar, aluminum, rubber, etc. Each family received ration stamps with which to make their purchases. Cissy remembers helping the war effort by making balls of aluminum foil from candy and gum wrappings, cigarette packages and wherever aluminum could be found. They would wrap cord string into huge balls. There were collection places in town to take these items.

During the war, there would be blackout nights. That meant everyone had to blow out their lights and cities had to shut off all electric lights. This was to practice caution should enemy planes fly over—so life would not be seen.

December 7, 1941, Japan brought the United States into the war with its attack on Pearl Harbor. First Cissy's uncles enlisted to serve their country and as soon as Cissy's brothers reached the age of 18, they enlisted, also. Fortunately, they all returned from the fighting war. Cissy's brother LeRoy had been wounded while serving in Okinawa and was considered 100% disabled. The people in the United States had been very fortunate that the war ended and did not reach U.S. soil.

There was a lot of Whoopy-doo when V-E Day and V-J Day arrived. Big celebrations were held in all U.S. cities and communities.

God bless America!

Da "Teef"
By Lloyd Gran of Erskine, Minnesota
Born 1948

Years ago when I was growing up on the farm in Polk County, our closest neighbor living to the east of us was Almer Anderson. He was elderly, had a shock of white hair, and was a dried up little old man, but he had a sharp mind and an insatiable interest in mechanical things. When he was 95 years old, his knees started bothering him, enough so that it was hard for him to get in and out of a car. Therefore, to get around, he bought himself a Honda ATV three-wheeler with a windshield. At the time, he was the oldest registered owner of an ATV in the State of Minnesota. He eventually lived to be 100 years old, staying on the farm until just a few months before his death in a nursing home.

I used to enjoy going over to his farm and visiting with him when I was a kid. He would tell me stories of how he ran a trap line in the morning when he was a kid, near the turn of the century, on the way to the country school he attended, and how he ran a trap line in the opposite direction in the afternoon on the way home. He saved the money he made from trapping to pay his tuition for engineering school in Crookston because he had seen the big impressive steam locomotives that the railroads used on their prairie runs and he wanted to become a train engineer. As part of the requirements for graduation, he had to construct a small-scale steam engine from scratch. I mean, literally from scratch, as he had to make all the parts on a lathe and get it to run. Somehow, he ended up farming without ever becoming a train engineer, but he used that steam engine—the one that he had made in school—to pump water on the farm for many years.

He used to tell me how, every fall, he and his brother would each buy a case of shotgun shells (500 shells) and hunt prairie chickens. One fall, between the two of them, they shot 527 prairie chickens. They didn't miss many, but when they did, it was made up for by several shots where they got more than one prairie chicken with each shot. Those birds were what fed his parent's large family through the winter. He would shake his head at the retelling, becoming apologetic because it was "overshooting" like that which led to the near extinction of the prairie chickens in our parts. In all actuality, it probably was the changing landscape from the original prairie grasslands to intensive farming practices that did it.

One of my favorite stories that he told me was the one about the time he caught da 'Teef' (as he pronounced it) stealing wood from him.

Being on the edge of the prairie, it was common practice to buy land a little further east that had some trees on it for much needed building materials, fence posts, and most important of all, heating wood to burn during the long, cold Northern Minnesota winters. Almer wasn't married at the time, so he bought an 80-acre parcel a couple miles away that had about 40 acres of woods on it. During the winter, between the morning and evening milkings, he would take a team of horses and a bobsleigh and spend the day in the woods on his 80, cutting the next year's wood supply. He always made a road into the middle of the woods and did his cutting there, as the woods still standing around the outside gave the resting team shelter from the cold north winds that seemingly blew all the time. Of course, it was all hand labor back then, using an axe and crosscut saws to cut down the trees and saw them to cob length. Then he would use wedges and splitting mauls to split the cobs into stove wood pieces. He could cut more stove wood in a full day in the woods than would fit in the bob sleigh, so he would stack the excess in a pile to be hauled home later.

In the dead of the long cold winter, one dark moonless night just before a storm was approaching, he heard his dog start to bark. Going outside to investigate, he heard the sound of a team and sleigh passing by his place (in a westerly direction) on what passed for a road in those days. He thought that was strange, because, at the time, the road past his place led to nowhere except to his 80 acres where he was cutting wood. There was no one living in that direction at the time; therefore, there was no need for anyone to travel that road. He shrugged his shoulders and went back to bed, to arise in the morning to find the world enveloped in a full-scale blizzard. It was many days before he got dug out and returned to the woods to cut more wood. When he did, he discovered that his pile of surplus stove wood was considerably smaller than he remembered. Someone must have loaded up a load and stolen it. The deed probably occurred the night he heard the team and sleigh go by his place right before the storm struck, which hid the tracks of da "Teef."

Almer went back to cutting wood again and soon had a decent surplus pile built up in the woods. One night, just before another big storm hit, he again heard his dog bark and heard a team and sleigh going past his farm in the dark of night. Again, after the storm was over, he discovered that his woodpile in the woods had been diminished.

He sat and thought a long time about who could have done such a thing and finally narrowed his suspicions down to a lazy bachelor farmer who lived in a shack several miles to the west on the open prairie and had no woods to cut wood in. He never seemed to have a sizeable woodpile at his place as most people did. Other people who lived west on the prairie sometimes cut wood further southeast of Almer's place in an area the called the "swamp," which actually was state land; there wasn't supposed to be any woodcutting there, but the locals figured that the Governor wasn't going to ski out to the swamp in the middle of the winter to check on his woods, so they cut wood there anyway.

Almer skied back into the swamp on the trail of a wolf one day and while there, checked to see if it was possible that the bachelor guy could have been cutting wood. There was no evidence of any recent woodcutting in the swamp, so he ruled that out. He figured that da "Teef" waited for an eminent storm to approach, then cut across the open prairie with an empty sleigh to Almer's woods and loaded up a load of stove wood. He then used the cover of darkness to hide his trip home, traveling the road because his sleigh had a heavy load on. Later, the raging storm would cover his tracks and tracking him down would be impossible.

Almer went to town and purchased a box of .22 caps. Now, today, we buy .22 long rifle shells mostly, but back in those years, you could also buy .22 longs, which were less powerful than the long rifles, and you could buy .22 shorts, which were even less powerful than the longs. .22 caps were very short, low-powered cartridges, less powerful even than the shorts and used mainly in shooting galleries at the country fairs where hotshot nimrods used to impress their girlfriends by picking off moving wooden ducks in the shooting galleries to win teddy bears for them.

He returned to his wood cutting project and before he left for the day, he drilled small holes in random pieces of stove wood and inserted a .22 cap shell in each hole, topped off with a twig broken off flush to camouflage his deed. Then he waited for the approach of the next storm, and sure enough, his dog barked in the middle of the dark night again, as a team and sleigh passed by his place once more.

After checking to see that his wood had been stolen again, Almer skied over to the suspect's (da "Teef's") shack. Da "Teef" invited him inside and brewed up some thick black coffee on the wood-fired stove while they talked farming and politics. The talk eventually turned to wood supplies for the winter and Almer said he had been losing wood in the woods as someone had been taking it without paying for it. Da "Teef" didn't bat an eye.

Then, Almer said that sometime the party that took the wood was going to be surprised, as he had laced the pieces with .22 caps that would explode in the stove. Da "Teef" still didn't bat an eye until, suddenly, there was a loud BANG from the stove. Da 'Teef' jumped about six inches in his chair, while the stove also jumped several inches off the floor and rust and soot rained down from the overhead pipe. Da "Teef" swallowed hard and shifted uncomfortably in his chair. Just then, another BANG sounded as another .22 cap went off, followed almost immediately by a third. Da "Teef" abruptly pushed his chair back from the table, put his coffee mug to his lips, upended and drained it, got up, walked over to a rough board shelf nailed to the wall, reached into an enameled sugar jar sitting there, extracted a wad of paper money, and peeled off four one-dollar bills (which was about the going rate for four cords of wood at the time), and handed them wordlessly to Almer. Then, still saying nothing, he refilled their coffee mugs and they resumed conversing about farming things.

A short time later, Almer tendered his "gud dag," slipped his five-buckle overshoes into the leather straps on his homemade wooden skis, and laughed all the way home as he thought about how there were still 47 shells to go off sometime in the future as da "Teef" heated his shack. Da "Teef's" not knowing when they were going to go off was probably as good a punishment as could have been devised for stealing the wood in the first place.

I reckon the events in this story took place over a hundred years ago. Almer told them to me around 50 years ago. Even though the years seem to stretch out, in my mind's eye, I can still see him as clear as day, sitting alongside his kitchen table in a straight back wooden chair, his left arm laying on the table, long, thin, bony fingers tapping the red and white checkered oil cloth covering the table, while his left leg was crossed over his right at the knee. He usually wore coarse black wool trousers held up by thin suspenders over a black and white plaid wool shirt. He always had the other arm hooked over the back post of the chair at the armpit. He would sit like that and tell stories for hours, waving his right arm and hand for emphasis. I remember how, after telling this story, he uncrossed his legs, put both elbows on his knees, propped up his chin and sat and thought for a few moments, then slowly sat up and shook his head from side to side, his tousled white shock of hair swaying, as if he was still in disbelief that someone would steal from a neighbor like that.

I'm glad he took the time to tell this story to a kid back those many years ago; and because he did, now YOU, too, get to share in it.

Minnesota Farming
By Connie (Strandlien) Riewer of Bagley, Minnesota
Born 1938

I was born at home near York, North Dakota on June 21, 1938. My maternal grandmother was a midwife, so she was present, as well as a doctor. I am the youngest of six children. We were all born at home.

In October 1939, our family moved to Shevlin, Minnesota to live with my paternal grandparents and take over their farm as they retired. It must have been a houseful with our family of eight along with my grandparents and an uncle. There were only two bedrooms downstairs with a big room upstairs. That was divided with a curtain between the girls and boys beds. There was a kitchen with a large pantry, a dining room, and a room we called the parlor. There was no bathroom. My grandparents soon built a smaller house on the same farm.

We had a heating stove in the dining room along with a wood box. Sometimes we burned coal. There was a register directly above the stove to heat the upstairs. I remember taking sponge baths behind the heating stove as the rest of the house was too cold in the wintertime. In the summer, Mom would heat water on the wood cook stove and fill a washtub for our Saturday night baths. I think several of us used the same water.

At one point, my father and brothers rigged up a shower of sorts. It was a barrel filled with water and put up in the air. The water was warmed by the sun. It must have had a spigot of some sort to open up when needed to shower down on us. It was on the backside of a building for privacy. Often we would just go to the Clearwater River for a dunking. This fun was spoiled by the hungry leeches that would attach themselves to us.

When it was extremely cold, we would close off the kitchen at night. In the morning, there would be ice in the water pail that we used for drinking and cooking. A dipper hung by the water pail and we all used that for drinking, dipping it back in the water pail. Not very sanitary, but that is the way it was.

My siblings and I all slept upstairs. We would do a lot of talking after we went to bed. Then someone would say, "I'm going to say my prayers now," so we would all be quiet, assuming everyone was saying their prayers. When each of us was done, he/she would say, "Done." After we heard six "dones," we could start talking again.

I remember the excitement when we got electricity. I think I was about six years old. We got our first refrigerator when I was fourteen. Before that, we kept food cold in the pump house in cold water. We got our first telephone when I was in high school. We were on a party line, which meant that if you wanted to use the phone, you had to listen to see if anyone was already on the line. You had better not say anything on a party line you wanted to be private. Each home had a certain number of rings you had to use to reach the home you wanted. This could be three long rings, two longs and a short, etc.

My parents worked hard to provide for us. Dad's special team of horses was "Dude and Beauty." We also had a horse named Dick. Dad took special pride in his horses. Eventually he acquired an Allis Chalmers tractor to use for farm work. We had dairy cows, pigs, and chickens. My dad also raised corn, hay, and grain crops. We raised all of our potatoes for the year and we kids picked them. This was actually a fun day. They were

Connie's father, Helmer Strandlien driving the car with his parents and siblings in 1920

brought to the house and sent by a chute down to the basement, which had a dirt floor and kept very well all winter. My mother raised a big garden and did a lot of canning.

I always had chores to do, but the chore I hated most was washing eggs. It seemed there was an endless supply of eggs to wash. After washing and drying, they were put in crates and brought to the store in Shevlin to be sold. This money helped pay for other groceries we needed. The cracked eggs were kept for our own use. There was no thought about salmonella in those days. I remember often having an upset stomach; this might have had something to do with using cracked eggs.

Washing clothes was quite an ordeal. Water had to be carried into the house from the well outside and heated on the woodstove, then put into the wringer washer along with homemade soap. We had two rinse tubs; the second one would have "bluing" added to make clothes whiter. In the summer, my mother would catch rainwater in barrels for washing clothes and in the winter, she would sometimes melt snow. My brother and I liked to play in the melting snow, making tunnels etc. The clothes were hung outside to dry. In winter, they would freeze partly dry and then we would bring them in to finish drying by hanging lines in the house. My job was to drain out the water when the wash was done and carry it outside, first washing the wooden steps in the summer and then the outhouse. We tried not to waste water.

Going to church was an important part of our lives. Sometimes in the winter, we would have to take the horses and sleigh as the roads were not plowed. Mom would put flat irons in the oven to warm and wrap them in towels for us to put our feet on as well as bring blankets to cover up with. It seems it was the custom in many churches for the men and boys to sit on the left side of the church and the women and girls to sit on the right. I don't remember when this changed.

I loved threshing time. The neighbors owned a threshing machine together and helped each other out. The women always made wonderful meals as well as providing coffee breaks. I liked sitting in the grain wagon and watching the golden grain come pouring out of a chute into the wagon and the straw flying out another chute.

When it was time to butcher pigs, we knew we were in for a special treat. My brother said it was his job to slit the pig's throat and catch the blood for blood sausage (klub). He had to hurry and add snow to it so it wouldn't curdle. My mother then would add flour, salt, and salt pork and we would scoop it into cloth bags that Mom had sewn from old sheets. Then they would be tied at the top, put in boiling water, and cooked. When they were done, they would be sliced and fried in butter. I could not eat that anymore.

Potato dumplings were another special treat. They were made from ground raw potatoes and whole-wheat flour, salt, and maybe some salt pork. They were made into balls and placed in boiling water. My brother and I would sometimes race to see who could eat the most. They were HEAVY.

One incident that happened on the farm stands out in my memory. My mother and I were in the house. We had a wooden porch with about three steps, which led to an entryway. The door to the entryway was open and the door to the kitchen had a glass window in it. I looked out and saw our Holstein bull part way into the entry. Apparently, he was too big to get any further. My brother was out in the barn and we worried that the bull had hurt him before coming to the house. My mother was cooking something and crawled on her hands and knees in front of the window to move whatever it was off the stove before it would burn. She did not want the bull to see her. I ran upstairs to see if I could see out the window if the bull decided to leave. Eventually, it did. My brother was okay and was unaware of the drama that was taking place at the house. This happened about 65 years ago and I can remember it very vividly.

I attended school in Shevlin for grades one through seven. I loved going to school there. We played kickball, jump rope, jacks etc. In the winter, the janitor made a skating rink for us, which was so much fun. I used a pair of skates that were my sister's and too big for me, but I didn't care as long as I could skate. We had wonderful hot lunches and great teachers. My one big fear was going into fourth grade and having to go down the fire escape. When you got to fourth grade, you were upstairs. The fire escape was a long tube we had to slide down. We had to be ready to land on our feet instead of our butt. After the first time, I decided that was fun, also. When we advanced to eighth grade, we were bussed to Bagley for the remainder of our school years.

We did not have very many modern conveniences growing up, but I think we were in many ways better off than children growing up today. We did not have television, only the radio and neighbor kids to play with. We played softball, kickball, anti-I-over, kick the can, Captain May I, Monopoly, and many card games. I know I have many wonderful memories.

Railroad Dreams
By Michael Holst of Crosslake, Minnesota
Born 1941

As a young boy, I grew up in Staples, Minnesota. Staples was not only a small town, it was a railroad town. I was fortunate to live there before the railroad's demise – at least the way I knew it – in the era of the steam engines. That end came a few years after I graduated and moved away. I have so many memories of the railroad during my growing up years in Staples. The railroad was to the town what the mines were to Hibbing and Eveleth on the Iron Range up north. It was a way of life, the financial backbone of the community and the surrounding area. My father, my father-in-law, my uncles, and almost everyone else in my family associated with and worked for the railroad. Those who didn't work for it indirectly prospered from it in one way or another. The town lived and breathed the Northern Pacific, and later, the Burlington Northern. It was called the "Rail Hub of the Northwest" on a sign on the east end of town. My dad, with Mom and all of us eight kids in the car, would slow down and read that sign with pride each time we came into town from the east. If you talked with Dad about the railroad, you would believe that golden spike had been driven right there in Staples and not out in Utah. If you took a long, deep breath, you could literally smell the railroad.

Dad worked in the car shops repairing boxcars, and each night after school, I could hear the quitting whistle blow in the shops. I would walk the half block to the main highway that separated the town and sit on the curb, waiting on him to come walking across the tracks. He was always dirty and smelled like creosote and oil, two of the tools of his trade. He would let me carry his dinner pail the rest of the way home. There would always be a cookie or a half a piece of cake in there that he would say he "just couldn't eat." His hands were always rough and calloused, but I would put my little hand in his, and we would walk home that way. It was ten minutes of my life when I didn't have to share Dad with the rest of the family. Young boys have a way of emulating their fathers, and I was no exception. I wanted to grow up and work on the railroad.

I used to walk the tracks in the summer time and dream of driving one of those big behemoth ten wheelers across the western prairie, its whistle shrieking at every crossing and clouds of steam seemingly leaking from every orifice in its mighty steel hulk. I envisioned where I would ride just like the engineers of old, with my arm out the window, a red kerchief around my neck, my striped cap pulled tight around my head, scanning the track ahead. The smoke plume from the mighty coal-fired boiler would play out behind me, like a black ribbon, from the engine to the caboose and beyond. Then I would pull my train into the depot and watch the conductor get off and put the stool down for the passengers to get off. I would sit there looking out the window while that steel giant belched smoke and steam, and then the conductor would yell, "All aboard!" He would pick up his stool, signal me with his lantern, and we would be on our way. The huge steel wheels on the engine would spin on the steel tracks, digging for traction, and then, slowly but surely, we would pull away into the night, our whistle shrieking at every crossing.

As a kid, I used to go to the roundhouse where the giant engines slept and see the huge turntable that turned them around to go the other way. I climbed the black-timbered coal dock with its hanging bins full of coal, where they stopped for fuel and water, and dreamed of the day when I would pull under the coal bins with my engine to get refueled. I remember going to the depot on a cold winter night and watching in awe as those mighty engines spun those huge steel wheels on the cold steel tracks, trying to set the whole train in motion once more. I watched the comparable small switch engines pulling boxcars around the yards, sorting them out like merchandise on store shelves. I would put my ear on the track to hear if a train was coming and then put a copper penny down to see it flattened as the train passed by. I would go inside the depot and watch the telegraph operator clicking out messages to some faraway place. I sat in the depot on cold winter nights, mesmerized by the clatter of the telegraph operator, sitting at his desk sending messages to some faraway place, but it was that engineers' seat in that steam engine where I belonged. I went to the union picnics in Pine Grove Park and drank the free soda pop and ate hot dogs and watermelon until I was sick to my stomach, while the speeches flowed throughout the afternoon like some kind of political rally.

But time moves on, and sleek diesel engines came along. Those old giants I loved so much now lay dead and cold on a siding, until at last they were hauled away for scrap. When they died, a big part of the railroad and my dreams died with them, at least for Staples and also for me. I have a little pewter statue of a railroad man on my desk. It reminds me of my father and all of the men who found railroading a way of life in Staples. If I close my eyes, I can still see my father sitting on the back steps of our house, reaching for his watch fob as he hears the bells clanging from up by the depot. "There goes the dinky," he says. "Right on time."

A lot of trains still go through Staples today, but they have no reason to stop anymore, and they barely slow down. The diesel units that pull them now can run from coast to coast without refueling. The cabooses, too, have been done away with, and now it's mostly oil, grain cars, and container cars. The roundhouse, the coal docks, and the car shops, along with the icehouse, the water towers, and the freight depots, are all gone. Most of the tracks have long been torn up. There isn't much left that resembles the railroad town it once was.

I do go back to Staples from time to time, but most of the people I knew then now reside in Evergreen Cemetery north of town. Gone, but never forgotten, just like the railroad.

Note: the "dinky" I referred to in this story was a small two-car train that ran every day from Staples to Duluth.

An Early Morning Walk to School
By Rose Niemela Taylor of Menahga, Minnesota
Born 1918

Our log schoolhouse was District #16, two miles north of our farm. The neighbor children would walk together through the woods and fields. Sometimes the older boys would stay home to help with the farm work. We felt better when they walked with us.

Sandwiches were made from the good home-baked bread made the day before. The butter had also been churned in the large glass jar and now spread on the slices of bread. Next came pincherry jelly. All this was wrapped in wax paper and put into an empty syrup pail for our school lunch. All would be devoured at noon recess.

Next, we put on extra socks, overshoes, hat, mittens, and a long scarf to cover much of the face to keep from freezing on our long walk.

The pale sliver of the moon still hung in the western sky although dawn was beginning to break in the east The Kinnenens, Puljus, and Torvinens soon joined us Niemelas and all of us trudged down the old logging trail, saying little, saving our breath, as the cold air stung our lungs.

As our group approached a clearing, the older boys suddenly stopped.

"Hush," they whispered. "Look."

In the clearing ahead, someone had cut firewood, leaving long rungs in a pile. On this, three or four wolves were running back and forth, nipping at each other as if they were playing tag.

"What shall we do?" someone gasped. "Shall we run home?"

"No," said one of the older boys thoughtfully, "Everyone bang your lunch pails and yell as loud as you can as we run toward them. Now! Let's go!"

"Hang on tight," my sister whispered as we ran toward the wolves. My heart was beating hard and my breath became short, rapid puffs. The wolves, surprised at being caught unaware, scampered off the woodpile and disappeared into the forest.

As we hurried on to school, looking back frequently, we found the teacher and some students standing outside.

"We heard wolves howling and we wondered where you were," the teacher said, looking relieved. "Let's go inside and warm up."

Even now, 92 years later, when I think of those wolves, cold shivers of fear run up and down my spine.

My Younger Life
By Jean Koppes of Staples, Minnesota
Born 1933

I grew up on a log house with five brothers and sisters. We had no electricity or indoor plumbing or running water. My mother cooked on a wood burning stove. When we took a bath, we used a small wash dish and took a sponge bath. We had to go outdoors to the outhouse, which was very cold in the winter.

My mom sewed my dresses from printed flour sacks. She would buy more than one of the same prints.

In the summer, I would walk in the pasture and bring the cows to the barn to be milked. We milked them by hand and carried the milk to the house, where we put it in the separator. You had to turn the handle on the side to separate the milk from the cream. It was my job to turn the crank. Dad would tell me if I was turning it too fast or too slow.

Before we went to school in the morning, I had to help do barn chores, like feeding cows

Jean with her brother, Harold

Norma, Jean, and Phyllis on the farm

and watering them.

After chores, we walked to school. It was a mile walk. We did not wear jeans to school. We had long brown socks. Sometimes it was so cold. Our teacher was Clara Schmidt. She was really nice. Sometimes she made us a hot lunch cooked on a small Bunsen burner. Other days we brought our lunch in a dinner pail. There were twelve or fourteen kids in grades one through eight in the school.

In the summer, my sisters and I would pick blueberries. We would pick a milk pail full in an afternoon, and Mom would can them and make blueberry pie.

We had a radio that ran off from a car battery. We had a phonograph to play records on. You had to crank it up with a crank on the side of it. Mom would play the organ, and we would sing. On Sundays, our aunts and uncles and cousins would come over or we would go to their place. This is about all I remember of my younger life.

School Days were Great Days
By Betty Holm of Sauk Centre, Minnesota
Born 1925

School days, school days, how I loved school. Our school was Dettler School, District No. 32. However, I remember it as the Bluth School. It was built in 1872 in Birchdale Township and closed in 1939. My brother, Sidney, and I walked three and a half miles to the school, which had no playground because it was located at a crossroad. My father and uncle rode a donkey to the school, and my grandfather built a small shed where the donkey spent the day eating hay that was brought along with them.

I went to school there the last six weeks in the spring before I started the first grade. We had double desks, and I sat with Don Peschel, who was in a higher grade. I think Iris Woodman was the teacher. That summer the school board bought an acre of land from Mr. Bluth, which was a half mile closer to our home. They added an entryway to the south and a wood room to the north, dug a well, and built two small buildings accompanied with paths to each one.

The school had a great playground where we played kitten ball and all the winter games. New single desks were nailed to 1"x4"x8' boards so they could be moved to the side of the room for meetings. The school had a water cooler and a basin for washing dirty hands. We brought a small towel from home, which we were supposed to take home each Friday (most of the time it was forgotten). The bigger boys brought in the water with a pail, and I am sure the wastewater was thrown outside. The school board would bring the wood to school, and the boys would rank it in the wood room. We had a big stove in the northwest corner that was enclosed with a steel sheet so the heat went up. There was also a cold air vent to the north, and our feet were always cold.

We all wore long johns (mine were inherited from my brother) and cotton stockings that would not go on smoothly. If the snow was deep, my grandmother would wrap my lower legs with strips of wool that the soldiers wore during World War I. Most of us carried our lunch in syrup pails, but some students also had store bought pails. In the later years, we had paper sacks. My brother, Sidney, was a year older than me so when he started school, he would come home and teach me what he had learned that day. My first grade teacher was Mrs. Art Bluth. We did not have a flagpole but a flag stood in the corner and every morning we said the Pledge of Allegiance. Pictures of George Washington and Abraham Lincoln hung on the wall. The last hour of Friday was art class and maybe singing; each teacher had a different schedule of classes. Our last teacher was Miss Randal, and she would not allow the girls to wear jewelry or bright ribbons in their hair (what would she think of today?).

The Christmas program was the highlight of the year and what work it was for the teacher. We all knew each other's parts by the time we presented the program. About two weeks before the big night, the school board members would come and set up the stage with planks and saw horses. The mothers furnished sheets, which were strung on a wire above the stage. What fun it was getting used to walking on the stage, learning the Christmas carols, and practicing our parts for the skits. On the night of the program, everyone brought their lanterns, which were all cleaned and polished for light. We always had a Christmas tree, which we made decorations for, and it was given to the school board member who furnished the tree. I always wanted it, as we never had a Christmas tree at home.

There was a school close to us in Round Prairie named Oak Haven that my grandmother attended, whose students would come to our program, and the older students from our school would attend their program. We always made sure the programs were scheduled on different nights. Many schools would have a basket social after the Christmas program. I attended one at the Diamond School the first year I was married. It was fun!

In the fall before school started, some of the mothers would go to school with buckets, soap, scrub brushes, old towels, and hot water to scrub the windows and floor. One mother would take the curtains home to wash and iron them or replace them with new ones. It was always nice and clean when we went back to school for another year.

I do think we got a better education at that time, at least the basics. If we did not learn it the first year, we heard it each year thereafter. My geography and history are better than some of my children but I will not mention math; however, I have always done the bookwork for our farm. We had a three shelf cabinet with glass doors that rose up and slid back which was full of books and I read most of them many times. At my home, we all read books. At Christmas time, everyone got books, and we read each other's and lent them to friends. Zane Grey was a favorite, and we had quite a collection over the years.

Our school day began like most of the farm kids. In the morning, our grandparents would call us before they went to the barn to milk cows. We would get up and get ready for school, and Grandmother would come in and fix our breakfast and pack our lunches. As we got older, Sidney went to the barn and I made breakfast of pancakes and canned meat and also packed our lunches. Sidney had cheese sandwiches and I preferred mustard. Cookies or a donut were always a delight. We all ate breakfast together before going to school. School was from 9:00 a.m. until 4:30 p.m. After school, I would peel potatoes for supper, and if Grandmother was working outside, she would leave a note for what else I was to do.

I loved school and all my classmates were good friends. It was a sad day when I graduated from high school, even though we had to walk five miles each way.

Mostly It Rains On Me
By Jacob Efta of Middle Rivel, Minnesota
Born 1975

At her funeral, Mrs. Elizabeth Rantenen's eulogy described her as the richest lady in the whole world. The eulogy went on to describe that her riches were not in the form of money, but in friends and values that most people dream of attaining. This was well represented by the casket bearers who were from every social class imaginable. There was a drug addict, an alcoholic, a crippled lady and gentleman and a German war bride. Other bearers included two with doctorates degree and three with master's degrees. They ranged in age from twenty to eighty years and each and every one was a beloved friend of Mrs. Rantanen.

Elizabeth Jane Kruger Rantanen was better known as Betty Rantanen. Betty was born on October 28, 1921 to Orrin and Ruth Matthews Kruger at Wadena, Minnesota. She was a delight to her parents and grandparents as their first-born child and grandchild. This fair skinned, red haired, blue-eyed child was dressed and groomed to be a real lady, but her family soon learned this little lady was a real tomboy at heart.

Betty's parents owned a grocery store in

Deer Creek, Minnesota until the 1930s. The depression provided little money for people to buy groceries, but her kindhearted parents could never turn people away who could not pay for their food. They knew the grocery business, during the depression, would be a very bad one. The family found someone at Warren, Minnesota who would trade their farm for a grocery store. This is where Betty's life and love of the land really began. At the age of eight years, she knew she was a farmer at heart and would be one until the day she died.

Betty Rantanen was educated in the Schey School near Argyle, Minnesota. School was about a mile across the country and she either rode horseback or walked to school. She attended school eight years of her life but was self-educated by our standards. She did this by reading. Among her prized possessions was her large library of books. She has many of the classics. A number of them were signed first edition copies. Many books were on the history of the Red River Valley, farming and the wildlife and nature books she referred to on a daily basis. Her most treasured book was an 1893 copy of Don Quinote Von Der Mancha. Written in German, this large beautiful book is illustrated on every other page. Always interested in learning more, she attended the University of Minnesota, by invitation, on a special program as a senior citizen.

Betty farmed with her father on the family farm until she was married to Arne Rantanen November 11, 1945. She was of German heritage and married into a Finnish household of family members that did not speak English at home. Adapting to another culture did not pose a problem for Betty, thus creating a happy family. The couple lived with her husband's family, whom she loved dearly, until they got a farm of their own. Betty and Arne had a farm and a well-known herd of registered Brown Swiss dairy cattle. Betty managed the herd and Arne ran the large farm. The children were cared for by what farmers called hired girls but people in high-class society called nannies. Six children were born to Betty and Arne, one who died in infancy.

Arne Rantanen died in a tragic car accident in 1957, when a school bus hit Arne's pickup truck broadside. Luckily, the schoolchildren were not hurt, but Betty was left with five children from the ages of three to nine years of age. Betty decided to continue to operate the farm however this was an unorthodox task for a woman. In the 1950s, women did not have credibility or a credit rating by most standards. Farming was very difficult for Betty. Banks would not loan out large sums of money to a woman without a male co-signer and some people just plainly did not want to do business with a woman.

The late 1950s and early 1960s were wet years. This problem got worse because Betty's farm was located next to Agassiz National Wildlife Refuge, which was known as Mud Lake back then. The ducks and geese that should have been in the refuge were eating off Betty's fields. What the birds didn't eat they

Betty and Bear in 1988

Elizabeth "Betty" Rantenen in 1989

career of farming. Among these was 1988 Red River Valley Farm Woman of the Year. This contest covers both Minnesota and North Dakota. She was the only woman to receive the Minnesota State Conservation Farmer of the Year (1973.) She was one of four people to receive the state 4-H Alumni Award 1971. The award is based on lifetime achievements in 4-H and community.

Betty Rantanen was best known for her kind and generous attitude towards others. She gave of her time, talent, and money to those who could not afford it. Those people were children, the elderly, and persons with disabilities. She was known to hand over a $100 bill to someone in need, no questions asked, and she did not expect anything in return. She was an accomplished artist and gave art lessons. She didn't charge children, old people, the handicapped, or anyone who could not afford to pay for the lessons. She often drove to nursing homes to give lessons and also provided the supplies. Betty always had a soft spot for he "underdog" in life and she helped out many troubled

trampled into the mud. There was no crop left to harvest even if it would have gotten dry enough to combine. She lobbied in the State Legislature to try to get compensation or pay back for what the birds did to her crops and that of other farmers, but none ever came. The rains did not quit and Betty didn't either. This is when Betty decided, "If you can't beat 'em, join 'em."

In 1960, Betty began a supervised hunting plan or what people today would call a hunting club. With the abundance of birds on her land, this turned into a profitable enterprise. She continued with her hunting operation until she died. Betty once said in an interview, "It rains on the just and the unjust, but mostly it rains on me."

Betty was given many awards and honors for her dedication and hard work in her chosen

persons, some of whom were drug addicts and alcoholics. She went so far as to travel 200 miles a day to help a jailed inmate, out on the Huber Law, get to work and back.

Betty was well known for her herds of livestock. She has a herd of karakul sheep, which is where Persian Lamb comes from. She also had a herd of purebred Nubian goats and imported some registered Brown Swiss. She had a flock of peacocks for the "purpose of enhancement and nothing else." She loved her animals and doctored many a sick one in her house where she could care for it day and night,

Betty died unexpectedly June 16, 1990. Her funeral services were at her farm upon the land she had nurtured and loved for so many years. Her casket was placed directly behind her prized Iris plant that was in luscious bloom. The animals fenced in the front yard so they could be a part of the services. Hundreds of folding chairs and three canopies were set up on the lawn. Friends and relatives arrived with arms full of wild flowers they had picked. The service began with a light mist and midway through turned into a downpour. The service went on and everyone crowded under the canopies to finish the service. That day it rained on the just.

Growing Up On a Farm as a Young Girl
By Irene Bromenshenkel Trisko of Sauk Centre, Minnesota
Born 1931

If I had a dollar for every childhood wish that I could live in town, I would have a million dollars. I grew up on our family farm, one of many siblings. There is always work on a farm, even work a child can do, and even though I suppose the same could be true of a child growing up in town, I often wondered what there could be without a big garden to weed, geese to tend, chickens to feed, grass to mow, and much more.

Of course, there was also the fun of having animals around all the time. Cats, kittens, dogs, puppies, horses, colts, cows, calves, and even baby pigs are so cute, but as a child, I didn't think of this.

In September, I remember walking home the mile and a half from school, not in the least bit of a hurry. We usually stripped off our shoes to enjoy going barefoot the last days of summer. We squished the sand between our toes and stopped along every slough to try our hand at skipping stones across the water, but I knew there would be work to do when we arrived home. I wished I lived in town. Those kids had nothing to do but play.

My mother had pulled the navy bean vines from the garden in early September and had laid them in the sun to dry. They were now ready to be threshed out of their pods. This was not done by machine, but by us kids using a 1 x 2 stick to pound them until every last bean was shelled from its pod. The vines were laid in a farm wagon box and we took the vines one by one and threshed the beans out. This took many an hour of our time to gather the 35 pounds of shelled beans that could now be stored without worry of spoiling. However, they did taste delicious during the winter made into soups or baked beans. As I threshed the beans, I wished I lived in town. Those kids had nothing to do but play.

One of my chores after school was to feed the chickens, which still free roamed the farmyard. This was to be done before they "roosted" in the willows for the night. Often, I dawdled and it got later than it should. That was until my dad found out I had been lax in doing my chore. Believe me, it didn't happen again; the chickens were fed on time after that. As I fed those chickens, I wished I lived in town. Those kids had nothing to do but play.

Towards the end of October when the weather turned colder, we had to catch these roosting birds and carry them into the chicken coop where they were kept until spring. Dressed in warm clothing, using a six-battery flashlight and a long wire with a hook on the end, we found the roosting chickens and surprised them by pulling them out of the tree, snaring them with the hook. We carried them to the coop, each of us carrying two or three chickens in each hand, their wings flapping against our bare legs and squawking in vigorous protest. They were as happy to be released, as we were to release them. This went on for several evenings until they were all safe and snug in the coop. As we caught the chickens, I wished I lived in town. Those kids had nothing to do but play.

Just before freezing weather, the garden produce had to be carried into the basement. This meant carrying large heads of cabbage into the basement. Some of the heads were so large we could only carry one at a time. With each trip down the steps, we also brought in heavy ground on our shoes, which had to be swept up later. Rutabagas and beets were carried down by the pails full. The pumpkins were put on a pile in the garden waiting their turn to be carried to the basement as well. As I carried produce to the basement, I wished I lived in town. Those kids had nothing to do but play.

Shortly after school started, the potatoes were harvested. The older of us kids had to stay home from school and pick up the potatoes, load them into a wagon box to be taken home. The potatoes were put through a side window in the basement and funneled into the potato bins. This was backbreaking work, walking barefoot behind the potato digger and carrying them to the large wagon box. We were tired out, our young bodies aching from all the bending and stooping. After a full day of this, we fell into bed, exhausted. Morning came much too soon. As I harvested potatoes, I wished I lived in town. Those kids had nothing to do but play.

In the winter when I was old enough, I shoveled grain from the wagon box into the feed grinder. I would shovel a load of grain through a window of the feed room into the grinder while my brother Robert scooped it into a bin. This was the food for the milk cows. Every three days we had to grind a wagon box full of grain. This, too, caused my back to ache, but going into the house for supper was wonderful. I remember the fragrance of stewed cabbage, stacks of hamburgers, potatoes, and milk gravy with boiled eggs. Suppertime was always a family time when we listened to our older siblings and learned from their experiences. As I shoveled grain, I wished I lived in town. Those kids had nothing to do but play.

About the age of 14, I had to ride the hay rake, guiding the horses down the hay meadow and raking the hay into windrows so that it could be gathered by another piece of machinery and put into stacks.

It was boring and time got very long. I remember one summer when sleeping sickness was prevalent in horses. My dad instructed me to keep the horses going, not to let them go at a slow pace. All that day I prayed that the team would keep a normal pace. Somehow, I felt responsible if one of the horses should lie down on the job. I don't know if keeping them going was the remedy, but I did as I was instructed to do, keeping them on their feet. I was glad when the day was through. As I guided the horses, I wished I lived in town. Those kids had nothing to do but play.

Later on, I was old enough to learn to drive the tractor. I drove the tractor and pulled the grain binder. My dad rode the binder, tripping the bundle carrier and watching so everything worked well. My biggest responsibility there was to watch for rocks that may be in the way of the binder and to carefully guide the binder over them. This was much easier than driving horses. As I drove the tractor, I wished I lived in town. Those kids had nothing to do but play.

As I grew older and worked off the farm, I began to realize that maybe the kids in town had chores to do too, albeit their chores would be different than mine. I began to realize what good training I had while growing up on a farm. I learned the satisfaction of having done hard work, the pleasure of being around animals, and the advantage of plenty of space to run and play in. I realized that I did have time to play and enjoy being a kid and, finally, I no longer envied the kids who lived in town.

Community Service
By Janyce Bakken of Goodridge, Minnesota
Born 1937

I have always felt the need to help the less fortunate. My childhood was rather rocky although I always felt very loved by my parents, and they were full of pride for me. We had little money and sometimes people would give us big boxes of clothing and miscellaneous. I never felt poor, as we had a lot of love, happiness, and God in our home. We rarely missed church and once a month we had "family night" consisting of programs, lunch, and fellowship. The church seemed to be the focal point of the community in those days.

My husband and I were married in 1960 and by 1965; we had been blessed with 4 darling little children; 2 girls and 2 boys. "The perfect family," I exuberated! I taught school for a while but the babies were more important, so I became a stay-at-home mom loving every minute of it. I jumped for joy every morning when the school bus went by and I could stay home. But with this newfound happiness came the fact that we had very little money coming in.

1962 was the worst. We earned and lived on $900 for the entire year. I thought very little about our financial situation, as I was busy with the kids and the day-to-day work. I had always learned from before. Be content with what you have. God will take care of all your needs. 1 Peter 5:7 says, "Casting all your cares upon Him, for He careth for you."

Marvin and Janyce Bakken on their wedding day in 1960

We had survey sheets that we showed when we stopped here and there along the highways. We were trying to find people in need of our services. People who were low income and struggling in some hardship. I took my job home with me many nights feeling so sorry for the people I had met that day. In those days, you didn't have to be afraid of people and I enjoyed my job very much.

I met many elderly people who showed me their arts and crafts. If they had no one to give them to, they just piled up and made a clutter. They were having a lutefisk supper in town one fall night. I gathered up all those arts and crafts, asked what price they wanted for each individual item and I priced them. Then I arranged two tables at the gym when the supper began and I sold every single item I had brought. I was a little afraid driving home

When my youngest child was four (1969) I saw an ad in the paper for the Office of Economic Opportunity, headquarters in Oklee, Minnesota that was looking for an outreach aid. The applicant must be from a low-income household and have a high school diploma. That fit me to a 'T.' I could go into lengthy detail as to how we fit into this category but it would be very depressing. Actually, it didn't seem so bad to us, as a lot of our friends were in the same boat that we were. Needless to say, I got the job!

It was a rather strange position. I was my own boss. I had to decide on my own what I would do each day. Of course, I had to report to the office exactly what I did do. That was once a month.

Marvin and Janyce Bakken with their children in 2000

31

Marvin and Janyce on their 25th anniversary in 1985

that night as I had collected over $1,000. My next week was taken up with bringing the money back to each rightful owner. The next month I reported on my project. I'm a rather sensitive person and one man blurted out in his loud burly voice, scaring me half to death, "Whadaya want? A medal?" I felt very intimidated and sad. Most everyone thought it was a very good idea. The radio station called me and wanted me to talk with Sylvia on her "Coffee Time Show," but that one man had ruined it for me and I declined.

However, that didn't stop my project. I was asked to set up shop in the old auditorium and other towns made places to do the same thing. It took off over the whole state. My town even built a new building for it. They called it "The Heritage Community Center." And it is still going strong. My little room and others like it were known as Craft Shops. These Craft Shops are phased in or phased out depending on which political party is voted in. And now you know the story of how the little Craft Shops originated. I would still like to take the credit for them, even if it is almost fifty years later. I'll just say I was God's servant doing the will of God. You have all heard that God has a lot to do. He sometimes softly whispers in your ear what it is. He needs our hands, our feet, our time, our talents, and our abilities. I have heard it said, "It is not our ability, but our availability that he wants."

Another rewarding experience I had was working at the bakery. The psychiatric department of the hospital sponsored a bookstore where these patients could work and learn the skills of daily living. I felt empathy for these people so when they came to get a coffee and a roll, and having no money, I just said, "I'll just pay for it and you can pay me later." The other customers jokingly asked me why I didn't do that for them. I'd answer, "You never know. Every dog has its day." I'd also say, "A dollar here, a dollar there isn't going to make or break anybody." I'd say, "If they don't pay, well then, that's my missionary work for today." But to tell the truth, I don't think I'm out a penny. As far as I can remember, they all paid the money back and I made some wonderful life-long friends who mean the world to me. Another worker in another store down the street would see me visiting with these people by the big front window. "How can you stand to visit with those people?" she would ask. Sure, some of them looked a little scruffy but so do I sometimes. Nobody is perfect. If they are, it's only because they think they are. I've had some very interesting experiences in my lifetime.

I worked in activities in the nursing home for ten years. After I retired, I wrote stories like this, and once a month or so I'd go visit the residents and read my stories to them as a volunteer. After every program, I'd conclude with this country song by Gail Davies. The song talks about there always something you can do, even if it's just praying. "Prayer Changes Things." That sign used to hang in my mother's bedroom. Now it hangs behind my kitchen table. Prayer, in my opinion, is the most important thing we can do.

I will conclude with this: one day when I was a sophomore in high school, I noticed a lot of people in this certain area. I was curious. Slowly creeping my way into the crowd, I was told that one of our classmates had been shot. I learned that he had been partridge hunting with his brother and some friends in the woods on the family farm. They had made rules as to where and where not to be. Marvin, the name of the boy who was shot, had the rules wrong and was just where he wasn't supposed to be. Needless to say, it wasn't long till he was shot. There was a lot of screaming and hollering in getting Marvin up to the house. His dad fainted when he saw him covered in blood from head to toe, leaving his mother and an uncle to get him to the doctor. It all turned out fine in the end. I felt so bad for him; I talked to him whenever I could and just tried to be nice. That was the beginning of a nine-year courtship and on July 23, 1960, we were married. It always pays to be nice. We will be celebrating our 56th wedding anniversary this summer.

Summers on the Farm in Fertile, Minnesota
By Daniel Thonn of Kirkland, Washington
Born 1954

Each morning I awoke realizing I was in a very different and faraway place with the distinctive warble of the mid-west songbirds coming from the front yard. There was no need for an alarm clock with the birds and chickens sounding their wake-up calls. In the morning, there was also the distinctive sound of the well pump cycling, cows mooing, and often shortly thereafter a tractor firing up or equipment moving around preparing for the day's work. Back in those days when our grandparents were alive, and the family was young, we took regular summer trips back to Minnesota to the family run farm in Fertile, in northern Minnesota and visits to the extended family. The year was 1968, and this year I was allowed to stay on the grandparent's farm for the rest of the summer. I was 13 years old and this was a completely different and fascinating world coming from Seattle on the west coast.

Grandpa Oscar was always up early having his meat and eggs for breakfast. No cold cereal for him as he wanted something hearty to begin the day. He usually wore a set of overalls, kind of a striped work outfit that had various smudges of equipment grease, and a matching brimmed hat that he wore slightly angled to one side that appeared to me similar to a train conductor hat but more soiled and worn. After Grandpa, the rest of us would come down the steep narrow stairs and eat quickly, eager to observe and be involved in the days' activities. I recall it was nice being heartily greeted each morning by the dog, Shep, as if he was reuniting with a long lost friend.

There were busy weekends there with lots of aunts, uncles, and cousins coming from the Twin Cities. Sometimes bringing their tent trailers and setting them up in the front yard. For this summer, the only other cousin who stayed longer was my cousin Grady, who was there up to the Fertile Fair. Grandma Ellen played the town drawing each week and reminded us that she had won several times. So there was an important trip into town each Saturday evening to listen to the drawing results at the Red Owl grocery. This was a big year as cousin Grady had won a bicycle at the Fertile Fair, which for the kids was the ultimate prize.

Grandpa was known as a mechanical wizard to keep the farm equipment running, which was old at the time and in present terms would be well valued at an antique tractor show. There was the 1945 Allis Chalmers WD 45, the 1937 Minneapolis Moline (possible a Model Z), the 1950 John Deere Two Cylinder Diesel "R," and the yellow Case Combine. I was mechanically inclined and was first given the job of greasing the equipment, tightening the belts, checking, and topping off the oil, etc. I was also fond of reading whatever maintenance manuals I could locate and learned models, years, and repair procedures for the equipment.

As I was a young kid, I was mainly observing during my first weeks there and doing the light mechanical tasks. Then one day, Grandpa brought me over to the granary and we laid out the old combine belts on the lawn. He showed me how to repair them by replacing broken slats, removing, and replacing the rivets. This was a tedious job and I spent several days pounding and replacing the rivets but completed all the work. Grandpa was pleased with this progress and I had, in effect, passed this test of doing real work, which then led to bigger tasks, and engagement in the main farm work.

The equipment needed regular repair to keep going. One day Grandpa gave me a lesson in pouring Babbitt (lead) bearings used in the pulleys. He told me to go to the pump house and prepare a fire in the shop furnace. I placed straw in a pile, lit it, and started it with large hand-powered bellows. Grandpa was a man short on words and as he walked in yelled, "Get that birds nest out of here!" Then he showed me how to light a stronger fire using wood splinters and coal pieces. He was known for his direct talk but he also was a favorite among the grandkids, who like to watch his activities.

Grandma had her own tasks and farm wife duties. I also had the opportunity to spend quite a bit of time with Grandma. She had this gentle patient manner and liked to tell stories, often humorous stories. I recall several stories on one of the local characters known as "Freddie." He went to town on the weekends, often became imbibed, and was known to show up in people's out buildings in the morning when he couldn't make it all the way home. One time he apparently had a date in town, he couldn't locate a car, and drove all the way to town and then down Main Street driving a tractor and wearing a suit. Apparently, this was during the fair so his antics were observed by many. Grandma seemed to always have a funny story to tell each time there was some type of project going in the kitchen, yard, or garden.

There was also church at St. John's Lutheran Church every Sunday. Once a month, there were the ladies aid dinners in the basement of the church. The best home cooked meals with homemade pies all for 25 cents. Also, there were traveling Evangelists that came through town. On one Sunday, we went to an Evangelist event at Bergeson's Nursery. There was a lady there speaking who had come from the cities for this event. I recall it was a hot day in August and we were sitting in lines of metal chairs lined up on the lawn with a platform in the front. I noticed Grandma was quite engaged, she was following closely, and nodding on the key points; Grandpa was sitting still and just stared straight ahead. By the time we left, it was dark and as were leaving down the driveway it was dead silent in the car and Grandpa was staring straight ahead driving. Grandma broke the silence and said, "Don't you think that was a really nice talk?" This was followed by a long silence and finally Grandpa responded, "Someone should have coked that woman!" Grandma said, "Oh no, that's an awful thing to say!" This was followed by a long silence the rest of the way home and no apparent remorse for such a statement.

In July, there was the haying and collecting of bales. We would place the bales against each other end up to dry out, and then go back later to collect them using the baling skid. Grandpa was driving; the older cousins and I were on the back throwing the bales in the skid, and then we would stack them back at the barn. We would catch gophers and collect the bounty from the county agent who happened to be our Uncle Vern. We would get paid as long as we could turn in a pair of gopher feet.

And then there were the junk piles. The most important junk pile was in front of the pump house. The pump house itself was a marvel of Midwest farm architecture and was made of the top part of a windmill. It was a round faceted multi-sided tall structure. And stepping in, you were never alone as there was typically a bird or two scratching around in the upper rafters. When inside you could scan 360 degrees and see the older relics such as harnesses and older relics hanging from the upper walls. The newer more readily used tools and metal implements hanging within reach in the lower sections, all hand operated including the large drill press. And the pieces that no longer warranted a place inside were tossed into a large pile outside. The first thing that caught my interest was a round headlamp from a 1920s automobile, glass still intact. With each day, I would dig deeper into the pile and resurrect an artifact. Grandpa didn't seem to mind and would provide the story of each piece, usually while sitting on the porch at the end of the day with the dog sitting at his side delighted to be included in this newfound ritual. There was an immense oil can and metal pitch fork that came from the days of steam thrashing operation that used to be run on the farm. And there were horseshoes, bullet molds, hand corn planters, kerosene lamps, a part of a copper pot brought from Sweden but the great grandparents, enamel ware, and various iron tools. There also were other stockpiles of junk and antiquities in the granary and areas behind the building were equipment beyond its useful life was retired, all for the dis-assembly and dissection of the curious kids willing to ignore the mosquitoes. And in town was more junk at Jim's Jungle where second hand items were affordable on a budget of gopher feet money. Grandma was amazed and at the same time dismayed at all this gear being dragged up to the house wondering where it would end up. Hanging in the garage was an old shotgun that Grandpa said he learned to hunt on and that his father had purchased it from a Native American for one dollar shortly after his arrival to Fertile in the 1880s.

The August harvest was delayed due to colder and wetter weather than normal. When it finally warmed up, Grandpa set things moving quickly and the home farm was combined first. The farm trucks were also older even in those times with a 1950 International pickup, and a larger 1946 era Chevrolet grain truck. I had been practicing with the grain truck for several weeks and was ready to assist. Grandpa ran the combine and would signal me over each time he filled the hopper. The weather held up during the combining of the main farm, but the forecast was starting to turn by the time it came turn to move on to the east farm. The east farm was heavily wooded and the fields were in various pieces interspersed with the woods and in the center were the remnants of the original building site. This farm had been homesteaded by Grandpa's mother in the 1880s. I later went to town with Grandpa carrying the loads of grain, the sideboards and top bulging and wondering if the old grain truck would make it all the way, but in spike of the noise and grinding it was able to make each trip. For Grandpa there was no question, it was business as usual.

I spent two summers on the farm in Fertile and one thing I remember was how fast the time seemed to go. Before I knew it, the summer had come to an end, and it was time to head back to Seattle. And each time I didn't want to leave, asking if I could stay and go to school there instead but unfortunately, that was an option that never came about. And going back years later, the farm continued to hold its fascinations. The grandparents had passed away and with each visit, the farm continued to hold its fascination. The original buildings were being torn down one at a time and the home site sold off. But the memories remain; the sounds of the tractors and combine, the lean of the vintage trucks as they negotiated the dirt tracks, Grandpa shouting over the noise of the raucous machinery, the home cooked meals, the fresh garden vegetables, Grandma sending off the kids to collect the choke cherries, the welcoming neighbors, and the song birds sounding off in the mornings.

Howard's Memories of Yesteryear
By Howard Tyrrell of Browerville, Minnesota
Born 1924

The farm was homesteaded in 1873 from descendants of early settlers that left England and came to America to start a new life. They were not on the Mayflower, but came very shortly after. The family names were Tyrrell and Pettibone. The Tyrrells were considered royal lineage from the House of Windsor. The Pettibones, on the other hand, were merely "commoners." Both families were out east. Truman Tyrrell and Sarah Pettibone fell in love and were married. This "mixed marriage" did not please either family to the point that Truman and Sarah were shunned. When the territory of Wisconsin opened up, Truman and Sarah anxiously moved on.

The Civil War started and Truman joined the Wisconsin Militias in order to serve. He was captured and had to spend time in a POW camp in Texas. While other POWs lost their lives from starvation, Truman had been wise and traded his whiskey rations for bread rations. Upon conclusion of the war, he returned to Wisconsin and in 1873 wanted to start his own farm. He wanted to go to where the rivers ran north. His land was patent deeded at 160 acres. The current house and barns sit in the middle of that property. They originally traveled with two horses. One of those horses died, so the remaining good quality horse was traded for a pair of oxen. The family made it about as far as St. Cloud when one of the oxen died. They were able to continue on with just

A black bear

The farm

the one ox. The farm is still in possession of both of the original ox yokes that were used to break the land for the farm. The tree under which the oxen were rested is still alive and is farmed around to this very day.

Interestingly, you will note that the farm was homesteaded in 1873, but the deed could not be filed until five years later. The reason being that Sarah and Truman could not come up with the three to five extra dollars that were required as a fee to do this. The deed was officially signed by President of the United States, Chester Arthur.

Truman passed the farm along to Hayden and Earl and eventually, Jay (born in 1877) took it over. Jay was Howard's father. The farm is now run by Howard's son, Dennis and Howard's grandson, Jakin. Over the years, the farm has been expanded to 1200+ acres. Howard, Dennis, or Jakin never asked neighbors to sell them additional land, it was always offered to them by the neighbors that had previously farmed it.

The original farm did not have acreage that directly touched the Long Prairie River, but it now runs through the entire farm. The river has a long history of having Winnebago Indians along its banks. The government had relocated them to central Minnesota. They were friendly, great neighbors to the early settlers. There did not seem to be disputes among the two. In fact, Howard recalls his father telling of many times when the Winnebagos were welcomed into the Tyrrell homes. He laughs that he is not sure how they would have communicated.

The neighbors have always been thought of as blessings even in the earliest settlements when there were not many neighbors around. In the late 1800s and early 1900s, the Germans and Polish arrived in large numbers. They were wonderful neighbors and became lifelong friends. Included in that group of settlers were the Itens (pronounced EEton) who became undertakers. They have continued to be good friends and have served the family in that capacity for generations. One member of that family, Ed Iten, even when he was fully grown, appreciated the fruits of the land, literally. He would come and help himself to the bounty of Stella's (Jay Tyrrell's wife) garden. On one occasion, he came to the door to inquire about whether Stella might have a knife to cut the beautiful watermelon he "found" (in her garden)!

Howard was born on the farm in 1924 in the home his uncle Hayden built. He has enjoyed the same neighbors most of his life. He brought his late bride, of almost 70 years, Marlys, out to the farm in 1945. They milked cows, grew the farm, and raised three children. He met Marlys in their sophomore year of high school and asked her out to a movie. He smiles when he says, "It was the quickest yes she ever gave him." That black haired beauty who knew all the answers and was Salutatorian of their class gave Howard almost 75 years of partnership, love, and devotion.

Howard, along with the three children: Eloise, Dennis and Lynette, all attended grade school in the same one-room school, Batavia District #54. Howard went to church and Sunday school at the Batavia Church of Christ in rural Browerville, Minnesota. When events took place at either the church or school, it seemed that everyone would show up whether they were members or students or not. They were the social hubs of the community. Marlys went to Normal Teacher Training and taught in one-room schools for several years.

One of the most fun events that took place in those days were "shivarees." Those events were times the neighbors showed up making loud noises (banging pots and pans, ringing cow bells, tooting horns) after a couple had just been married and were least expecting it. The couple would have to provide treats for the attendees. While the newlyweds were busy figuring out what they could serve, the guests would create mischief by doing things like short sheeting their bed, filling it with rice, and other disruptive behaviors. Howard and Marlys were shivareed on their 50th wedding anniversary for added memories!

Memories of the river flooding in the spring also come to mind, but the most vivid memories were the flash flooding of 1972 when approximately 14 inches of rain came in 24 hours. The usual, gently flowing, Long Prairie River became a raging river, nearly three miles wide in some places. Boats were used to go from one side of the farm to the other, over cornstalks that stood eight feet high. If you looked down, you could see northerns and carp swimming among the stalks. You could travel by boat down the middle of the roads for miles on end. Because of the very sandy soil, the river receded very quickly. Most of the corn crop was destroyed; however, farmers were able to access the highland corn at harvest time. The debris left by the flood had to continually be picked up in the fields for years after. Daughter Eloise, and husband Mike Thorson, had water lapping at the back door of the house they were living in at the time.

The farm is surrounded by virgin white pine that was native to the area. The family has managed the 18 acres to now be 35 acres of white pine. It is harvested regularly to keep it growing properly. One incident that stands out for Howard and Dennis is the winter that they were cleaning up the trees after a fierce summer storm that blew many of them down. It was late December and had been an unusually warm fall and early winter. Dennis and two of his sons were cutting trees for lumber. There had been a number of bear sitings in the area that year. Much to their surprise, their attention was grabbed when they saw a black bear sitting on one of their logs, not more than 50 yards away. The bear had probably been stirred from its slumber by the sound of the chainsaws. The bear seemed to be quite drowsy, so they were able to take dozens of pictures before returning to the cutting up of the trees.

The next morning as they were preparing to go back to work, Dennis wanted to investigate which root ball holes might have been the bear's den. Many of the trees were over 100 feet tall so the root balls were large enough for the bears to be using. Dennis happened upon a hole he thought looked used, and called to his son. Peering into the hole, Dennis saw the

Long Prairie River flooding

bear open his two big eyes and look directly at him to which Dennis said, "Dude, go back to sleep!"

It should be pointed out that the river attracts wildlife beyond imagination. Animals seen on the farm over the years include bears, coyotes, wolves, cougars, wild turkeys, elk, moose, white tailed deer, and bald eagles. All types of waterfowl including Tundra Swans have also been observed.

Often neighbors would be blocking the middle of the road conversing about the goings on in the countryside. As "retirement" neared, many of these same neighbors would spend winters in warmer climates and laugh about how they had to travel hundreds to thousands of miles to spend time with the neighbors from back home where everyone was too busy with their own farming operations to take time to visit much.

The stories are too numerous to share them all, but suffice it to say that Howard would not trade any of his 92 years on the farm for all the money in the world.

Sugaring the Sugar Maple Trees
By Jim Frick of Cass Lake, Minnesota
Born 1943

Let's begin this historical adventure of a non-typical profession of sugaring or tapping the Sugar Maple trees of Northern Minnesota. This venture was a two men or person undertaking. It would start in early February, when my wife and I would walk out with shovels in hand to attack the snow that had accumulated through the winter months. Of course, the clothing was not of summer attire, but the typical attire to combat the elements of Northern Minnesota. The Northern Minnesota weather could reach minus 50 degrees or lower with wind chill on top of that. That type of cold drives right through the winter attire.

Anyway, back to our trip out to the Sugar Maple with our shovels in hand. We lived on an 80-acre parcel of wooded land in the Chippewa National Forest, in the back northeast corner of the parcel, and the Sugar Maple stand was in the front southwest corner. The course was to trudge through the accumulated snow. Snowshoes would have been a more convenient mode of transportation but were not available. The route of the trudge was to proceed from the northwest corner towards the southwest corner, which entailed movements oriented around swamps and trees (the easiest path of resistance). This forged path would be traveled many times through the sugaring season.

When we got to the end goal of our trudge or human snow plowing expedition, we would be at the sugar shack. The sugar shack had been established during the summer months. It was made of plywood panels, open at one end, attached to a frame made with Popple trees. The back had several openings to accommodate a stovepipe. The roof had several removable panels also. This brings us to the boiling implement. It was a 55-gallon barrel cut in half lengthwise, with a welded steel frame that sat on a firebox. The firebox was an old steel sink cabinet. The cabinet was open on top and at one end. We placed this in a dug out area in the sugar shack. The boiling barrel would be placed on this cabinet. The sides of the frame of the barrel had tin sheets that flared out to collect the heat off the firebox. The back of the frame had a stovepipe opening that accommodated a stovepipe elbow. The elbow had 4 straight stovepipe sections connected to it, to get it above the walls and out of one of the sections of the removable panels of the roof or windows in back.

The next task was to shovel paths to the 200 Sugar Maple trees surrounding the sugar shack. The total stand of Sugar Maples numbered around 400 trees. But we only tapped around 200 or so. We would alternate stands year by year as long as we gathered sap. Besides shoveling paths to the 200 or so Maples, we would shovel snow away from the south side of the trees. This wasn't a necessary endeavor, but if it was done one gets a longer run of sap. This is done to allow the ground to heat up faster so the sap flows up and down the trees. This whole process needs days above 32 degrees and nights below 32 degrees. The snow removal would take several daily sessions to complete the task. If the weather was really adverse, we'd forego that day.

The next task after the shoveling would be to show up with a chainsaw and axe and begin to cut up fallen or standing dead trees. This would be stacked up on the sides of the sugar shack or wherever convenient to pile. After that, the next task would be tapping the 200 or so trees via the use of a brace n' bit. The best tap is one at an angle off a feed root on the south side of the tree, between knee and waist height. We used plastic pails with covers. We would connect about an 8-inch piece of plastic hose to the spile and drill a hole in the plastic cover and feed the hose into the pail. The reason we did this was because the trees seem to shed bark and one never knew when it might snow and moths! We learned from past endeavors wherein we would come out to gather the run and there would be 5-10 moths floating in the pail. The powdery material on their wings had mixed in the collected sap. We had to throw this sap out.

After all of this was accomplished, we'd wait for a 32 degree or above day and a below 32 degree night. If it snowed we'd have to clean away the snow from the trees again. When the weather was accommodating, we'd go out and gather the sap that ran down to the roots on cold nights. We'd throw out the frozen water in the pails and gather the concentrated sap. This gathered sap was put in holding containers until we had around 50 gallons of concentrated sap to boil down.

When this came about, I would head out very early in the morning, around 5:00 AM. I would get a good fire going and then place the barrel over the fire, fill it about 4 inches from the top, and keep stoking the fire until I got a rolling boil. We learned that if one killed the boil because you were adding very cold sap, it took a long time to get that boil back. Thus, we came up with a pre-heater. We had an old enamel canning kettle that we punched a small hole in, made a frame to sit in on, on top of the barrel. We'd fill this with cold sap, which would trickle out at a slow pace, and not kill the boil. When the canning kettle heated up its contents and started evaporating also we'd pour that into the barrel and start the process all over again by filling the pre-heater with cold liquid. Thus, we kept the boiling going. There was a foam that would gather on the boiling sap and we'd strain that with a stainless steel spoon that had holes in it.

My wife would come out later with breakfast and a noon meal. We would boil down, get wood, and pick up the runs, as the storage containers were emptied. In the afternoon she would head back home and I'd continue to boil down until the sap reached a certain boiling point on a candy thermometer. I would fill as many 5 gallon pails as I could carry and head for home around 4:30 PM. We would finish off the boiling at home until it reached the necessary degrees of syrup. This was jarred and sealed in various sized containers. Then we would hit the hay and get ready for another day.

The sugar shack was always quite warm during the boiling times and sometimes quite hot if the temps were up during the day. It takes about 40 gallons of sap to make about 1 gallon of syrup. This depends on the sugar content of the trees. A run would go until the trees start to bud, then the sap takes on a bitter taste. The sap coming out of the trees is semi-sweet.

There is a bird called the Yellow-Bellied Sapsucker, it's a problem because they drill holes in the trees and the trees leak sap out of those holes. If these holes are over your tap, your run will be greatly decreased. Even if a branch breaks it will run sap at the break. Some trees produce a lot of raw sap. We could count on certain trees to have the pails full to sometimes overflowing. And other trees to be quite slow at filling the collection pails.

We could have a lot of visitors during the day. The deer were curious about this strange endeavor. And chipmunks, they would show up and run all over the sugar shack. The squirrels, snowshoe hares, and once in a while a porcupine would visit. Of course, a mouse or two would venture into the scene. The birds had to check out what was going on. There was one chickadee that was especially fond of sunflower seeds and he/she would fly in to eat out of your hand. Once while out gathering a run, a friend was helping and he had an eagle try to pick off his cap as a prey. That was quite a sight to see, as I observed the eagle swooping down towards him and swerve at the last minute when he must have determined that this was not a prey.

One year, we were extremely busy and we didn't pull the pails and spiles at the end of the run. We were planting trees for the Chippewa National Forest and the starting date for this came right at the end of our maple sugaring season. So, we left everything at status quo, until we had a break to tear down and pack up. This was about a week later; we headed out to pull the spiles, pack up the pails, and set everything in order for the next year. As we approached the sugar shack we saw things knocked over and scattered around. It was obvious a bear or two had come out of hibernation and ventured upon a miracle. There was still sap in the pails and the bears had assisted us by tearing down every pail. They clawed or bit the pails to enjoy their miracle. Some pails were a long way from the trees and some pails were completely torn up. They must have swatted some pails because the spiles were torn right out of the some of the trees. We had to search for some of the spiles because they weren't lying by the tree. Well, we learned a lesson from that and didn't leave the pails out after that excursion.

Raised in a Chicken Coop
By Marlene Mattila Stoehr of Shoreview, Minnesota
Born 1932

AARP's 50th anniversary ad read: "Founded on the simple premise that no one should have to live in a chicken coop." I was born in a chicken coop and lived in that chicken coop until high school age. It didn't seem all that bad then. Neither does it now.

My parents married on New Years' Eve 1920 and rented a small house near my mother's parent's farm. Two babies were born there. The little family shared its next home with my dad's brother, and soon bought adjoining acreage. The first building on the farm of their own was a 16- x 36- foot concrete block chicken coop.

A third baby arrived, and so did the Great Depression. In time, the children numbered eight, and of necessity, the chicken coop, which never housed a chicken, housed a growing family. Buildings important to the farm operation were built. A log barn for milk cows. A hog house. A granary for field crops. An actual house had lower priority, always on hold, always in the future.

In its own way, the chicken coop was rather charming, framed by a stand of poplar trees, a cluster of lilacs, and transplanted rows of wild plum and pin cherry trees. A magical moonflower bloomed at night, sweet pea vines climbed on a birch trellis and zinnias and moss roses formed a mass of variegated color in my mother's flowerbed.

Free-range chickens, having lost the race for space, cackled from the grass to foolishly reveal their hidden nests. Up to 15 farm cats ruled the outer space, a wren sang from the birdhouse on the granary, and a friendly dog announced when a car drove up the long driveway. Likely as not our mother would say, "Girls, make a one-egg cake," or "Girls, make a two-egg cake," depending how much company food we had on hand.

The coop's 36-foot length was divided into three spaces: a kitchen, whose doorway led into the "front room," whose wider doorway led into the bedroom. In winter, fire in the wood-burning cook stove and another in the front-room heater warmed the house, yet the cold crept in. On the windowless north wall, furry frost outlined cracks in the concrete blocks; elsewhere frost painted delicate fern-gardens on windowpanes.

Space was at a premium. By the time

The chicken coop home

40

my memories begin, a small screen-porch had been added to house the DeLaval cream separator and the noisy gasoline-powered Maytag wringer washing machine in warm months. In winter both were moved into the kitchen, the cream separator on one side of the door that we locked at night with a butcher knife stuck in the casing, the washing machine on the other. Mother's black treadle sewing machine with gold letters spelling out "Singer" spanned a window and stopped just short of the first dividing wall.

The wall telephone hung there, its long mouthpiece our coat rack. When the phone rang two long rings for 1F7, our number on the party line, we lifted off the coats and jackets and perched on the sewing machine to answer. If we wished only to rubberneck - listen to other people's calls to get the neighborhood news - the coats remained in place as a sound barrier.

The cook stove, heart of any farm kitchen, resplendent in black with chrome trim, was centered on the kitchen wall. A reservoir at one end warmed water; we washed dishes in dishpans over that reservoir. On the stovetop, we heated heavy flatirons, toasted bread, and popped corn in a long-handled popper. In the oven, we heated bags of salt to warm icy sheets on wintry nights.

Before we began to drive regularly to my grandparents for Saturday night sauna, we bathed in a galvanized washtub in front of the stove. Taking turns, youngest to oldest, we added hot water from the teakettle to keep the water warm.

Our wood box sat behind the stove, a hungry mouth waiting to be fed. While the older children helped with milking our small herd of Holsteins, we younger hurried to finish carrying in wood in time to listen to Jack Armstrong, All-American Boy, and hear The Lone Ranger ride again.

An iron pump stood over a sink in the third corner of the kitchen. Water drained into a galvanized pail and although we carried water out, we did not have to carry it from an outside well, as was common in the community.

Objects of both beauty and practicality filled the tall cabinet on the north windowless wall: a built-in flour bin with sifter, mismatched dishes and flatware, the much despised cod-liver oil in its oily brown bottle, a small pewter pitcher filled with wondrous bric-a-brac we kids loved to sort through, and a magnificent cut glass bowl received as a wedding gift that had held the water for all the children's home baptisms. In early spring, Mother started tomato seedlings in crates beneath the cupboard and baby chicks spent their first hours there after being delivered by the mailman. Weak baby pigs or frail bottle lambs were also nursed to health in the warmth of the kitchen.

Beside the cabinet, a curtain screened a pantry where we stored supplies of all sorts: bags of dry cereals, sacks of flour, kerosene in a metal spouted can, "farmer matches," and Red Wing crocks in which we made sauerkraut and dill pickles. Mason jars filled with canned vegetables from our garden,

Marlene Mattila, Mary Ellen Mattila, and Kayo Mattila

sauce from wild strawberries and blueberries and juice from chokecherries, pin cherries, and plums waited here before being moved to the dirt cellar below a trapdoor in the middle of the linoleum-covered floor.

We had no electricity; a kerosene lamp lit the room with a yellowish glow. A rectangular table was pushed against the east wall; beside the table, backless benches. For many of my growing up years my oldest sister worked in the big city, so the family at home numbered only nine. Three children sat on either side of the table, my parents on one short end, and my younger sister on the windowsill at the other.

A square heater stove, a round oak pedestal table with wonderfully sprawling legs, and my parent's metal bed took up most of the space in the front room. Between the stove and a closet was The Box, a wooden bench with a hinged top that stored items not used every day. Cast-off fur coats from my mother's younger city sisters and old overcoats that Mother sewed into children's snow pants and mittens took much of the tiny closet space.

The table in front of double, lace-curtained windows was crowded with a kerosene lamp, a Philco tabletop radio, back issues of the Sebeka Review and The Farmer magazine, houseplant slips taking root in metal cans, school books, Montgomery Ward "wish books," and half-finished embroidery projects. Often a pair of knit woolen socks waited there for Dad to "turn the heel," a skill Mother never needed to master as Dad's Finnish-immigrant mother taught him to knit while he was bedridden with a childhood illness. Beneath the table were my little brother's lengths of wooden 4 x 4s, his "horses," with names that echoed those of our father and uncle's teams.

Chairs ringed the table, and it was there, after a hurried clearing of clutter, that company was served cake and coffee, so important to Finnish hospitality.

The youngest child's white iron crib sometimes filled the corner or sometimes traded places with the dresser and mirror at the foot of my parents' bed across the room. Cardboard boxes beneath their bed provided additional storage, one always full of socks with holes in the heel. My sisters and I learned to darn with the contents of that box.

A clothes rod spanning the double doorway to the bedroom held the family's entire wardrobe, pushed aside at one edge for space to walk through. My three older brothers shared the bed to the right, the bed I shared with my two sisters stood on the left, between them a dresser. There was just enough room at the end of each bed for a stack of old magazines and catalogues, precious material for cutting up for paper dolls.

A two-seat outdoor toilet, furnished with prized peach wrappers and the remains of last year's catalog stood at the end of a path behind the house.

Those were demanding times for parents, with grasshopper infestations, fear of foreclosures and acute shortages of hay and grain. But for children, protected from these grim realities, life was good. Fall and spring were times of eagerness for school to start and eagerness for school to end. Summer brought glorious barefoot freedom, splashing in puddles, swinging on the hay rope, catching fireflies and playing house with cardboard boxes and old clothes stored in the granary. Undaunted by circumstances, my mother held unto her deferred dream of a real house, some day. My parents pored over house plans from the lumberyard. But only after five of their eight children had graduated from high school did the dream become a reality.

Today, after nearly nine decades, the chicken coop's concrete block walls still stand, but only three sisters remain. We tell stories of our childhood to the younger generation, and, strange as it may seem, our stories never mention feeling crowded.

Pa Saves the Day
By Hazel Cartier of Red Lake Falls, Minnesota
Born 1928

My sister, June, was born in September of 1931. When she was a toddler, she got in to the hired man's room. We were not allowed in there. He had a bowl of Lysol solution sitting on the windowsill. It was the perfect height for her to reach and she swallowed the poison. The country doctor came and said her throat was so swollen he could not get the lavage tube down to pump her stomach so she would have to go (die). What a horrifying pronouncement! Our father could not accept that verdict. He got some egg whites down June's throat to coat it and prevent more damage when the Lysol solution came back up. Then he fed her home churned unsalted butter to make her throw up the Lysol solution. Up it came. The roof of June's mouth was so burned that the skin hung down in strips. She had a long time of eating only broth and thin custard while cradled in our mother's lap but eventually made a full recovery thanks to Pa's home doctoring and Ma's home nursing.

What's In Town?
By Michelle Bickford of Cohasset, Minnesota
Born 1973

When I was growing up in the 1970s and 1980s, there was an amazing older lady who lived at the very end of the road. The tarred part of the road ended three quarters of the way down the road. So she actually lived on the dirt road. It was about a mile from our house. We used to go for walks down to her house to visit her. She was a farmer. She was really good at raising animals. She had horses, sheep, chickens, and a couple of milking cows. She also had an amazing German Shepard dog that went everywhere with her. I loved to go see what was new at her house. She always showed us around and visited about what was happening on the farm. Then she would invite us into the house for "coffee." Having coffee with her consisted of having a big glass of milk with a tiny dollop of coffee and homemade cookies. And we would visit some more. It always bothered me though, that she would only go to town one Saturday a month. That's it. She never went to town more than once a month. She would get in her truck and drive at 20 miles an hour the three miles to town. She must have got whatever she needed then and was done for the month. I was in town as a kid almost every day and I was amazed that she didn't go to town more often. So over the years, I asked her in as many different ways as I could, why she didn't go to town more often? She always replied, "What's in town?" I never could get a different answer no matter how I asked. I realize now that she had everything that she needed. She had good friends and neighbors that went to visit her, so she probably didn't get lonely. She had really nice animals to take care of and plenty of food. It was amazing though; she lived all by herself and did so much at home. I think now she might have been right, "What's in town?"

The Things I Remember
By Helen Kuester of Alexandria, Minnesota
Born 1930

We had an outhouse; I was 8 years younger than siblings, my dad made a board with a small hole in it so I wouldn't fall in the big hole. The toilet paper was the yellow pages from the Sears Catalog. It was thinner than the other pagers. Also used were peach wrappers. Another help was the chamber pot if it was a night emergency. Castor oil was used for constipation. *Amos and Andy* and *Ma Perkins*, were favorites. Also, Cedric Adams delivered the noon news.

We had party lines with your own ring, like 2 longs and 1 short ring. We could tell who was getting called. We didn't listen in but if we did, it was called "rubber-necking." Our clothes were homemade, except for coats. In winter, we had overshoes that were made of rubber. I know my mom used S&H Stamps. I believe for sugar and gas purchases. Mom used to bring eggs to grocery store in exchange for groceries. It was called trading. We always had cats in the barn and a family dog. They were never allowed in the house. They slept in the barn. Snakes were common and accepted. Swimming by my Grandma's place on a Lake Chippewa, picnics on Sunday. Our house was a place where several young men came to play music. My brother played accordion. My brother, cousins, and neighbors were drafted into the Army and Navy and they all returned safely.

Storms were accepted. Holidays were fun. One old lady called, Mrs. Gurena Melby, she lived way in the middle of "Melby's Woods." Young people used to tip the toilets on Halloween.

I attended a one-room schoolhouse for 8 years. Then it was on to high school in town. There were 2 outhouses out back in the country schools.

We started raising our six children and a root beer stand, and the drive-in theatre was a weekly treat.

The Blizzard of 1966
By Jeffrey D. Sorenson of Newfolden, Minnesota
Born 1957

It was March of 1966 in the little town of Viking, Minnesota and I remember it well. The blizzard of 1966 will go down in history. My father came home from work one evening and said he had heard there was some bad weather coming. (Forecasts were pretty much not accurate as technology was not what it is today.) Dad said he would park out on the street instead of the garage so he could get to work if our driveway plugged up with snow. As one family of 4 boys and 2 girls (ages 4-13) snuggled in, a light snow was falling and a gentle breeze whirled in the air. In the middle of the night, we were awaked by the wind howling outside out window. The blizzard had begun!

Dad did not go to work and school was cancelled as whiteout conditions raged on for two full days. On the third day, we woke to blue skies and below 20-degree temperatures but the wind had settled down. Dad told us to bundle up, as we had to help him dig his car out. The only part of the car we could see was the antenna sticking through the snow! Taking our turn to shovel, we found the car but he could not go anywhere. What a winter wonderland as 10-foot high drifts of snow were everywhere. We could walk right on to the roof of our garage and slide down the roof onto the ground. I begged my mom if I could walk the four blocks to the general store to get a treat. She said if I wear a facemask, scarf, and layers of winter clothes, I could. On the way home, my facemask was hard to breathe out of so I rolled it up. Little did I know my ear stuck out of one the eyeholes and by the time I got home, my ear was frozen.

As I sat by our woodstove and thawed out, tears gently rolled down my cheeks as blood began flowing in my ear again. Those of you who grew up in Northwest Minnesota know what I mean by the pain. I had had my fill of the blizzard by now and was content to read books for a while!

Country School Christmas Memories
By Melinda K. Taylor of Edina, Minnesota
Born 1943

I went to Medina County School District 285 in Menahga, MN, a one-room country school with grades 1st through 8th. It was a good experience and I think we learned as much as the kids do in the city schools of today. We learned by doing common ordinary things such as reading, arithmetic, and writing. I remember learning to write by the old Palmer Method, lots of practice every other day.

The time between Thanksgiving and Christmas was an exciting time for us. It was spent preparing for the big event of the school year, the Christmas program. Reading the Christmas stories was our reading class and making Christmas decorations was our art class. Practicing and reading skits was our memory work. This was at a time when America believed Christmas was the celebration of the birth of Jesus Christ, our Savior, so our music classes consisted of learning all the beloved old Christmas carols. We also had a rhythm band that had simple instruments, brass horns, tambourines, and drums. These were taken out only at Christmas time. I can still taste the metal from that old horn in my mouth. Somehow, we were able to make music with them. Our stage curtains consisted of old sheets strung across the front of the school on a wire. These sheets were held up with old fashioned safety pins. The older boys, which consisted of seventh and eighth graders, had the job of hanging these up a week or so before the program. They would open or close these between each skit and song. I think the teacher was holding her breath hoping that they would not come down.

At last, the long anticipated day of the Christmas program was here. It was usually held the Friday before Christmas vacation started. It was a community event. People came from miles around whether they had children in school or not. They also included all the old bachelors that lived in the vicinity. One year, our old Model T wouldn't start so Grandpa had to hitch the team of horses to the bobsled. It was really cold outside but nobody minded, we were warm with nice warm blankets and the straw made good insulation. It would have made a wonderful Christmas card. No wonder when I tell people about when I was growing up they ask if I knew Laura Ingalls Wilder.

We would always start the program by singing, "Joy to the World." The school kids would present skits, carols, and the rhythm band. It seemed like every year my Mom would play the guitar and my sister, Donna, and I would sing. One year we sang that old song by Doris Day, "How Much is that Doggie in the Window?" Everybody would sing Christmas carols and we would also end with "Silent Night." The curtains or sheets would close and that would be the end for another year.

After the curtains closed, Santa Claus would show up, usually he was the teachers' husband. We were each given a paper bag with an orange, some candy, and nuts in it. Everyone would visit, have coffee, eat a few Christmas cookies and bid each other a Merry Christmas and be on their way home with happy memories floating through their minds. I remember the stillness of the night, only the crunch of the horses' hooves in the snow, the stars and moon seemed so bright and beautiful. I wonder if it was on such a night out Savior was born. How I wish we could go back to the simpler times when we remembered what Christmas was all about, without the consumerism and shopping that there is these days.

Richard's class with bags of milkweed pods

was 4 years old, I remember the Army troops camping in our garden one night on their way to Camp Rejuly.

One 4th of July when I was 10 years old, I went swimming in the river. It was 104 degrees, I sure got sunburned. I also remember the Armistice Day blizzard. The big Caterpillars plowed the road. We got electricity, it was great. Two of my brothers made some homemade wheat wine. They put the mash out in the yard. The chickens ate it. It was so funny. Some just sat there and some tried to walk they just staggered and clucked like there were singing. I got my first car when I was 16 years old. It was a 1938 Chevy and it cost $40.00. That's all I can remember.

Growing Up on the Farm
By Richard Koppes of Staples, Minnesota
Born 1937

I grew up with four older brothers and a sister. My mother passed away when I was 14. I walked to school ¼ mile from home. I wore bib overalls. There were about 30 kids, grades 1st thru 8th, with 1 teacher. We each had a job to do, mine was doing farm chores. My brother, Jerry, was the cook and he would be at the neighbors and come running home about ½ hour before supper to cook. When I

Jonny's Lost
By Joan Johnson of Havre, Montana
Born 1934

My brother, Jonny, was 6 at the time, a student at the country school in Malung #3, Roseau, Minnesota, located 12 miles from the Canadian border. It was 1942. Ours was a huge two-room country school, 4 grades to a side, requiring two teachers. The total enrollment was between 50 and 60 students. At the time I was a 3rd grade big sister. It was the habit in those days to let the first graders out a bit earlier than the rest of the kids at the end of the day. Perhaps they could play without competing with the big kids or perhaps their attention span necessitated the early break.

So, on this particular day in question,

The sudents of Malung School #3 in 1940

Jonny and his first grade classmates are outside enjoying playtime. Suddenly Clifford rushes into the school to tell their teacher that Jonny has fallen into a toilet hole. The school had two outdoor toilets, one for the boys, and one for the girls. They were well maintained, that is, the holes were deep. After all, these small buildings had to provide for the needs of all those kids for the whole school year.

The frantic teacher, with flashlight and two of the big boys in tow, raced out to check the reported accident site. The expectation is that they will be fishing a small child out of a terrifying spot. They checked the boy's toilet first. No Jonny. Next, the girl's toilet (just in case). No Jonny. A search was made of the grounds, the woods surrounding the school, and every nook and cranny of the building. No Jonny. He was apparently lost. I am thinking that this must have been very stressful for the teacher. She is responsible for all her charges. The school had no telephone so there was no way to call for outside help. Could he possibly be under that mass of brown stuff in the outbuildings?

Soon the school day ended and I as big sister was instructed to go home and break the news to our parents. Dad was not home but Mom was. It was a sad assignment for a small girl. Mom didn't get excited at all when I broke the news that Jonny was probably buried in the toilet. She said, "Dad went by the school about that time to get a load of hay, he probably picked Jonny up as he went by." Indeed he had. We found out later when they came home with a big load of hay.

Poor Clifford. I guess he lost track of his friend and just assumed the worst. And what could be worse than falling down a toilet hole to the scary depths of what lay below.

Blame it on the Snapping Turtle
By Jerry Huebsch of Perham, Minnesota
Born 1948

Long before calls to 911 existed, or homemade videos became common, or cell phones in everyone's hand, an event happened to me when all three of these modern conveniences would have come in handy. The year was 1954, maybe 1955.

Just after church on a Sunday in May, our family was to have a family photo taken at my mother's parents' farm south of Perham, Minnesota. Arriving early, dad decided to see his parents too, only living 2 miles away on Rush Lake. Dad wanted to find out how fishing was since the ice recently left the lake and fishing season just opened. Dad told mom, "I'm going down to the lake and I will take Jerry and Tom with me. Be back in a few minutes." I believe I was 6 years old, maybe 7, and Tom was a year younger.

We arrived at my grandpa and grandma's

cabin on Rush Lake and Grandpa Mike wanted to take us fishing on Boedigheimer Creek, just a short half mile west of the cabin. With a short ride in grandpa's car and a small jog through the woods, all of us were at the creek. Water was high at the time but we all had our fishing poles, bait, bobbers, hooks, and fished. I stood on a culvert and Tom was about 10 feet or so to my right and dad was just beyond Tom. Grandpa was a few feet on the other side of me. I remember dad telling Tom, "Hang onto your fishing pole. Don't let go."

Me, standing on the culvert in my Sunday best clothes, wearing my baseball cap, both grandpa and dad would say to me, "Jerry, get back. You're too close to the water. You will fall in." I backed up and of course, inched forward again. Looking down in the water, I saw a big snapping turtle swimming into the culvert. I watched him, the biggest turtle I ever saw. Leaning forward and looking into the culvert, SPLASH! Down I went into that cold 6 to 8 feet of water. Immediately dad ran towards me, jumping over Tom's fishing pole, only to stumble over the pole, and Tom faithfully holding his fishing pole, flipped into the creek too. Grandpa Mike came from the other direction and jumped in to rescue Tom while dad jumped in to rescue me. All four of us were in the drink, splashing, with all kinds of commotion. Dad pulled me out. I looked at Tom and couldn't figure out why he was in the creek too. And Grandpa Mike was in there with him, all in our Sunday best. Tom was still hanging tight to his fishing pole. I lost my pole. My baseball cap was floating away towards the lake. Needless to say, fishing ended. Back to the cabin we went and the look on grandma's face said it all seeing all four of us drenched in wet clothing. "What happened?" she questioned. Immediately, grandma wrap Tom and I in some warm blankets and she took our wet clothes and hung them out to dry.

In the meanwhile, mom is at the farm and unaware what had happened, waiting for dad to come back for the family photo. Those few minutes we were supposed to be gone, turned into a few hours. Mom was very upset with dad to say the least. I believe dad was not pleased with me. Tom was upset with dad flipping him into the creek. Grandpa sure wasn't out there to get wet. Me, I was obsessed with the snapping turtle. The snapping turtle got scared and swam away. And the fish scattered and were happy because no one was fishing now.

Fast forward 60 or so years later, the year 2016, I finally had the courage to come clean. I asked Tom, "Remember that day when you and I were kids and we fell in the creek?" "Oh yes," he remembered, "Dad and grandpa kept telling you not to get so close to the water." I replied, "Well, I was watching a big old snapping turtle swimming into the culvert. He made me fall in." And now a few days later, I told my dad and mom what really happened. Oh, how they both remembered that day. "Mom and dad, a big old snapping turtle made me fall in!"

Blizzards and Bad Storms
By Dennis Gordon of Verndale, Minnesota
Born 1940

Today, January 16, 2016, I just came in from outside, where it is 12 degrees below now before noon but around 6:00 AM, it was 16 degrees below. Yesterday the pastor called, he lives in another community, and said that Sunday morning service was cancelled for the forecast is 40 degrees below. I tell you that to tell you at age 75, I dress with long underwear, 2 pairs of socks (1 cotton and the other wool), and 2 shirts both flannel. The weather hasn't changed. My wife is making a meal to share with her mother, who is 99

Uncle Oscar with Dennis, Judy, and their dog

Leon, Muriel, Dennis, Judith, and David Gordon in 1944

soon to be 100 on February 5th. I have the '94 Ford pickup plugged in so the motor will turn over having warmed up the engine. All this to say the weather still gets cold and we have got older.

I also have an '84 Ford pickup that I haul firewood with in the season. But I do remember a bygone day of cold and storms. The road to school would blow and drift and we walked or my uncle would take Bonnie, a bay horse, and Nellie, a black horse, bigger, but Bonnie was the boss. My uncle would hitch up to a single bobsled with a box on it and put hay on the floor of it for us to sit, it also worked as our sled when we cleaned behind the cows almost every day and take a trip to the field, unload by hand and return with one or two shocks. (One shock was a number of bundles of corn and food for the cows and hogs.) We would remove the ears of corn for the pigs and then the remainder of bundle were fed to the cows outside if weather allowed.

Today I am flooded with these memories, examples and just a moment an aside from the last church I pastored in Vining, Iowa. An older gentlemen, Grandpa Herb Gettle, each Christmas sends me a calendar of monthly pictures of different breeds of draft horses pulling machiner, Grandpa is in his 90's. Riding in that sled, we dressed warm but the teacher would have the big wood stove putting out heat. There were approximately 30 plus students. We all were farm kids; we fed and milked the cows by hand. We bathed once a week and being the oldest of five of us, my sister being the only girl used the water first and then us 4 boys. As I said, I being the oldest, after each one just added a little warm water, we stood by the old wood cook stove. Years later same way but we had Home Comfort stove, half wood and half gas.

One final note, my Uncle Oscar when we had a cold spell he stayed up and slept very little but would keep wood barrel stove so even glowed so the old house would "snap" and "pop" because it was so cold. I will forever be thankful that my uncle and his wife took my sister, brother and me into their home to live because our father was killed serving our country as a Marine in WWII on the island of Iwo Jima. They adopted two small boys plus my Grandma and his brother, John. A total of nine were all around the table together. We

Oscar and Vida Sorum

48

worked, we ate, and all eight of us piled in the 1946 Chevy or older and went to church together. God truly has blessed as He lets me serve Him still in a country church.

We had outhouses and chamber pots. The time of these happenings is in the late 1940s to early 1950s. My Aunt Vida and Uncle Oscar lived in North Central Minnesota. He had been a bridge builder and continued to do so but he had bought a farm, 160 acres with Red Eye River running through it. I tell you about the river as it gave us many experiences.

But back to my subject, there was a total of eight up in the family, my grandma who was in her sixties, is important in this story. It was a big farmhouse, 3 bedrooms upstairs, where in each bedroom we had a 'thundermugs' (chamber pots) and we after the other chores, washing up for school, we had to get them out to the outhouse where grandma took cleaning pail and whatever and she washed and hung them upside down on a post. In country schools mostly we walked 1 ¾ miles to school. In later years when we or some attended upper grades in town and rode a school bus. We had to have this chore done before the bus came lest we would get caught.

One thing, very special about this place (the outhouse) where we had business, one could do a lot of 'musing' if someone else was not waiting to be next. Oh! Lest I forget we received some big catalogs, Montgomery Wards, Sears & Roebuck, and Garden & Farm Journals.

My secret interest was to buy a double work harness out of Montgomery Ward's catalog at $99.95 for a lot of our farming was done with horses. I just remember we did put a stool in the basement, it was a chemical toilet, and we named it Mary Jane. It too had to be taken outdoors to be emptied.

January of 1982
By Mary Lu Stephanie of Lake Bronson, Minnesota
Born 1959

Everyone knows Minnesota is notorious for its record breaking winters. Like January 20-21, 1982, the snow storm that left 17.4 inches of snow. Followed by January 22-23 storm, which left another 20 inches of snow. My story is not about those storms, but the days following those storms.

I was a young widow, left to raise three little girls alone. My daughters were a year apart in age. At the time of this story, they were three, two, and almost one years old. We lived on a little farm about five miles from town. Every day I would put the girls in their little buntings or snowsuits, wrap them in quilts, and put them on a toboggan. I would drag them outside wherever I went. I would also drag the girls all the way down the driveway, little by little, shoveling snow as we went. We had a shed at the end of the driveway near the road. I always wondered if that were the reason the shed was built there. Maybe the previous owners would park their cars in it during bad weather. Otherwise why else would a person put a shed in such an odd spot at the end of the driveway placed so far away from all the other out buildings? So when I heard there was a blizzard coming, I would park the car in that shed. Just in case the blizzard brought to much snow for me to shovel. Well the January of 1982 blizzard did just that. It left a ten foot drift of snow right in the middle of the driveway. The huge mountain stood between me and the shed, were the car was parked.

Every day I would load the girls on the toboggan, drag them over the mountain of snow and attempt to shovel the car out. Thank God I moved the car to the shed. I would also start the car to make sure it started. One time I was nearly done shoveling and SWOOSH! The snow plows came by and with that one swoosh, I was snowed in again. I would try again tomorrow. Then finally the day came and the car fit through the tiny path I had shoveled for it. It was late so I went back to the house. Tomorrow I would attempt to head to town with the girls.

Tomorrow came. I got up early dressed the girls and loaded them on the toboggan. We headed over the huge mountain of snow… when POOF…down I went. The mountain of snow swallowed me up. Not the girls, just me. I still had one hand on the sled and held tightly to the rope. I was stuck in the ten foot drift and couldn't move. I couldn't see the girls and didn't hear a peep out of them either. First, I just stood there motionless, thinking of the predicament I was in and how in the world I was going to get out. How will anyone find me? No one knows I'm here. Will anyone notice the girls? I couldn't afford to let these thoughts control me. The girls needed me. I had to get out.

So I began to rock my body back and forth. While taking my arms and packing the snow away from me, I did this for what seemed like hours. I kept thinking how long have I been down here and the girls up there alone in the elements. Still I heard no peep from the girls. What would I do if I did hear a peep? "Just keep packing snow," I kept telling myself. Then finally I packed enough snow away from me that I could put my arms down. I also packed an area big enough for me to move my arms around. With my feet I packed and built a step for me to step on. After much more work and packing, I finally had two steps built. I could almost see out of the tunnel. I needed to now build a platform for me to climb on. Eventually, I did build the platform and climbed up on it. I was free! I pulled myself out of the hole. I didn't stand up for fear of plummeting through the drift again. So I lay on my side and rolled sideways down the drift, pulling the toboggan along with me. Thinking as I did, still no peep from the girls. I ran and started the car and loaded the girls one by one into the car, checking each daughter as I loaded them. They were fine. Thank God! I stayed in the car with the girls and sobbed as the car warmed.

Kittson County Memories
By Allan R. Gustafson of Hallock, Minnesota
Born 1924

I remember as a little boy living on a farm, and a doctor came to deliver a baby at our house. I was three years old playing on the floor, when he was ready to leave I asked him, "Aren't you going to take your baby with you?" He left the baby, turned out to be my brother Jim; I already had three brothers and a sister. We all went to school at the "Grasshopper" School District 54, it was given the name in the late 20s because the grasshoppers were so thick and they covered the fence posts and the buildings too. It was a mile and a half from home and not one tree all the way, just prairie.

This was in the early 30s and the grasshoppers were very bad, I remember men spreading poison bran mixed with Arsenic, I think, they spread it along section lines on dirt roads; we did not get much rain in those years so it did not wash away

Sometime after I was in school, I herded cattle during the summer, a lot of the land was not farmed so was all grass, I rode a pony, and it was my job to watch that the cattle didn't stray into fields that were in crop. I was too small to be able to get on the pony so if I got off I had to wait till she put head down to eat grass then I jumped on her neck, she lifted her head I was on, just had to turn around and was ready to ride. I made a lot of miles on horseback. We had at least sixty head of cattle and half dozen horses that we had to pump water from a well for, it was a tiresome job so we took turns pumping. We finally got a gas engine and a pump jack that did the work. The well was not deep so the water was not real good but we drank it too. Dad brought our first radio home in the late 20s; it was operated by dry cell battery and had a very large speaker that sat next to the radio. He put a wire for an outside antenna from the house to a pole it worked very well. We got a Station, WLS from Chicago and they had a program LULUBELLE & SCOTTY, really good music and songs, we always listened to them.

Mother did all her grocery shopping, cream and eggs paid for the groceries and bought some of our clothes in those days. Jim and I each got a quarter that took us to the movie a dime, popcorn a nickel, and we had a dime to spend for candy which was hard to buy, there were so many different choices of penny candies. We lived closer to Lancaster than Hallock, so our folks did nearly all their business in Lancaster and on Saturday nights, there was hardly room on the sidewalks. So many people in town were shopping and visiting and at the time, the stores stayed open 'til 10 o'clock. Jim and I also ran over to the Depot to watch when "The Flyer," the SOO Line passenger train, came from Winnipeg to St. Paul. The Customs men always searched the coal tender, they sometimes pulled a guy off who was trying to get in to the USA, and we thought that was pretty exciting. At that time, Lancaster had a very wide main street and they parked the cars in the center of the street and drove next to the sidewalk on both

The home farm in the 1940s

sides. One Saturday night, Jim and I were sitting in the car waiting for the folks to come and a barn caught fire it was behind the hotel not too far from us and was really burning, anyhow it scared us, we were in no danger but we did not know that.

When I was 10 years old, we moved to a farm a mile and a half to the south, now we had lots of trees around us and the North Branch of the Two River ran through the farm. We had a telephone for the first time, we kids thought that was awesome, but mother said, "No rubbernecking." The winter of '35 and '36, it stayed 30 below zero for six weeks in January and into February. Jim and I walked to school every day, we did not know what wind chill was back then. It was about a mile and a half. When we got to school the teacher kept us all huddled around the stove for an hour or so until the room warmed up some. There were about 20 students in that school from 1st grade through 8th grade and there were no partitions, just one big room. There was a coal shed with an outhouse on either end of it, boys and girls, there also was a barn with three stalls for our ponies. We brought our noon lunch; we used empty syrup pails for our lunch pail. The teacher must have brought water to drink; we had a water jug with a spigot on it in the school.

The summer of '36 was very hot and we had no electricity on the farm so no fans, no fridge. Mother had an icebox to help keep food cool it was all country people had, it worked, but not too well. Lots of people just hung milk and cream down in the well till it was in the water but not covered and that worked too. We bought ice that was cut on the river in Hallock, the ice blocks were about 2 feet square and hauled it home by truck and filled the ice shed then packed with sawdust all around about a foot thick. We cut chunks off to put in the top compartment of the box, the

Allan Ray and his brother, Delbert on the combine

University of Minnesota in 1933

ice cakes lasted all summer. Dad bought a gas generator that was kept down in the basement along with 16 large batteries it was a 32-volt system, then they bought a 32-volt electric fridge and we had electric lights in the house. The engine was both noisy and smelly, so he had a wind generator put up in 1937, it was a 32 volt too so they got rid of the engine, the next year he got a bigger 110 volt that was put out in the shop, whenever we used anything 110 volt, the engine automatically started. We used that until REA (Rural Electric Association) came in 1946, which was a God send. The generators and motors were expensive and troublesome. We never had wells with good drinking water so we made cisterns and hauled water from town. The cisterns only held 3,000 gallons so we had to haul every 3 weeks to a month, and when we ran out, we had to get water right now, without water we could not brush our teeth or make coffee. Many times the trucks were loaded or the weather was bad, it was not unusual to have to make a torch too thaw the faucet in the winter time, as it would freeze up on the way home. We got water piped to the farms in 1980, now we have water and electricity to every farm that wanted it, was that ever nice, it seemed we ran out water on a holiday or when we were having company for a meal.

In 1937, dad bought a new Minneapolis 12 foot G3 Combine and Swather on rubber tires for $1200. Dollars, at that time, it was one of the bigger Combines made. It had a 12 foot header and had pickup fingers that picked the swath off the ground. Today they use headers with a sickle that cuts the standing grain. The large combine today with header costs close to $500,000.

The folks went to the movie on Tuesday nights so Jim and I got to go ice skating, the ice arena was built in 1934 so it was a great place for public skating and lots of kids there.

In fall of 1938, I started high school at the Northwest School of Agriculture at Crookston, Minnesota, about 75 miles from home. I was 14 years old and my first time away from home, I was very home sick the first six weeks. There were nearly 400 students enrolled, we lived in dormitories and ate in the dining hall. It was an education of its own to live and eat together and learn to get along. After the first six weeks it was home to me, I met many new people and made a lot of lifelong friends. I went to school there because we lived out in the country, had no relatives in town to stay with and too young to drive, the school term was only six months, October through December and January through March. I was home for both spring and fall field work, we had to have a summer project at home such as trial plot of grain or fertilizer home beautification and other choices too. The school had shop courses that the small towns did not have at that time. It was a branch of the University of Minnesota. There were four such schools over the state. The cost for room and board was about $130 for the year, and it was not easy for my parents but they did it. After 4 years, we graduated with regular high school diploma and could go on to college and many did. The dorms had three beds in each room, 2 or 3 chairs and a small table; it was up to us to keep the room clean. We scrubbed the floor every Saturday, no classes Saturday or Sunday. The school was also an experiment station so they raised a good part of the food we ate; the food was actually pretty darn good. They served us home-style, passed around in bowls and platters, we sat 8 to a table, senior boys and girls had be at the head and served as host and hostess. For sports they had both boys and girls intermural basketball for all four grades. Boys' basketball, football, hockey, and wrestling with other schools in the area. We got black and white television reception in the early 50s and color in the early 60s, before that the reception was snow and shadows.

I have lived at the very best time in history, I think. I saw the first ball point pen, I have seen so many great inventions and improvements and technology just boggles the mind and they may not have scratched the surface yet, I regret that our generation has lost our morals, in the late 30s or early 40s the movie *Gone with the Wind* came out. In one scene, Clark Gable said to his co-star "My dear I don't get a damn" and every one thought it was awful. Well today, the movies and the books all have language that would make a mule skinner blush, I do not think it adds a thing to the story and nobody seems to give a damn. What happened?

Country Girl
By Bertina Hanson of Bagley, Minnesota
Born 1938

I was raised in Bagley, Minnesota on a 120-acre farm. I am 78 and a widow. I was just a country girl who got the cows in for milking after school. I learned to run the tractor at 11 years old helping my dad with the farm work. There were western movies on Friday night that were never missed.

I do have to reflect on my parents as they settled here and a big part of our hometown. My parents were born in Prague, Czechoslovakia. They came over at different times. My dad lived in Chicago and often told of Al Capone and things that happened. His wife was ill and was advised to come to Minnesota for the clean, fresh air would be better for her. However, he forgot about the cold weather. She passed away and Dad advertised for a housekeeper, as he had two small children. My mother answered the ad from South Dakota. My grandpa wouldn't let her go unless my dad married her; so thus, she became a "mail order bride."

I have to backtrack a bit. My mom had a farming accident and lost her leg at age nine. She wore a prosthetic. The doctor said she could never carry a child, but here I am. She was a most extraordinary lady.

They were married for 49 years. I always thought my parents worked very hard, and they did. They brought their eggs and cream to town. I always had good food and clean clothes. We had our own meat and garden, however, I was always the country kid in school.

My husband and I lived in Chicago for ten years, but came back to our roots, so to speak. We lived on a farm close to my parents for 42 years.

Working and Playing on the Farm
By Violet Hagen of Clearbrook, Minnesota
Born 1929

I am one of eight children who grew up in Clearwater County in Northern Minnesota. Our farm family appreciated the basic necessities, which our parents were able to provide. We really weren't aware of the modern services of electricity, plumbing, school buses, etc., as our neighbors and friends lived like we did.

Our country school had one teacher, eight grades, and all brought lunches, most likely in syrup pail lunch containers. Church services and Sunday school were held in the country school.

Our chores were shared by all of us. We would have to carry wood, bring in water in pails, and pick wild plums, blueberries, strawberries, and raspberries, which Mom would preserve by canning. We helped in the garden and did housework. We tended to the younger brothers and sisters and helped Dad with many farm jobs. Chickens and animals needed tending, especially bringing cows home to be milked. We always expected to meet some of the wild bears and wolves in the woods. Our trusted dog, Fritz, was always along to protect us.

We played, too! Dad would make tire swings from trees in the yard. Games and toys were scarce, but we had a wagon and checkers to entertain us. Winter snow on the hills was our ski area. Sometimes Dad would tie the sheep buck to a tree in the yard. We had a game where we rolled a tire at him. He would come at it headfirst and we would have a "ringer" on his neck! Of course, this angered him and we had to watch our rears when he was loose later! More than once, we paid for our mischief!

Looking back, life was simple and enjoyable. Families and friends visited more and seemed healthy and happy. Card parties, picnics, fishing, swimming—we were not in need of anything!

The Little Log Home
By Clarence Sindelir of Baudette, Minnesota
Born 1933

I was born June 5, 1933 in Olivia, Minnesota to Godfrey and Emma Sindelir. Brother Roger was born April 28, 1936. That same year, Godfrey moved his family with his 1930 Model A Ford north to Lake of the Woods County where he had acquired 120 acres of un-cleared land several miles southwest of Pitt, Minnesota.

Our first home was an unused 20 ft. by 20 ft. log house located about 1 mile from the 120 acres. Godfrey began work on the government W.P.A. Program. At the same time, he started hand clearing a trail into the 120 acres, which was about 1 mile from a traveled county road. He purchased an old Fordson tractor that he used to travel the trail into his property. All the time not working on the W.P.A. job was spent hand clearing with a bow saw, ax, and a grub hoe. The Fordson was used to pull stumps and trees.

In 1939, I started grade school in the Peppermint Creek School which was about 3 miles from the little log house. The school was very small. One-room, one teacher, and eight grades. A total of about 25 students. The school was heated with a wood burning barrel stove. There were no electric lights and no running water. Out back there were boys and girls outdoor toilets, a woodpile, and a hand dug well. A neighbor, Alton Grund, had an old bus and hauled kids to and from school. Often times, when roads were bad, we had to walk to and from school. I walked the 3 miles many times. In 1942, the Peppermint Creek School was closed and consolidated with the Pitt School.

Roger started his first year of school in the Pitt School. Like the Peppermint Creek School, the Pitt school was heated with wood. There was a woodshed out back, boys and girls outdoor toilets and a hand dug well. The Pitt School had two-rooms, two teachers, eight grades, and about 60 students. In both schools, kids brought lunch from home. Unlike the Peppermint Creek School, the Pitt School had electric lights.

My sister Donna Mae was born in 1942. By this time, the county had put a road through by the 120 acres. We had moved from the little log house to a larger house dad had moved on the property and we had electricity and a telephone. Some of the land had been cleared and dad was doing some farming with the old Fordson tractor.

The Pitt School District #117 was consolidated with the Baudette School District in 1968.

Farmyard Work and Play
By Peggy Rattei Donahe of Wahpeton, North Dakota
Born 1940

We grew up on a farm in North Dakota. We have lots of memories from our time back then. There were six of us with very creative minds.

We had a very large garden that had to be weeded every day. Since we all were out there, we decided to play as well. We built roads, bridges, and barns. We each had our own fenced in area in which we would haul the weeds to until we were done weeding for the day. The trucks and tractors were small, so we made lots of trips. Sometimes we would meet and have lunch together or even help each other out.

Pretty soon, we made canals and rivers so we could water our crops. Sometimes we had

Peggy's brothers, Jayen and Jordon Rattei

to build our bridges bigger.

Another adventure was when our folks went to town, we would ride the horse, or a sheep ram. Buster was pretty smart. We would take him to the barns so we could get on him. Three would get on at a time. The first one would hold on to his mane. He would take us around the yard once and then he would head for a small incline we had in the yard. You guessed it! We all would slide off!

The sheep was a different story. Only my brothers would ride him, even if they weren't supposed to. So whenever Dad was out in the field, they would let the ram out and ride him. The funny thing was that whenever Dad was in the yard, the ram would butt him. For the longest time, Dad could not figure it out. Why was he the only one that got butted? My mom didn't know the boys were riding him, either.

Our mom raised chickens to sell at the store. Three times a week, we were up very early to dress out 20 chickens so they were ready at 10:00 A.M. for the driver to pick them up to take to town. We had one very colorful rooster who would strut around the yard so proudly, except when our youngest brother was outside. If Mom wasn't around, the rooster would chase him back to the house. We don't know why he picked on Tony; maybe it was because he was small and the youngest.

The Rattei family

We had so many fun stories to tell at our last family reunion. My sister, Nancy, wrote a poem for Mom's birthday a few years ago:

A Testament

She's a lady without fame or grace
I will never forget my mother's face
She lived on a rocky road
Most often carried a heavy load.
Eight children needed fed
She prayed to God for daily bread
Living each day one at a time
With reason, but without rhyme.
Many things were left undone
A better race she could have run
Even these things have shown us how
And helped to make us what we are now.
If you give my words some thought
We learned a lesson that she taught
For we are the testament,
That her life was well spent.
A thousand children passing by,
Taught by teachers, Peggy, Rachel, Viola, and I
To feed the people of the land
Bringing the harvest was Gerry and Tony's plan
In the darkness of the night
Jaycen helps provide the light
While we were all at our station
Jordan served to protect the nation.
Now as we all gather around
We are the jewels in Mother's crown.
Only in our silent dreams
Forever she will be a queen.

The Monster Storm
By Arlis Bresnahan of St. Anthony, Minnesota
Born 1937

Every November in Minnesota, we are reminded in newspapers, TV, and radio of the 1940 Armistice Day snowstorm, which left 50 people dead. Many of those who perished were duck hunters.

But there was another monster storm four months later, this time in the Red River Valley. Saturday, March 15th was a spring-like day. The weather forecast predicted light local snow with a cold wave and strong northerly winds…and the winds were! They came roaring down from Canada up to 85 miles per hour. And the snow fell! People described it as a blanket draped over the car. The cars were immediately stopped, and the temperature plummeted to below zero degrees.

Seventy-two people perished, most from exposure, CO_2 poisoning, or suffocating on blowing snow and dirt. Thirty-eight people from North Dakota succumbed, 28 from Minnesota, four from Manitoba, and two from Saskatchewan!

Being Saturday, many farmers and their families were in various towns shopping. As they drove home, the storm hit. Their cars became disabled and many left their cars to find their way home. Their bodies were found the next day.

A train crew south of Pembina, North Dakota were unaware a dead, frozen 13-year-old girl was on their cowcatcher. They found her sister further on the tracks. The girls had been in Pembina and were walking home on the tracks.

Stephen, Minnesota (my hometown), a small town of about 1,000 people and located 50 miles east of Grand Forks, North Dakota, was fortunate not to have any deaths.

Since it was March, high school basketball tournaments were being played. Stephen was hosting district tournaments. The storm hit during the game. By the end of the game, all 700 spectators were stranded in the gym and school overnight and well into Sunday. Members of the commercial club made several trips downtown to the restaurants. The restaurants were on 24-hour shifts and provided food for the stranded teams and fans. Coffee was provided by the school.

The Roseau Team didn't show up for the final game. Eleven players, superintendent, and coach were found Sunday morning, all in one of two cars in a ditch south of Stephen. Only two boys suffered shock and chills from exposure.

My family lived about ten miles northeast of Stephen in the little community of Happy Corner. My parents and 20 other couples were in Moorhead attending the farm crop shows. They had returned as far as near Grand Forks when the snowstorm covered the car like a blanket. They were unaware I was not at our neighbor's but at home with my brother Bob. I had asked my neighbor to go home because the weather was so nice. I was three and a half years old and Bob was 13 years old.

Our house had two stovepipes. The one on the kitchen blew over, so the wood cook stove didn't work, which was fortunate because we were not affected by the CO_2.

Bob heated water on the wood-burning heater in the living room and made me oatmeal. He tried once to go to the barn to tend to the cows, but returned when he couldn't make it.

On Sunday, two neighbors arrived to bring Bob and me to their farm. They had a bedspread and formed it into a hammock to carry me. Bob stayed in the hired men's bunkhouse. I wanted so badly to stay with Bob, but the neighbors wouldn't let me. I remember being in bed with one of the women as she told me stories of her childhood.

I don't remember when my parents returned or any more of the storm. As I reflect on this, I see how well Bob took care of me… with the help of angels, of course.

Escapades of a Swedish Farm Girl
By Elizabeth "Betty Faye" Anderson Lindsay of Clearbrook, Minnesota

I am sitting here reminiscing about early life in Northwestern Minnesota. Do I have anything special that I can share with readers? I come from a very normal Swedish upbringing that centered around family, church, school, 4-H, and community activities. As I continued to delve into my past, I shared a chuckle or two with myself. I have entitled my epistle "Escapades of a Swedish Farm Girl."

My first recollection was awakening in my crib, pulling back the covers, and looking at my legs. My cousin, who was a few years older, had talked me into eating fish food the day before and told me in the morning I would turn into a beautiful mermaid. That was my first major disappointment.

Swedes love their coffee and I started "imbibing" at an early age. After coffee parties, I would go around and drain every drop from the cups until Mama caught me. It didn't stunt my growth, as I turned out the tallest in my ninth grade class.

Being my name is Betty, I was always baking "Betty Crocker," which consisted of flour, salt, and water baked on a coffee can cover on the old wood stove. Poor Mama and Daddy ate my burnt offerings and most likely suffered in silence, but grinned and bared it! Much later in life, I did a weekly recipe program on the radio station where my husband worked. Needless to say, I had advanced from my creations of yesteryear.

Music on the radio got me dancing at an early age. When my Baptist minister grandfather visited, Mama made sure the radio was off, as dancing was a Baptist "no-no" back then.

My brother was a good-looking little boy. I would pinch his cheeks to make them rosy and sometimes gave him "hot boxes" heated on the stove. Needless to say, today I would probably end up in kiddy court for sibling abuse.

Another memory, I recall, is a cold, rainy Easter Sunday when I was five or six, and my brother was two years my junior. There on the porch next to our Easter baskets lay the Easter Bunny with an injured leg. Our little minds were so impressed as Daddy exclaimed that he had been hurt while delivering our Easter treats. With tender loving care, he recovered and hopped away.

Fun times were had licking the salt block and mooing like a cow, walking on stilts, learning to ride a bike with all those skinned knees, and whistling duets with my brother at Farm Bureau meetings.

I was fascinated by the big console radio in my upstairs bedroom. It no longer worked, so the "innards" were removed and I would crawl into the back and perform a soap opera or two. Little did I know, but much later, I married a radio announcer.

When I was young, I had long hair. (Come to think of it, I still have my braids tied with a plaid ribbon in a little memory box.) One time I recall my hair getting caught in the wringer washer. Luckily, Mama was there to rescue me before I got scalped! While sitting under the big oak tree drying my tresses, a bat flew in and got tangled in my hair. Mama had to cut him out with a scissor. Thus, my great fear of bats!

Frog legs were a delicacy back in those days. I recall my brother, a friend, and I killing a frog, skinning the legs, and frying them on a coffee can cover on a bonfire. Last fall, a frog hopped into our dwelling and while chasing him, I had fond memories of those delicious morsels of yesteryear!

I began writing in grade school. One of my poems, "Days of the Week" was published in our local paper. Through the years, Mama would send me yellowed copies of poetry I had penned. The last poem I wrote was entitled "The Girls with the Grandma Faces" in honor of my Aunt Signe's 90th birthday.

We had a large cattle tank out by the barn. One time a friend came out, dunked me in the tank, and said, "This is how the Baptists do it." Thus, I became a Lutheran-Baptist!

Back then, I was fascinated by crawly things. I wrote an essay entitled "Ode to an Earthworm" for a high school project. The cover was nicely decorated with a worm made out of buttons. I became the proud owner of a wooden snake with 28 segments, so I named it Anacompopolitan Dur Dur O'Durley, a letter for each section. I had forgotten about "Ana" until five years ago when we were cleaning out they old farmhouse. My husband exclaimed, "I found your snake!" "Ana" was still in good shape for a snake!

A big thing way back then and still continuing are church suppers. I remember my first experience with lefse (a Scandinavian bread made with flour, potatoes, butter, and cream). It does resemble a white napkin after being thinly fried. "That man buttered his napkin, rolled it up, and took a bite of it!" I exclaimed to Mama, with eyes as big as saucers. Lefse is now on my favorite food list.

Everything was better with butter back then. Nobody thought about clogged arteries. Margarine was a bad word, especially for dairy farmers. I wanted to join a contest, which required sending in two Blue Bonnet box tops. Daddy was so upset that his daughter would stoop to buy such a disgraceful item.

One Christmas season, I recall my younger brother coming home from Sunday school quite disturbed. "Mama, why did they give manure to the baby Jesus?" Mama exclaimed it was gold, frankincense, and myrrh. After all, he was a farm boy!

Way back then, we didn't have TV, so my girlfriend and I would go to a home with a little black and white set while our dads were at monthly church board meetings. How we loved watching boxing and wrestling (our only choices)!

We had four horses, Topsy, Bessie, Maude, and Colonel. I used to ride Colonel who was big, slow, and had the heaves. Once atop Colonel, my brother tied him to the porch post. He pulled and away came the huge porch pillar between his reins. I can still visualize the sagging porch and a terrified yours truly!

One summer, I went to Bible Camp down by the big city of Minneapolis. We stayed at our chaperone's relatives on the way to our destination. When arriving, upon opening my suitcase, lo and behold, a set of false teeth presented themselves. How they got there remains a mystery to this day. Agatha Christy to the rescue!

"The Boy with Green Hair" with Dean Stockwell was showing at the local theater. As Mama drove up with us three kids in tow, billowing smoke was pouring out of the theater, so no movie that day and never again.

One of my high school teachers was very handsome and some of us gals had a crush on him. I recall disguising my voice, calling on the phone, and asking him to drink champagne from my silver slipper. My partner in crime gargled in the background, imitating champagne bubbles!

I spent six weeks on a Minnesota-Mississippi 4-H Exchange Program upon graduating from high school. Being I hail from Clearwater County, which contains the source of the Mississippi River (where I have waded across) and then to see the mighty river empty into the Gulf of Mexico on the other was quite an experience! Friends and family detected a Swedish southern accent upon my return!

"You can take the girl out of the country, but you can't take the country out of the girl." I put my nursing skills to action both in the big city and on the farm. "Nurse Betty sticks it to them" was the theme every now and then as I gave shots to young pigs. Needless to say, my sterile technique went out the window, but I am happy to have contributed to "hog health."

I have traveled all over the United States, Canada, Mexico, the Caribbean, and twice across the pond, but a Swedish plaque on my kitchen wall sums my life up the most accurately: *Bort er Bra Men Hjemme er Best* (Away is Good, But Home is Best).

As my memoir ends, I am thankful every day for growing up in a God-centered family in Northwestern Minnesota (even though back then we were Democrats!).

Seasons of My Youth
By Ardell Nyhus Lewis of Bemidji, Minnesota
Born 1941

My name is Ardell (Nyhus) Lewis. I was born September 19, 1941 in Bagley, Minnesota, to my parents Harry and Eveleth Nyhus. I grew up in the Debs area, which is 30 miles northwest of Bemidji.

I can remember in the spring, many times roads and culverts would wash out. They were all dirt roads in our area. There was one time my neighbor girl and I decided to walk down the road about two miles to visit my aunt. We did not ask our folks if we could go. A culvert had washed out and we walked across the creek on boards, there was a lot of water in the creek. Our parents had a search party out looking for us; we paid the price dearly and never did that again! We both got our back-ends spanked when they found us.

Summers were busy living on a farm. On hot days, my folks milked the cows, by hand, outside of the barn. The milk was put in a separator, separating the milk from the cream. The cream was put in cream cans and brought to a creamery. The milk (other than what we used in the house) was fed to the calves and pigs. My brother, sister, and I would churn butter. I remember enjoying the buttermilk; it was sweet tasting with tiny chunks of butter in it. I can remember all the wild berries we'd pick, raspberries, strawberries, blueberries, etc., with my mother canning them into sauce, over a hot wood burning range. She also canned the garden vegetables, and meat.

We also had to carry water into the house from a well and the only bathroom was a backhouse, which in the summer you'd find a snake on the floor. In the winter - you'd freeze your back end, anyway it felt that way!

In the fall, before school started, we'd get a big box of clothes from an aunt in California. Her kids had outgrown them, and we were excited to open it and try them on.

We had to walk about a mile or so to meet the school bus. Sometimes it was so cold and we'd wait for that bus and it wouldn't show up (bus probably wouldn't start) so we had to walk home and thaw ourselves out by the wood stove.

There was a lot of deep snow in those days. One time my neighbor girl friend and I were running on top of the hard-

Ardell with her brother, Ralph

Ardell with her sister, Marilyn

crusted snow, my leg went through clear to my crotch, and I couldn't pull my leg out. My friend ran to get her mother. Her mother came and jokingly she told me she'd have to hook up the horse and pull me out - boy - it wasn't long before I figured out how to wiggle that foot and leg out!

We didn't have a television, but listened to a lot of stories and music from the radio. My sister and I played on an old pump organ we had, and we'd sing.

There were a lot of hard trying times with illness with my father and sister and then my mother. But we were always a family with good humor and belief in God that gave us the strength we needed to carry us through. Life was tough in those days but it made us strong in spirit and thankful for the good things in life too.

The Old Grey Mayor
By Lynn M. Jeffers of Cohasset, Minnesota
Born 1945

My mother's name was Edna Comstock. She was the cook at the Cohasset School. (My dad was janitor and I was a student there back in the early 1950s.) People kept coming to our house and saying that my mom should run for mayor of our town. She did run and won by a landslide!

Edna Comstock

Edna Comstock as Justice of the Peace

Back then, it was uncommon for a woman to have such a position. I was in third grade, I think. The kids came to school and teased me—not in a bad way—they just never heard of a woman having such a job! All the kids loved my mom and because she was a cook at the school, they all knew her well. They teasingly called her "The Old Grey Mayor!" (Mare)

Things went well for her as mayor. Before my dad and I knew what was happening, she became the deputy sheriff of our town. If there was a fight at the liquor store, they'd call Mom. She'd strap on her pistol, snap on her badge, and hike down the block and break up the fight. Looking back, I kind of think of her as the Barney Fife of Cohasset. I know she had a pistol, but I never saw a bullet.

Before Dad and I knew what was happening (again), she was the Justice of the Peace! She could—and did—marry people right in our living room! (My dad tolerated her being mayor pretty well, but because he liked his meals on time, I'm guessing that he was one of the very few that voted against her!) She was a busy gal!

From the Woods to the Whole World
By Janice Knight Evensen of Effie, Minnesota
Born 1922

Life in the Northwoods of Minnesota in the early days gives the modern world much to think about.

Our family lived by the Big Fork River

on land homesteaded by my father, James Knight. My mother came here as a country schoolteacher. My father decided he would marry her the first time he saw her.

My father was the first one from his family married, so he was expected to produce a child. This child, a baby boy, was born a year later. The extended family gave him an old family name, Jere Knight. Many people have read the name Dr. Jere Knight with no idea of his humble childhood.

Jere walked a mile and a half to school with his brother and sisters. The country school concentrated on academics for grades one through eight. What a challenge for a teacher! One boy came to school speaking only Norwegian. He remained in first grade for three years before he learned English so that he could move on.

Jere was always very curious. We had no electricity, but we had a telephone attached to the wall operated by a battery. Our shop had many tools and gadgets, including a telephone and battery. Jere tinkered with the old phone and was surprised to get a shock. Leave it to Jere to think of something to do with the phone. The outdoor toilet was behind the shop. Jere pounded a big nail on each side of the toilet hole. He found enough wire to attach the old telephone to the underside of the toilet seat. Jere kept a close eye on traffic to the toilet so he could turn the crank. A neighbor girl was very nervous. I took her to the toilet and Jere turned the crank. Dorothy jumped up and screamed, "Chipmunks!" Jere tried to wire the fence for the cattle, but that was not allowed for our prize Guernsey cows.

Jere was a very good student who graduated from Bigfork High School. He went on to Hibbing Junior College and then to St. John's University near St. Cloud, Minnesota where he graduated with a degree in chemistry. This was followed by graduate school in the University of Minnesota. This is when our parents received a letter stating, "I am in the University of Chicago. Do not tell anyone where I am." We did not know he was part of the Manhattan Project where they split the atom to make the bomb that ended WWII. Shortly after the end of the war with Japan, the war with Hitler's Germany was also over.

After more studies, Jere was now Dr. Jere Knight. He was invited to make a presentation at Oxford University in England, and meet with laboratory scientists for a week in Moscow, Russia.

All this was before Dr. Jere accepted a position at Los Alamos, New Mexico. This is known as the atomic city on a mountaintop by Santa Fe. Los Alamos is an interesting city where the atomic bomb was also developed. For many years, the only entrance to the city was guarded by the military. Visitors had to be very specific about who they wanted to visit and why. Children of the families in Los Alamos lived very different lives from children in other cities. A boy we met had received a pet snake for Christmas. The snake was emotionally and visibly attached to the boy. He preferred to be coiled around the boy's leg.

Los Alamos was where Dr. Jere met his wife, Sylvia. She was also a scientist who had escaped from Cuba on the last plane Castro had allowed to leave. Both Jere and Sylvia were part of many important activities in Los Alamos.

This makes one wonder what is being done now in Los Alamos and why.

A Family Saved by Faith
By Bernard Lewis of Bemidji, Minnesota
Born 1934

My story began in Albert Lea, Minnesota, where I, Bernard "Jim" Lewis, and my twin sister Betty, were born in 1934.

My dad and mother were farming on my paternal great uncle's farm. We were born in the farmhouse and that house is still in use with new owners. The barn was a big stone basement barn, which is still standing to this day.

In about 1936, during the depression, my folks had a sale, selling the cows for about $4.00 a head.

My dad's father had a general store in Steven's Point, Wisconsin. He bought 40 acres of land in the Bemidji, Minnesota area for my father. (I still live on this land.) There were no buildings, just all woods.

My dad, mother, and four children (two older brothers and us twins) were moved up to the Bemidji area in a Buick car and a Model

Bernard's mother, Agnes Lewis in 1950

T truck, pulling a trailer with one horse and three cows in it. My parents rented an old shack of a house where my youngest sister was born in 1937. These people they rented from sold the house in the late fall in about 1939 when snow was on the ground. My dad had to quickly build a log house on top of frozen ground. He tried to plaster between the logs, but it froze and fell out. Then he used paper on the inside of the house and cow manure on the outside, and soon a lot of that fell out, too.

I remember my two brothers and I sleeping together in the same bed. We would wake up in the morning with streaks of snow across our blankets. I remember our mother could only wash the floors on warm days because on cold days, the floors would freeze over with ice. The water pail would have to be emptied every evening; otherwise, it was frozen by morning. Before a well was dug, my folks hauled water home from a neighbor.

We had real tough times, but my mother had a lot of faith. Food was very scarce, but we always seemed to manage somehow. There was one time I remember that there was no money to buy a bag of flour to make bread or cream mush (which we ate a lot of). In a day or two, my mother received a five-dollar bill in the mail from her sister for her birthday. Someway, the folks got to town and bought a bag of flour.

There was a side hill that my father dug out with a dump scraper for the cattle barn. Then, for the roof, we had poplar poles lumber over the poles, tarpaper, and hay. There was a wall built in front made of poles and lumber.

My grandfather helped to pay for a well to be dug and a hand pump. I remember we walked two and a half miles one-way to a one-room schoolhouse. We were a close-knit family who helped each other to pull through those tough times.

We all grew up with a background of hard work and all have done well. Of the five children, four are still living except my twin sister who died of cancer at the age of 72.

I am 82 years old and still help my son who owns my farm now with the beef cattle and putting up hay and other farm projects. The farm has expanded to 400 acres. We rent another 100 acres. This is a three-generation

Bernard "Jim", his cousin, Betty and Joann

farm with a granddaughter who wants to someday make it a four-generation family farm.

My Favorite Teacher
By Lawrence Torske of McIntosh, Minnesota
Born 1933

The greatest man I ever knew was the superintendent of our school. We all called him Piney. He would come into our rooms and teach. He would ask the question and then give us the answer, so he would teach us besides being superintendent. Also, if there was a dispute in school, Piney would get it settled.

He was a magician. Piney would fold newspapers and balance them on the end of his fingers.

I drove to school, and when Piney wanted to go somewhere, he would have me drive him there. He was my driver's education teacher. So the highway officer came and gave me my driver's test in front of the school. So Piney is the gent that got me my driver's license.

A member of the school board said Piney didn't get much wages, and he never asked for more. He just liked our town so he wanted to live out his life here. He blended in with everyone. He didn't live high. He lived conservatively and was a Christian man. Piney was the greatest influence in my life.

This is the story of R.L. Edwards, the superintendent and mayor of McIntosh, Minnesota.

What a Dog!
By Karl Kuebelbeck of Long Prairie, Minnesota
Born 1961

In the late '60s, my parents moved from the "city" (Cold Springs) to a hobby farm in the country. Being the ninth child in a family of twelve, the openness of a larger house was a great relief for me and my siblings. My mother raised (besides children) ducks, geese, and chickens – not counting the 12+ cats and Tuffy the dog. Tuffy was a German Shepherd/wolf mix. He was the size of a small horse.

Our milkman, Scooty, delivered "kegs" of milk to the house. The kegs were put into a small refrigerator. The milk was hooked up to a spigot, and when you turned on a faucet, the milk filled up your glass or pitcher. This was our family "cow."

One day the family came home from church to find Scooty sitting in his truck and Tuffy sitting next to his driver seat door.

We came to find out that Scooty, who came to deliver the milk like always and knew the dog well, tried to walk up to the front door where Tuffy was guarding. Tuffy gently grabbed Scooty by the arm, led him back to his truck, and held him "prisoner' until the family came home.

Just another day in the country! What a dog!

Windy and the Marble Mallards
By Jeanne Roberts of Coleraine, Minnesota
Born 1940

I have many precious memories of growing up as a young girl in Marble, Minnesota. The one that never leaves me is the memory of the Marble Mallards playing a home baseball game on Sunday afternoon. The ballpark would be full, and people would have to park along the highway and walk a short distance to enter the park. The adults would pay a small fee, and there was no charge for children. Pop, beer, hot dogs, candy, and chips were available, and the fun was to begin.

The Marble Mallards were first organized in 1909. In June of 1976, the ballpark was dedicated to the memory of Billy Knight and Donald "Todd" Anderson, two local young men who gave their lives in the service of our country.

The Mallards had many great managers. I recall the greatest of my era, Robert "Windy" Anderson, who managed the Mallards from 1938 to 1969. Windy devoted his life to baseball and provided Marble with some of the finest entertainment.

Windy had many young men hoping to make the team. One incident still talked about when baseball folks congregate happened in the 1950s. A thin young man visiting his grandparents in Calumet, our neighboring town, tried out for the Mallards. Windy cut him; "Not good enough for the Mallards," he said. This young man grew some, moved to North Dakota, and is now a legend. We know this young man as Roger Maris. Windy had a hard time living that down.

Marble folks were very proud of their Marble Mallards and were upset to read the sports page of the *Hibbing Daily Tribune* and find the writer casually mention the next game, Hibbing Greyhounds vs. Marble Mallards, and stating that the Mallards looked like a bunch of Hell's Angels out on the field.

There was a lot of friction between Windy and the Greyhound manager, Al Nyberg. They loved each other, but not on the field. There was never a dull moment when the two of them were in competition. They would argue over the most trivial issues. One of my favorites was the time they argued over who was the most "fit," each of them being overweight. That issue was solved when they decided to have a race. I have to report that Al won the race but the Mallards won the game. As the game ended, the sportswriter ran to his car as I, a young mouthy teen, hollered (embarrassing her mother), "How was that for a bunch of Hell's Angels?"

Many of the players of the Mallards of my era have passed on, and many of the living have many, many happy memories as mine. Windy is no longer with us, but his memory lives on. I am proud to say Windy is my dad, and you can bet he is pitching that ball around heaven's doors.

Thanks, Dad, for the memories!

Marie with her mother

ran to my mother, and she said it wasn't a rain cloud but grasshoppers. I didn't understand what she meant.

The next morning, I went outside to find my daddy. I was always following him around. I found him out in the field. The field that was full of tall, waving grain yesterday was nothing but stubble and sticks. My dad was on his knees, so I thought he was praying. As I got closer, I saw he was also crying. I became so frightened, as Daddy never cried. So I started to cry, too.

My dad put his arms around me and said, "Don't worry; we'll always have something to eat."

We were always hearing about children who didn't have enough to eat!

The Cloud of Grasshoppers
By Marie Engen of Thief River Falls, Minnesota
Born 1932

I grew up on a farm in northern Minnesota. This was in the mid-thirties in which there were very difficult Depression years.

I was so afraid of thunder and big dark storm clouds. Late one evening, I looked to the west and I saw a big black cloud coming. I

Uncle Frank's Milk Route
By Dennis E. Nordstrom of Long Prairie, Minnesota
Born 1951

I was born in the sleepy little river town of St. Paul, Minnesota, in 1951. My mother was a St. Paul native, and my father was born on a farm near the town of Browerville, Minnesota.

My parents loved St. Paul. So they settled there and raised a family with five children in it there.

My father was born into a large family, eleven siblings in all. Most of them were born and raised on a farm that my grandfather bought in 1920 just east of the central Minnesota town of Browerville. My father left that farm around the age of sixteen to seek his fortune elsewhere and to explore other worlds not found on their poor farm. Some of his siblings did the same. Some left the farm and went to the Twin Cities. Some stayed in the area they were born in and started farming themselves.

Farming is a lot of work. Hard work. And you have to stick to it if you're going to have a chance at some success. This was very apparent at the three farms my relatives had near Browerville. My aunts and uncles worked their hind ends off to get by. Besides taking care of their children, cows, pigs, chickens, crops, etc., some of them found jobs off of the farm to supplement their income. A couple of these people were my uncle Frank and his son Gene.

Frank and Gene had jobs hauling fresh milk from farms to creameries. One of the creameries was located in the town of Randall, Minnesota, and the other one was in Browerville. I think it was every day except Sunday that Frank or Gene had to drive to numerous farms and pick up milk. They did this in big trucks designed for hauling milk cans. These trucks were also called deuce and a half. They were big and powerful. The men would drive these trucks to farms all over the area. And at these farms were cans of milk that had been recently taken from cows. The milk needed to be taken to the creamery as soon as possible to keep its freshness. Hauling milk is an important job. And my uncle and cousin were good at it.

Every so often, when I was a young boy, I'd get to ride along on the milk routes. It was a special thrill for a city boy like me. I think the tires on the milk truck were taller than me when I started riding along with Uncle Frank. When I was up in the cab of that big truck with Frank or Gene, I was on top of the world. I got to go to so many different farms, some nice, some sort of trashy, and some in between. I met a lot of nice people who lived on all those farms. I got to know their pets, too. Uncle Frank would warn me beforehand on whether or not it was safe to get out of the truck and pet any of the dogs or cats that were at the farms we stopped at.

When we stopped to pick up milk, Frank or Gene would go to where the full milk cans were kept. This was usually in a wood staved tank filled with cold well water. Each can weighed about 90 pounds when full. I was too small and puny to carry one of them. But my Uncle Frank could carry one with each arm. He was very strong and could whip those full milk cans up into the truck with no problem.

When we finished our route, and we had a lot of cans of milk in the truck, we headed to one of the creameries. That was another special treat for me. When Uncle Frank had finished unloading and sending the full milk cans into the creamery, he'd take me inside to show me the workings of the place. I remember the steam, the stainless steel, the tile walls, the tile floors, and the smells. Then he'd treat me to a bottle of fresh chocolate milk, probably bottled just minutes before. After that, we'd load up some empty cans to exchange for full ones and head back out. I think that there were two trips to the creamery a day.

I wasn't the only one to go on ride-alongs on the milk route. Cousins and other family members went along from time to time. I'm sure that they had fun and have wonderful memories as have I of it.

Uncle Frank is gone now. So are the milk routes of the type Minnesota had years ago. Back then, there were a lot of small dairy farms that trucks like my uncle's had to visit and get the milk from. Now it's go big or you can't make it. That means large dairy producing farms with a large volume of milk that's kept in very large, clean, bulk tanks. Now, huge bulk trucks take the milk to large processing plants. Those old milk cans are now collector items. Those small town creameries are gone. Many of those farms we stopped at are no longer farms. A lot of those dusty dirt roads are still here. And so am I. I built and moved into a house two miles away from the farm my grandfather had. So I'm close to where all those memories were made. And one of my fondest memories is of going on the milk route.

In My Glory
By Barbara Olson of Litchfield, Minnesota
Born 1936

I started teaching in a one-room country school when I was 19 years old. I had always wanted to be a teacher. My dad wasn't living, and my mom didn't have the money to send me to college, so I went to "teacher training" in Madison, Minnesota, for one year.

When I "got" my school I was just in my glory. I taught all seven grades. I had never been in a country school before I went there. The pupils were so nice (the parents, too!). I'd go outside at recess and play games with them. One game was pump, pump, pull away. One side had to guess what the other side was doing. They were shoveling. We never did guess what they were doing. They were digging a grave for their former teacher, who was very old.

We had great times at Christmas. We put on a play for the parents. We had a curtain strung on a wire.

One of my "highlights" was watching a mouse jumping up and down in an empty milk bottle in the entry room. I asked who wasn't afraid of a mouse (I was). Many hands went up. A fifth grader captured it for me.

In October, after I'd been there a while, I made coffee for the parents one night. I'm sure it was "tasty." They drank it though.

I had so many memories. One was going to the outhouse and a cat was in the hole. Did I jump up fast!

I wish I'd kept a diary of all the things that happened. I wonder where my pupils are now. I'm almost 80 now and think of the "good old days!"

Barbara Kern Olson

Going Visiting and Having Company
By Carol M. Kofstad of Warroad, Minnesota
Born 1944

Oh yes, I remember the outhouse and the chamber pots from the "good old days." My sister and I used to go out to the outhouse after a meal and sit there for quite some time hoping that Mom would do the dishes before we got back into the house. But it never worked; she would out wait us, because she knew what we were doing, and we'd still have to do the dishes when we got back inside. Trouble was, by that time the food had dried on the plates, and it was harder to clean the dishes.

Party lines, oh yes, you never knew who was listening when you made a phone call, so you didn't dare say certain things on the phone because that person might be listening – rubber necking, we called it. So to get around that, my friend who was on my line and I would set up a certain time to pick up the receiver, and we would talk without ringing the phone. At that time there was no dial tone; it was an open line for talking, and if we didn't ring each other no one would know we were talking.

"Old neighbors" – oh yes, I remember our old neighbors. They were my mother's aunt and two bachelor male cousins, and they would come over to play cards, or we would go over to their place and play cards. They were very unique. "Auntie" would excuse herself after playing one or two games at their house, and then she would make "lunch." When we had finished the next game she would have a many course "lunch" to serve all of us. When I was home from school in first grade with pneumonia, the one cousin would walk over – yes, it was January and very cold out – and he would play Canasta with me to keep me entertained for hours. I was bored out of my wits but couldn't go outside and play, so he entertained me by playing cards with me. One winter, we had so much snow that they were blocked in for months, and "Auntie" couldn't walk the distance to the road so hadn't been anywhere for months. One sunny day, my family and I walked in from the road – they had a long driveway – and we played cards all afternoon. She enjoyed seeing other people and visiting for the afternoon.

Drive-in movies – oh yes, I remember the drive-in movies at Malung Hall. No, it wasn't the same as drive-in movies they have now. There were only the large speakers on the top of the concession stand, and you had to keep your windows open in order to hear the movie. Trouble was we also had mosquitoes. Sometimes it was hard to hear the movie over the buzzing of the mosquitoes, because you couldn't have the windows open more than a crack in order to keep most of the mosquitoes out of the car. But it was fun! That's where we met our friends and socialized during the summer.

Yes, I grew up with homemade clothes and hand-me-downs. No one ever threw clothes away; you handed them down to cousins or neighbors who had children that they would fit. My mother was a very good seamstress and could alter clothes to fit when needed. She did sewing for other people, too, so she had a lot of scrap material. Flour was bought in sacks made from material, and my mother would sew us blouses and dresses from the flour sacks. We were happy to have our "new" clothes, and because everyone else was "in the same boat" no one made fun of us.

"Visiting" was a pastime that my family did a lot of the time. Cousins, neighbors, and friends would come over in the evening, or we would go to their houses. No one waited for an invitation. We would just "drop in" and visit with them or they would come to our house to visit. Summer was especially good for that because there was no school to go to the next day, so we could be up later at night. My family loved "company," and we had visitors as often as we went visiting. Sometimes my mom would say, "Can you mix up a cake and put it in the oven so we've got something for lunch?" And that is what we would eat later on when "lunch" was served. Mom made her own homemade bread that was the "hit" of the neighborhood, so we always had bread and butter with jam, jelly, or luncheon meat, too.

Saturday night in the summer, the stores in town were open until 9:00 p.m. That was a time to socialize. We would go in early to get a parking spot on Main Street, and then we would "shop." Friends and cousins would come in, too, and we would walk all around town talking and laughing. Around 9:00 p.m. when the stores closed, we were careful to stay away from the side of the street where the car was parked because Mom and Dad might want to go home, and we weren't ready yet. We were having so much fun walking with our friends we didn't want to go home.

The Travels to the Lake
By Peter Donald Gravdahl of Northwood,
North Dakota
Born 1993

In the summer of 2014, my aunt, JoAnn Guerard, passed away from lung cancer at the age of 84 after fourteen years of battling emphysema that started fifteen years after she quit smoking. Then on June 16, 2015, my grandmother, Shirley Ann Sanderson, passed away as a result of her dementia and severe arthritis that started out as fibromyalgia when she retired from teaching in 1980. These two ladies who I was very close to for the 22 years of my life had one thing in common as sisters. They in their golden years both had a lake cabin or a summerhouse in Minnesota.

Grandma Shirley had a lake cabin that she and her late husband, Grandpa Otto, built in the 1960s and took care of even as she turned it over to her son, Uncle John, (Mom's brother, the family dentist). Mom and her side of the family made many trips to the lake in the 1970s until the 2000s when Grandma's health started to decrease rapidly following her 80th birthday on February 9, 2001.

I can remember starting when I was two years old in 1995 that we travelled to the lake cabin owned by Grandma Shirley. The cabin had a main open room to the left that contained the dining room and living room with the couches, chairs, and an end table that had so many playing cards, along with two bedrooms, a bathroom with a shower, and a kitchen that had an old GE fridge and an antique stove, both from the 1960s when

Peter's grandmother, Shirley Ann Sanderson

the building was built. The property also had a bunkhouse that also housed the outboard motor for the fishing boat and other fishing accessories. I can also remember when we went out on the outboard motor that I was scared of falling over and drowning. Those were the memories of a three year old also in 1996.

One memorable trip that I can still think of is when I traveled with Mom, Grandma Shirley, Aunt Jane, and my cousins, Matthew, who was still in college and graduated from Michigan State University in Kansas in the class of 2001, and his sister, Mary, who graduated high school in Lansing, Kansas, in the class of 2001, also. This trip took place in the summer of 1998, when I was five and Grandma still lived at home.

One thing we always did was drive down to Walker, Minnesota, from Cass Lake, where the lake cabin was located at Little Wolf Lake in Beltrami County, Minnesota.

At times, we drove Grandma's beige colored 1983 Mercedes four-door sedan to visit Aunt JoAnn, her sister, who had a condo in Walker, Minnesota, south of Cass Lake on Highway 271 next to Leach Lake. I believe this year we drove Aunt Jane's car, a 1996 GMC Safari minivan to visit Aunt JoAnn. The year before Aunt JoAnn moved to Walker, she had another lake house on a hill that was also spacious but located by Cass Lake, the lake actually of which she sold the property before relocating to Walker, Minnesota.

I can remember the last time we went to see the lake cabin before Grandma turned it over to Uncle John was the summer of 2002. Also, it was the last time Grandma rode with us to Fargo to get the Mercedes's oil changed at the Valley Imports dealer in Fargo.

I can remember the last time I actually visited Aunt JoAnn's condo in Walker was in the summer of 2004, in which Aunt Jane and Mary spent the entire summer with us visiting and taking care of Grandma as her health declined. I can remember pedaling the paddleboat that Aunt JoAnn had way out southward to the south end shore and paddling the boat back. It was cool, but Mom was scared for me, as I was a young guy at the time. As we also visited, Aunt JoAnn also took us to very nice places to have dinner and such. She also took us to Crazy Days shopping in Walker where all the stores had their street side sales. It was very interesting and out of the ordinary as I saw it at the time. The last thing we did before leaving Walker was we ate at a restaurant that was decked out all in white and looked like the interior of a wedding reception hall, because the place was actually a bakery, also.

There are very fine memories that I have of my Grandma Shirley and my Aunt JoAnn. I was very close to them for many years, and they looked out for me as I got along with them for so long. I miss them so much, but I still pray to be with them when I return home to be with them. For being there for me in my 21 and 22 years of life, I thank them very much.

As I move on in life to more accomplishment, I can look back on very fine memories from my childhood of spending time at the lake with my family in the better times before declining health and such did not make that possible anymore. As I close this writing for now, I shall move on and keep focused on the here and now and not think about the past too much.

My Life Story
By S. James Berg of Goodridge, Minnesota
Born 1942

My grandparents came from Sweden and homesteaded in 1895. My dad was the youngest of eleven children. He had eleven sisters, and they were all schoolteachers. I was born on May 15, 1942. I was born in Brocket, North Dakota, at my grandparents' house, Herman and Anna Kaliokoski. A midwife delivered me at a cost of $5.00. I have two older sisters and two younger brothers.

I lived in Doyon, North Dakota until I went to college at North Dakota State University in Fargo, North Dakota. I graduated in 1964, with a major in animal husbandry and a minor in economics.

I was married on September 19, 1964, in Devil's Lake, North Dakota, to Joni Magnason, whose mom came to North Dakota in 1937. My wife passed away in Fargo due to bone cancer. I have two children, Jodi Smithwick, who lives in Moorhead, Minnesota, and Jeff. Jeff is married to Becky, and I have two grandchildren, Logan, who wants to be a commercial pilot and works at Polaris, and Aly, who is going to college in South Carolina. I am retired and worked at Artic Cat in their River Falls plant for eleven years.

James Berg at age 1 1/2

Animal Memories
By Joan Sethre of Newfolden, Minnesota
Born 1930

Our church group went caroling every year at Christmastime. A couple of the places we went were Bachelor Farmers—one had pigs and the other had llamas. The farmer would come out to hear us sing or would already be outside doing chores. We'd start singing and the pigs would line up against the fence. Same with the llamas, but when we'd sing "We Wish You A Merry Christmas," they'd leave. It seemed like they realized it wasn't a Christ song.

Some years ago, we had a golden retriever who loved when I went to the piano to sing praise songs. He would ease himself into the living room and almost up to the piano before I'd notice him. The dining room and living room were off limits to him and he knew it.

I belonged to a Praise Team that went to nursing homes to sing and read for them. We would take turns reading an inspirational poem for them. I would practice my reading out loud in the game room and after a while I'd look to the side and there sitting right next to me was our dog.

Shivaree

We were married on December 31, 1950 at our church with only family present. We were both in business and would have to invite the whole community if we had had a large wedding in our small town. Ball games were the chief entertainment and every able person attended. The next game after we got home from our honeymoon, the Firemen (my husband was a volunteer) planned a Shivaree after the game. They hid in the church across the street from our upstairs apartment, and watched until we turned the lights out. Then, they put the firetruck ladder against the building and pounded on the window of our bedroom, and turned on the siren and lights of the firetruck. Everyone in the town had been tipped off on the goings on, except us. My husband, being a diligent fireman, jumped out of bed, and then realized what was going on. We got dressed and went outside where they had an animal cart from the locker plant to tote us all over town. We gave out 35-cent coupons for all to have lunch. In those days, 35cents would have been enough to buy pie alamode and a beverage or a cheeseburger and a beverage. They gave us a community party a few weeks later. Those were the Good Old Days!

FDR and the WPA
By Grace Sonstegard of Beaudette, Minnesota
Born 1942

I was born in 1942—2 months to the day after Pearl Harbor. During my life, I heard my father say that "Franklin D. Roosevelt saved this country." He set up social security and WPA, etc. and brought this country back from starvation. Young people all over were struggling to eat, to get a job (any job). They "rode the rails" just trying to find something to make a few bucks just to eat and to send a little home for the family. The Great Depression and the "dustbowl days" were killing this whole country.

My dad was fortunate enough to get a job in 1936 working for the Lake of the Woods County Highway Department building roads and bridges in this far-north, undeveloped area. They had dug ditches to try to drain some of the underlying "farmland" and they built roads on the ditch grades so people could more easily travel into new homesteads. It took a lot of very hard work.

The WPA began to build things to improve the infrastructure of this country—roads, sidewalks, buildings, etc. Next to our house in the little town of Williams, Minnesota, they built a city park. It wasn't large but it was nice. They built big log picnic tables, stone fireplaces, and a well with a pump. They also built a big wooded ski-slide on a hill above the creek that ran thru the park. We loved that park and played there almost every day of my childhood. It's gone now, but it was there until the 1970s. People still came there to slide in the winter. Everybody would come bringing their toboggans, sleds, and big pieces of cardboard to slide down the ski-slide and hills. There was a 4-way fireplace in the middle of the park that had a tall chimney and picnic tables all around. My dad would build the fire in the fireplace and Mom would bring hot chocolate from our house in this big, old, blue enamel coffee pot. Everyone would bring their hotdogs, if they had them, and their marshmallows to roast. The good old Campfire Marshmallows in the blue, wax paper covered box that puffed up 3 times their size. Or sometimes, we would just have peanut butter sandwiches that Mom would help us "toast" on the fire. The big jack pine trees all around us, the smell of the wood smoke, the cold cheeks and chilly fingers, are still fresh in my mind. The organization around town used the park often too. Summers and winters, the Boy Scouts, the Girl Scouts, the Luther League, and the 4-H Club would all have sledding parties or weenie roasts in the old park. We spent many hours just playing around the creek. It wasn't really deep but it was so cold. The water meandered around twists and turns and ripples and little waterfall spots. It was great to take off our shoes and socks and dangle our feet to cool off. Sometimes we would jump in- clothes and all- to splash around.

We would play great imagination games. We would crawl thru the towering fiddlehead ferns (being careful to avoid poison ivy). We'd break the ferns off and string the together with cord to make grass hula skirts and we'd capture each other and drag the prisoners (usually a "maiden" like the movie stars of the day) to the top of the ski-slide where we would throw them, screaming, into the blazing volcano. Many days we would play "escape from prison" where we would gather all our children (dolls) and drag them thru the jungle (ferns, again) to escape and hide from either the Germans or the Japs prison camp. Hiding, keeping the terrified children quiet, avoiding the "soldiers" (neighbor boys who were always trying to sneak up and scare us). Remember, this was post World War II and we saw it in the newsreels at the Pines Theatre, and we listened to the conversations of our returning "boys." Nearly all of my uncles were in the war (Army, Navy, and Marines).

Ours all came home, some were badly broken but alive, and back.

Politically correct wasn't part of our vocabulary then. We knew about Patriotism, homeland and saving "our boys." So different from today, and yet, somehow, the same.

The WPA also built parts of our local school, which was just up the street from our wonderful park. Sometime, walk around the sidewalks in some little towns and see if you can find a stamp in the cement that says "WPA 1940" or 1941. We have them here. And if you drive out thru our Beltrami Island Forest area, once in a while you may still find a tree-shaped wooden sign that says "Norway Pines" or "Jack Pines planted in 1941 by WPA." They ae getting to be fewer but everyone once in a while you may find one still there. AAs they harvest those trees, the signs disappear but they were there.

Dad always said a lot of the roads and bridges were built on the backs of the WPA. Firewatch Towers in this area, as well, because of the timber.

Dad passed away in July 2012 at 103 ½ years old. He told me many stories of his day-to-day life and it is amazing the hardships they survived to make this country what it is today. I believe that all his hard work and caring for his family and his little community made him the man, he was. So when he told me, "Franklin Delano Roosevelt was one of the greatest Presidents the United States ever had," I believed him.

Students and the teacher of Theresa's one-room school in 1953

read, "clean hands," you would have to go around the room checking everyone's hands. If a student or students had dirty hands, the teacher would turn their photo around for the day and they went to wash their hands.

We were quite fortunate to have an inside toilet and not an outside one. The toilet was in a little room and sat over a deep, dark hole. This was quite scary for us little ones, as the thought of falling in was scary.

We would play games at recess such as, gray duck gray duck, ring around the rosey, and pump, pump, pull away. We would bring bag lunches (mine was mayo and sugar between two slices of Wonder bread) and the teacher would supply small cartons of milk.

I graduated in 1965 from Burnesville High School with the classmates I had at this one-room school. I also have a class photo with the teacher in it. It always brings back fond memories.

One-Room School 1953
By Theresa Kunze of Bemidji, Minnesota
Born 1947

When I was in the first grade, my older sister, Victoria and I went to a one-room school located in Orchard Gardens, Minnesota (which was south of the twin cities). There was only one teacher, Ms. Chocolate, who taught all 12 grades. I was one of eight first graders and my sister was one of two second graders. There was one third grader.

On one wall hung our photos and a chart with cards in pockets. Each day, a student was chosen to go to pick a card, and turn it over to see what it revealed. For instance, if the card

Our Story—A New Way of Life
By Evelyn A. McKeever of Warroad, Minnesota
Born 1925

When we went to Flag Island to live in 1944, it was a new way of life for me. There were just David's folks, brother, Charles, and Uncle Charley living on the island. There was no electricity, which meant no washing machine, dryer, iron, vacuum cleaner, or TV. There was no telephone or running water. There was no bathroom, only a path out back to where the outside toilet was located. All the water we used was dipped out of the lake in the summer and out of a "water hole" chopped through the ice in the winter.

We did have a battery radio. We had a wood burning cook stove for cooking. I really got pretty good at building fires. We also had a wood burning heater, either a barrel stove, an airtight stove, or a parlor furnace for heating the house. Having a big woodpile was a must. The men spent several weeks getting the wood out of the woods and chopping it at different lengths for the stoves. Making sure you had dry wood for the fire was really important to the cook.

After we had our new houses built, the men decided we should have some sort of electric plant on the island. David's father would be the one to take care of the light plant. We got a little gas light plant with a 1.5kw motor that Grandpa would start up a little while each day so we could do our ironing or the vacuum cleaning, and have a couple hours for the lights in the evening. That was for the four houses. In our new houses, I really enjoyed that we each got a new gas stove to cook on. No more cooking on the wood stoves and building fires early every morning to get breakfast ready. No more wet wood or a wood box in the kitchen, or taking out the ashes daily. We also got gas refrigerators. No more carrying in ice blocks for the old icebox. These were the same ice blocks that the men had cut out of the lake in the winter. With the icebox, we always had to remember to empty the water pan from under the icebox after the ice had melted. We continued to use bottled gas even after electricity came to Flag Island.

We were able to have a type of telephone just between houses after the war years. They were army surplus called field phones. We had four homes with a line between the houses. They were battery operated, a square wooden box and outside covered with leather, with a crank that we could turn to ring the other houses. One ring for grandparents, two rings for Joe, three rings, for Charles, and four rings for us. The phones worked great to find out where the children were playing or if someone needed help right away at their house.

Life of Flag Island was isolated in the winter. In the spring of the year, after spending all winter on Flag Island, I wanted to go to Warroad to get some groceries and see a movie. We had a Willis Jeep and David agreed to take us to town, across the ice. The ice was good, but there was about 6inches of water on the ice. Having water on the ice meant that the ice was still good. If there were holes in the ice, the water would go down. We took the boys and started to town, about 45 miles away and there were no other cars on the lake. Everything went well until the spark plugs got wet halfway to Warroad. David had to try to dry the plugs out. While he was working on the engine, the boys were monkeying around in the car, and one of the boys hit the horn, which sounded where David's head was as he was working on the Jeep. Needless to say, David was not happy, so as soon as he got the Jeep fixed, we headed back to Flag Island and never did get to Warroad.

Fine Squaw
By Chris Wahlberg Goodson of Roseau, Minnesota
Born 1944

When she got the telephone call, Hazel danced around her dorm room in utter delight. She got the job! Oh, how she needed that job. While attending college during the Great Depression, she often resorted to making a meal of soda crackers in her room, and giving up trips home to save bus fare. Now she had finished college and someone had hired her to teach.

The school was located 450 miles north in Minnesota, but she didn't care. It was a job. She learned there had been many applicants, but she was the lucky one chosen because she could play the violin and the school wanted to have an orchestra. Again and again, she thanked her parents who had insisted on violin lessons in spite of tough times. Now she was on her way to her teaching job, the beginning of her career, and a decision that would change the course of her life and, ultimately, mine.

Teaching high school English and directing the orchestra went well for her, as did her social life. The educated young lady made many friends in the town of Warroad. However, it was a young businessman who caught her eye. She met him in the local hardware store where he partnered with his father. Often when she dropped in the store, he was conversing with an old Native American man. The hardware man was friends with many Native American people of the town of Warroad. He even learned some phrases in Chippewa. She wondered about this hardware man who was so friendly and loved to tease. But, she soon learned that the hardware man had a great outgoing personality. She grew to like him so much. It wasn't long before they were an item. Wanting to make an impression on and needing acceptance, she asked the hardware man to teach her to greet the Native American in his own language.

It took a while, but she finally mastered the words, "Kow win," and, "Nisa shin." So when she saw the old Native American in the store, she confidently greeted him with the words that the hardware man had taught her. He exploded in laughter, slapping his leg repeatedly. He was speechless. Finally, he recovered and told the hardware man he had a fine squaw.

Puzzled and suspicious, the genteel teacher asked the hardware man what she had said. He replied, "Oh, you just said, 'How the hell are you?'"

Eventually, the hardware man married her and they became my parents.

A Letter That Changed the Course of her Life

Have you ever received a letter that changed the course of your life? My mother, Hazel Dornfeld Wahlberg received a letter many years ago which propelled her life in a wonderful and happy direction. My mom's family lived in North St. Paul, Minnesota, in the late 1920s and early 1930s. They owned a small grocery store right across the street from their home. Many people thought they were rich because they were storeowners, but the truth is, they were just hardworking people who made a comfortable living. My grandfather, my mother's father, was a shrewd businessman though, and was able to invest much of their money in the stock market. My mom and her sister worked in the store in their spare time, but my grandmother was a strict taskmaster who expected her two daughters to excel in school and also in music. Mom chose the violin, and her sister chose the piano. Grandma made sure they dutifully practiced for at least an hour each day.

After high school graduation, my mom was accepted into a private college, St. Olaf, not far from their home. Her sister chose, instead, to get married and raise a family. Mom loved college and even played the violin in the college orchestra. It was at this time that the unthinkable happened, and the stock market crashed. Now Grandpa didn't have the funds to keep Mom in college, but fortunately, somehow she managed to graduate. She often talked of eating soda crackers for meals because she didn't have the money to eat in the cafeteria. You can imagine how proud her family was when she was finally awarded her diploma.

At this time, teachers were a dime a dozen. She now had to start the arduous talk of sending in her resume and hoping for an interview. After many rejections, she finally secured an interview 400 miles north of the city in a little town named Warroad, Minnesota. She had to look it up on the map, and even then thought it was the end of the earth. Well, she boarded a train and arrived at the interview two days later. She thought the interview went well, but she knew there were many teachers applying for the job. The principal didn't give her any indication of her chance for the position. She went home rather discouraged. A few days later, a letter arrived in the mail. This is the letter that channeled her life in a completely different direction. She got the job, but to live in Warroad, Minnesota, so far from home? There may even be wild Indians living there, she thought. Thus, the name Warroad.

She arrived in Warroad in the fall with all her belongings. In meeting with the administrators the next day, she was somewhat chagrined at the assignment they gave her. She was to teach English, biology, music, and social studies (all on an English major). She was to give violin lessons and start an orchestra. She didn't dare balk at the assignment in light of all the prospective teachers vying for the job. The principal told Mom that the reason she was chosen over all the others was because she could play the violin. She did well in her first teaching assignment; and met and married my dad to-boot.

That letter was the beginning of a happy teaching career and a happy marriage. About 65 years later, I was teaching adult education in the same school building. On my break, I sometimes sat outside in the spring. I sat outside on the same steps Mom probably did, and think about how that letter changed our destiny.

Love Thy Neighbor
By Cindy Pazdernik of Alexandria, Minnesota
Born 1948

Cindy's mom and dad with Ed, Cindy, and Sue in 1954

I was so excited! We bought our first house. Moving in on a cold October evening, a short disheveled man leaped out from behind the hedge dancing like a fighter in the ring. With fists clinched he said, "Do you want to fight?" I hustled the three kids in the house and watched as he disappeared through the hedge to the small house next door. We had just met "Ole."

Later I learned this recluse man did odd jobs, was an alcoholic, and was a bachelor. He was a quiet man, often hiding, peeking out from behind trees or the corner of the garage, watching over comings and goings. However, when he had his fill of liquid courage, the polka music blared and he could be very vulgar and mean.

One day I saw him lying in the driveway, bike tipped over, and his head bleeding. I went over and asked if I could help him in the house. We struggled and staggered up the three steps; I opened the door and got him into a chair. He smelled like an outhouse accented with stale alcohol. I looked around at this hoarder's paradise with a bare mattress to sleep on, stacks of papers, books, and cardboard beer cases. There was the odor of uncleaned cat litter, and the back door was propped open for various cats to come and go. I asked him if I could come over now and then and clean up for him. He said I could. That day began our true neighbor relationship.

In the following days that extended to 12 years, I became a cleaning lady, cook, and friend to Ole. I found frozen baby kittens, individually packed in sandwich bags in the freezer, and skeletal remains in the various crocks in the basement. He would come over to our house when on a "bender" to taunt the kids, and I would call the police to come take him home.

Over the years he stole our dog and refused to give him back; the cock-a-poo named Bear became Ole's sidekick. They were an item around town. Once, in downtown Alexandria, Ole was over served at Ben's Bar and laid on the sidewalk. Bear circled his disabled master to protect him and the police had to be called. Many were the times that I saw the police car drive up, Ole riding shotgun and Bear bouncing in the backseat (they had spent the night in jail).

I would get him his groceries and booze in later years when he couldn't ride his

Cindy's parents in 1943

Cindy's dad's farm horses

bike anymore. He over-indulged on alcohol but always wanted to eat healthy. Among constants were two kinds of cheese, Raisin Bran, liver worst, cat food, and vitamins. He went from ginger brandy to blackberry brandy and always beer.

This is the same man who was kind to me. On a 95degree summer day, he mowed my lawn. After a 10 inch snowfall, he scooped my sidewalks. The later years, I mowed his lawn and scooped his walk when he was failing physically.

Over time, I hung curtains at his windows, made his bed with sheets and pillows, gave him a cookie jar, and kept it stacked with homemade cookies.

He will always be one of many life lessons. A true reason to not judge. Ole will remain in my heart always, with hundreds of stories just about him. He lived to be 97.

Growing Up

On the farm,
Life wasn't always easy when I was growing up,
Simple people in a farmhouse, old car, and Chevy truck;
A loyal Collie dog, cats and kittens everywhere
Patched clothes to play in, one church dress to wear.
Clothes sewn from printed sacks that came with chicken feed
Always a way to stretch a dollar, an answer for every need.

On the farm,
There were chickens in a coop, piglets peeking through the fence
An old orange tractor and wagon with signs of wear and dents.
The roads were mud or gravel, corn grew straight and tall,
There was haying in the summer, and "pick'n" in the fall.
We had loyal, caring neighbors ready to lend a helping hand.
Potluck suppers at the church, ice cream socials with a band.

On the farm,
Life was hard, yet simple. Friends and family stopping by
Bringing fresh eggs or produce for a slice of homemade pie.
TV had four channels, favorite programs planned ahead.
Always gathering for supper, homework done, then off to bed.
Saturday nights we went to town, got our shopping done on time.

We hurried in and out of stores because they closed at nine.

On the farm,
Life seemed safe and honest, counter checks and a man's word.
Most business done in good faith, the term "foreclosure" never heard
Because people cared about others, were forgiving and allowed some slack.
There were good times and good harvests, to make up for the seasons that lacked.
Those days were long ago, yet seem like yesterday.
I can still see the farmhouse, and smell the fresh cut hay.
Days of living within your means, not caring who had more or less.
Everyone seemed more equal, not under so much stress.
Those memories are dear to me, will always warm my heart
The days of simple living, I am glad I was a part-
Of growing up – on the farm.

The Autopilot Milk Truck
By Thomas Salomonsen of East Grand Forks, Minnesota
Born 1962

One of my earliest memories as a child was the summer of 1965. We lived in a mobile home park on the outskirts of Crookston, Minnesota. On milk delivery day, when we heard the diesel engine of the milk truck getting close, all the kids on our block would come out to greet the milkman and his magical milk truck.

He would begin delivering down our street by jumping out of his truck, which was still rolling; to deliver the first home's order. He would greet the kids in the yard, jump back into his truck, grab the next order, deliver, greet and so on. There were a couple of empty lots before the end of our street, so he would stick around goofing around with us kids, while his truck was still rolling toward the intersection! This would get all us kids excited and would start yelling that his truck was going to crash! He would quick, run to the truck, jump in, and turn just in time to continue with the next block's deliveries.

Looking back, I know the truck was only going a couple miles an hour and didn't have power steering so it would go straight, but it was a truly wonderful memory that makes me shake my head and smile to this day. This is one of the most exceptional memories that I cherish of my childhood.

My Grandparents: My Angels
By Dan Bartsch of Thief River Falls, Minnesota
Born 1967

I was born in Thief River Falls and was taught that there are angels among us. When I was growing up, I had two angels that were a part of my life—then and now—my grandparents, Lloyd and Ellen Spray.

My grandpa was my best friend. He was always there for me. Every time I visited him, he was reading the Good Book and read passages to me. I can hear my grandpa's voice when I am asked to read the lessons at church. My grandpa also taught me to be loyal. He loved listening to the Minnesota Twins and he and I would work in his garden listening to the game on his transistor radio. He told me, "No matter what, Dan, always root for your home team, especially with their ups and downs." So, to this day, I am a loyal fan of all Minnesota teams—the Lynx, Timberwolves, Wild Vikings, and Twins. My grandpa was called home in 1978, but I know he was with me when I heard the Twins win the World Series in 1987 and also in 1991 on his transistor radio. It still works to this day.

I have a wonderful story about both of my grandparents. I had a case of the chicken pox when I was six and my mom brought me over to my grandparents' house to keep an eye on me. My grandma was working at our local newspaper, and always came home for dinner. One thing she liked was watching her favorite soap opera at 12:30, but you see, she had a problem: her show ran for an hour and she had to go back to work at 1:00 P.M. So, she begged by Grandpa to take notes for any stories that she missed.

Well, my grandpa wasn't a fan of "soaps," but he took the notes for her anyway. Needless to say, I couldn't talk to my Grandpa for an hour as he was writing his notes. Yes, he dished on the stories, but also he would write about the kids singing about Coke, how mothers like peanut butter, and why a store manager was worried about folks squeezing toilet paper. My parents wanted to buy my grandparents a videocassette recorder, but my grandma said no. Truly, she didn't need it.

I got close to my grandma and was there for her whenever she needed me. She was called home in 1998. I know they are both looking down from heaven and bragging to anyone around them, saying, "That's our grandson." I know my grandma is with me in the stories I have written. Their light will always shine on me and I love them both very much.

Left Behind: A Childhood Memory
By Darlene Greendahl of Erskine, Minnesota
Born 1945

On cold winter mornings, I would come in from the snow to the warmth and sweet aroma of hay, straw, cows, and a horse, mixed with a scent of fresh manure. The cows would turn to see who was coming and usually I would get a greeting from the horse.

Of course, our several cats would give us salutations as well. It was such fun when the "Ma Cat" appeared, all skinny and meowing, as if she had something to tell. The search was on! Where were the new kittens? As soon as we found them, they would be moved to another secret place. They were usually found in the manger of the empty stall next to the horse, but sometimes she would fool us and they would be hidden in the hay upstairs. One time we even found them under the stairway inside the feed room.

What a fine room that was! Oh, I can just smell corn and grain being ground. Tasted pretty good, too. Almost like chewing gum, a good mouthful would last a long time. I always made noise before entering, just to scare the mice, of which I was deathly afraid.

Hanging on one wall were the currycombs. I liked the round one the best. What satisfaction when the entire night residue was finally scraped off the cow's hindquarters, the hair so nice and smooth, and making the tail end all wavy and silky. I would receive an appreciative look from Bossy. A big fascination of mine was the cow's tongue. What an enormous reach! Never needed a hanky!

There was a special shelf against the far corner wall. Never knew what you'd find there! Some of the things I never knew what use they held. The radio was there as well as some clothespins, twine, and something very special —a tin of carbolic salve. The joy of opening that tin (I can still feel today) and breathing in the sweet aroma of that salve. I can't remember ever going to the barn without opening that tin for a sniff of heaven. It was like a magnet and I could not resist its pull.

The windows were another fascination. I would study the different spiders of many shapes and sizes with their fancy webs. Sometimes, I was lucky and would see a live fly buzzing and trying to break free. Most of the time, they were already dead. I could not figure out how something as pesky and quick as a fly could not escape something as fragile-looking as a spider's web—that is—until getting caught in one myself. Super glue should work so well.

Sometimes we would have calves and would get to feed them with special pails with a nipple at the bottom I didn't get to do that too often, as the little ones were pretty strong and would bunt the pail. I had a hard time hanging on. I can still feel the pressure in my fingertips while letting one of the calves suck on them. Felt like the blood was going to come right out the ends. I thought if I let them, they would probably take my whole arm. Such innocent faces and trusting eyes.

Barn cleaning day brought many delights, especially in wintertime. The backdoor was opened and the wonders you could see. Warm air rushing out or cold rushing in—I don't know which—but what a wonderful sight! It was like magic being performed as it made such beautiful clouds close enough to reach out and put your hand right through. The bright sun made the snow sparkle, almost blinding your eyes. I squinted so I wouldn't miss a thing. I can just see the steam rising from the freshly cleaned gutters and dancing upwards as the manure was piled outside in the cold. Stalagmites building their way upwards by the door glistened a beautiful amber color. What riches.

Another specialty was the salt block. Never mind that the cows had been licking on it, too. Just look for a dry spot. Then I would take a trip to the flowing well. That ice-cold, salty flavor! Always had to have just one more sip!

The stairway was special, too. Made of rough-cut lumber, you had to be careful for slivers. At the top was another wonder—the wooden nail keg. I always had to take a peek inside. It never changed, but I still had to look. Oh, the wide expanse when I got upstairs. The high rounded ceiling, watching dust particles floating in the sunbeams peeking in. That "good" itchy feeling after rolling in the hay. Climbing the bales seemed like a mountainous climb. I was feeling on top of the world, as if I could almost touch heaven from way up there. Sliding on that beautiful floor was another wonder. Slippery with hay, a short run and a good slide would carry you a long way. Oh, and there's the rope on the pulley. That was big time! You could be Tarzan for a while and even visit the jungle. You could fly inside and out. Looking out the hayloft door was the best place to yell, just to hear yourself yell or to listen for your echo as it resounded across the yard. So high up and powerful you felt standing in that doorway up so high. You could be the king of the world practicing your yodeling skills or seeing visions unseen by any other.

In summer when the cows were out to pasture, you could have the whole barn to yourself. Several western sagas were played out. The dividers between the stalls made perfect horses. Riding with my best friend, she being Roy Rogers, and of course, I was Gene Autry. What wonderful adventures we had. Then came the stanchions. What was it like to be a cow? Well, stick your head inside and lock yourself in. You could slip your head right out if needed, it being much smaller than a cow's, but more fun to think you were locked in. We would chew on hay for a while and would then try to bring up some cud so you could chew some more.

Behind the barn was another treasure, the pasture—the great wild west. We would play horse and gallop to our heart's content with not a care in the world. Margie was Trigger and I was Champion. Two finer horses you never would find. We performed such magical feats. Faster than the wind we ran.

When the evening came, we would listen for the tinkle of the cowbell. What a delightful sound, just like a homecoming. One of my favorites? Those wonderful cow pies. Stepping in a nice fresh one and feeling it squish up between

The barn as it sits today

your toes, giving them a wiggle to get the full effect. Then I'd run over to the flowing well to rinse off my feet in the ice cold running water. What a delight!

Further out in the pasture were the plum trees. Eat to your heart's content and sometimes your stomach's demise. There were even some wild grapes, but I never acquired a taste for them. They were fun to squeeze 'til they popped. Beyond was the junk pile. Oh, what treasures were hidden in there! That could take up the better part of a long afternoon. It even had a special horse. I didn't mind that it was missing its head, but it sure made for some wonderful rides. I was told it was used in the repairing of harnesses at one time. I couldn't understand why it had been tossed aside, as it had so much use left in it.

Off to the river. I remember sneaking in for a swim in just your underwear so Ma wouldn't know, not thinking the dingy gray color they had become would be noticed. I always kept a watchful eye out for Minnie Woods, as you never knew when or where she would appear.

Crossing the river on the fallen tree. Crawling on hands and knees, hanging on for dear life. The triumph of making it to the other side only to realize you had to do it all over again to get back home.

Roaming the pasture was wonderful. Whenever I thought I was lost, I would look for the barn. It was like a beacon. You could travel the whole wide west and never leave home. All you needed was a pasture and an imagination. You didn't need TV or a lot of fancy toys if you had a mystical barn with a pasture full of imaginative happenings and places to explore. You would listen to Roy or Gene on the radio and fill the next day with a whole expanse of treasured memories, go places only dreamed of and experience things only in a child's mind.

You may read of some of these things or maybe see some in a movie, but nothing can compare to experiencing them. They were riches that money cannot buy.

Oh, what a wonderful, magical place was the barn. I see it today and it seems so sad. I would just like to tell it that although it was left behind, it has not been forgotten. Its treasured memories will last as long as I will.

The Race that Wasn't
By David Steinhorst of Mizpah, Minnesota

I went to a country school in Minerva Township in Clearwater County for the first eight grades. The last day of school there was a very special day. The whole community gathered that day for a big potluck dinner, lots of visiting, and in the afternoon, there was the traditional softball game between the married and single folk, both young and old. It was a special day you didn't want to miss.

When I was in high school, my good friend Art and I decided that we would skip school at noon and go to Minerva's "last day of school." So, at noon when the bell rang for lunch, we headed for our cars. Art had his own car, a 1938 Ford with its 85hp flathead V-8 and twin straight pipes. I had my dad's 1952 six cylinder Chevrolet. Well, we got in our cars and headed south on Highway 92. It was 12 miles to the corner where we turned onto the county road to go the mile up to where the school was.

We raced out of town to see who could be first to the school. I don't know if you could call it a race when our top speed was 75 miles per hour. If we tried to go faster, the engines would get hot and threaten to blow up Somehow, I beat Art to the corner where we had to turn onto the county road.

About a quarter of a mile up the county road was a BIG frost boil that covered the whole road and I slowed down to five miles per hour to negotiate the frost boil. I was navigating the best path I could find when I heard this ear-shattering noise on my right. I glanced over in the ditch, and here came Art in his '38 Ford with those two straight pipes just a bellering. He was in second gear with his foot on the floor when he passed me in the ditch with the car bouncing all over the place, the mud flying everywhere. He pulled back up on the road ahead of me and beat me to the school! We arrived and enjoyed all the festivity of the day. I was thinking that Art sure hated to lose a race and his determination to beat me was a little over the top.

But, that's not the end of the story. About 50 years pass. We graduate and go our separate ways: the military, working our jobs, raising families, etc. Then comes the time when we reconnect in retirement. Art and I get together for lunch, reminiscing old times, and I bring up that race and tell him that I knew he never liked to lose a race, but that he went a little overboard to beat me up to Minerva school.

Then he told me. "Winning the race had nothing to do with it. When we were coming up on that frost boil, I tried to slow down, but found out my brakes got hot slowing down to turn the corner onto the county road and I didn't have any brakes left, so it was either run into the back of your car or take the ditch. I decided to take the ditch and hope for the best. And I did beat you, didn't I?"

End of story.

On the Milky Way to Oklee
By David G. Holmbeck of Grand Rapids, Minnesota
Born 1948

In June 1970 shortly after my college graduation, I needed to find a job to feed my wife and six-month-old son. The University of Minnesota posted several teaching positions available in rural Minnesota seeking candidates with bachelor degrees, but that they did not have to have a teacher certification. Forty-five years ago, the shortage of teachers in rural towns allowed school districts to hire college grads on a one-year basis—and I needed the money to feed my family. In July, I applied for a science position at Oklee High School and was soon contacted by Superintendent Carl Quist for a job interview with him and Principal Marvin Bronken the next week.

At the time, we were renting a house in Chisholm, and on the day of the interview, we planned to leave our son with grandma for the job interview, not really knowing how far Oklee was from Chisholm. On the state highway map, the two towns were only a few inches apart and Oklee didn't look very far away at all. My wife was breastfeeding our son, who of course demanded that he be fed with regularity; so we left him with grandma and a diaper bag full of Curity all-cotton diapers and some of Mom's freshly-bottled breastmilk. This, however, would be the first time the boy's mom had left him alone, and everything seemed to be going as planned for us young, absentee parents; and we were very excited about my potential new job.

I learned on that very hot July day, though, that Oklee was a long 3 and a half hours from Chisholm, to Grand Rapids, to Bemidji, to Bagley, then to Oklee. My scheduled interview time with Messrs. Quist and Bronken was fast approaching. It seemed like no sooner than when we got to Grand Rapids, when my wife complained of the discomfort of too much milk and that she wasn't feeling well. I quickly stopped at Globe Drug in Grand Rapids, bought a breast pump, and sped off, trying to make up time while my wife began the process of suction, followed by discharge out the passenger wing window.

At the time, we had a 1964 maroon Chevy station wagon. From the day I bought it, my wife didn't like it because it had been in an accident, always pulled to the right; and she said it looked like a Highway Patrol car—an ugly station wagon model. Back then, most State Patrol cars were a one-color maroon. After traveling for one hour at 55 MPH and the suction/discharge process, it is easy to imagine what our car looked like. My side was a deep, unscathed maroon, but my wife's side was a cloudy milky color, a top layer of breast milk baked by the hot July sun. We made it to Oklee on time, but crept into the school parking lot, embarrassed, and hoping no one would see our two-tone car.

My interview went well, and I got the teaching job for the 1970 to 1971 school year, but only after a pre-admonishment from Superintendent Quist. He told me that he did not want to see any of his Oklee Public Schools teaching staff entering or leaving the Municipal Liquor Store.

Furthermore, if I wanted any alcohol, then I should buy it somewhere out of town. What good and lasting memories I have about the students, parents, and great people of Oklee.

Go Bobcats!

The Old Country School of Yesteryear
By Carolee Bruder of Oakdale, Minnesota
Born 1935

A narrow winding gravel road led to the one-roomer
That once held eight grades of local farm kids.
The metal flagpole was front and center
Holding a forty-eight starred red, white, and

The old country school

blue. Circled by a large patch of green lawn
Used for fun and games.
The weathered door led into a narrow entry
Lined with coats and boots in winter,
And rain gear at other times.
A several gallon water filled crock with rusty spigot
Sat regally on a four legged metal stand below
A wooden shelf used for lunch pails.
Inside and up front loomed a large teacher's desk Holding books, attendance record, and a small bell
That when rung got everyone's attention.
The small wooden desks aligned in a row
All Sported inkwells in the upper right corners.
Chalkboards with dusty erasures abutted windows
And a large globe hung from an anchored rope pulley, Allowed for any age to use,
While world maps attached to a front wall
Rolled down to reveal countries being studied.
At the rear stood a huge wood burning heater
The teacher stoked for comfort needs.
Yes, the old school now paint starved
With splayed siding, and broken windows
Tells a silent story that nothing lasts forever.

Do You Remember

When daylight came, and your eyelids were stuck shut Because you had pink eye
When in spring you wanted to kick off your shoes and go barefoot
But Mom said no, 'til you see the first dandelion bloom
When in winter and snuggled under tons of quilts Mom's last call for breakfast meant a mad dash
From your cold upstairs room to a toasty warm kitchen below
When in summer a car ride to town with Dad
Meant an ice cream cone to savor on the way back home
When a new dress meant hurry up and empty the feed sacks
So Mom could cut and sew
When a trip to the doctor meant you were near deaths door
And Mom's home remedy worked no more
When left over oatmeal from breakfast
Meant fried mush for supper
When getting up early meant You got the socks without the holes
When Saturday night fun was popping corn on the old wood-burning cook stove
While listening to Gangbusters, Inner Sanctum,
And always, The Grand Ole Opry
on the A battery radio
I remember!

Olden Time Outhouse

The outdoor toilet in olden times
Sported a quarter moon cutout
Gracing the weathered door
And usually sat on rear property.
It had many a name
From Grandma's term privy
To others, the outhouse
or backhouse.
Most had three holes, ours two
With one smaller for kids.
Wiping paper consisted of
Newspaper or the Sears Roebuck Catalogue
But during canning season
Peach papers were the choice
They were ultra-soft!
Without electricity
Night visits proved scary

Lest a flashlight or
Stick matches were handy
A hard stomp on the floor
Scared any and all critters away
Yes, it truly was olden times

A Little Girl's Courageous Run for Help
By Andrea Hepola of Duluth, Minnesota
Born 1956

"Selina, stay close by, I may need to have you take a letter to Grandma."

Papa had left for town, seven miles distant, to take the cream to town and bring groceries back. Hitching up the team of horses, Nellie and Spot, he hoped to be home by one or two o'clock. The older children had gone to school; they would return by four if they did not loiter or play at the neighbors. Only Selina and her little sister, Alma, would be at home with Mama.

It wasn't long before Mama called, "Selina, I want you to take this letter to Grandma. Be my mailman and go right away."

"Mama, can you go with me? I don't want to go alone. Fido will come and bark at me,"

"I know Selina, but you are the only one here. I cannot carry Alma. Just go straight to Grandma's. You will be there sooner than you think. Fido won't hurt you. He knows you. There, that's my good girl. Grandma may have a cookie for you."

"Here's the letter; don't drop it. Grandma will come back with you."

Selena took the letter and hurried out the door. Passing the chicken coop, she wondered if the surly old red hen had had her baby chicks yet. She was reaching for the door hook to take a look when she heard Mama calling. "No Selina, you must go straight to Grandma's. Hurry and give her the letter!"

Selina started up the narrow one-car trail. Her feet got soggy from the water that was running across the road from the meadow. Reaching the rail gate, she wondered, "How do I get through?" Mama would open it by pulling the rails back—she could not do that, so she quickly got down on her hands and knees and crawled under the barbed wire fence. Her dress didn't get caught; brushing off the grass and dirt that clung to it and grabbing the letter from the ground, she cut across the wheat stubble field, then through the pine grove, and past the potato and rutabaga field. Her heart was pounding hard as she would run at times because she felt afraid. Finally, she was at the long lane leading to Grandma's house. Fido, napping in the sun, sat up and then ran to welcome her.

The big door was open because the sun was warm. "Grandma!" Selina called through the screen door. Grandma came hurrying, "Child, what is wrong?" as she opened the door, Selina in tears of relief, handing the letter to her. "On my," Grandma said as she turned to Grandpa. "I must go right away to Marie's.

By now, Selina had gone to the toy box, ready to sit and rest while playing.

"No Selina. Here, eat a cookie and some milk, and then we must go to help your mother," as she hurriedly put things into a pillowcase.

It was nice to have Grandma walk with her. She wasn't afraid now. She was tired and wondered why Grandma walked so fast back through the potato field, the pine trees and the field of grain stubble. Grandma opened the gate and soon they were home. Mama met them at the door.

"Thank God," she murmured as Selina and Grandma came in. "Selina, you did so well taking the letter to Grandma. Thank you."

She then said to Grandma, "I have everything ready. I don't think it will be too long." A big kettle was on the stove, the water gently boiling.

Why was the bedspread off the bed thought Selina?

"Take Alma outside, Selina. Play in the playhouse."

Selina was tired but soon was having a good time, making pretend cookies so they could have cookies and coffee later. Mama and Grandma could have cookies and coffee, too.

Later, Selena hear a baby cry. "Oh, come Alma, I hear a baby cry!" They ran to the house. Opening the door, Grandma held a baby, ready to give her bath. They stood looking in amazement at this little baby with the loud cry.

"Girls, come here," Mama called. "You have a new baby sister. We will call her Rose." Rose had dark hair and soon would have rosy cheeks. Selina's heart was happy to have a baby sister. She would help care for her.

Her courageous trip to get Grandma was often repeated as the sisters and brother reminisced of days gone by.

Selina (my mother) was born November 2, 1912, and passed away September 21, 1967.

Meeting Kennet
By Jinny Foldoe of Waubun, Minnesota
Born 1947

I opened the cabin door to an animated face and burst of words. "There's someone you've got to meet! I'm going over there now, why don't you ride along?"

How could I turn it down? I was a New York City gal who had a bad case of March cabin fever after my first winter ever in Minnesota. I lived in a sixteen by seventeen foot log cabin that once was used as a goat barn but now without electricity or running water and was heated by a wood cook stove. We were tucked back on an old logging trail in the woods and my nearest neighbor, Diana, had driven her pickup all the way down in the muddy thaw.

Back out at the mailbox the truck turned right, onto the gravel then right again on the tar road. Less than two miles up the road, we turned into a familiar driveway.

"Diana, this is where he guys refill our five gallon milk can with spring water."

"Where?"

"Up front by the road."

"Have you met her?"

"Who?"

"The lady that lives here?"

"No."

"Well you're in for a treat."

As we climbed down from the vehicle and slammed the doors, a woman opened the door and hobbled out onto the paint peeled porch.

"Darlings!" she said coming over to greet us as my friend flashed me her I-told-you-so smile.

"Fenanda, this is my new neighbor Jinny. I wanted her to meet you."

The lady's weathered face had eyes that glittered behind her glasses and a head of younger woman's chestnut wavy hair. She took my hands in hers and pulled me towards her wide smile.

"Come in, come in. Papa's just awoken and ready for a little lunch. I made some soup; you must have some."

I raised my eyebrows and traipsed behind Diana as we entered the cozy small kitchen.

Fenanda's balding husband, with long wisps of white hair awry was seated at the wooden table. Fenanda said, "Papa, we have company," and fetched dishes, ladled soup from the stove into bowls and placed it in front of us. Then she stooped over "Papa" and started to spoon feed him.

"I yust want some coffee," he protested and sputtered the dark goop from his downturned mouth.

"Yah, yah," she said shaking her head while wiping his mouth and lifting the coffee mug to his lips. He drank.

I averted my gaze to my place setting. I wasn't sure what was in the bowl. It didn't look any like soup I'd ever seen. Raisins, peaches, and what looked like gelatin fish eyes stared back at me. In my mouth, it was sugary and warm.

"Good sweet soup" Diana said eating hers. And for my sake. "Those balls are tapioca, right Fenanda?"

"Yah, it tickens it nice."

After Papa retreated back into his bedroom, Fenanda showed off some of her kitchen knick-knacks and wall hangings. She tapped a postcard tacked to the wall with her bony finger. "And dis is my Kennet," she boasted.

"She means her son Ken," Diana interpreted. "He lives in Alaska with his four daughters and wife where he builds log cabins and carves totem poles." I could see that indeed he did. He was kneeling down amidst a dozen or more totem poles painted with bright animal faces arrayed in front of a small log cabin surrounding by woods.

That indelible memory of immigrants, who had made their home and life in a place to which I was just beginning to adjust, left a warm spot in my heart. I wasn't as hearty or far from my native home, and not too many years later, I moved back east to be near family in upstate New York. Ithaca was a perfect balance between my big city roots and the deep woods of my recent past. One late summer day I drove up into farm country to pick blueberries and a waft of manure came to me suddenly through the open window. It triggered a memory of my funky north woods life and tears came to my eyes.

That same unsuspected tug came to me when my former supervisor contacted me saying he was upstate New York at a Special Olympics national competition with a couple the clients I worked with in Minnesota. I was able to drive and attend the track meet and enjoy the brief reunion. After two years of working at an Ivy League university and learning the middle class way of life again, I was unprepared for the homesickness I felt for my Midwest life.

I asked my former boss if I could work for his program again with the clients and he got an okay from his board members to rehire me. When I told my mother, her pale blue eyes rimmed with red and her brow furrowed. "Whatever you do," she warned, "don't marry a farmer." I shook my head and reassured her, "Mom, I promise to get a phone this time, okay?"

An old friend let me live in a tiny house with her until I could find my own place nearer town. There was an appealing ad in the local paper to rent a basement apartment in a home on Walkerbrook Lake Road, close to my old neighborhood. When I went to view the rental, I was surprised to discover it was the totem pole carver's home. He came to the door, took one look at me, and was grinning ear to ear. Seems he had inherited his mother's hospitality and friendliness. He wore a broad stiff brimmed hat, even in the house, had a moustache that was a bit bushy and the color my mom called "brassy blonde."

Kennett "Ken" with his totems in Alaska

"Waal," he drawled, "let me show you the place." Before he showed me the apartment in the basement, which had its own entryway, he told me, "You can park in this garage." It only had room for one car, but he said he had a two vehicle garage not attached to the house that he used.

Ken led me up a few steps and opened a door that led to the kitchen, through another door that descended into the basement. He reached into a room full of wood and grabbed a log, opened another door and there was the living room.

"This is it." He lifted the latch to the wood furnace in the middle of the living room, and tossed in a log. "I fill it first thing in the morning and before I go to bed at night. You might hear it, but I won't be a bother. It saves on the electric heat."

Around the corner was the master bedroom. The kitchen was small and functional; there was a second room for an office and a household laundry room. It had everything. Then, ascending the stairs, he asked if I was hungry and told me to fry myself a hamburger. I fried one for each of us.

At the table, I expected to hear about his family, but instead I listened to his story of divorce sadness, while his facial expression pinched. After a brief meal, he escorted me around the corner from his kitchen into a huge living room that was at first sight, a hunter's paradise. It was the full width of the house, and unlike the other rooms with average ceilings, it was a cathedral shape decorated with huge antlers of caribou and moose. "We ate the crab" he chuckled nodding at its two foot diameter.

"And the moose and caribou?" I asked. "You hunted them for food?"

"Waal, sure." Ken replied. There was a mountain goat preserved by taxidermy just above his head. It was standing on plaster pedestal next to the huge stone fireplace looking down.

I realized he was truly as colorful a character as his postcard as I listened to his Alaskan tales. When he told me he was 48, the first contradiction I noticed was the loose skin sagging from under his chin. I was a poor judge of age so I let it slide. Back in the kitchen, I washed up the few dishes and drove home.

I called him the next day to ask if I'd left my watch there and could I pick it up.

"When I saw your watch on the window sill above the sink I told myself, 'She'll be back!'" Ken said when I arrived.

A week later, I moved in to the walk in apartment, and I became his cook and we shared meals together.

One evening we stopped at the grocery store to buy food. I chose a loaf of cracked wheat bread, and then Ken tossed in five more packages into the cart. "We'll keep em in the freezer." Then he took me out for dinner at the classy restaurant in our small town.

I leaned a trick from a New York City friend called breakfast in a glass. It was a milk shake of sorts, which included an egg, frozen strawberries, a spoon of instant coffee, milk, and honey. Gulp it down with a vitamin and I was finished in five minutes. One morning after I'd brought Ken half a batch of "breakfast in a blender" he joked about such a cold drink on such a cold day. I was wearing my New York winter jacket. "Hey it's way below a goose egg today. Why don't you wear my parka?" I started to resist, but he got up, lifted it off the peg by the front door, and helped me slip it on. It was a bright red down parka from Eddie Bauer and he had trimmed the hood with wolf hide. It was a bit large for me, but so snug and comfy, I wore it proudly. Then just before Christmas, he gave me the diamond ring. It was a stone set on a stage that reminded me of the space needle at the Seattle World's Fair because the stone was high and lifted up. It seemed the house was a bounty and Ken couldn't give me enough protection from the world.

A full five years had elapsed since I entered Kennet's parents' cozy cottage with a friend. This time it was with my fiancé, who insisted on showing my brand new engagement ring off to his folks.

Fenanda looked at it and then gazed into my face and called me an angel. When I held out my hand to show Papa who was resting on the living room sofa, he looked up at me, then at my much older fiancé and said, "You're full of prunes."

I turned toward Ken and said, "He doesn't believe it."

It was rather incredible that I was marrying the man I'd seen in the postcard long ago. But it was true, and you can ask him today. He's 94 and only recently ceased building cabins. He still whittles totems though.

"Show" Money
By Eileen Olson of Baudette, Minnesota

Many people consider Brainerd to be northern Minnesota but we who reside in Baudette, Minnesota, know there are many miles between Brainerd and Baudette before you get to our neck of the woods, which is REALLY northern Minnesota!! Our neighbors to the north are our Canadian friends in Rainy River, Ontario, Canada. We can look across the Baudette River and see some of their homes and farms. They shop in our town and we shop in their town. Many sporting events go back and forth. We hear their fireworks on July 1st and they hear ours on July 4th. They are, indeed our northern neighbors.

It is true that we have four seasons and the most challenging one is our winters when it can get down to -40 degree and much colder with the wind chill. Now you may think that most people would stay home by a warm fire on such days or evenings, but it seems to be almost the opposite. I think a lot of us must like to prove that we are resilient, and events go on regardless. Sometimes it feels and sounds like the tires on our vehicles are square as we drive in these conditions. But every day and evening, there seems to be something we don't want to miss out on attending.

Baudette boasts a population count of around 1000. Baudette is in Lake of the

Woods County and we also believe to be the only county in the state without a single stop light in the entire large county. We commonly hear people ask us what we possibly find to do for entertainment in a small town and so far away from any metropolitan area. We can only chuckle at these remarks because most days and evenings we have to make a choice of what event we should attend.

My story is from the early '50s when I was 11, 12, and 13 years old. My family had lived on a farm until this time and then we moved to town for those few years. It was really new to us kids and I really got interested in the movie theater and all the movie stars lives. There wasn't hundreds of actors and actresses like there are now and you could write to them and ask for a picture and you'd get one in the mail with their autographs. It was a fun thing to do and we'd tack them on our bedroom walls. We loved going to the movies and there weren't too many that we wanted to miss. The same movie was shown on Sunday afternoon at 2:30, again on Sunday evening and Monday and Tuesday. Then a new movie on Wednesday and Thursdays and another one on Friday and Saturdays. There was always a good preview of the movie to be shown next, so we'd get really excited. There was only one problem, and that was that the movies cost 14 cents and we didn't usually have any money. We did some babysitting and some odd jobs but we always had to save that money for school clothes. I did, however, figure a way to make things work for myself and my two younger sisters. Soda pop came in glass bottles back then and if you returned those bottles, we would get 2 cents at the grocery stores. We didn't have the luxury of buying pop but we could find bottles, which other people discarded instead of bringing back to the stores. But I felt really lucky because I always knew of a few bottles that would be laying out behind the Hartz Grocery Store in the alley. I thought it was unbelievable that people discarded their bottles there so often when all they'd have to do is bring them around to the front and get 2 cents apiece for them. I thought they must be rich if they didn't attempt to get their refund back! I would pick enough of them up and go in the store and get my money. Life was good! My sisters and I could go to the movies. I did this time and time again. I brought them in to Wes Hoscheid, who worked in the store and he also knew and loved all the young kids in town. He had nick names for all of us. He'd always ask me, "what movie are you going to see now?" and I would tell him what was playing at the theater. We called it the "show" back then. I suppose "theater" was too sophisticated. Anyway, this went on till we got older and started spending more time with school activities and sports instead of the movies being our biggest thrill.

It wasn't until many years later as an adult, that I found out that I was actually recycling those same pop bottles that were behind the grocery store! I'd cash them in at the store and Wes would put them out back. I'd get them again the next week and he'd put them back out there. It was a cycle and he knew all along what I was doing. But, as I said, he loved kids and I guess it was his way of letting me think I was working for my "show" money.

So this was just one of the entertainments for us kids many years ago. Sometimes we even sold enough bottles to buy some popcorn!

As kids, we all made sure we got to Wes and Lucille's home on Halloween when we were trick or treating because he gave out pop and a candy bar.

Wes is in his heavenly home now but his wife, Lucille, resides in our Care Center. Wes resided in the Care Center for a short time. I was employed at the adjoining hospital at the time and I informed the Care Center nurses how much Wes enjoyed giving out treats on Halloween and they provided him with lots of treats and invited the kids to come and visit and get treats! I felt like it went full circle for Wes and I.

Farm Life
By Connie Sell of Sauk Centre, Minnesota
Born 1947

The year was 1871. My great grandfather Ole, a 21-year-old, came to this country from Norway to pursue a new life as a farmer. After staying in Red Wing, MN for one year, he took homestead near Osakis, in Gordon Township, Todd County, MN. His father Mikal also came to America and settled there that same year.

They built a house and helped to build a

Connie's grandparents, Olga and Mikkal Olson

church, in which my great-grandfather and great-grandmother's marriage was the first in 1873. His wife Johanna died 11 years later, leaving him with five small daughters. A year later, Ole married Mali and had five more daughters and two sons, the oldest of which was my grandfather Mikkal; who later, along with his wife Olga, took over the farm.

Together my grandparents raised nine children, three boys, and six girls on the family farm. A second home was built. My great-grandparents remained on the home farm until their deaths - she in 1930, and he in 1940.

Some of my mom's fondest childhood memories are of her grandparents. Living in the same house, they had a big influence on their grandchildren. Great grandpa was a music lover, and all the grandchildren played instruments or sang for him. Per his request they even sang to him the night he died.

My mom Katherine, was the second oldest child - oldest daughter. She told many stories about those days like only having one dress to wear, one pair of shoes, that when the shoes got so worn the toes came through. They put cardboard inside to cover the hole, then used shoe polish to make it look like part of the shoe. They were poor farmers, but proud, God-fearing Norwegians.

Grandpa did maintenance at the church, and Sunday service was a must. Mom also told of how he would drive the team to church on cold days with the kids all covered in the back of the wagon. Or how when it was really cold, their dad would walk the older children to school, wrapped under his coat, or let them put their hands in his big fur mittens to keep their hands from freezing.

Mom only finished 8th grade, then worked, first cleaning, cooking, and babysitting for relatives, then as a waitress. Her earnings went for the most part to help support the family. Another of her stories tells of how one year she desperately needed a winter coat. When she gave her earnings to her dad, he insisted she keep money to buy a coat. She so loved her parents, and felt like her dad's gesture was most generous, which only strengthened her respect for him.

Eventually my eldest uncle Merlin took over the farm. He never married, and my grandparents continued to live there with him (as had great grandpa and

Ole's father, Mikal Olson

grandma before them).

Electricity was first introduced into the house in the early '50s, so before that everything was done after dark with kerosene lamps. Heat was provided by a combination of coal/wood burning furnace in the cellar. I'm told grandpa shoveled enough coal into the burner every night to keep the fire going all night. To get heat to the second floor, where all the kids' bedrooms were, there were holes cut into the ceiling/upstairs floor with cast iron grates in them so no one could fall through. In the kitchen stood the big dual-purpose wood burning stove (heat and cooking). At one end of it is where grandpa would fill it with wood. The other end had a 'reservoir' which was filled with water which got hot from the burning wood, so there was hot water to wash dishes - one metal dishpan for washing, and one for rinsing them. Then someone dried them with the dishtowel that grandma had made from the sacks flour they bought came in. Those flour sacks were made into clothing, too. There was no running water in the house all the years my grandparents lived there.

Side note—The building site and a few acres were sold after Merlin's death, to another brother Raymond, who later sold it again and the man who bought it lives there STILL without indoor plumbing. So like my family before him, he 'pumps' water outside and carries it into the house in buckets. Grandpa lived on the farm until age 80 when he died, and grandma stayed until about age 78, when she moved to an apartment in town, at the insistence of her children.

The water for drinking was carried in with a white porcelain pail, which sat on the cupboard in the pantry. The dipper hung on a nail next to it, and just think – everyone drank from the same dipper.

On washday, water was again carried in by buckets and put in a very large copper cooker, which was put on the top of the stove to get the water hot, then bucketed out again and carried to the wash machine. A wringer-type machine was used, and was hand-cranked both for agitating the clothes, and for wringing them first into the rinse water, then the wringer was lifted off, turned, and the clothes were wrung again before hanging them to dry. The same wash water was used for all the laundry - first the baby clothes, then the whites, next the colored clothes, the darks, and finally the rugs from the floor - load after load. Grandma made her own laundry soap from lye, shaped into bar form, then shaved into the wash water. I remember grandma adding 'bluing' to the rinse water to help keep the white clothes bright. The clothes were hung outside on clotheslines. Sometimes they actually freeze-dried.

The 'toilet' was called an 'out house' and was several yards down the path from the house. Toilet paper used was catalog pages (not so much like the pages of today). In the spring a real treat was being able to use the nice, soft paper the peaches bought for canning, were individually wrapped in. Grandma kept a 'chamber pot' in her bedroom closet. It could be used during the night or if the weather was so bad, they couldn't 'go' outside.

There was a phone box on the wall in the front hall, but it had no numbers on it to dial. In order to call out, they clicked the receiver hook a few times until the operator picked up and connected the call. It was called a 'party line' because several nearby farms all shared the same line. They each had a certain number of

Mikkal and Olga with their nine children

rings so they knew when the incoming call was meant for them. Grandma and Grandpa's ring was two long and one short. However, most of the ladies were not beneath picking up and listening in on their neighbors' conversations. Actually often times they would then be asked to join the conversation. Later phones added a 'rotary dial' and they were given a 4-digit phone number. Now they could place their own local calls. Long distance calls still had to go through the operator.

Beside working the family farm, which was all done with very basic equipment - even to milking the cows by hand, and church maintenance, grandpa was a member of the cattlemen's association, and hauled cattle to the 'yards' in South St. Paul. Uncle Merlin who took over the farm had an accident with the corn picker while on leave from duty in the US Army. He lost left hand. So he was discharged from the Army, but still worked the farm. Grandpa helped with many of the daily chores, even after his son took over.

The Event that Changed My Life
By Nancy Pepin Kjeldahl of Sauk Centre, Minnesota
Born 1940

I grew up on a dairy farm in Morrison County in the '40s and '50s. In the fall of 1940 my parents, Lloyd and Luella (Johnson) Pepin had moved "down the road" from their rented acreage and house to their very own farm and house. The house was modest-one bedroom with no electricity or indoor plumbing. I was born in that farmhouse on Nov. 1, 1940 and my grandmother Nancy and an aunt and uncle were also staying overnight— they were sleeping in the unfinished attic and the only way to get to it was to climb a ladder to a square access opening. My now almost 96-year-old uncle often reminds me that he heard my first cry!

The weather was warm those first days after I arrived and my dad was busy getting everything moved to our new home. And then on November 11, everything changed and the infamous "Armistice Day Blizzard" hit. For years, I thought it was my fault, as my grandfather would always tease me about bringing the blizzard. Dad would tell how he sat up all night feeding the wood stove to keep us warm but he didn't have a blazing fire for fear of the house burning-the chimneys in those days were brick without a liner and chimney fires were common. He also said that when it got light in the morning, there was a small snowdrift inside the house in front of the door where the snow had blown in through the key hole. He was very glad when the snow stopped and the wind died down and relieved to find out that none of the livestock or chickens had perished in the storm. I think they were all appreciative that everyone, including 11-day-old Nancy, had made it through. Over the years, there would be many snowstorms, but none like the Armistice Day Blizzard.

Within the next year, our farm was wired for electricity and we soon had running water. We realized how fortunate we were as our farm and my grandparent's farm across the road were the last to be wired before it became impossible to get copper because of World War II. Many of our neighbors had to wait until 1946 or later before "the electric" came. My dad soon built a small bathroom and also a 2nd bedroom as well as stairs to the attic and to the cellar so we no longer had to go outside to go to the cellar. The wood burning stove in the living room was replaced with an oil burner. In the late '40's our kitchen wood stove was replaced with an electric range, which meant that in the winter, there wasn't any heat in the kitchen and it was a cold kitchen! To help remedy that a "rubbish or trash burner" was put in alongside of the new electric range and as well as burning the trash it was fed both wood and corn cobs to keep us warm. So as a child, I do not remember life without electricity, running water, and indoor plumbing. I was one of the "lucky ones." But I do remember cold floors and cold beds. Mom would heat a flat iron, wrap it in a towel, and put it at the bottom of the bed to keep our feet warm. In those days, no one ever thought of taking off their shoes when they came in the house-no way would you go stocking footed on those cold floors! Mom would often mention how cold the kitchen floor was and that when she scrubbed the floor it was so uneven that the scrub water would run to the edges and freeze! No wonder she complained about chilblains on her feet and even resorted to wearing "felt shoes."

The first 9 years of my life were pretty uneventful. I rode the bus to "town school" as our one-room country school closed in 1942, as did several others in the school district. We attended church in a small country church and Ladies Aid meetings were a social event as it was a time for the neighbor kids to get together and play. The ladies would also meet to roll bandages and do other things for the war effort. I remember one time my mom sewed a blue star on the flag at church in honor of her brother. I remember there was at least one gold star and not understanding what it stood for but thinking it was so pretty, I said something like, "Oh I hope Uncle Herb gets a gold star." It did not take long for Mom to explain why we did not wish for a gold star. Uncle Herb did not get one and is the only relative I have left from that generation.

Another neighborhood activity was 4-H. My mom was the main leader and I waited to be 10 so I could join. My older brother was an active member. 4-H was a wonderful organization for rural youth. We learned how to conduct a business meeting, keep records, how to get up in front of a group and give a talk or a demonstration, and kids of all ages learned to work together and to learn from each other. We were proud to take our projects to the county fair and to even earn some money! Of course, we learned to cook, bake, sew, and take care of a garden as well as to take care of cows, chickens, and pigs. As we grew older, we were always hoping to win that wonderful "State Fair Trip."

On January 30 of 1950, my uneventful growing up changed in one big event. It was 30 degrees below zero that morning and I was getting dressed for school in front of the oil burner in the living room. Mom and Dad had a "good fire" going in the trash burner when my brother came running down from the upstairs yelling "Our house in on fire!" We soon saw fire coming out of the walls that were around the chimney and we knew we had a fire. Although we had electricity and running water, we did not have a telephone, so my brother quickly dressed and ran across to my grandparents to make the call. In those days, our "social media" was the party line and when you wanted everyone to listen, you rang "5 shorts" which was called the General Alarm ring, and everyone was to listen. So the 5 shorts were rung and all the neighbors soon knew Lloyd Pepin's house was on fire. By the way, there was no rural fire department to help fight the fire. While my brother was running to my grandparents, my folks and I got into our '47 Ford, which had been parked in front of the house overnight, with the few things we had been able to grab on our way out. Miraculously the Ford started and Dad took us to my grandparent's home across the road and then returned to watch his home go up in flames. By the time he had gotten back, the neighbors had already started arriving to help in whatever way they could. They were able to crawl in on their hands and knees to pull a few things out of the porch including the wringer washing machine and the barn clothes and boots. They soon noted that there was a strong south wind blowing the sparks toward the barn. Shortly before this, there had been a strong wind and the big door that covers the haymow had been blown off and Dad had not been able to put it back in place. Several neighbors grabbed the washtubs and filled them with water and went to the haymow to put out any sparks that flew that way. Other neighbors were able to put the haymow door in place and an even larger catastrophe had been averted. Other neighbors grabbed the milk pails and did the morning milking probably leaving their own chores undone so they could help a neighbor. Soon the school bus went by as we watched from Grandma and Grandpa's window. Some of the neighbors left to go home to their own work and others stayed to watch as the house burned to the ground. It was a hot fire and we learned later that the walls in the old part had been insulated with sawdust!

We knew we had a home to stay in and were soon settled in at Grandma and Grandpa's until a new house could be built in the summer. That same day some of the neighbors came over with clothes for us, as we had nothing except what we were wearing. A cousin of mine who was a couple of years older brought me 2 of her dolls and their wonderful wardrobe that had been sewn by her mother. I returned to school the following day-and even had my schoolbooks, which I had taken with me, after all I was getting ready for school! There were many acts of kindness in the next weeks and months. I had more clothes than I had ever had before-mostly hand me downs but for the first time in my memory I had two new "store bought" dresses that arrived in the mail from my aunt in Milwaukee. Up to this time my clothes were either "homemade" (mainly from feed sacks) or hand me downs from my cousin. I was so proud of those "store bought" dresses. Neighbors had a shower for my folks with gifts of bedding, pots and pans and other essentials. My mother never let us feel sorry for ourselves reminding us that we had all escaped the fire, we had a place to stay, and none of the farm animals had been destroyed so we still had our income. We were also looking forward to having a new house with 3 bedrooms, warm floors, and we would have a telephone and that would make 22 parties on our party line!

That event did change my life in many ways but it has always made me thankful that I grew up with caring neighbors and family who worked together to move forward and not dwell on the past. I've learned that it isn't the material things we have that are important, but what we have in our hearts.

Nancy's grandparents, Andrew and Addie Sophie Remer Olson

When They Met
By Nancy (George) Rudd of Grand Rapids, Minnesota
Born 1954

My mother was originally from Grand Rapids, Minnesota and my daddy hailed from Springfield, Missouri. My mother, then Isabel Florence (Remer) West, had taken her two children, Tom and Bonnie, from an emotionally, abusive first marriage, to Los Angeles, California. My daddy, Jesse Floyd George, a third cousin of the infamous outlaw Jesse James, had just completed his stint in the Navy as a Gunnery Mate. He also made Los Angeles his home. My daddy was a longshoreman and my mother helped manage a small hotel for room, board, and pay.

The Germans had surrendered in May of 1945. My mother and daddy met sometime later at the hotel. My daddy frequented the hotel for my mother's Sunday fried chicken dinners, made in her room. It didn't take long, even considering the thirteen year age difference, for them to get married on July 23, 1945. My mother wore a dress and my daddy a suit. Mae, the owner of the hotel and her husband, were witnesses in their casual Justice of the Peace marriage. The four of them celebrated that evening at a local bar and restaurant.

Shortly after, Tom, the younger of my mother's children was checked out by a doctor. The doctor diagnosed rheumatic fever, and said that they needed to live where there was cleaner, cooler air. The solution was to move back to Grand Rapids, Minnesota. They took the bus back, my mother already pregnant with the first of the five George siblings. My daddy was used to big cities and towns, and as they were coming down the hill entering Grand Rapids, my daddy asked my mother where it was. The answer: This is it!

There is a large, family home on a corner lot, four blocks from Grand Rapids proper and it was built by my great-grandmother's father, Herschbach just after the start of the 1900s. It was then a one family house. My mother had grown up in this home. My grandma was Addie Sophie Remer Olson Jenkins and later, she owned this large home. None of us ever knew my grandfather, as he had died when he was just twenty-three. My mother was two, and my Grandma was pregnant, when his family from Hudson, Wisconsin came and

Nancy's parents' wedding celebration

took him home to die from some lung disease. The newlyweds had lived in Nashwauk, and Andrew Olson had worked as a bookkeeper in the mines. When he left, my grandma moved back to the family home.

Mother and daddy followed suit, as my grandma had, and moved back into the large family home. We lived in half of the downstairs. It was quite crowded, with five rooms for eight of us. By the time I had been born, Bonnie had married and moved with her husband. My grandma lived in the other half, and the upstairs was rented. We never called my parents mom and dad in the northern Minnesota vernacular. We used the southern mama and daddy. As we grew up, we switched from using mama to mother, but my dad was always daddy to all of us.

After my grandma died, in March of 1973, my mother inherited the home, and now my youngest brother owns it. It is remodeled and back to being a single family dwelling. We can still go home for Christmas.

Paying the Doctor

We weren't the very poorest in town, but we far from the richest. My grandma owned a large, two story house on a corner lot close to town. The house was quite long and about half as wide. It was built on a double lot. You would have thought that the eight of us would fit comfortably in such a sprawling home, but the upstairs was for renters. We would have been worse off had we not shared half of the lower level with my grandma.

My parent's wanted the best in life for all of us, so Mama took in altering from the men's stores in town and babysat. My Daddy made what little money he could by being self-employed. He painted houses inside and out, usually coming up with the color schemes himself. He advertised his services with a large, hand-painted sign on top of our copper colored Dodge. It read: JESSE GEORGE - PAINTER AND DECORATOR.

As you can imagine, with six of us being children and my Grandma getting on in age, we often needed the services of a doctor. Our

Nancy's Great-great Grandma Remer, Great Grandfather Edward Remer, Grandmother Addie Sophie Remer Olson, and her mother, Isabel Florence Remer Olson in 1919

92

doctor was Dr. Andrew Grinley. This was a time when a phone call would bring the good doctor to our front door. He held his black bag in hand, ready to treat whatever ailed us, and many trips he made!

My Daddy's job came in handy when goods and services were needed, because he often bartered a paint job for payment, or reduction in a bill. Dr. Grinley's office painting was a part of this exchange. I'm sure we received the better of the deal.

When an office paint job just wasn't needed and money was short, as it nearly always was, we would keep the good doctor and his wife well supplied with homegrown vegetables during our short, summer months. Green beans, being the garden's most prolific producers, were the vegetable of choice.

When other vegetables weren't as plentiful, my younger brother and I would take a large, brown, paper grocery sack, full to the brim with green beans to the doctor's home. Dr. Grinley and his wife would always accept them graciously. Then in turn, they would give my brother and me some silver money, usually a nickel each, for the short walk to their home.

To this day, I'm not sure what two people would do with so many green beans. Once again, though, I'm sure we received the better of the deal.

The Dime Store Ring

I can't recall whether the machine was a penny machine or a nickel machine. That fact blurs in my memory, but it is the kind you would find in the old five and dime stores. The machine contained gum or prizes. Our five and dime, was named Kremers. These stores existed before the chains came into town and gave shopping that impersonal feel.

What I remember clearly, however, is the anticipation on Daddy's face each summer day. After work, he would start his walk to town. He was older, because he was fifty when I was born. He would put on a hat, tipped to the back of his head, grab a bit of change, put it in his pocket and begin the six block walk to Kremers.

Daddy's goal was not to gamble for prizes. It was sentimental. He wanted a ring for Mama. The ring in the machine had a big, green stone that resembled an emerald. It has a pewter colored setting, with an adjustable band. He knew it wasn't a real emerald, but he wanted it as a gift for his wife.

Heaven knows, he couldn't afford a real emerald. If it weren't for the summer garden, and his painting jobs, there were times he could barely feed all of us. Daddy still saw value in that ring.

He spent most of his time that summer walking to town, five days a week. If I had been him, I certainly would have given up, but Daddy didn't.

One day, he came home shuffling faster than usual. He wore a lopsided grin on his face. I knew he had his gift!

Even though he tried to keep the purposes of the trip a secret, Mother must have realized the effort and love behind the gift. When she died, although the contents of her jewelry box were sparse, she had kept the dime store ring.

Growing Up on an Indian Reservation
By Cynthia L. King of Red Lake, Minnesota
Born 1955

When I think about my life and growing up, I feel very lucky that I survived all the things I went through. It seems as if hardships were the normal part of life growing up on an Indian Reservation.

My mother and father (Mary Louise Northrup and George Wilford King) were sweethearts in their teen years and when my father went off to Korea; my mother went off to Flandreau Indian School in South Dakota and waited for him. Many letters later, my father was severely wounded, earning him a Purple Heart and a year of rehabilitation in San Francisco. My mother was into her senior year and knew once she graduated, she was going home to marry him. They were married on November 4, 1953 at St Mary's Mission Church in Red Lake. Two years later, I was born and baptized in the same church that is still standing today.

My first recollections of life was sitting on the ground on a quilt and watching my mother do laundry on a wringer washer and hanging them on the clothesline. All of a sudden, there were these great big bugs coming toward me. My father was planting flowers and trees and came running toward my screams. My mother was horrified and ran to get me only to watch my father gently brush away a few daddy long

Cindy with her mom, Mary Louise King in 1955

legs and some ants.

We lived in a three-room house, which consisted of a bedroom, living room and a kitchen with two large tables and some chairs and a big wood stove. We didn't have indoor plumbing back then, but we did manage to have electricity. My mom was lucky to have an indoor pump for water, which was very cold and had to be heated on the wood stove for bathing. She used to bathe me in a small, round basin when I was a baby until there were more of us, and the little basin turned into a big steel tub. Bath times were in pecking order and the oldest was always first, when I think back on that I was so very lucky!!

Since we had no indoor bathroom, unless you count the big metal slop pail in the kitchen for nighttime duties, we had an outhouse. This outside toilet was near the house, but not too close as to smell it. We always had a used Sears's catalogue inside, either to look at or use. My mom always kept it clean with pine-sol. In the winter, the hole was always flushed with hot water to melt the frozen points protruding upwards, so as not to hurt us.

I always loved to look through the Sears catalogue and wish for majorette boots. Little did I know that the time I spent sitting on the "O" would not be in vain.

We were one of the first families to buy a television. My mom was so happy! We were so happy! My majorette boots had arrived in the mail and I now thought that this was the best of times. My mom immediately began planning a gathering of friends and relatives to come watch the "telly" with us. She would make the popcorn and I would provide the entertainment with the green skirt she made for me out of her lampshade material. I was proud to dance on top of the table for everyone wearing my little green skirt and my beloved majorette boots.

Soon it was time to leave our little home and venture on to Thief River Falls where my father would attend college, and we would be living in a new home. Wow, this was great! We had a bathroom and bedrooms of our own and hot running water. Life was good. I started kindergarten and made friends that weren't related to me. Soon came bikes and a swing-set On weekends, we would motor back to Red Lake and see relatives who would listen wide-eyed to all the things we were doing and experiencing and I realized then, that I felt guilty. I wondered if my life would ever be the same. I missed my people and my

Cindy's dad, George King with his children in 1959

gramma Squay who was the strongest woman I had ever known.

Eventually, we moved to the "City" and my dad had a nice job and again, we had a nice home. We went to Catholic schools and wore uniforms and I became obsessed with becoming a nun. My favorite teacher was Sister Mary Robert who encouraged me to excel in my studies and win prizes for using spelling words in a story. She put the fear of God in me.

It was during this time that we got our first colored television and went to the drive-in movies on the weekends. I also noticed that my father had nightmares every single night; they were so bad that my mom had to wake him. I learned later on that he had PTSD from the war. I prayed and went to church every day, even in the summer for him.

Along with the Beatles, came a desire to play guitar. My mom saved Gold Bond, and S&H green stamps to buy me that guitar. I lost interest the summer I was thirteen and kissed a boy who lived down the block. I knew it was wrong and I was so ashamed. I had to tell my mom that God didn't love or want me anymore and that I was now going to have a baby. Once I told my mom about that first kiss and the baby, she laughed so hard she had to hold her belly and rolled around on my bed laughing until she cried, all the while telling me that I was not going to have a baby and that was not how you get pregnant After that she proceeded to tell me about the facts that I never knew. How embarrassing yet how fondly I recall the good old days.

1950s Well Digging
By Carol Birkeland of Baudette, Minnesota
Born 1942

The house in which I grew up during the 1940s did not have year round running water in to or out of the house. In the summer, we had water from the cistern coming into the kitchen sink and a pipe under the sink took the grey water downhill outside to the pasture. During the winter months, we hauled all our water in from Grandpa's farm and hauled it out in a five-gallon bucket. Around 1950, Dad decided it was time for the family to get a well, so he hired Leo Bleau from Warroad to do the digging.

Mr. Bleau showed up one day with his forked red willow tree branch to witch the property for water. He walked all around the calf pasture near the barn until the branch bent towards the ground indicating the location of where he should drill. The next day he returned with all of his well-digging equipment which consisted of the drill, several long pieces of pipe, a wooden A frame contraption from which the pipes and drill went into the ground, a long boom sticking out from the platform, and a horse. A horse! Why in the world did he bring a horse?

He proceeded to attach everything together and build his platform. Once he finished that, he was ready to begin drilling, but how was he going to get that drill into the ground? The horse had been leisurely eating the grass around the area while Mr. Bleau prepared everything. Now, it was time to put the horse to work. When you need horsepower, there is nothing like the real thing. Mr. Bleau hitched that horse to the boom and had him walked around in circles for two days while the drill went deeper and deeper into the ground. It was a sight to see. People going by on the highway stopped to watch; people came from town to watch as the poor horse kept going in circles. Every couple of hours or so, Mr. Bleau stopped the horse, gave him some water and let him rest for about five or ten minutes, then it was back to work again.

After two days, he still had not hit any water and the horse was too tired to continue. Now, what to do for 'horse' power. Dad got on the old John Deere tractor and he began to go around in circles. It reminded me of the tigers in the Little Black Sambo story where all the tigers wanted his fine clothes and went around and around until they turned into a circle of tiger butter. I was hoping that neither my dad nor the horse would turn into butter by going around in those circles.

They finally struck water at around the 200-foot deep level. Dad dug a trench below the frost line to bring the water from the well to the house and to the barn even during the winter months. Dad also installed a drainage pipe from the kitchen sink below the freezing level so we finally had running water inside the barn and the house all year long.

Awe, Spring
By Donna M. Erickson of Baudette,
Minnesota
Born 1942

I was a kid in the late 1940s living in Pitt, Minnesota, a small spot just a handful of miles from the Canadian border. Spring was my favorite time of the year because it meant the end of another harsh winter and the beginning of a busy new year.

Spring was always full of awesome sights and sounds, and our small farm produced many of both after several months of "hibernation" of the lush green foliage, wildlife, domestic animals, and even people. The sounds, though, were especially memorable for me.

Over the winter, the county snowplow had made a few trips down our 1/4 mile-long driveway into our yard. By spring, the banks on both sides of the road were higher than our car, and the plowed snow mountain by our house was my playground, my snow fort. When the snow began melting, I remember not the visible sign of spring but the audible one.

As the ditch beside mom's clothes lines opened up, the melt began trickling down the bank behind our house to the Winterroad River. At first, it was the sound of a babbling brook, which soon turned into a roar. I remember thinking it sounded like Niagara Falls, although I had never been there. The river overflowed its banks, and the moist ground along those swelled banks became a blanket of yellow color of cowslip flowers. Those brightened our table long before our lilac bushes bloomed or the dandelions covered our lawn.

Spring also saw the emergence of JoJo, the crow. My brother had rescued him as a baby bird in a tree about to be cut down by my dad and brother as they cleared land for farming. The baby crow, still in the nest, was brought to the house, and JoJo became our family pet till we left the farm many years later. He spent the cold winters inside the chicken coop and became one of the flock. His contribution to the sounds of spring was his coming out of the coop crowing like the roosters he had lived with rather than cawing like the crow he was.

But the best spring sound was the phone call letting us know the baby chicks my folks had ordered had arrived at the Pitt store and post office. When we picked them up, the peeping of hundreds of chicks could be heard long before we entered the store. Although only 100 of them were ours, the rest of the chicks had been ordered by our farmer neighbors. At home, the chicks were our houseguests for a while because it was still too cold and they were still too small to be outside. Dad built a wooden box about five feet square, on four foot legs and a plywood sheet cover. He cut a hole in the cover and hung a large light bulb

Donna M. Erickson building a snowman

in the hole to heat the box to keep the chicks warmer than our potbelly wood stove in the living room could. We watched the chicks closely and separated any being "bullied" to a smaller section of the box before they got hurt too badly. For quite a while, the peeping chicks serenaded me nightly as I slept in my bed just a few feet from their box.

Awe, spring. Sounds like those of many years ago bring back many memories, and I miss them all. Spring is still my favorite time of year even though the sounds of the season are much different today.

up to the top of the garage. It certainly caught my attention and, of course, after my lecture they did not do that again.

In the early years, there was no plumbing, and I hated that trip to the outhouse. My dad was a teaser and always reminded me there might be a bear waiting inside for me. On one occasion, I did find a snake inside. I hated them so much that I think I would have welcomed the bear.

Equally unpleasant was filling the old tub for a Saturday night bath. Oh, how I appreciate running water!

Trading with Judy Garland's Dad
By Richard Bullock of Grand Rapids, Minnesota

Back in the '30s, my parents were neighbors of the Frank Gumm family, parents of Judy Garland. At that time Frank owned the movie theater in Grand Rapids where, between movies, little Judy performed on stage.

It was during the Depression and money was in short supply. My dad did mechanical work and Frank Gumm needed repairs on his car but didn't have enough money to afford it. Since many theater patrons were also short of money, they would pay for theater tickets with vegetables raised in their gardens and farms. Frank therefore paid my dad with those same vegetables to get his car repaired.

It all worked out well in a time when nobody knew what a popular movie star Judy Garland would become in the future.

Minnesota is Not for Wimps!
By Helen Nemzek of Moorhead, Minnesota
Born 1926

My main reflection of living in this area is that one could not be a "wimp." I remember one storm in March so horrible that it went on for two days. We lived on a corner lot with a small garage on the edge of the premises. I looked out a day after the storm and saw my kids, ages four and six, walking on the drifts

The Man in the Tree
By Harold Freyholtz, Jr. of Hewitt, Minnesota
Born 1948

My father's side arrived in this country in the 1880s from Pomerania and settled north of the Minnesota River with other German families. The land they farmed was open prairie with no trees, so in order to have fuel some settlers would purchase a few acres in the Minnesota River Valley, which was heavily wooded. They would take wagons to the valley when time allowed to replenish their fuel supply.

On one occasion, a very large old hollow tree was cut down with a crosscut saw. When the tree fell, my ancestors saw a pair of feet in the stump. They opened up the tree and found the mummified corpse of a man. A note on the body told the sad tale.

In 1862, during the Sioux uprising, the man was being pursued by Indians and, remembering the hollow tree by the river and fearing for his life, he climbed the tree and dropped inside. He successfully evaded the Indians but could not climb back out of the tree. He obviously had paper and a writing instrument and was able to leave a note instructing whoever found him to send the money he had on him to his family. His body wasn't discovered until the early 1900s, and his family members were by then deceased.

This story was related to me by a relative who was just a boy and present at the time this discovery was made. He swore the incident was true.

He Called Me Lightning
By Andy Boessel of Wirt, Minnesota
Born 1949

We moved to Minnesota in 1966. I was the oldest of seven kids. I still am. The youngest, a brother, was two weeks old when we came here from Indiana.

We moved into the biggest house my dad could find. It was built he same year my dad was born, 1922. It had "central" heat, by which I mean all the heat came from a wood-fired furnace in the basement and up through a grate in the floor in, approximately, the center of the house.

Since we arrived in August, getting firewood was high on the list of priorities. We cut a lot of our firewood on our own land, plus we picked up more that was waste wood left behind on logging jobs.

I was helping split some wood at a neighbor's house one day when he said, "I'm gonna start calling you Lightning."

I said, "Because I'm so fast?"

He said, "Because you never strike twice in the same place."

Now, over forty years later, I'm still living in that same old house and still heating it with wood. I'm better at splitting wood, now.

The Water Pail and the Slop Pail
By Fern Jackson of Clearbrook, Minnesota
Born 1935

Oh yes, we carried the water from the outdoor pump to the house, and we carried it out again. On the one end of the cupboard counter stood the water pail with the long-handled dipper in it. It was common to go to the water pail, dip a little water and drink it, and put the dipper back in for the next person to use. It was just the thing to do, and we never thought about germs.

We might not like to admit it, but everyone had a slop pail too. Now there went all the peelings from the potatoes and other veggies. With no sewage system, the pail filled up quite fast, as it included the dishwater too. This would be taken out and fed to the pigs, and they could choose to eat what they liked from it.

Also, the outdoor dog was fed the leftovers from the table. Never did we buy dog food. The dog was fed well because living on a farm there was plenty of milk, meat, eggs, and vegetables.

I am from a family of eight children. We learned to work, walked two miles to school, walked to church and Sunday school, and had the highest respect for our elders. Even though times were tough, we never felt poor. We worked hard, played together, and loved and laughed together. Life was good.

The Day Grandpa Tricked the Hunters
By Tom Shaughnessy of Coleraine, Minnesota
Born 1943

My grandfather, Herman Brandon, lived in an old log cabin in Balsam Township. He was well known throughout the area as a great storyteller and had many visitors each evening stopping by for the newest story.

One of my favorites was the deer hunter story. Ernie Bittner had a resort close by my grandpa's place, and deer hunters from out of town would stay at the resort using Ernie as a hunting guide. My grandpa and Ernie were not great friends, mostly because Ernie tended to guide his out of town hunters near or on my grandpa's land.

So one morning, Grandpa heard Ernie telling his hunters that he planned to take five of them to make a deer drive. The remaining four hunters would be in stands. Ernie lined up the "hunting drivers" approximately 150 yards or more apart. Their instructions were to listen to his voice, start moving when he said go, and listen for "hup" to stay in line and not get lost in the woods. There was no snow that weekend so it was hard for the hunting drivers to stay in line except for the voice of Ernie.

The hunting drivers started on Ernie's "go" command. As Ernie was leading the way on one end of the line, my grandpa got on the other side around ¼ to ½ of a mile from Ernie's end. Ernie would holler "hup" and after a couple hundred yards, Grandpa would holler "hup" just loud enough for three of the hunting drivers to hear.

Ernie went straight, and Grandpa went

right. Every five or ten minutes Grandpa would holler "hup." Eventually they were led in to a spruce swamp about two miles from Ernie and his group. Grandpa hollered, "Hope Ernie can find you!" and left them there.

Ernie never knew for sure it was my grandpa, but he never went close to my grandpa's land again!

Early Memories of My Childhood Home
By LaVerne Halverson of Minneapolis, Minnesota
Born 1925

T'was a small farm on the prairie where I first showed my face.
Until I was five, we lived on the place.
Photos and now my maturity, picture it primitive and stark.
But I remember love and play, and the song of a meadow lark.

For Mom and Dad there was always work from dawn to *beyond* setting sun.
Life was hard. For them there was little time for fun.
But I was free to roam, to play…enjoying each new discovery.
I was alone, but my dog Carlo always kept me company.

There was the thrill, the high, the feeling of mirth…
Finding where Mother Cat chose to give birth.
Newborn kittens, small balls of fur,
Eyes still shut, cuddled in a spot she though obscure.

In the granary, partially filled bags scattered about…
Slumped like fat old women all tuckered out.
Musty, dusty, course burlap sacks,
Leaning, sagging, resting their backs.

The modest, frame, three room house,
Built for eight hundred dollars was where Dad brought his new spouse.
From the makeshift porch, Mom tossed the household suds.
And in the cellar below, they stored the spuds.

Keeping flies out of the house was really a chore…
So tacked to the top of the wooden screen door
Was a fringed oil cloth, last year's table covering,
That flapped in the breeze scaring flies that were hovering.

Fondly I recall kerosene lamps, wood stove, linoleum floor.
But the oak dark brown leather davenport I did abhor.
It was my bed…when it got unrolled.
Not comfy or cozy, it was hard, stiff and cold.

So Mom warmed flat irons and wrapped them well.
And tucked me in with a story she'd tell…
Then before I'd finished "Now I lay me down to sleep"
I'd be there…before I'd even asked God my soul to keep.

And there was a well house dark, cool and dank
Where in the center was a bottomless tank
With drinking water from a natural spring, but also it was just the thing
To keep our milk and butter cool in wire baskets hung above the pool.

Today, I've shared…but am appalled
At another memory I've just recalled…
Of my audacity and childish sin
Of curiously peering over that water bin…
and mischievously SPITTING IN!

My First Hour at Fort Polk
By James B. Allen of Swanville, Minnesota
Born 1945

The year was 1966. I was in the United States Army and stationed at Fort Sam Houston, Texas. I finished school to be a medical corpsman and the training to be a surgical technician. Three of us were sent to Fort Polk, Louisiana, for on the job training working as surgical technicians. We took a bus from Fort Sam Houston to Fort Polk and arrived there on a Sunday afternoon.

As we arrived at the headquarters of the hospital, we saw a dead armadillo on the road. When we reported to the "charge of quarters," he asked us how much education we had. Two of us said just high school and the third soldier said he had two years of college. The CQ "charge of quarters" handed the guy with the two years of college a shovel and told him to bury the armadillo.

After he buried the armadillo, we were assigned a bunk in the barracks. I introduced myself to a soldier sitting on a bunk next to mine, and he asked me where we were stationed before coming here. I told him Fort Sam Houston, Texas, and that we will only be at Fort Polk for four weeks for on the job training in the operation room and will be assigned elsewhere after that. He told me the only way you get out of here is to die of meningitis or if your time is up. He said, "The morgue is across the street from the barracks, and they've been hauling a lot of bodies in there lately."

It was mid-July and hot and there was no air conditioning in the barracks. I asked him if there was a pop machine near here, and he said there was one in the hospital and told me where to find it. He said, "There will be an out of order sign taped over the slot but you put the money in. Pay no attention to the out of order sign. Just lift up the sign and put the money in and you will get your pop. We put the sign there on weekends so the patients don't buy all the pop and we won't have any." I did what he said and got my cold bottle of pop.

That was how my first hour at Fort Polk, Louisiana, went.

Hope from the Buried Clothes
By Joanne Williams of Alexandria, Minnesota
Born 1930

This is a true story as related in person by Lillian Blomberg to her niece, Joanne Williams, and in writing to her daughter, Lil.

October 12, 1918, is a day I will never forget. I was 15 years old and living in Brookston, Minnesota, with my parents. Dad had left for Superior, Wisconsin, just a few days before to work in a lumber mill. My sister and her six children were visiting. Sis sewed school clothes while they were there and had folded them in to a neat pile. I was setting the noon table with dishes my parents brought from Sweden.

Midday, on the western horizon, it looked like the world was burning up. My mother and sister grabbed shovels and began digging holes in the backyard where they buried the newly sewn clothes.

The phone gave five rings. That meant "emergency" and everyone answers that ring. A man's voice said, "Drop everything and anything you are doing. Hurry to the depot. A coal train is waiting to take you out of town." Because we could not carry any luggage, Mother put on seven skirts, one on top of the other, so she would have something to wear in the future and use some for clothing for the family. I will never know how she climbed up those iron rods and into the coal car because she suffered from serious rheumatism and was being weighed down by the seven skirts.

Our family of nine rode the coal car to Cloquet, Minnesota. The wind was very strong and flames were jumping form treetop to treetop, faster than the train could go. At one point, a trainman jumped from car to car, telling everyone to lie down and cover as best they could, as we were going through fire. A hole was burned in my coat.

One family, the storekeeper, wife, and son, didn't ride in the coal car. They had too much money that they wanted to save so started driving and hit a windfall that deposited a tree on to their path. The mother was thrown from the car, broke her neck, and died. The father and son lay face down in a wet ditch while flames flew over them. (Lillian did not elaborate so we do not know how or if they survived.)

In Cloquet, we left the coal car for a passenger train to Duluth. Here, we were driven to the armory to register and also to apply flu masks, because this was during the flu epidemic. The Red Cross took over. Electricity was cut off in both Duluth and Superior. Lamps and lanterns were used for lighting. We were comfortably settled on army cots when aroused at 3:00 a.m. and told to leave. Cloquet was now on fire, and the armory was needed to treat fire victims. We were driven to a lovely home where all nine of us stayed together. Duluth, at 3:00 a.m., was buzzing with taxicabs and cars transporting people from the armory to private homes.

The Red Cross located my father in Superior, despite the fact that all means of communication were dead from wires burning down. Within a few days, our family was reunited. The time came when residents of Brookston could return by train, but not everyone made this choice when there was nothing left for them to return to. They chose to start over somewhere else.

We rode the train quietly and dismounted when told it had arrived at Brookston. Nothing reminded us of our hometown. Buildings and trees were replaced by flat land with no landmarks. We walked in the direction of our old neighborhood. Then, someone spotted what appeared to be the dishes from Sweden, melted by the fire but recognizable. From that clue, they shoveled holes nearby until the school clothes appeared, still in their original condition. With that little hope, we felt comfortable about beginning again and building a new home and a new community where we already had good memories.

Itasca Ski and Outing Club
By Doug Maki of Coleraine, Minnesota

The Itasca Ski and Outing Club, Inc. is celebrating its 111th year this season.

The ski club was formed in 1905 with a ski jump being built on Slush Dump Bay near the southeast side of Coleraine.

The club has a rich history in this area and could very well be the oldest club in Itasca County that is still active today.

Back in 1908, a wooden log ski jump was built on the hill down to the lake on the south end of Lakeview Boulevard. It stood for only a couple years being replaced in 1910 with a large iron ski jump to host the National Championships that same year with hometown favorite, Barney Riley, "The Wild Irish Rose," winning the Class B title.

The ski club flourished for years to come with the ski jump right in town. The club produced many state and national champions during this era. Rolf Managseth won the

The old jump in Coleraine

National Junior Class title in 1923, 1924, and 1925. Stylish rider, Gene Wilson, was noted as one of the top ski jumpers in the nation for several years. Gene won Class B at the National Championships in 1936, which were held in Red Wing, Minnesota.

The jump was dismantled in the summer of 1941 and moved to just west of the community. The area is now known as Mount Itasca.

As ski jumping throughout the nation started to decline Mt. Itasca started to struggle as well. During the 1960s, some local youth, including the Maki boys, John Hanson, Bill Hershbach, Nate Salisbury, Rick Anderson among others, stepped in to save the club. They were unwilling to watch it crumble. Through a great deal of hard work, energy, and enthusiasm the club forged on.

Eventually the club produced two-time Olympian, John Maki, who competed in the 1976 Olympic Games in Innsbruck, Austria, and the 1980 Olympic games in Lake Placid, New York.

In 1977, the jump was condemned due to structural safety reasons and a salvage company tore it down in 1979.

A new, modern ski jump was built at Mt. Itasca in 1990 with plastic mats being added in 1999 to allow for summer jumping.

The new jump was named after one of

the clubs founders and ski champion, Ole Mangseth.

The club has also provided downhill and cross-country skiing since 1950.

The club has produced many National Ski Jumping champions for over a century and continues to do so. Club member, Somer Schrock, earned the National Junior Champion title in 2014 in Anchorage, Alaska.

The Itasca Ski and Outing Club, Inc. would like to thank the past, and present volunteers who helped make our ski club historic and have help keep Mt. Itasca going.

The Country Store
By Nancy Dahlquist Harris of McCall, Idaho
Born 1933

My dad was one of seven children born and raised in Roseau. I don't know the history of the Sjoberg brothers except that they had stores in Roseau and Badger.

Israel Sjoberg and his wife, who built the "castle" next to the old courthouse, had no children and took a liking to my dad. He spent a lot of time with them and helped them out at the store. When Mother and Dad married in 1922, Dad was working for Israel, and they lived in an apartment over the store.

Forward to 1941. At some point Dad had quit working for Israel and was working for the Regional Farm Credit Bureau, which took the family to Bemidji and later to Grafton, North Dakota. In 1941, Israel asked Dad to come back to Roseau to manage the Roseau store. We moved back in the summer of 1941, and Dad managed the store until it was sold in 1950.

It was a wonderful store. Starting at the back left corner was Dad's office, and next to it was an open office where Hulda Roadfeldt did the bookkeeping. Then there was a section (somewhat small) of dishes and kitchen utensils. The grocery section was next, and the practice of the day was to hand your grocery list to the clerk behind the counter, which was promptly filled by said clerk and you could be on your way. If you needed something like vinegar that came in bulk, you brought your own bottle, and the clerk would go down the wide wooden stairs to the basement and fill your bottle from a barrel down there.

After the groceries was the women's and children's section. That was served by Irene Ebner, Barney Ross's sister. They had everything: shoes, dresses, lingerie, coats, fabric by the bolt, and everyday things like gloves, socks, etc. The men's section was on the other side of the front of the store. As with the women's sections, they had everything for men and boys. I don't remember the name of the man who worked in the men's section, but I do remember thinking he was the handsomest man I had ever seen!

I remember many times when Mother needed some groceries she couldn't wait for Dad to bring home so I was delegated to take my red wagon downtown to get them for her. How I hated pulling that noisy wagon down the sidewalks. Once at the store, however, I got to help myself to what I wanted out of the bulk supply of cookies and/or candy.

Then across the street where the post office is today was the farm machinery part. I don't remember who ran that but again, they had most everything for the farmer's needs. Gerald Miller worked somewhere, perhaps he was in the farm section.

After the store was sold in the 1950s, Dad and Mother opened the Fairway Market in the new Roso shopping "mall." Irene Ebner opened Irene's Fashion Shop in the same location.

The Creek – the River – the Railroad
By Ruth Johnson of Kensington, Minnesota
Born 1947

I was raised on a farm in Section 24 of Land Township, Grant County, Minnesota. My parents purchased this farm in 1943 after it had been lost by a previous owner during the Great Depression and drought of the 1930s. However, it had been homesteaded in 1870 by Swedish immigrant pioneers who built up a farm.

What an interesting farm to live on for me in the 1940s, 1950s, and 1960s. It was a hilly farm but had the Chippewa River running through it on the western edge of the 160 acres. The Chippewa River and surrounding area had been home to the Ojibway (Chippewa) Indian tribes. But more interesting was the creek, which came through the pasture from east to west and flowed into the Chippewa River. In the southwest area of this farm along the creek was a very flat hay meadow. It was here I envisioned a village for the Ojibway Native Americans as many artifacts were found all along the creek, the Chippewa River, and around Wilson Lake located just to the northwest of our farm.

The creek would be shallow in late summer and fall if it had been a dry year, but in spring, especially if it had been a heavy snow winter, the creek roared through, and we were warned by our parents not to go near it for fear of being swept away in the strong current and in to the Chippewa River.

The creek divided us from our closest neighbors to the south of our farm. In early spring, my dad and uncle stood on our side of the creek and hollered across to our neighbor to visit after a long winter. To actually get to our neighbor's meant a long trip around on township roads. There was a small bridge across the creek that we would cross to get to our neighbor's farmyard but not in spring when the creek was running high.

However, the most interesting part was the old railroad bed, which had been built through our farm. In 1886, the Minneapolis and Pacific Railroad Company constructed a railroad line from Minneapolis-St. Paul to Lidgerwood, Dakota Territory. Between what became the villages of Kensington and Hoffman, the railroad track ran through our farm from the southeast to the northwest, with a bridge built across the creek and a larger bridge to cross the Chippewa River in Section 13 north of our farm. It was in 1887 when the villages of Kensington and Hoffman were founded when W.D. Washburn, a builder of the rail line, surveyed and platted the villages.

In 1907, the rail line was straightened and rebuilt between these two villages, and the new rail line bypassed our farm to the north. The old tracks had been removed, but the raised rail bed remained. One could walk on it and even drive a car or tractor on it. It was a great place to do some more exploring!

And so it was for this farm girl in the 1950s and 1960s to spend my days during nice weather exploring and dreaming of how the landscape of our farm had looked from the time of the Chippewa Indians inhabiting the area, to the early Swedish pioneers who broke the sod establishing a homestead, to the building of the first railroad line and all the interesting artifacts that could be found in my searching along the creek – the river – the railroad!

I did not spend much time in the house!

Tarpaper Shacks and Porcupines
By Virginia Wilcowski Long of Pennington, Minnesota

My name is Virginia Wilcowski Long. I was born in 1938 near Pennington, Minnesota. I spent all but fourteen years of my life in Minnesota.

The first I recall was living in a tarpaper shack in the woods near Blackduck, Minnesota, where Dad and my uncle, Jim Morrison, a brother to my mom, were logging. I remember hearing the porcupine chewing on our shack at night.

Mostly Dad was a musician and sang and played guitar, fiddle, and banjo, in Swatara for the Grange. He used to mention towns like Kettle River, Remer, and many more. Dad always moved us from one place to another. He used to sing and play to put us to sleep at night. That was very enjoyable.

When Dad, Elmer "Bud" Wilcowski, was in the service in the Navy in World War II, Mom bought a farm near the old Goodland School and close to Grandma and Grandpa Morrison. We loved that place. We had 60 acres to play on. Sometimes we would find baby deer in the woods. Mom, Ethelyn Morrison Wilcowski, had the farm built up to 23 head of cattle, two work horses, pigs, and usually 500 chickens, most of which ended in jars in the fall, along with the vegetables we grew, berries we picked, and jams and jellies. We really loved that old farm and living next to Grandma and Grandpa.

I remember after Dad returned home from the service he tried farming and had an oat field that was six feet high, and it waved in the wind. But farming wasn't Dad's thing, so he sold it all and moved us in the middle of Remer. His brother, Erwin, lived there, and he had a sawmill which Dad helped him run. We didn't live there very long. My brother Ken got shot in the foot. Mom lost her third baby, so we ended up back in the Bemidji area in another tarpaper shack. Dad's sister and brother-in-law owned a place with another tarpaper shack, but Uncle Roy had an itchy foot too and sold the place to Dad for $300.00 for 38 acres. That's where we lived when Dad died at 44. He was logging and hauling junk at the time.

Dad always had his music and Mom the household. Food she cooked was absolutely delicious. Sometimes we had partridge or venison or fresh caught fish. After Dad died, it was very hard on Mom trying to raise us five kids and keep us fed. She would sew our clothes from flour sacks, which was cloth back then. They fit the best, and we loved them.

Mom had a five-month-old baby girl, Sandra, when Dad died. I don't know how she made it through caring for us five kids. Ken was the oldest at fourteen, I was twelve, my brother Laverne was ten, and Bobby was seven or eight. We had a half brother, Lyle, too by Dad's first marriage.

One time Mom went off the road with her car and sent me home to get another. I didn't know how to drive but somehow the car got to Mom. I remember having to get up in the middle of the night to go out in the woods and get wood for our heater stove. We could hear all kinds of animals around us. Back then, even bears would come around the house.

My Grandpa Wilcowski had a sawmill somewhere near Bigfork, and Grandma used to be cook in the lumber camps.

I could write a book about the happenings in my life, but for now, this is enough. God has brought me this far to my 78th year, and I thank Him for all I've been through. It has made me a stronger woman.

The old 1940s "ringy-dingy" phone on the wall

Entering the Age of Technology
By Marlyss Rivard Hernandez of Freeport, Florida
Born 1944

I didn't think growing up in northern Minnesota in the late 1940s and 1950s was so different from other places in the country. There wasn't anything unique or special about it. I later learned that we were just a little behind the rest of the world. We didn't have Bell telephones or year-round running water, paved roads, or commercial transportation. We didn't even have television until the late 1950s, and when we did get television, it was very cloudy. One needed a 200-foot antenna and a receiver just to get that. The only channels we could get were the ones from Winnipeg, Manitoba. What we did have was a safe environment in a very remote area of the United States. We always knew where the car keys were- in the car ignition- and our front door never did have a lock on it. The only crimes, if you care to call them crimes, were moonshining for deer out-of-season and/or fishing with more than one pole. We would be gone from the house nearly all day, riding our bikes all over the gravel country roads, skin our knees, catch bullfrogs in the deepest hole in the ditch along the road, swipe some rutabagas from the neighbor's field, fill our bellies with berries, and be home before dark. No one sent the sheriff out searching for us. Since there was no TV to keep us indoors, we were always running around outside. A part of Lake Of The Woods County did not get electricity until the mid-1970s. My grandfather, William Thomas Rivard, was very instrumental in getting the Rural Electric

Association started and bringing power to our side of the county in the late 1940s so we had electric lights, and even an electric clock on which my parents had to pay personal property taxes! It was a great place to live.

I grew up in a house built in 1904. It did not have indoor plumbing and had no heat for the upstairs bedrooms. We had a two-hole outhouse (without the moon on the door) down the hill from the house. Dad hauled water from Grandpa's for us to drink and to use for cooking. We collected rainwater for washing clothes and bathing. The cattle had the Rainy River, (boundary between Minnesota and Canada) from which to drink. We also had a cistern that held water for them. We would melt snow on the woodstove during the winter months for some of our needs. Our "freezer" was one or two garbage cans out in the snowbank. We kept the beef, venison, and fish in a "locker" at the local creamery where Dad sold cream. We canned all of our homegrown vegetables in glass jars. About the only store-bought items were cereal, sugar, flour (which came in sacks that we later used for dishtowels and other things) and butter.

Around 1954, the state paved the main highway going past our place so that made it easier and faster to get to and from town, which was five and a half miles west of our farm. Most people travelled long distances by train back then. The Canadian National Railroad went through town and the trains would stop in town to pick up passengers going to Winnipeg, Manitoba, and to the Port Arthur/Fort Worth, Ontario area. Today these two cities are one, knows as Thunder Bay. The trains no longer stop in Minnesota.

In my senior year of high school, I went to Mankato, Minnesota to take an entrance exam for nursing school. Since there was no public US transportation from Baudette, I had to catch a ride to Grand Rapids, Minnesota with some friends. There I caught the bus for Mankato. I was traveling on my own for the first time. I didn't have much money, so instead of buying a meal in a restaurant (there wasn't any McDonald's or fast food places around there), I went to a grocery store and bought an angel food cake and a bag of apples. These were things I really liked and never got at home. What a crazy, terrific diet! However, there was no one to tell me I couldn't have what I wanted. I arrived late at night in Mankato, walked to a hotel, and got a room. The next morning I had an interview. On Saturday, I took the nearly daylong test and went back to my room.

Early on Sunday morning, I got up and walked to the bus depot, only to learn that the bus I had intended to take north did not run on Sundays. I had to wait four hours to catch the next bus to Minneapolis. It was the end of February and freezing cold outside. I missed the connecting bus to Bemidji by about 15 minutes, which meant I had to wait 6 hours for the next bus going north. My parents were to meet me in Bemidji, which is 110 miles south of my hometown.

I sat in the bus depot, freezing as the doors were constantly opening, trying to do my homework, and staring at the public telephones that lined the wall in front of me. I knew I should call my folks, so I went over to the phones, and read the instructions. Only it was so confusing to me. I had never used a phone like this. Our wall-hung phone at home held huge dry cell batteries, was "cranked" up on the right side, and had the receiver on the left side with the mouthpiece in the center. A small ledge stuck out in front. One long crank and the operator would come on asking,

The Bell telephone in 1962

"Number, please?" You would tell her the number you were calling, and she'd literally plug you into that number. There were about a dozen families on our party-line phone, plus two resorts, so you seldom got through when you wanted too. "Rubbernecking" or listening in on other people talking was a very common thing to do. I sat in that bus depot, reading my history book, looking at those phones, and wondering, "How do I contact my folks?" I could barely move when I got up, as I was so cold. By this time, I was also getting rather hungry as my angel food cake was gone, and I was down to just two apples. I could not figure out how to operate that payphone, and I didn't know what calling collect meant. At six o'clock that evening, I boarded the bus to Bemidji for the six-hour ride north.

My parents were at the bus depot when I got off the bus around midnight. They had learned from the man there about the Sunday schedule and figured I'd be on the late bus, so they had gone to a movie and just waited around for my arrival. We got home around two o'clock Monday morning to find my sister frantic with worry. My parents had not called her to let her know we'd be late. When we hadn't arrived by 10pm, she got on the phone to the operator. The operator called the sheriff, the hospital, and the local officials along the route between Baudette and Bemidji. There are actually only three very small towns along this extremely remote 110 miles of bog. If someone has an accident along that route during such cold weather, he'd freeze to death before anyone found him. This was why my sister was so worried and everyone went on alert, all because I didn't know how to use a payphone. Today everyone carries a cell phone, and one hopes to have service in that area. We heard about phones that would take your picture, but I don't think too many people believed that these phones would actually be here in our lifetime. It was progress just to get off that old party line, "ringy dingy" phone and go to a rotary Bell phone in 1963. Although we were still on a party line, we had fewer families and no resorts on it. Now those little handheld gadgets (phones) can do a multitude of things, everything from being a phone to a computer and a camera, and it will come as no surprise that I still don't know how to use one.

When I was in high school, we had manual typewriters and learned to type instead of poking at the keys of electronic toys as a three-year-old child does today. We didn't even have ballpoint pens until I was a senior in high school. We first used the pen dipped in the inkwell of a jar of ink, the kind often used for special calligraphy, with different sizes and types of pen points. The hole in the school desks that one sees in museums was there to hold that bottle of ink. After that, we had the pens with the little rubber inserts with a lever for sucking the ink up into the rubber insert. The pens that held a plastic cartridge of ink that one inserted into the pen followed, and finally, we got the ballpoint pen in the early 1960s. If a girl wanted to be a secretary, she learned shorthand compared to learning how to transcribe from a recorder today. Cable television is available to most customers up there now, even those who live in the country. What a contrast to the days of the 1940s and 1950s.

In 1958, the Air Force built a radar site just south of Baudette, and officially classified this base as a "semi-remote" assignment; one-step up from "remote." Growing up in this "semi-remote" area, so far removed from the rest of the United States, may have been why I have always enjoyed traveling and seeing new and different places. We did not miss what we did not have.

Today people lock the front doors of their homes, and they do not leave the keys in their cars while parked in their yards, or on Main Street. One must program their cell phones to take the signal off the tower that is several miles south of town instead of the one just across the river in Canada. If you don't program your phone, your server will bill you for an international call.

There still isn't any public transportation from this area to the rest of the state. The Canadian trains ceased stopping in Baudette years ago. Therefore, some things have not changed much at all. One still must take a long lonely drive south to get to Bemidji while keeping an eye out for wildlife jumping out in front of you, or drive 70 miles to International Falls to catch a plane. It just takes one less time to drive these distances due to better road conditions. Kids can still ride their bikes, and stay out all day without their parents panicking and calling the sheriff, but most kids spend more time in front of the television or computer than playing outdoors.

Seeing and living in other areas has made me realize that growing up in northern Minnesota during the late 1940s and 1950s really was very unique and special. It has given me more appreciation for what we have now and has made me see what we who lived in a "semi-remote" area missed or maybe it was those who lived in more urban areas who missed the best part of those days. Modern technology has made life a lot easier, and has helped to shrink the world in ways we never imagined back in the 1950s, but I'm glad I grew up in that "semi-remote" little town of Baudette.

Logan getting encouragement from his mom, Andrea

Taking and Giving Inspiration
By Andrea Mackey of Coleraine, Minnesota
Born 1979

Logan Mackey is 10 years old and ski jumps with the Itasca Ski Club in Coleraine, Minnesota. He is a friendly, generous, and sweet kid, passionate about ships, sirens and ski jumping, and loves life to the fullest. He joined ski jumping as a first grader when we were trying to find ways to help him manage his anxiety and to help advance his learning and motor skills as he had been diagnosed with a Developmental Cognitive Disability. Neither medication nor therapy had helped enough, so why not try ski jumping?

Junior coach, Sue Kavanagh, was so supportive and engaged with Logan at that very first Learn to Ski Jump Day and there was no doubt about him joining the team. As he continued to practice, his ability grew as well as his confidence and social skills. His younger brothers, age 6 and age 4, then started in the sport, and Logan was able to help take on a teaching role with them, which also increased his confidence as well as his communication and his ability to lead. As he mastered the 10m hill, I thought he'd be too afraid to even go over to the 20m hill. But with the confidence given by Coach Sue, and 20m coach, Doug Maki, Logan went down the 20m landing with barely a hesitation. He then proceeded to ski from the 20m half bar by the end of that practice, and a week later, he was able to ski from the top of the 20m, I am amazed at what he has been able to accomplish.

The benefits of this sport go beyond athletic ability and skill gained from going to practices and tournaments. It teaches responsibility as kids help take care of the equipment and the hills. They learn how to support each other on and off the hills. They are surrounded by positive role models as they watch and interact with the "big" kids that jump the 40m and 70m hills. And it makes them part of something bigger as they carry on the tradition of ski jumping in Coleraine.

As I see him developing into a responsible, mature, happy, young man, I am, and will be, forever grateful, not only to his current coaches, Sue Kavanagh and Doug Maki, but to all that have kept the sport alive in Coleraine, Minnesota, for the last 110 years. From Ole Mangseth and John Greenway to present day Shrock's, Denney's, and Rick Anderson along with many others, a lot of dedicated parents and volunteers, including those of you at Central and USA Ski Jumping, that put their time, energy, and efforts into providing this amazing sport for my children as well as many others'. I sincerely appreciate everything you do. Thank you!

Peggy on the Piano
By Sandra Renollette of Bagley, Minnesota
Born 1950

My name is Sandra Faith Wilcowski Renollette. I have a great husband and 2 children, 9 grandchildren and 2 great-grandchildren. My husband and I and our

Sandra with her mom, Ethelyn Wilcowski

children were all born in Bemidji, Minnesota in the old hospital, which is now Baker Apartments. I spent my whole life in Bemidji except the last 27 years in Bagley, Minnesota.

I think I had about the best childhood a person could have. My mother was Ethelyn Mae Morrison Wilcowski and she was amazing. I never went to school without a good breakfast and my hair braided. My father died when I was just over 4 months old, so my mom raised 4 children older than me, plus me, on her own. I have lots of good memories- not many before I started school though. I went to Buck Lake School until 5th grade then went to Bemidji. I grew up in Sugar Bush Township, east of Bemidji.

I remember when my mom would really get into cleaning. She would set chairs outside and they made a good train for me and my dolls. I remember walking with Mom to pick wild strawberries and blueberries and any extra she would can. She always had a big garden and cows and chickens. My favorite cow was Susie. She was a Guernsey and very gentle. I used to sit on her a lot and I remember when they eventually got sold. I stood looking out the window crying.

I liked to watch Mom milk the cows and was so totally amazed by the separator- how the milk and cream came out separately. Then we would make some butter and it sure was good.

My mom was a very hard worker. I remember going with her to pick up pine knots for firewood and she picked pinecones for extra money and cut boughs. She was always busy.

I always thought we had the biggest Christmas tree and after I grew up I found out it wasn't so big. But one year I had a beautiful walking doll I had asked for earlier and Mom said she couldn't afford it. I was pretty excited. I named her Peggy and when I took her to school my teacher put her on the piano to keep her safe. My teacher was Miss Laura Rako and I think she was the best teacher ever.

My Uncle Jim and Aunt Arda Morrison lived close and they lived by the river. In the winter, they would bring ice and we would make ice cream. We took turns cranking the machine and it was wonderful when we were at the eating point. It was always fun when they came. I enjoyed the time with my cousins. Sometimes we played games like carom or cards.

I remember the hand pump at the kitchen sink and the cellar when Mom kept her canned goods. Sometimes, she put carrots in a barrel of sand. There was always lots of food down there.

The Electric Fence
By Joyce Flermoen of Spring Lake Park,
Minnesota
Born 1931

My husband, Ken, grew up on a farm three miles north of Winger Township in Northwestern Minnesota. He had one older brother and four sisters. They had an electric fence to help keep the cows in the pasture.

One day while Ken and his brother, Louie, were outside they noticed the crows landing on the electric fence. They stood there and stared at them, trying to figure out why the crows were not being electrocuted by the fence.

Louie, being the "older and wiser" one, thought there must be a problem with the fence. He thought maybe someone had turned the fence off or that it was broken. He walked over to the main switch for the fence, looked, and saw the fence was on, leaving him quite perplexed.

He told Ken to go over and grab the fence with both hands, and he would try turning the fence off and on to see if they could figure out what was wrong with it. Ken did what his brother told him to and went over and grabbed the fence. Louie had turned the fence off before Ken grabbed it. Then he turned the fence on. Low and behold, Ken started vibrating.

Ken started yelling at him to shut off the fence, but by this time, Louie was laughing so hard that he didn't want to shut the fence off! It was too funny watching Ken trying to get loose. Ken would work one hand free from the fence, but he couldn't let go with both hands at the same time. He was yelling to his brother about what he was going to do to him when he finally broke free from that electric current running through him. Louie was laughing so hard he never noticed their dad had come out of the house. He was standing on the back step watching them and shaking his head.

Their dad calmly and quietly walked over to the switch and shut off the fence. Louie was rolling on the ground laughing when Ken was finally able to break free from the fence. Ken was running toward Louie when Louie finally noticed he was free. Louie looked at him and saw how mad he was and got up and started running.

Their dad made his way back over to the back step, and now it was his turn to laugh as Ken chased Louie all over that farm that day until they were completely worn out.

Moving to the Farm

It was the summer of 1945 when my parents decided to move. We moved from the Twin Cities of Minneapolis and St. Paul, to a farm in rural McIntosh, Minnesota. McIntosh was a small community in the northwestern part of Minnesota.

I was 14 years old and would be starting ninth grade in the fall. I should have been a young lady helping Mom in the house, but since I was the oldest child, I became my dad's farm hand. The neighbors called me his hired hand. Every morning at 5:00 a.m. I had to milk five cows by hand and again every evening at 5:00 p.m. My dad believed if you milked at exactly the same time every day the cream was better on the milk. My younger brother, Myron, also had to milk cows. He had more cows to milk than I did so Dad had him use the milking machine. My younger sister, JoAnn, didn't have to do any chores. She always got out of doing chores by crying. My dad would feel sorry for her and tell her to go in to the house and help Mom. I would never have gotten away with that because I was the oldest.

In the summer, I would help my dad in the field. I helped shuck, bale, and stack grain. I rode on the binder hooked to the back of the tractor. My job was to make sure nothing got caught up in that binder while we went through the fields. The binder tied the bundles of grain. After the bundles of grain were shucked, we had to go out and stack them to dry. To stack them was a balancing act. We had to stand them up and lean them against each other like little tepees in the field. Once the bundles were dry, Dad would come though on the thrashing machine. We would load up the bales of grain and send them through the thrasher. They would then be ready to take into town for sale.

I also ran the mower to cut the hay. After cutting the hay, I rode the rake to make windrows. When Dad and I were done making windrows, we would take the stacker out to the field. We would pile the windrows into haystacks and leave them throughout the field.

In the wintertime when the snow was too deep for the school buses to get to the road by the farm, my dad would hook our horse up to the bale sled (a flat sled used for hay bales). He would bring us out to the main road where the school buses could get us. We sat on hay bales and wrapped ourselves in wool blankets to try to keep warm as we were being pulled across the fields. We lived north of town but the school buses went into town from the west. I was the first one picked up by the school bus for the high school. We would drive east from the main road through all of Hill River Township, making a large circle, picking up other students along the way. When I left school for the day, we would once again travel through Hill River Township to drop off the other students. I was the last one off of the bus. My bus ride was two hours long to and from school daily.

Ice in the Icebox
By Clarence Horsager of Verndale, Minnesota
Born 1929

Years ago at the age of 14 and in the year of our Lord 1943, our family moved from North Dakota to Minnesota. Our house was only a stone's throw from the Leaf River and the "Old swimming hole." Neighbors used our yard as a staging point for teams and sleighs to haul the heavy loads of ice up the bank and on to their farms, and for placement in their icehouse. The process was very interesting especially to a kid who had lived in North Dakota through all of the '30s and the dust bowl. I had hardly seen water- much less walked on it.

The process went something like this: In late January, the ice would be about 24 to 30 inches thick, perfect. Chop a hole and sharpen up that big ice saw. The saw was about five feet long and had huge teeth. One of ours is still laying somewhere at the bottom of the swimmin' hole. Work out a row- maybe 16 feet by 2 feet and then cut at right angles to that as far as you need to go. Others will probably be working off the same hole. This way one end will be cut off and you will cut on two sides and use an ice chisel to pop the other end off. You should not chew snooze and spit on the ice. It was kind of like a little fraternity down on the ice or a wood sawing crew, or a threshing clan or silo-filling.

Anyway, that's when the grunting started. Each piece weighed several hundred pounds so the guys with the most beef found it easiest to get the rhythm up and land the chunk on top of the ice; then on up the plank and onto the sleigh. You would unload the cakes in your icehouse- place them tight together-cover them with three feet of sawdust, and with a little luck, you might have ice for the icebox into July.

I've got to tell you, my dad, who was not so young as he was 45 when he got married; seemingly, he was destined to be another one of those Norwegian bachelor. All true until this Norwegian beauty left Minnesota to teach school on the North Dakota prairie, meet my dad, and make my existence a reality. Well, just the two of us were down putting ice and sluicing it out with those big tongs. He lost his footing and into the frigid water, he went. He was scrambling and I was pulling, and all is well that ends well.

"Those were the days my friend. I thought they'd never end."

Agnes's Miracle
By Ethel Mindermann of Fergus Falls, Minnesota
Born 1942

A long time ago, my mother, Agnes, her mother and father, nine sisters, and one brother lived in a four-room house. This was on a farm east of Menahga, Minnesota.

One day, Agnes was playing with her sister, Rose. Then Agnes didn't want to play anymore. Rose could not understand why Agnes didn't want to play with her. Agnes was tired and did not feel well. She just wanted to lie down. Agnes had contracted a serious infectious disease called Poliomyelitis or Polio for short. Sister Rose would sit on the bed with Agnes and would try to entertain her. Even though they spent a lot of time together, Rose never got Polio.

My mother told me that, at that time, they believed "it was in the water." There were two additional families in the same school district, each of which had one child who also contracted Polio.

Soon Agnes wasn't able to walk, as one of her legs was affected by the disease. To move around the house, she used a kitchen chair as a crutch.

A doctor advised one of the neighbors that the best treatment for their child was rest. Agnes' mother had her own idea as to what the best treatment was for her child. Agnes' grandmother walked across the fields to help her mother care for Agnes. They massaged the leg with oil, which they had purchased from a traveling salesman. They called it "skunk oil" because of its foul smell. While massaging the leg, they warmed some middlings in the oven. Middlings was a coarsely ground grain which was used to feed livestock. The middlings was put in a cotton flour sack. Then her mother and grandmother placed this "hot pack" on Agnes' leg. They did this faithfully every morning and every evening.

One day, a big truck filled with lumber came driving into the yard. The children wanted to see the big truck, and so they all went running to the window. Agnes forgot she couldn't walk and she ran to the window, also. In the following days, Agnes walked and ran as much as she was able to, and continued to improve.

From 1911 to 1918, a nurse known as Sister Kenney worked at developing a treatment for Polio. Her method was to stimulate and reeducate the muscles. This was quite controversial among the doctors at the time. Agnes' mother and grandmother had never heard of Sister Kenney or her method, when they basically used her concept in treating Agnes's leg.

My mother grew up to be a beautiful woman with auburn hair, a contagious laugh, and straight, strong legs. She lived to be 92 years old.

Tim with his parents, Dorothy and Lester Renollette in 1949

The Best of Times
By Tim Renollette of Bagley, Minnesota
Born 1944

My name is Tim Renollette. I was born in 1944, May 17th, in Bemidji, Minnesota. I don't remember much before 1948 or '50. I grew up in a time and place, "Northern Township," where you didn't have to lock your door or worry about home invasions. Folks could carry their gun out in the open for the honest world to see. I have never been without a gun, dog, or horse, since I was 10 years old.

When I was a lad, I think people tried harder to keep their word or promise. I went to Northern School, Bemidji High School, and Bemidji State Teacher's College in my formative years. During that time, I never came across any drugs or any kind of sexual abuse. I think that says a lot for those times. I feel I grew up in the best of times, around a lot of good people.

It was after the Depression and World War II, and before Vietnam. I lost friends in that war and I think, good or bad, it changed America and people's thinking.

When I was 5, in 1949, I was privileged to be in the centennial celebrating Minnesota becoming a territory one hundred years earlier. I played a frontier kid. My mother was a frontier lady, and my dad was the scout of the wagon train. In fact, I still have the boots he wore- rumored to once belong to Buffalo Bill, but that's another story

In 1969, July 27th, I married the love of my life in Bemidji at Assembly of God Church at the corner of 12th and America, but it is no longer a church. As I write this, she is still putting up with me and if I behave myself, maybe that will continue some more. I hope.

We have two great children and a great life with no regrets. I attribute that to our growing up- both of us had hardworking parents with outstanding values and ethics. Back then, we only chased the almighty buck in deer season. Now we have to chase the almighty buck of a different kind.

Where I grew up, the landscape hasn't changed except for more houses, but the people have, somewhat. Growing up there was more physical hard labor. It took more effort to get through the day. Those Old Timers seemed up to the task and this easier life, I think, has had a negative effect on people. After all, it takes more effort to keep your word or promise. Although the times have changed and some values may have changed, I am not unhappy with my life, past or present. I do believe I grew up in the best of times and wouldn't want it any other way. When I say people put out less effort, I am no different. If a tree falls in my yard, I am the first one to reach for a chainsaw rather than a swede saw, as in days gone by. I'm a happy camper in Northern Minnesota.

Lizzy was My Daughter. Lizzy is My Daughter
By Heidi Lamb Castle of Crookston, Minnesota

I had looked for her… waited for her. There was some cosmic connection between our spirits. I knew she was coming even before she was born. I knew she would be in Minnesota.

A birth mom connected with us from Saint Paul, Minnesota. I can only imagine the difficulty of her situation; trying to decide what is best for her child, trusting someone else enough to love, to truly and deeply love her child. I thank God for the birth mothers in my life. Each one of them made an incredible sacrifice to give life to the beautiful children that I mother. I am the benefactor of their months of sacrifice, their pain of birth, their labor of love.

We nervously drove down to the cities to meet Lizzy and her mother. I held her. I held her for the first time. And I loved her. Her birth mom made her decision and signed the papers then and there that September day. Thrilled beyond words we took Lizzy home.

But…In the State of Minnesota birth parents have two weeks to revoke their decision - two weeks to change their minds.

The pain of returning Lizzy to her birth mom, was….well, it was all I could handle. Then, trying to explain to three-year-old Ruby Catherine why her baby sister was going away. How do you do that? It just isn't something that you can Google for helpful tips or read a book about (how to help your child deal with giving away her baby sister?). There are no resources.

I stayed in contact with birth mom. I sent blankets, formula, toys, and love. Weeks later to my surprise, she contacted me again and said she is going to place Lizzy for adoption. Her mind was made up. This was the right thing to do, she said.

My heart skipped a beat. I don't trust easily anymore, but with so much at stake and not being in any position of control, I had to trust. And hope and pray.

Once again, our crib was filled with a warm bundle of love. We were a family complete. I went about nesting, loving, and mothering. The innate joys of being a woman. Yet, still in the back of my mind was the countdown two weeks until the paperwork is complete, legal, and cannot be changed.

It was a Wednesday evening when I received the dreaded phone call. I was at home with Lizzy. I saw the name of the adoption worker on my phone screen. NO. No. NOOO!

Again, Lizzy was returned to her

Heidi Lamb Castle and her daughter

birth mother. The following months were excruciating. I did not keep contact with birth mother. It was beyond my strength. I felt so alone. No one really knew what had happened or what I was going through. Her empty crib stood cold. And I wondered, is she crying for me? Pain in my chest. Does she think I abandoned her?

There was nothing I could do. I prayed. I still felt that cosmic connection.

Christmas 2012 when Lizzy was nearly seven months old. We brought her home to stay. The social workers involved found out that birth mother was going to place Lizzy for adoption again, and they allowed the two-week waiting period to lapse before calling us. It was truly a Christmas Miracle.

Lizzy brought a peace to our home and to our family that is indescribable. Her personality, joy, dancing, Oh her dancing!! And most of all her peace. Peace profound.

Just three weeks before her second birthday is when it happened. Unfathomable. Totally unexpected. A parent's worst nightmare.

Saturday morning about 8:00 a.m. I went into my girls' bedroom to wake up sweet Lizzy. The room was filled with her peace. Ten thousand angels were with me holding me up. I heard a soft whisper, "She is okay. Things will be okay." I peeked over her crib and gazed down at her peaceful body cuddled up to her blanket. She had gone home. Her real home. The real home for us all. She is in heaven.

I don't know why God planned it this way but I do know that God has a plan.

We are all one. We are all children of God. Love is all that really matters. I look forward to the day we can be together again.

I wrote the following to Lizzy the morning of her funeral.

Forget-You-Not
I had looked for you, waited for you.
I just didn't know this was your part
A huge role you are playing baby girl
Although your time on stage was short

I found you Elizabeth,
My wise Oak Tree
Now, with your help,
I am finding me.

You are helping me find my missing parts
Making me complete

Showing me the best things of life
Honoring what's most sweet

Living life with No Regrets
Making the most of each day
Elizabeth is printed on my heart
And there you always will stay.

Reminding me to live in the moment
To soak up the light when it shines
To brave the darkness, allow the hurt
This little light of mine~

You're teaching me to honor my dreams
Your light within burns with hope
Reminding me that Jesus redeems
It is only through Him we can cope

To make the most of what we have
To honor each moment we're given
You bring out the best in our family
You are Peace, Love, and Forgiveness

With the ones I have now, I will treasure my time
Your memories I will keep alive
Knowing one day, there will be no more pain,
When Jesus will finally arrive.

When living seems too painful
Will you bring me the gifts that I need?
After the rain comes the Son
To Him we are blessed to concede.

Jesus Lives.
My baby does too.
With me for just a short while,
You came and brought your gentle peace.
Your gift makes all the pain worthwhile.

I know now, the question I wondered…
Is it better to have loved and lost?
Absolutely yes Elizabeth!
You are worth the cost.

Sweet Dreams my child.
My little girl.
You are in my heart to stay.
We'll be together again, this I know.
For God has planned it this way.

Love, Mama

Letter to Ole - 1991
By Dennis O'Gorman of Coleraine,
Minnesota
Born 1945

Dennis O'Gorman wrote this Letter to Ole in 1991. I was Master of Ceremonies at the banquet in 1991, which was in honor of my grandfather. I failed to call on Dennis to share this letter with the audience. I regret the error on my part and sincerely hope that including it in this publication will mean as much to you as it did to me when I first read it. –Kurt Mangseth

I thought that I should write you this letter to let you know what's happening with ski-jumping in Coleraine.

You probably don't remember me as a little kid skidding down the alley from Gram and Gramp Mjolsness's house. You would always greet me kindly in that old Norske accent. I guess even way back then we considered you a ski-jumping champion. Townsfolk say that you came from Norway and settled in Red Wing, Minnesota, and that John C. Greenway himself recruited you to come to Coleraine to ski and work. Townsfolk say that even the Red Wing landing was introduced by you. Folks around have often used the name Ole Mangseth synonymous with the sport of ski-jumping in Coleraine. Anyway, ski-jumping in Coleraine was famous; big as the County Fair, they say. Fact is, there used to be a sign coming into Coleraine that made claim to this proud heritage. It said, "Home o Ski Jumping Champions." It was our sport, and you were considered King of the Hill. Well Ole, the sign ain't there no more, but, by God Ole, ski-jumping is alive and well in good old Coleraine.

Now I must tell you the truth. There have been a few yarns spun about this sport. I don't know of any kid from Deer River to Ely that didn't ride that jump when they were 12 years old, and boy, the distances they jumped and the falls they took, well… we'll leave that alone. Did you know Bob Demaris jumped 398 feet on that hill? I haven't got time for the others. All kidding aside, Ole, I must say to you with pride that even though we all dreamed of following in your footsteps; many Coleraine ski jumpers have successes in the sport. Of course, you remember your son, Rolf, as a National boy's champion, and many of your grandson's winning special events in the sport. That young Wilson boy, Eugene, went on to join you in the US Hall of Fame and is still considered by many today as one of the most graceful ski riders of all time. The junior ski slide is named in his honor. (I do hope that St. Peter told you of your induction into the Hall of Fame.) A young flying Finn from Coleraine named Jim Maki became a two time Olympian skiing all around the world. He even did some ski flying and jumped near 600 feet in distance. Calm down, Ole, I know that's a bit further than your US National record.

Coleraine ski-jumping has produced high school winners time and again. In the last years, we have placed four junior jumpers on the Junior National Ski Team. I know that you will love to hear that a young Irishman (and, no Ole, his name isn't Riley) has won your prestigious "Ole Mangseth Memorial Trophy." Ok Ole, calm down, he is Norwegian on his mother's side.

Getting on to more ski-jumping… Ole, I must tell you, by golly, that ski-jumping has indeed changed just a little bit. Ski-jumps now come in different sizes. They call them meters.

Ole Mangseth in flight in the mid-1920s

The jump no longer has an upshoot, but they say it hangs at a certain degree. You don't land with a red wind, but you used something called a telemark. Actually, you see that very little these days. The jumpers these days wear funny looking suits and hard stocking hats in case they fall. By golly, Ole, them there pants don't even flutter and make that ski jumping noise anymore. And you can't hear them land all the way over in Taconite. Something about following the hill and landing softly. The guys and gals jump on plastic skis with fancy names and use something on the bottoms called graphite. The wax from the jam jar is out. Them there bindings are just about as fancy as you can imagine. No more leather straps and rubber clamps. Well, don't get too discouraged. I think the bindings are made in Norway. Well, one thing you taught them still applies- you jump hard, you go far.

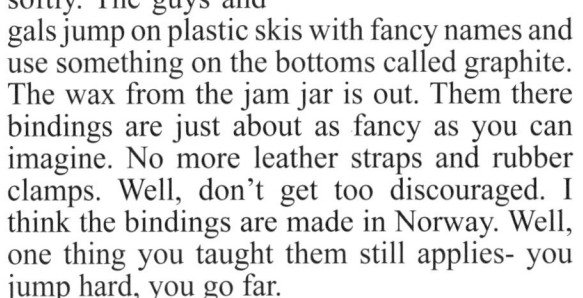

Well, Ole, I guess I had better close this letter. Coleraine has their big ski banquet tonight and I want to get there on time. I know how much fun you all had in the old days. Is it true that Rolf would have won that meet in 1939 if he hadn't went to the d&%n banquet? Your son, Ron, and grandsons and granddaughters, are also going to be there tonight. That crazy Kurt thinks he is going to ride in the tournament tomorrow. I know, I know, you always thought something happened to him when he fell on his head skiing at the "Breakneck Hill" on Trout Lake. Anyway, as the old song goes, "We'll take our fun where we find it!" Oh ya Ole, I almost forgot the most important part of this letter. The ski-jumping tournament tomorrow is in your special honor. We will dedicate the new "Ole R. Mangseth Hill." We think that some

Ole Mangseth and his sons, Rolf, Otto, and Ron in 1920

good jumpers can jump 250 feet on your hill. As I said earlier, I won't tell you what the new US distance record is, but I will tell you that you no longer hold it. I know you wanted it that way. One final question, for the record... did you really ride the jump with your baby daughters under each arm? Now I know where Kurt is coming from.

Well, Ole, I have to get running along. If you see any of those Beattila boys up there, tell them Coleraine says hello. Tell Barney Riley they still talk about him in Eau Claire. Our best also, to young Jeff Wright and Roy Larimie and anyone else you see up there. Thanks Ole, for bringing ski-jumping to Coleraine. You have made winners out of many young men and women who have had the opportunity to stand at the top and push out of a ski-jump. Ski-jumping is truly something special in Coleraine. Tell the Chief of Competition up there that we need some more of that white, fluffy stuff, but to hold off until after our tournament. Well Ole, take care now. I know you will be with us tomorrow as all the jumpers compete in good old fashion Coleraine ski-jumping.

Ole Mangseth died on September 24, 1952 at the age of 74.

Thank You, God, for These Blessings
By Sister Mary Jean Gust of Fertile,
Minnesota
Born 1927

Growing up on a farm about ten miles north and east of East Grand Forks had many advantages and, looking back, perhaps just a very few disadvantages!

I am the third child in a family of eight - an older sister and brother followed by a sister (who was about 13 ½ months younger than me) and then four brothers. I remember so well when my last two brothers were born. They were born in the hospital while the rest of us were born at home with the help of a family friend who was a midwife.

Tim was born in January, and the day my dad brought Mother to the hospital in Grand Forks became very stormy. Dad had taken my brother Bob along (perhaps he was five years old) and on the way home they followed a truck as Dad couldn't see the road too well due to the blowing snow. Bob often reminded us how they watched the rear lights on the truck. The day Dad brought Mother and Baby Tim home was so exciting for all of us. We could hardly wait to see our new baby brother, and we were ready to help take care of him. Mother always told us to be careful when we touched the baby's head because his skull was still so soft!

My youngest brother Philip was born in July so the weather wasn't a problem when Dad brought Mother to Grand Forks. During the winter months of that year, one Sunday when we were on our way to Mass in Tabor, I can still hear Dad say, "Hold on! We're going in!" About four miles away from home, our car went into the ditch on the driver's side and in some way rolled up and back again. There we were – Mother, who was pregnant; Dad, who had a cut on his head; my younger sister, whose leg was bleeding; and the rest of us, stunned at what had happened. My older sister told my brothers Gerard and Bob to run across the road to our neighbors for help.

In no time, we were all in cars and on our way to Grand Forks to see our doctor, Dr. Ralph Leigh. I remember being in the doctor's office and he and his nurse took one look at each of us and then took care of Dad and my younger sister, who had a large gash on her leg, and then checked the rest of us to see if we had any injuries. Finally, he checked our mother! He told her he waited to check her till the last because she was in a state of shock as she watched the rest being taken care of. He was concerned because she was pregnant but was so happy to be able to tell her that nothing had happened to her or the baby!

When parishioners arrived at church, the question was, "Where is the George Gust family? They are always here early." I do not recall who gave our priest, Fr. Zellekens the information, but during the afternoon, he came to our home to see all of us. By that time, neighbors had pulled our car out of the ditch and brought it back to our farm behind our granary so we wouldn't have to see it. Some neighbors also brought food for us.

What had happened and how did it happen? As always during the wintertime, Dad would tuck a heavy blanket over the hood of the car to help keep the engine warm. Apparently, in some way the blanket got loose and caught in the front wheel, which caused a problem with the steering. That is the only explanation Dad could give. Remember, in those days cars didn't have heaters so all families had to create ways to keep the engine from freezing!

Going to school in a one-room schoolhouse was a joy! We walked to school about a mile each way, along with our cousins who lived just across the road from us. Our grandparents (Dad's parents, Jacob and Anna Gust) lived just a short way from the school. On our way home, as we came closer we could smell fresh baking. Several times, we would stop to see our grandma and grandpa and, of course, there were always fresh cookies or donuts or rolls that she gave us. Mother always told us not to bother them, but we just knew they loved to see us, and Grandma would give us some kind of a treat!

I believe I read every book in our library. I couldn't wait to get to the next book on the shelf. One of my favorites that I read many times was <u>Heidi</u>. I pictured myself walking in the hills watching sheep and being Heidi. Yes, someday I would go to Switzerland and pretend I was Heidi!

During the wintertime, we went to school by horse and sleigh. Many times my dad or one of the other dads would lead the horses right across the fields and then to the school. We were covered up very well, but I remember I always had frostbite on my cheeks and my feet suffered from the cold. After school hours, one of the dads came with the sleigh and two horses to bring all of us back to our homes.

Our teachers were the very best! Dad was the school clerk, and he was always able to find teachers who cared for us and taught us well. All of us enjoyed Friday afternoons because the teachers had Manual Training for the boys and taught us (the girls) how to embroider and to do other creative things. We always made some special gifts for our parents and learned how to keep secrets for long periods of time!

Christmas programs were a time when each child had a special part to memorize. I remember when I was in the first grade I sang "Jolly Old St. Nicholas" as I sat on Santa's lap. The most important words were "Don't you tell a single soul what I'm going to say" as I shook my finger at Santa. Such memories!

One time our Uncle George Pribula (Mother's brother) came to our farm during the harvesting or haying season. He wanted to take us (my sisters and myself) to East Grand Forks to see our aunt and uncle and then to buy ice cream for everyone who was working in our fields. We had been playing outdoors and were without shoes and our uncle said that is just fine, but Mother had us quickly wash our feet even though we would again be barefoot when we got to town. We visited at my aunt's home for a while, and then he stopped at the Bridgeman Creamery and bought at least three kinds of ice cream to take to our farm. What a treat! Dad and my brothers and farm helpers came in to the house, and we sat around the table eating ice cream until it was finished. We made our own ice cream during the winter months, but this ice cream was BOUGHT and it was summer time! No, we didn't have an icehouse so what was bought had to be eaten.

The opportunities of being in a one room school led me to move forward with my education at Sacred Heart High School in East Grand Forks. Our parents wanted us to have a good education. My older sister was the first in our area to go to high school. At that time it was felt that children should stay at home and work on the farm, get married, and go on with life. Our parents had different ideas and made many sacrifices to help all of us go to high school.

When I was a sophomore and my older brother was a junior we were determined to make enough money to pay for our tuition. For several days, we picked potatoes for one of our uncles. Never will I forget how in one day Joe and I picked 125 bushels of potatoes! They were larger potatoes, but nevertheless we had to fill the buckets. He had me fill the buckets as fast as I could, and he carried all of the bags. Working together, we had a full day and we survived. I am sure we slept well every night!

Milking cows in the morning before school and doing chores when we came home from school was a routine. But our mother always had something for us when we came home from school: fresh cookies, fresh bread, or a roll or two. She'd always warn us not to eat too much or we would spoil our supper, which she was preparing.

Our dad was a born teacher. Many evenings we would go outdoors, and Dad would point out the various star formations. I remember the Milky Way. Now why was it called the Milky Way? Because there were so many stars close together, it looked like a trail of milk!

These memories and many others have been shared with family and friends over the years, and I always say, "Thank you God for my parents who taught us, guided us, and taught us how to become responsible individuals at home, in school, and wherever we would be in our adulthood!"

Pity Sakes- Smells Like Limburger Cheese
By Patrick T. Doll of Perham, Minnesota
Born 1938

I grew up on a farm near Rush Lake, about five miles south of Perham, Minnesota. We did not get electricity until the fall of 1948, so our necessities and work were basic. I was the youngest of eight children. All of us kids had chores to do. One of my jobs each week was to help Mom with washing clothes.

Mom stoked up the kitchen double boiler cook stove with wood from the wood box. Then, I went to the pantry to get the well water that our chugging horse and a half gasoline engine on the well pump jack had pumped. I filled the pails with water and carried them into the kitchen, then poured the water into a big copper boiler kettle on top of the stove. After the water was heated, I used a suitable sized tin dipper to take the hot water out of the kettle and put it into a pail. I carried the pail of hot water to fill the Maytag washer that was in the unheated farmhouse porch. The Maytag, square topped, double roller, wringer washer was powered by a noisy, Maytag gasoline engine. Dad connected a flexible, steel like hose to the gas engine exhaust so that Mom could wash on the porch without having to wash outside in the winter months. After washing, I could flip the hose up along the wall to store.

The gasoline had to be mixed with Maytag oil to fuel the engine. I took the sparkplug odd the gasoline engine and placed the ignitor tip on the edge of the woodstove firebox door. After the ignitor tip was heated, I tightened the sparkplug back in the engine. The Maytag washer seemed to start easier when the sparkplug tip was hot. Mom then step-jumped on the pedal, similar to how many motorcycles are started. She never liked to do that because it often took several step-jumps before the engine fired. It always sounded as if a motorcycle was popping in our porch every time we washed clothes. I don't think Mom ever had any ambitions to be a "motorcycle momma."

After the washing machine did its job, Mom would wring the clothes through the double rollers into two tubs filled with cold water for rinsing. In the summer, she hung the clothes outside to dry and in the winter, she hung the clothes inside. I tipped down the gravity hose from the washer to drain the dirty water out of the machine into a pail. Then, I carried the dirty water from the Maytag and tubs outside to pour on the ground.

Now, my dad, who is of German ancestry, loved Limburger cheese, and my mom, who is of Irish ancestry, found it disgusting.

Limburger cheese originated in northern Europe during the 19th century. It was first made by Belgian Trappist Monks, but the Germans liked it so much they embraced it as their own. The problem with Limburger cheese is that when cured, it creates a bacteria that is the same bacteria partially responsible for body odor and stinky feet in people.

Mom would not allow Dad to keep any Limburger cheese in the house. Dad kept it in the cow barn in a medicine cabinet where he kept medicines for the cows. The barn cats never slept by the medicine cabinet, but the cows didn't seem to mind. Dad would buy his Limburger cheese in blocks, maybe four to six inches in length, at the Perham Locker Plant. He would cut off a chunk with his jack knife and eat the cheese with soda crackers.

One wash day in 1946, when I helped Mom with the clothes washing, this experience happened that I have never forgotten. After I carried one pail of hot water from the kitchen stove and poured it into the Maytag washer to fill, I returned to get another bucketful. When I opened the Maytag, square lid to pour in the second pail of hot water, a stench came out that made my eyes water. Right away I told Mom there was such a terrible stink out there that you wouldn't believe. Riled, she exasperatedly said, "Pity sakes- smells like Limburger cheese." My mom was madder than a wet hen. Dad had brought home some Limburger cheese. He intended to take it to the barn when he went to do his milking chores, but forgot he had hid it in the Maytag washing machine.

I drained all the hot water, heated more water on the woodstove, and Mom spent hours scrubbing out the old Maytag washing machine with her homemade soap. Needless to say, it was a smelly mess and Dad never hid his Limburger cheese in the washing machine again.

Precious Memories
By June E. Gartner of Park Rapids, Minnesota
Born 1955

I grew up in Squaw Lake, a small northern Minnesota town. The sign on the outskirts of town seemed to proudly boast, Population 100.

Our family of six lived the lifestyle of a pre-sixties era in some aspects. Although most people in the sixties had indoor plumbing and television, we didn't. The one good thing about an outhouse was there were no accusations about someone spending too much time in it. *Especially* when it was twenty degrees below.

I believe that a combination of things as I was growing up molded my character:

June's parents, Joan and Fannie Sandberg with Steve and June

Mom worked hard as a homemaker and mother. She kept our home immaculately clean and the four of us children as well, despite the fact that we didn't have running water indoors. She cooked, baked, and heated water on a wood stove.

We had a wringer washer, and at a young age, this would become one of my chores. I felt proud to help Mom wash clothes, but quickly learned to heed her warning about the wringer. One time of my hand and part of my arm being caught between the rollers was a lesson that I didn't need to be reminded of again.

My oldest brother and I both had chores such as chopping and carrying in wood, pumping water outdoors, and bringing in many buckets of water every day. I would also help Mom with cleaning and cooking. Shoveling snow, mowing, etc., were expected.

Even though Mom was busy the majority of each day, she always found time to spend with us. We couldn't wait to get home from school for the fresh baked bread or hot rolls that were waiting. Summer evenings were spent outdoors, many times with Mom. She would talk to us kids about God, the stars and the universe, explain different animal sounds, and tell us about her life as she was growing up.

honesty, pride, being considerate of other people's feelings, a positive attitude, and a great sense of humor.

My dad worked long, hard hours as a timber cutter and often worked at the sawmill. Occasionally he was a fishing tour guide. Dad was an honest, proud man who would never consider the idea of getting financial help from the government or by any other means. He would tell us children that nothing in life was free.

Dad was also a strict disciplinarian. If we did or said anything that he perceived to be wrong, we got the belt, or as he called it, the razor strap. By today's standard, he would have been sitting in jail. However, we did not think of this as abuse; just the consequence of what happens when you do something wrong.

June, Nancy, and Steve Sandberg

The radio was our source of keeping informed about events happening in our country, such as the first moon landing with Neil Armstrong and Buzz Aldrin, which we also were able to watch on television at school. I was amazed at such an accomplishment.

Sometimes events were not good news. The assassination of our president, John F. Kennedy, was heard about in school. I was too young to grasp how serious this was. We were released from school, and when we got home, our dad was on a work break. When we told him, he quickly turned the radio on, and I saw tears in his eyes. My parents had many friends and were used to company coming over quite often. On this day, however, friends were gathering, and the house had an aura of sadness. There were more tears and questions as to who could do such a horrible thing.

For a while, I almost hated the radio. This would not last long, because I couldn't wait until Saturday night to listen to the *Grand Ole Opry*. From this and Mom singing to us or with us, I learned hundreds of songs. I dreamed of becoming a singer. Later in life, I was able to partially fulfill this passion by singing at fairs, various nightclubs, and festivals for a few years. I also wrote songs and had one recording.

As my siblings and I were growing up, we knew that recreation and playtime activities were not bought for us. My oldest brother was very innovative and made carvings, fishing poles, and walking stilts. We built tree forts, made our own swing sets, played softball, etc. The chores we had made us feel important and appreciate other aspects of our lives more.

In 1970, my dad decided to move the family to Park Rapids where my grandma lived. There were more job opportunities with better pay. We knew this was a difficult decision for my parents. I believe the whole family was devastated to leave such a beautiful area with its towering pines, so many good friends, and all the good memories.

However, it didn't take long to make new friends and realize that this area was quite similar to what we'd left behind. The town's size and population were huge in comparison but offered so much more than we had seen before: drive-in movie theaters, ice skating rinks, pinball arcades, and more. Those were wonderful times.

After a few years, I married and had three precious children. I talked to them about how life was when I was growing up. There were no computers, cell phones, iPads, or DVD players in our home. Time was spent with family and friends. Even though we were able to buy my children much more than I had ever dreamed of, they seemed to think my childhood was fascinating. I agree with them, and time will never erase those precious memories.

The Barn
By Leonard Vonasek of East Grand Forks, Minnesota
Born 1952

My story is about a building. My story is about much more than a building; it's about the memories and the influences of a young boy growing up on the farm homesteaded by my great-grandparents, my grandparents, and their family on a quarter section of land between East Grand Forks and Tabor of Sullivan Township in Polk County, Minnesota. It was one of several buildings in the yard: a house, of course, a garage, a machine shed, a chicken coop, two granaries, brooder houses, and an outhouse. The outhouse lasted until 1962 when yours truly, while playing with matches, burned it to the ground, making my father very proud of me! But that is a story in itself.

The barn is the building that is in the background of all the family pictures taken in the yard: maybe the Saturday night baths in individual galvanized wash tubs; maybe picnics, baptisms, confirmations, birthdays, graduations, anniversaries, weddings, first cars, or the 4th of July.

Built in 1926, it is an elite round roof barn, with curved laminated rafters over a tiled first story. The tile is clay block, hollow for insulation value and glazed for maintenance free exterior and interior. Grandfather Rudolph Vonasek, on the original Vonasek homestead, built this barn and was told by the builder that it was to be grey in color, never red or white. Originally, it was grey. I don't know when it was first painted red, but as far back as I can remember, it was red with white trim, and it

The barn in early days

barn. I estimate that distance to be about 120 feet and from the well to the house, being longer, maybe 140 to 160 feet. I don't remember this being done, but it's the best recollection as told to me by Grandpa V. (probably while sitting on the running board of the blue 1948 Dodge truck that brother Terry still has, waiting for a hopper full of grain during grain harvest). Dad was combining with the KTA tractor, now brother Wayne's, and a MM G4 combine. I've got off the subject some by thinking as a boy, but I can't write as fast as I can think.

The barn is also the place where eggs were gathered twice daily from the chickens, washed, and candled by mother Martha and sold to stores, restaurants, and people in town. We watched the birth of calves and pigs. It's the place where cats and family dogs spent their nights during cold Minnesota winters. In the barn, we helped hold small pigs while they were being castrated, because they were not to be breeders. They were meant to be feeders, and their meat would be much more tender

was repainted twice that I remember; once by my father, Leonard Sr. and Joe Brda, who also hand painted a painting of the barn showing it in grey as original. This painting was on the wall of my grandparents' house until their deaths in 1975. I have not seen it since.

I have a lot of memories in this barn of calves in pen, hand milking a few cows, chickens in one corner enclosed specifically for them and gathering eggs, and driving our MM 445 with manure spreader through the alley and stacking manure on it and then driving out and spreading the manure in the field. When the snow was deep, the tractor would spin and slide around. It was great fun for someone ten or twelve years old!

We had a milk house where milk was strained into ten-gallon milk cans and sold. It was picked up by someone in a milk truck every two days or so. We had water piped into the barn from our artesian well (flowing well) that Dad dug in by hand. The way I heard it, he shoveled the trench one pipe length (21 feet), six feet deep, and two feet wide per day, from the well to the

The barn in present day

121

and flavorful this way.

In the barn as boys, brother Wayne and I would do the chores after school and help Dad when chores were done, sometimes Dad would pick a fight with us, and we would box, hitting very softly, mostly in each other's shoulders, just for fun. Then we went into the house for supper.

The barn was the place where when loose hay was being brought in by overhead sling and rope and dropped to the loft floor, a young boy pretending to be Superman jumped to the floor from a haystack and had a rack of hay dropped on him. Sister Becky screamed so loud, Dad came running up, and I could not be seen. I was really scared! Dad told me to kick as hard as I could, and when I did, he grabbed my feet and pulled me out from under the haystack. I think we saw Superman that day, but it wasn't me.

I was in the Army in 1972 when the barn was lowered and the tile walls were removed. It was re-shingled, a new overhead door was added, and new hand mixed concrete poured from the west end in about 20 or 24 feet and the gutters filled in. From that time forward the barn became the "Quonset" for almost everyone but not me. It will always be the barn.

Now brother Terry has refaced the Quonset with maintenance free siding, new shingles, soffits enclosed, cupola intact, west sling peak in place as original, loft doors outlined and trimmed, and it looks outstanding. It brought tears to my eyes when I saw it. It was partly the building, partly the memories, and partly the family. Altogether, that's my picture of the barn.

I was raised on this farm in rural East Grand Forks. I never farmed; being the oldest of three sons and the second oldest of five children, I could see that this small farm would not be able to support all of the family in this generation. So I spent my working years in the construction industry as a building, remodeling, and concrete contractor. In my spare time, I restored vintage Minneapolis Moline tractors and still have a collection of them and scale model (toy) versions of them.

I still live in rural East Grand Forks with my wife of 41 years, Gayle, in the home we built in 1977 and where we raised our three children, Katie, 41; Blayne, 38; and Abby, 33. We are proud grandparents of four grandchildren from 20 years to 12 years old.

I have been active in township and county zoning and now retired from construction, spend most of my time working for and helping the Catholic community of Sacred Heart in East Grand Forks as an administrator and witnessing my own and other families grow in the eyes and the protection of our Lord and Savior.

On Grandma's Farm
By Andrea Searancke of San Diego, California
Born 1970

My mother was born in 1940. She told me stories about life on the farm in Minnesota where she grew up.

In those days, the majority of people obtained their food from gardening and raising their own animals. They raised cows, pigs, and chickens. It sounded like a lot of work to me, and made me appreciative of current times.

The cows and pigs were sent to a slaughterhouse to be butchered. They then cut them into steaks, roasts, hamburger, chops, etc. and were picked up by farmers when the service was completed.

One summer we took a trip to the farm to visit Grandma. There was a big berry patch and garden. We helped Grandma pick strawberries, raspberries, rhubarb, and vegetables. I loved the berries- the vegetables, not so much. The berries we picked were made into jam, eaten fresh, or made into desserts. The vegetables we picked were cucumbers, beans, and potatoes. Cucumbers were made into pickles, beans were made into soup, and potatoes were boiled for salad or fried. Now I know why my mother has a garden.

Then came the big surprise. It was the day for chicken plucking. Once a year, in late summer, it is the time to stock the freezer for winter. From coup to freezer, it took 3 hours to kill and clean 40 chickens.

My cousin and sister were in the coup and caught 10 at a time. My uncle would chop their heads and dunk them in water. From the bucket of water, one of my aunts would

Andrea's grandma, mom, and aunts cleaning and cutting chickens

Blue Grass, I Love It
By Mary Ann Uselman of Sebeka, Minnesota
Born 1934

I'm Mary Ann Kern Uselman. I was born 8-22-34 and raised in Blue Grass. I was the youngest of nine children born to Peter and Suzanne Brockpalher Kern. My parents were a perfect, caring couple. When my mama was 6 months pregnant with me, the doctor said they would have to abort me or we both would die because Mom was so sick. But they said, "No. This baby is alive and if it's God's will, we both will live." I'm 81 and Mom lived to be 100 years and 8 months old. I think God told the world something.

Blue Grass is a small settlement located in the geographical center of Wadena County, 10 miles north of Verndale and 13 miles northwest of Wadena.

In the beginning, it was a heavily wooded area settled by Indians. The settlement was known as Lotta. The Leaf River Township was the boundary line of the Indian Territory. My grandfather said if they were going to be gone awhile, they would bury the women under the hay in the manger so the Indians wouldn't scalp them.

Chauncy Hill was the first white settler in the area. He farmed ¼ mile north of Lotta. As time passed, he decided to change the name to Blue Grass because he came from Blue Grass, Kentucky and because there was a lot of blue grass growing here. Chauncy retired in his little house, which still stands behind the CCD Building in Blue Grass.

In 1879, three brothers, Anton Kern, Joe Kern, and Mox Kern, migrated to the area. The Kern brothers decided to settle here because it was a beautiful, dark forest with tall trees which one sees now only in the national park. Land was cheap at $18.00 and they bought 160 acres. They cut the trees and started a sawmill.

Blue Grass was a growing community, which attracted many businesses. The post office was to the north. Raymond Lee was the postmaster.

John Rice built the first grocery store. It was the Rice Store. We also had a hardware store.

Vaudeville shows from Nevis, Minnesota came every summer and set up a tent and performed every night. Children weren't

put them thru the plucking machine. It was a power wheel with flying rubber fingers that pulled all the feathers off. Then another aunt would carry the chicken to the table that was set up. It was about 10 feet long. My grandma, mom, and 3 aunts were waiting. One would cut off the wings and feet, pass to next to pick the pinfeathers. Then Grandma and Mom would do the messy part. They would take out the guts and put the chicken back in water. The next step was cutting. Each one cut off a certain piece and would pass the chicken on. All the individual pieces were put in water and washed. The parts then reconstruct the chicken to wrap in freezer paper. Wings, legs, and other parts had been kept separate so it didn't take too long.

The crew consisted of myself, Grandma, Mom, Dad, my sister, 3 uncles, 4 aunts, and 3 cousins. The cousins were too young to do much so they played games and got tractor and truck rides from an uncle.

Early in our visit, we attended a cousin's wedding. There were over 350 people at the reception and there was a pig roast. They put two pigs, 1000 pounds each; in the roaster from 2am to 5pm., Beverages were put in a cow tank with ice to keep cold. They had beer and soda. When the beer was gone, they had a tapper beer truck.

For entertainment, they had 3 horseshoe courts, 3 volleyball courts, and a softball field. After eating and later in the evening, there was a band for dancing waltzes, polkas, schottische, and a limbo contest.

The farmers work hard in the fields during the weekdays, but know how to party in the evening and on weekends. A good time was had by all.

Blue Grass when Mary Ann's grandfather, Anton Kern came to the area

allowed in. He sold a cure-all ointment.

A dentist came every summer and had his office in the Woodsman Hall. It was used for many things. It was were all the meetings were held.

The County School kids came to Blue Grass for play day. The 8th grade exams were taken in the Lutheran Church. We also had a baseball team and we played in Simon Scheuer's pasture on Sundays.

John Kern built a garage to service the area. Art Thompson purchased it and it later became a grocery store. Then Paul Kaplin built a cement garage. There was a misunderstanding about a leak in a gas tank so he closed it and built across the road. The building is still standing.

Simon Scheuer built the last grocery store across from the parking lot. Frank Kaplin bought it and now it's the home of Tim Flagg.

In 1904, the Blue Grass Cheese Factory was incorporated. Later it became a creamery but as years passed, the farmers took their milk to creamery, so they sold it and in bigger towns, it's now the Nimrod Grocery in Nimrod.

The Catholics had no place to worship so Chauncy Hill donated 4 acres for them to build a church. Grandpa Anton Kern donated the lumber. Henry Westley built the church.

Blue Grass was home to the County Garage for years. Many people lived here. There was also a feed mill that sold lots of feed to the farmers.

Grandpa raised bees and sold a lot of honey. It was used for sugar when we were rationed. We would get tickets and that had to last us a month. With our big family, we were always short so Grandpa Kern would give us some of his stuff and we had to hide it in the attic because that was against the rules.

We had no running water or indoor bathroom. Our baths were in a washtub in the kitchen. Mom heated the water on our wood burning stove. We had to use the outdoor toilet. We were happy when peach season canning came because the Sears Roebuck catalog was pretty hard.

In the fall, Dad butchered five pigs and a cow for our meat. He also hunted rabbits, and fished. He smoked the fish, ham and bacon, and packed the cured meat in a barrel of salt. Mom canned the rest. Our milk and butter was lowered into the cooling tank. We also had an ice shed for making ice cream and frozen food.

My sister and I also had to get the cows home for milking and Dad said no one was to take any smoked fish, but one night we were so hungry that I stole one and got a bone stuck in my throat. Mom finally got it out but we learned our lesson.

Our radio was battery operated so we could only use it so much each day. We listened to the Lone Ranger. We had no phone so we would go to the store to make a call.

Our laxative was castor oil or Senta leaf tea. They would pick the weed, cook it, and to this day, I can't stand tea. Goose Grease was for chest colds.

Yes, Dad used the razor strap on the boys and the one that laughed got it too. He only pulled the girls' ears.

My youngest brother was in the Korean Conflict. The rest were in World War II. While serving overseas my brothers met up, they weren't far apart. Thanks to one sergeant who made the arrangements. But us kids at home better have been on their knees at 8 pm to say the rosary for a safe return. And our prayers were answered.

When I was 14, I had my first spinal fusion and after a year in Gillette State Hospital, they would only let me go home if I got schooling. So every Friday, Mrs. Citel would bring the 8th grade class to my house for a week of lessons. She was my favorite teacher.

Mom sewed all our clothes. If she didn't have enough of our fabric to make a coat, she would piece cut in different shapes. They were our coats of many colors. Dad made our Christmas toys.

S&H stamps made the down payment on my engagement ring.

We had a one-room schoolhouse. Our hot lunch was a can of beans or soup on top of the wood burning furnace.

We had a creek running through our land that was our swimming pool, but the cows also crossed it to get home for milking which made it a little dirty.

At one time, Blue Grass had a lot of houses and businesses but today it's a quiet town with two churches and one business. But I still love it.

The Lord Giveth, and the Lord Taketh…
By Jacob Harvala of Hanford, California
Born 1953

I was born on a very cold day in Detroit Lakes, Minnesota, on December 19, 1953. The temperature for that day could easily have been 22 degrees. Minnesotans will know what

Jake with his sister, Jean in 1954

this feels like. Another -8 degrees lower and one may stand outside in the dark and starry night and hear the trees "crack" and "pop."

My parents brought me home, 30 miles east of town, to the family homestead and farm in the Smoky Hills. It was a farm of eight cows, a summer garden, and enough fields to make summer hay to feed the cows and calves in the winter months.

My father was not a farmer, my mother was. After my birth, my father left home to work construction on the Alcan Highway in Alaska. He drove a D-8 Cat clearing trees for the road ahead. Prior to this, he worked in Thule, Greenland working heavy equipment on the Air Force base.

I was born, the 8th and last of the children in the family, known as "the baby" long into my teens.

My family was of Finnish origin. Our territory, if you will, was a Finnish community in a 25-mile radius. Not a true radius as to the north was Chippewa, to the east was German and Norwegian, and to the further west, a mix of Europeans. Even the Finns, though connected by origin and blood, had our own separations. Separated by religions, drinkers, and non-drinkers, extroverts and introverts, and some all mixed into one.

The year was 1955. It was a rainy spring in the month of June, and our church services were held once a month with travelling clergy/ministers. Services were held Saturday evenings. The other weekends of the month, the travelling clergy were in the Minneapolis area-200 miles south or the Duluth/Cloquet area, 180 miles to the east, or in Wisconsin or the Upper Peninsula of Michigan.

Our church did not have a lunchroom at the time, or a gathering/Fellowship room as commonly known. Thus, after service, congregants would go to people's homes for sandwiches and cinnamon rolls and cookies with coffee and Kool-Aid. Here the men would visit outside in the dark, starry summer's eve and, perhaps, smoke cigarettes while the children ran around outside.

It was too soon for the smell of cut hay and alfalfa, but just in time for the wolves of Smoky Hills to howl their songs back to the children outside and the hymns starting to be sung by the ladies and men hymn-masters in the home. Windows were slightly ajar to move air in the beginning of summer- humid air. Homes were small for the most part, meaning the house was full of people, elbow to elbow, knee to knee. The living room was full, the kitchen full, the landing, and its four steps full. The outside at the front and back door occupied.

Songs were in Finnish. Later years, people would sing in Finnish and English. In 1955, Finnish was still the primary language among adults.

I was in the bedroom, just off the living room, lying in my parents' bed. I was 1 ½ years old.

My aunt's mother-in-law, my cousins' grandmother, had the gospel revealed to her through the Holy Spirit. Ida stood and sang, waved her hanky, and wailed with appreciation that her sins were forgiven. A few more would rejoice with her. Then Ida was struck dead on the spot from a heart attack. There was no reviving her. Ida was moved to the bed where I was sleeping until the coroners could show up. Our home did not have a phone. A man drove to the neighbor's, ½ mile away that had an old, crank phone that would reach an operator and called in her death.

In the meantime, there was nothing else anyone could do but keep praising Jesus for the gift of everlasting life He has given, and they kept on singing. Word is the other neighbors to the northeast, a mile away, could hear the singing get louder and louder in the early June summer night.

A strong remembrance from that night; the driveway was clay and little gravel. The spring had been late and rainy. The hearse was barely able to spin his station wagon wheels along the ½-mile driveway and needed men in white shirts pushing it out of the muddy rut-ridden yard on his departure with Ida.

Meeting Roy Acuff
By Sarah Carson of Park Rapids, Minnesota
Born 1935

When I was growing up in Motley, Minnesota I used to listen to the Grand Ole Opry on the radio on Saturday nights. One of my favorites was Roy Acuff. Later I moved to Park Rapids, Minnesota and had a family. In 1979, I heard that Roy Acuff was going to have a show in Nevis, Minnesota and I was excited to go and see him in person. So after the show, I went up front to see if I could meet him. My youngest child at the time was my daughter, Traci, who was about one and a half years old, so I carried her as I went. He looked at my daughter and said, "Hello, Honey. You're the prettiest thing I've seen tonight." That made my day. I got his autograph too, and I still have it.

An Amazing, Once in a Lifetime Event
By George Newton of Grand Forks, North Dakota
Born 1925

I was a paratrooper during World War II serving in Europe. We were returning to our base camp in Mourmelon, France, and shortly after settling in, I received orders that a member of our troops in REG 502 101st Division would get a pass to Paris.

The day we left camp was sunny and bright. We always had a buddy with us in a civilian area and left camp in four trucks carrying about ten troopers per truck. The weather was perfect, and we wore our dress uniforms.

Our hotel was in a large business area of the city. I could see from my hotel room on the second floor this large open square with businesses all around and a USO among the other buildings. The day after our arrival was spent viewing the city and interesting sights.

The next day was bright and sunny, and I was looking out of my room in the hotel after a bath. The hotel had only one bathroom per floor, and it took two hours to get a bath. It was around noon, and I heard shooting, screaming, and loud shouting. The radio in my room was on, and I heard the war in Europe had ended. As I looked out the window from the second floor, I saw women screaming and men shouting like I've never heard before. It was amazing to hear and see the steady noise and roar of the crowd that had assembled. The crowd was a mixture of servicemen, businessmen, shop owners, local people, and residents, all shouting and hugging each other, as I've never seen before. It was an amazing, once in a lifetime event.

Booms, Rumbles, and Roars
By Delores D. Smith of Alexandria, Minnesota
Born 1918

There were some strange noises being experienced by people who lived on the western edge of Minnesota in the early 1950s. Usually these loud, explosive "booms" happened on a sunny, clear day. Their terrific, bombastic "BOOM" literally shook buildings with such a force as to crack the plastered walls in houses. The rumble and roar after the original "boom" would reverberate for miles away from the airplane or "bomber" as people called them. These were government (Air Force) planes, no doubt testing whatever. These huge planes would fly so low over the land and at a very reduced speed so as to "break the sound barrier."

Our family was a farming family at the time and our property was in the flight pattern. We had the usual farm animals- cows, horses, pigs, and chickens. On one of the flights over the barnyard, the plane flew so low, and at the right angle from the sun, so as to cast its huge shadow on the ground. The chickens must have believed the planes' shadow was that of a chicken hawk because they squawked and flew to the chicken coop. The cattle ran to the far end of the barnyard enclosure.

One other time, one of these planes flew over the cattle yard at milking time. The terrific roar of the plane permeated through the barn, scaring the cows in their stanchions to bolt causing the cows who were in the process of being milked to upset the milk buckets. What a mess! It was not a happy experience.

When these planes first appeared in the western area of Minnesota, it was quite the discussion of the community, but people soon became tired of hearing the booms and its reverberating rumble, and not to be overlooked, the damage inflicted. But we hardy Minnesotans joked about how the loud plane noises and booms were upsetting their fishing trips. They scared all the fish!

A Bucket List
By Glennys Medenwaldt of Wahpeton, North Dakota
Born 1930

Do you have a bucket list? I really am not sure what a bucket list is. I know what a grocery list is. I know what a to-do list is and a wish list, and even a Christmas list... Wouldn't a bucket list be the same as a pail?

The pail/bucket was a necessary item on the farm. Before milk machines, you sat on a one-legged stool with a pail/bucket between your knees, and proceeded to extract milk. The pail was used to carry water from the pump to the house. It was also used to carry water from the cistern to water the flowers and the garden.

Before cesspools, it was also part of the kitchen décor, better known as a slop pail. With all the modern inventions such as trash compactors, and garbage disposals, they have almost obliterated the use of a pail/bucket. If your pail/buckets sprung a leak, you didn't throw it away. There was a store item called "Mendits," a screw with a round disk of different sizes to fit the hole. The screw and disk were inserted into the hole and on the underside; you added a nut, thus adding a lot more service.

Now that I have an idea of what a bucket list might be, I have done some research as to what might go into a bucket. If you are a bit long in the tooth, so to speak, you probably don't need a very big bucket; however, a younger person might need a milk bucket. It might be things you need to do or things you would like to do in the future. What would be in your bucket? I asked a few people for ideas that they might have- visit the Holy Land, get a horse, go to Vermont in the fall, and win the lottery!

Crank Wall Phones
By Sandra Carlson of Staples, Minnesota
Born 1949

I wonder how many people under the age of 50 know what a wall phone looks like, especially the wooden ones with a black mouthpiece and receiver for listening?

Every home and farmhouse in our small town, then the population 312, of Upsala, Minnesota had one mounted on the wall, often in the kitchen.

They were called "party lines" which meant many people were on each line and responded to a different set of rings of the phone, such as 3 short rings and one long, or 2 long rings and 2 short rings, of the phone.

You would pick up the receiver and listen to whomever was calling and speak back into the bell shaped, black mouthpiece. However, anybody and everybody else on your line could pick up their receiver and listen. If your conversation wasn't very interesting, you would hear the "clicks" when they hung up their receivers.

In our home before 1968, we had graduated to a smaller, 10 to 12 inch mounted wooden box connected to a sleek black tabletop phone. Some people in our hometown though, still had the old wooden wall-mounted crank phones when the entire town went from that obsolete phone to the "state of the art" touchtone desktop phones with one-party, private lines and all fiber optic buried phone lines. It was amazing at that time! First fiber optic in our state.

Now, fast forward 50 years and generations of teenagers and younger adults with their "smart" iPhone would not have a clue what their grandparents used for phones. They carry their phones around in pockets or clipped to belts with access at their finger's touch.

Just for nostalgia, we have on the wall the original phone that was used in my husband's home 80 years ago. It is a conversation piece and intrigues our grandchildren.

Jim Carlson with the crank wall phone

Fear Comes to Town
By Lisa A. Lundquist of Rochester,
Minnesota
Born 1959

I was born in Alexandria, Minnesota, in 1959. Alexandria was a fabulous place to grow up; we went swimming every day in the summer and loved lying in the sun and reading books on the beach. It was an idyllic childhood.

But one summer, fear came to town. I was in high school when the miscreant dubbed "The Screen Streaker" began his reign of terror. It was all over the news: someone was creeping around in the dark and running his (we were convinced it was a man) fingernails over the metal window screens of sleeping homes. Everyone slept with windows open; air conditioning was for the rich. No one I knew had it. We were mostly okay. We lived out in the country, and the trees shielded our house from the sun (no help with the humidity, though; we suffered through many hot nights).

Back to the Screen Streaker; he came to our house one night. My mom, my sister, and I had discussed our plan of action should the occasion arise, but we didn't seriously think he'd come. But come he did. I heard him, inches from my face – my bed was up against the window – and I was instantly awake. And paralyzed with fright. The plan (to get Mom) evaporated from my mind. I pondered pretending I was still asleep. That seemed wise, and I went with it. When I heard him move away, I slipped out of bed and headed for my bedroom door.

I put my shaking hand on the knob, which would not turn because someone was turning it - from the other side. My heart stopped. He was inside. Inside the house. On the other side of my door. Panic does not describe the ice-cold dread in the pit of my stomach.

Then I heard it – a whispered "Lee?" It was my sister. She'd forgotten the plan, too, and when she heard him, she had come for me. I opened the door, and we grabbed each other.

Mom was not all that happy to be woken, but she was game to get the dog, a big golden retriever named Dinah (she could not be alone in the kitchen when she was a puppy) and go outside to investigate. The four of us trooped around the yard with a flashlight. We found nothing, of course. No screen streaker. He was a wily one.

The next day, I examined my screen from the outside. There was indeed a faint scratch running down its center.

Interesting Things on the Old 59
By Marvelyn M. Burtwick of Grand Rapids, Minnesota
Born 1932

I was born in St. Louis County in 1932. At the age of four months, my family moved to Red Lake County, where I grew up on an 80-acre farm, between Brooks and Plummer. Our farm was bordered on one side by the Soo Line Railroad and right by the farm, for a mile and a half, ran the 59 Highway, which is now called Old 59. The new 59 Highway was started about 1940, which took several years to complete.

We had interesting things happen along these lines. There were railroad hobos who would come up looking for a meal or food of any sort; also bums walking on the Old 59.

And we were visited frequently by gypsies, which were given the bums' rush. The road became quite muddy in the spring, one place especially, a curve near our place, which entailed many vehicles getting stuck or mired. We had horses that went out numerous times to pull rigs out; some were too big. I remember when I was eight or nine a family from Canada got mired and spent the night with us. It was exciting for a kid.

I went six years to a one-room school, classes one to eight, District 214. It was three miles to school, but we were lucky to be able to ride a bus, which my parents paid for. The school ended after it consolidated with Plummer School, which was called Pershing, grades one to twelve, where I graduated in 1950.

One unique feature in Plummer was the four churches in a row. I was a member of the Immanuel Lutheran, where I was confirmed in 1946.

We had cattle and milked cows. I learned to milk by age six. We hauled milk by ten-gallon cans to the Brooks Cheese Factory, where they made butter and cheese. It's now long gone.

We lived about five hundred or six hundred yards from Lost River. We spent a lot of time swimming in summer, skating in winter, also skiing and sledding. My mother made us a neat deal on the river, putting down a post and letting it freeze, and then attaching a long pole with a fastened sled on the end. We pushed the pole around and boy was it fun. Sometimes we'd ski holding a long rope behind a horse.

I'm 83 and the last remaining of my family, which are buried at the Emarville Cemetery. I now live at Grand Rapids, Minnesota, on twenty acres and raise a garden and flowers.

The Christmas Angel
By Lorraine D. Niemela of Minneapolis, Minnesota
Born 1929

My story took place in 1938, when I was almost ten years old. Our farm with its log buildings was east of Menahga, Minnesota, in the northcentral part of the state. There were eleven children in our family, ten girls, and one boy. I was the tenth child. Here is my story about Christmas in 1938 (I didn't turn ten until February of 1939).

It was the year I was going on ten. The excitement of the school Christmas program was over. I was happy I had not forgotten a line in my Christmas recitations.

The annual Christmas shopping trip had been made to the county seat, Wadena. Secretive activity in the small log house had ceased, and neatly (and some not so neatly) wrapped packages were hidden here and there. The greatest cause for curiosity and temptation were the packages that had arrived from some of the nine other sisters who were living away from home.

However, in all the excited anticipation of Christmas hung a dark cloud that belied the cheerfulness displayed. It must have been in October, for it was potato-picking time that Mother had left for the cities. Our doctor sent her to a place called "the university" to help her feel better. Sometimes in the loneliness of night, I wondered if Mother would ever really come home.

It was now Christmas Eve. There was no dawdling doing chores. Even in our hurry, each baby calf would get an extra splash of milk and a gift of the sweetest smelling clover that could be found. A hurried supper of creamed lutefisk and we were ready. With bated breath, we watched sis Agnes light the real candles on the fresh Christmas tree, which reached the ceiling. The kerosene light was extinguished, and we gazed in awe at the beauty of the tree. The candles were soon smothered, and it was time to open the gifts. Woolen mittens, a coloring book, a doll dress...all done, our eyes fell on the stack of unopened gifts.

"Do you think Ma would care if we opened them very carefully and then wrapped them up again?" we whispered to each other. Papa was already asleep, sitting in his chair by the potbellied stove.

Several minutes later, the packages lay all unwrapped and examined, when a soft knock was heard at the door. Who could it be? No car was heard coming down the long lane and not a bark from faithful Shep.

I ran and threw open the door...the Christmas angel...except she had wet feet... and Mother's smiling face! The vision of the opened gifts was before me as I stared with open mouth...and suddenly I was in Mother's arms and I knew everything would be all right.

Farm Chores - Memories of Yesteryear
By Patricia Berg Hanson of Middle River, Minnesota
Born 1938

As I turn back the pages of time on the farm, I can recall the days and times our family worked together.

In the summertime, we had to watch the cattle when they went out to the pasture and call them in when it was milking time, twice a day. Once the milking was done, it was time to separate the milk and cream which was processed through a hand-cranked separator. Then the cream and milk were put in a flavoring well cooler until it was sold or used. It sometimes got to be a debate who was to clean the separator after the chores were done.

Wintertime chores with the milking of cows was a bigger project as sometimes it was very cold! We had to milk the cows before we went to school, and needless to say, the barn odor wasn't easy to get rid of.

Cleaning the barn gutters in the wintertime was a job no one really liked to do but we knew it had to be done.

Dad had a nice team of horses, which did

Ernest Berg with his team of workhorses

a lot of the work on our farm. We learned how to use them for raking and stacking hay. They were used to put the hay up into the barn via sling ropes. Oh, yes, there were run-aways and broken harnesses.

Our farm was like Old MacDonald's. We had cows, calves, sheep, lambs, pigs, chickens, cats and dogs, and at one time, we had a couple of goats. We learned how to care for and love these animals and pets.

Our parents taught us the values of life and that hard work doesn't hurt anyone.

Dad would cut and haul wood home so we had to cut that into blocks and split them to dry for use.

Harvest time brought neighbors together sharing in the labors. We learned how to shock the bundles of grain in the proper way and needless to say, we spent hours out in the heat of the day. Someone always delivered lunches out to the workers as well as water. I recall the jar of coffee Mom put in a sock so it was easier to carry for us kids. We always hoped for a plentiful harvest.

Farm chores taught us the values of life and our parents were great teachers.

Slip and Slide Kickball
By Jack Burt of Jacobson, Minnesota
Born 1951

My story begins in the spring of 1957. I was a precocious 1st grader at a small, rural school named Wendigo. The school had six grades but there were two grades in each classroom. My classroom had both the 1st and 2nd grades in it. My teacher, Mrs. Hector, was a middle-aged lady who I thought was a good, but strict, teacher. On more than one occasion, I had my knuckles rapped by her 12-inch ruler.

In the spring of 1957, I learned a very valuable lesson. That winter we had a fairly large amount of snow. The parking lot in front of the school had a very thick layer of packed snow. On the edge of the parking lot were large piles of pushed up snow. When the snow melted, the packed snow of the parking lot turned into an icy sheet. The piles of snow melted and created a sheet of water on top of the icy parking lot. The parking lot was also the place the 1st and 2nd graders had recess. The combination of a thin layer of water on an icy sheet created a chance to play slip and slide kickball for myself and my fellow 1st grade boys. My friends and I had the time of our lives on that icy, wet sheet of water. By the end of recess, we were soaked from head to toe. When we came into class, Mrs. Hector took one look at us, sent us into the cloakroom, and said, "Take off those wet clothes." Needless to say, we were shocked. How can we be told to get out of our clothes? She came back with six large towels, took our wet clothes, and put them on the steam radiators to dry.

For the rest of the afternoon, we sat in those towels. Even though Mrs. Hector tried to keep the rest of the class from teasing us, we still took our share of ribbing about our situation. The 2nd graders were especially tough on us.

Well, being the smart 1st graders we were, Mrs. Hector would not get away with having us sit around class in a towel. We decided to go home and tell our parents about what happened. Of course, we did not say anything about getting ourselves soaked at recess- only that Mrs. Hector was so mean to us that she made us sit in towels all afternoon. I was sure my mom would tell Mrs. Hector a thing or two.

It soon became obvious to me that I didn't think this through very well. My mom did call Mrs. Hector. Mrs. Hector gave her the rest of the story. After my mom's conversation with Mrs. Hector, not only did I lose recess privileges until the parking lot dried up, but sitting down was not an option for a period of time.

I learned a good lesson that day. If I did something god at school, I might share it with my parents, but if I got into trouble, I just faced up to my mistake and if the school wanted my parents to know, they would tell them- not me!

Dad's Close Call
By Gaylan Witt of Henning, Minnesota
Born 1957

I grew up hearing about my dad's close call with death during the Armistice Day blizzard in 1940.

Dad was working for Simon Produce in Battle Lake, hauling turkeys with his truck.

131

On the morning on November 11, 1940, Dad and a fellow-worker were to drive out to Glendalough Game Farm to pick up a load of turkeys but they couldn't get there because the storm had already moved in so they returned to Battle Lake.

In the meantime, Simon Produce had received a message from Dad's folks, that they needed feed for their turkeys. There were not many phones in the country at that time yet, so they had gone to the neighbors to do their telephoning. Knowing the lives of many turkeys were at stake, Dad loaded the truck with turkey feed at the elevator. He left Battle Lake at about 10:00 in the morning. About 3 or 4 miles northeast of Battle Lake, he got stuck. He was near a farm so he walked there. Not many farmers had tractors in those days. The farmer tried to pull the truck out with a team of horses but could not. Dad decided to leave the truck and walk home. Of course, the farmer insisted that Dad wait out the storm at his place, but Dad was determined to go home so his folks wouldn't be worried. He estimated it was noon when he started his 7-mile walk home. He recalls that at some points the snow was so deep he could touch the telephone wires overhead. There was no electricity in the country at that time yet, so no electric wires.

The last few miles were a nightmare. In the meantime, the neighbors had helped the folks with their turkeys but they couldn't do much. The storm was too severe. Dad's folks lost about 1000 turkeys.

The neighbors were in the house at the folks' waiting out the storm. At about 5 o'clock in the evening, one of the neighbors was gazing out the window towards the road. Suddenly, he saw a figure s tagger and collapse. They went out and carried Dad in, and revived him. It was just good fortune that someone was looking out the window at the right time to see Dad fall.

Snowplow service wasn't too good in those days, so it was two days later when Dad and his brother were able to try to get the truck. The snowplow hadn't gone on the road where the truck was, but the truck was on a 2-foot high pedestal of snow. All the snow around it had blown away. They opened the hood, and it was packed solid with snow. It took quite some time to chisel it all out. It was cold enough so the motor didn't get wet.

I was always grateful to the neighbor that saw Dad fall or I never would have had the opportunity to enjoy the life that I have had.

The Christmas Fire
By Elsie Olson Lindgren of Cass Lake, Minnesota
Born 1937

The excitement of Christmas pervaded the Olson household in December of 1950. The long standing tradition had been to spend Christmas Eve with relatives. This year we went to Cousin Bernice's where we visited, played games, and opened presents until well after midnight.

The two sisters, ages 12 and 6, were sleepy and cold, so they went to bed with their long stockings on.

Early the next morning, Dad got up and built a fire in the parlor woodstove. Then he went to the barn to milk the cows and tend to the other chores. As he headed back to the house, he looked up to see flames shooting out of the chimney. He ran into the house, doused the fire in the stove while shouting to us to get up quickly and dress. Since we did not have a telephone, Dad ran a ½ mile north to a neighbor who had one. He told us girls to run to a closer neighbor to the south so we would be warm and safe.

In those days, one had to "ring central" and immediately people would pick up their hones to find out who was calling; many found out then that Gilbert Olson's house was on fire. Since this was Christmas morning and 25 below zero, volunteer firemen were hard to locate so there was some delay in their arrival because it was nine miles away from New Folden, so a few neighbors, who had "rubber-necked" starting arriving to help our parents.

Meanwhile, our mother began to carry things out of the house- a rollaway bed filled with bedding, a sewing machine, some clothes, and other items. She was able to take out very heavy items with "super human" strength. Among the things rescued was Janice's special gift, a "magic-skin" doll, although it did get one singed arm. She still has that doll today, 67 years later.

When the fire truck arrived, they realized

the house was too far gone and saved the water "in case the wind might turn" and would spread the fire to the barn.

One of the neighbors wanted badly to rescue the piano with which he had entertained us many times. The other men had to literally pull him out of the burning house. Its jumbled-wire remains among the ashes is still vivid in our memories.

We spent that night and several days at our aunt's house. I saw my dad cry for the first time. Yes, it was a tragedy and we were homeless, but each Christmas we are reminded to thank God that no lives were lost and that we had such good neighbors, friends, and family.

Our closest neighbors' house was empty so we were able to care for our livestock easily. The following summer when the neighbors returned, we lived in the woodshed until our new house was livable.

Our parents passed away a few years back, Mom at 90 and Dad at 101. Every Christmas we are reminded how blessed we are to have survived all these years later. I think every house we lived in after the fire had to have a telephone, not only for convenience but of necessity.

A Life in Fosston, Minnesota
By Josiah Hoagland, Sr. of Fosston, Minnesota
Born 1986

I was born and raised in Bemidji, Minnesota. I began to live in Fosston, Minnesota, by chance of a former high school prom date who was serving as the pianist at New Journey Church (formerly Fosston Baptist Church). I was home on leave from a tour to Afghanistan with the US Army Reserves as a chaplain's assistant with a route clearance battalion conducting route clearance (bomb finding) in the Kandahar province. I remember my first drive to Fosston since coming home on leave from Afghanistan. I was staying with my parents in Bemidji, Minnesota, in the spring of 2011. I began my drive down Highway 2 at a cautious speed of 50 miles per hour (I was used to much slower speeds down the mine infested roads of Afghanistan). When I finally arrived at the church, I did not realize that one day I would be the preacher at the Baptist church in Fosston.

I remember first smelling the Minnesota Dehydrated Vegetable plant nearby upon arrival at the church. The wafting smell of dehydrated vegetables mixed with the lingering smell of spring time spraying and planting left me partially unawares in this nostalgic community. My only experience with Fosston prior to this had been on drives from Bemidji to Grand Forks for concerts or the several eventful drives form Bemidji to Winnipeg, Manitoba, in search of adventure and fun. As I drove through this community on this particular drive I was there to attend church with my then very new romantic interest, and unbeknownst to me, my future wife and the mother of my two children.

I studied both Bible at Oak Hills Christian College in Bemidji, and social studies education from Bemidji State University while in college. My love for history prevailed as I looked around this historic small town and future home. I quickly fell in love with the church and community while attending church with my future bride. I began to fall in love with this eclectic small town farming community at the fringes of the Red River Valley. In fact, my future bride and the small town of Fosston, Minnesota, were on my mind quite a bit as I left to go back to Afghanistan and finish my tour of duty. It would be the longest four months of my life as I finished out that tour of duty. The humorous tales of the smells of the Minnesota Dehydrated Vegetable plant helped pass the time in Afghanistan while living on the Kandahar Airfield base enshrined with its own self-proclaimed "poo-pond."

Upon returning home to Bemidji, Minnesota, I would continue to attend New Journey Church in Fosston, Minnesota, with my bride-to-be. Eventually, the church would ask me to come on board as a part time worship pastor and eventually as a full time senior pastor. The adventure was invigorating. I eventually would transfer to the Minnesota Army National Guard as a chaplain candidate while simultaneously pastoring and working on seminary through the denomination's seminary, Bethel Seminary, located in St. Paul.

This small town congregation taught me a lot about the history of Northwestern

Minnesota during my tenure. I saw two of the church's matriarchs pass away. Doris Anderson and Martha Roue passed away within a couple weeks of each other, both at the age of 96. Both of these beautiful matriarchs would tell me about the history of the church throughout my time visiting with them. Doris once told me the story of how her family first became connected with the church. When she was just a young girl, her father helped a man from the then Rosebud Baptist Church get to church after his horse went lame (this was before the modern "horseless carriage" was to become widely popular!). This then connected her family with the Baptist church in Fosston. Many of her descendants are still at New Journey Church to this day.

One of my favorite trips is that of going up to the church's Bible camp in Karlstad, Minnesota. Way up in a land of few grocery stores or gas stations, Karlstad is the home to New Life Bible Camp (formerly Lake Bronson Baptist Bible Camp). On the drive up, I listen to the stories of yesteryear with those more seasoned congregants. I would hear tales of moose sightings on Highway 59. In fact, every time I make that drive to this day, I keep an extra sharp eye out for those infamous moose, though I have yet to actually make a spotting). I would also hear about the dangerous railroad crossing where destructive past crashes wreaked havoc and left an indelible impression upon passersby. I also was able to lay my eyes on the famous Mattracks headquarters that I grew up hearing about and salivating over when I would see a truck with those huge tank-like treads go rolling by.

From visiting farms to performing marriages, baptisms, and funerals, Northwestern Minnesota and specifically Fosston has now become my home. While I do not know what the future holds, the Fosston community has become an indelible part of my family history. Working at the church that has a 120 year history has been one of the greatest challenges and joys of this young pastor and his family's lives. While I cannot say whether I will live to be the age of Doris or Martha, if I do, I pray that I too will be able to encourage young people and tell the stories of what life in Fosston was like "back in the old days" while preserving the important history and heritage of Northwestern Minnesota.

Our Christmas Customs
By Arlene Jenkins of Henning, Minnesota
Born 1947

My parents provided us kids with memorable Christmas customs. We never had much money but we had a lot of family togetherness. I have been working on my family history since I retired. The following is a write-up of a typical Christmas from my childhood that I put together for the family history.

It's Christmas Eve in the 1960s in rural Minnesota. It is cold outside, probably around 10 degrees below zero. The sky is covered with vividly shining stars, the air perfectly still. There is a beautiful silence over the farm. Company will be coming for supper; it is time to do cooking and cleaning in the house, and it is time to do milking and chores in the barn.

As I go into the barn, my glasses steam over from the heat put off by the cows. It is peaceful to break the bales of hay and spread them out in front of the cows as Dad does the milking. The cows make comfortable chewing and snorting sounds as they patiently chew the coarse hay. But it is Christmas Eve and I am eager to get back to the house and get ready for the coming evening. As I walk to the house, the snow crunches underfoot and the stars silently shine overhead.

When I enter the porch, I smell the kerosene lantern (lit specially for Christmas

Christmas Eve in 1969

Eve) burning a welcome scent to all who enter. And when I enter the house, the aromas of roast turkey and stuffing and sweet potatoes and fresh baked bread fill the air. And there is Ma, scrubbing the kitchen floor- one of the last tasks to be done before the company comes and spreads tracks over her freshly cleaned floor. But she was satisfied knowing it was clean when company came.

Soon the company arrives for the evening, bringing in piles of gifts to put under the tree. There are usually about 18 people in all for the evening. Once everyone arrives, Ma sets out the huge feast she has spent the last couple of days preparing. It is delicious as usual. It is a sit-down meal with bowls mounded high with food being passed around. The adults sit at one end of the table and the kids at the other. Chatter abounds as everyone eats their fill. Afterward, the women work together to clear the tables, wash and dry the dishes (there was no electric dishwasher) while the kids do final preparations for the program they will present. Every year the kids sing a few songs and act out the Nativity. It is a short program and then the entire group sings Christmas carols. While we finish the last song, Silent Night, Dad suddenly says he heard a noise on the porch. The kids race out and there are sacks of fruit, candy, popcorn balls, and nuts from Santa. But Santa has slipped away before anyone arrives on the porch. He does that every time!

Now that Santa has arrived, it is time to distribute gifts. In the earlier years, Grandma distributed the gifts and then later Ma distributed the gifts. Usually one gift at a time was handed out with everyone enjoying the opening and appreciation of each gift. We each got 2 or 3 gifts, depending on the year's finances. There was usually one gift from Santa, one from the parents, and one from whomever had drawn a person's name. It was especially nice when one of the gifts was a good book. It took a few hours to pass out all of the gifts. The company left by midnight or so, but then we spent a few more hours appreciating each gift we had received. We usually went to bed around 2 or 3 in the morning, tired and content.

Christmas Day arrives for each of us as we wish. Dad and Ma get up for chores and making breakfast but the rest of the day is spent playing games and relaxing. Dinner is leftovers from Christmas Eve- all just as delicious as the eve before. It is probably even better than the evening before for Ma since she didn't have to cook the meal from scratch.

The entire week from Christmas through New Year's is devoted to playing games and enjoying the break from school. This routine was so ingrained in me that even now when I am retired, I expect to have the week between Christmas and New Year's seem different from the rest of the year.

One-Room Schools
By LaDelle Neal of Staples, Minnesota
Born 1932

I'm writing about some special memories of my eight years in a country school. We lived two miles from the school and got there by walking.

One weekend there was a big blizzard but Monday morning dawned bright and sunny and no wind. I don't know if my parents had a thermometer but I know it was a frigid morning. Us three oldest siblings (at the time there were seven siblings in our family) bundled up in our snowsuits, overshoes, etc., and set out for school. There were drifts across the road in places that we walked over but with the sunshine and no wind, it wasn't bad getting to school. However, when we got to school, there was no teacher and the school was locked. Our teacher roomed with a family about 1/8th of a mile from the school but because of the weekend, she'd gone home to her parents Friday night and they lived about 10 miles away. With the drifted roads, her dad was having a hard time getting her to school. My brother, sister, and I, grades 1, 3, and 4, were the only students who had braved the elements to get to school by 9 am. We stood on the south side of the school where the sun reflected off the white siding so it was a bit warmer there, but our feet were freezing. When the teacher and her dad finally made it to the schoolhouse, we went inside where it was also cold since the fire in the big woodstove had been out for a couple of days. Her dad quickly got a fire going and I remember him putting me on top of the stove to warm my feet.

My teacher in the 8th grade was such a nice person. She did many things to make school fun for the students.

One day she asked if we'd like to have a taffy pull. I'm sure many of us didn't even know what that was but the answer was a big YES! So, she got the taffy cooked and asked who'd like to be first to start the pulling. A 7th grade boy stepped up, no doubt thinking, "Yum! Taffy!" She had him butter his hands and then put a spoonful of taffy in one hand. I don't know if it was actually too hot or if this boy just wasn't prepared for it to be so warm, but he started shaking his hands vigorously and bits of taffy went flying everywhere. Our poor teacher felt so bad.

Encounters with Critters

I grew up on a 240-acre farm but half a mile away was another farm my dad rented.

One day, a couple of my siblings and I walked down to the creek on the rented farm. While playing in the creek, we came across a big snapping turtle. We knew a man who would buy turtles to eat. So, how were we going to get this turtle the ¾ mile to our house? It was ½ mile to the rented farm but another quarter mile to the creek, so we were ¾ mile from home.

Well, we found a sturdy stick about 3 ½ feet long. My sister held one end, I held the other, we put the middle of the stick right in front of the turtle, and sure enough, he snapped right on to it. We then, each holding one end of the stick, began the walk home. The turtle let go a couple times but we just repeated the process until we got him home. We called our intended customer and he came, got the turtle, and rewarded us with 25 cents! That's the most money we made all summer!

Memories are Good and Life is Good!
By Marilyn Dahl of Loman, Minnesota
Born 1933

With the flip of a switch there is light; a turn of a handle and water flows or a toilet flushes; the twist of a wrist and there is heat; the push of a button brings news and pictures of instant happenings all over the world.

Time marches on with progress, new technology, and social media. Life for me – an 82-year-old product of the Depression years – is sometimes unbelievable.

Simple words such as Twitter, Tweet, Skype, iPad, smartphone, and Facebook take time to digest and put in place. Perhaps that is one reason I like to go back in memory and reminisce…and then be grateful for those responsible for making progress and technology, which makes life easier.

Looking back 75 years to a typical day for me, a farm girl of seven years of age living along the Canadian border in Koochiching County, northern Minnesota…

I reluctantly crawled out of a warm, cozy bed to stand on a metal floor grate where the wood furnace in the basement blew warm air under my flannel nightgown. My dad would bring me a cup of warm, fresh cow's milk when he came in from milking our eight cows by hand.

A quick wake up as I made a hurried trip to the outside toilet. There, as I sat, I crumbled pages from the Sears Roebuck catalog to soften it. Toilet paper was a luxury, but in the summer, we were lucky to have tissue from fresh fruit crates to use!

My dad drove the school bus to Loman School for 34 years. The school was only six miles from our house, but he had a 40-mile route to pick up students. This meant leaving home at 6:30 a.m. and getting home in the evening at 6:00 p.m. with an 80 mile per day ride.

I had a few chores: feeding chickens and pigs, and I turned the handle on the cream separator after milking. Our cream cans were kept cold in a natural spring in the bank of the Big Fork River. Our house was located on these banks. Cream was taken to a creamery in Loman where butter was made.

Homework was done by kerosene lamps at the kitchen table. Electricity didn't come off the main line until I was in grade ten.

Bath time was in a galvanized tub by the wood cook stove that produced warm water. My brother and I took turns at who was first in the tub!

Entertainment before bedtime was often listening to the battery operated radio. A favorite program was *The Lone Ranger*. We also played games and cards. In the summer, I would dress the barn cats in doll clothes, including diapers and bonnets. I would push the cats in a doll buggy until they jumped out and lost their clothes. I also made paper dolls cut from catalogs and carved miniature items from homemade bar soap.

There was a lot of family time and love shown. My elderly grandmother lived with my folks, my brother, and me.

One incident showing a parent's love was in the early spring of 1948 when the ice in the river broke up and jammed up at the mouth of the river, causing the water to rise high. Ice and water surrounded the house (but not in it) and went across the county road. Cars didn't drive across for several days. My dad took me on his farm tractor across the water on the road to meet my date to go to a movie in International Falls. And he came and picked me up after the movie. That is love!

I am wondering what my youngest grandchildren, in 82 years, will recall as memories of "their good old days." Memories are good! Life is good!

A Christmas so Long Ago
By Sandy Henrickson of Goodridge, Minnesota
Born 1940

We stood with our faces pressed to the window, watching the snow gently falling as the squirrels were scampering around gathering the last acorns from the old oak tree on the riverbank close by. Ah! Christmas would soon be here and my brother, Bob, and I knew exactly what we wanted… Skis! Only one gift was what Dad and Mom said because money was scarce and our family was still growing. I selfishly thought if there were not so many babies, there would be more presents. However, Mom reminded us that Aunt Selma always brought a special box filled with nuts, ribbon candy, chocolate drops, California oranges, and, best of all, fruitcake. She also tucked in some educational books and toys. She wanted us to have keen and alert minds and to keep out of mischief. Then Uncle Albert and Aunt Florence would arrive and bring us colors and coloring books sometime during the Christmas season. The most poignant memories of all are the wooden tops and whistles our father carved for us out of wood… long gone but the memory of the worn hands carving remains forever. Even so, we still thought we needed skis.

Christmas was rapidly approaching. Our tiny tree with tinsel and real wax candles so carefully clipped to the branches was placed on top of the library table out of reach of tiny hands. I remember the fragrance of the twisted wax candles as they burned so brightly. How wonderful it was. Bob and I kept sneaking around the tree trying to locate some boxes that would resemble skis, but alas, there were none to be found. However, two wrapped boxes finally appeared under the tree and they were for Bob and me. Mom gave us a hint. She said they were brown and black.

We knew it. Our summer had caught up with us and we were getting Bibles, and a pair of skis was a lost dream. We slowly climbed the stairs and went and sat on the bed in the room my brothers shared. We talked about the past summer. How many commandments did we really break? At our age, there was quite a difference between skis and a gift of bibles. We both recalled that our neighbor, Roger,

Gordon, Geno, and Gloriana standing by a '39 Chevrolet super deluxe

Roger, Janice, and Sandy

was a partner in crime so we certainly could put the blame on him, especially when it was his idea to cut off the tops of the beets in the garden to make play cigarettes. That really was not so bad, but then we took some of Dad's blue lined tablet paper, armed ourselves with farmer matches, and climbed down the bank to where the Indian tobacco grew. We carefully rolled the paper, stuffed it with Indian tobacco, and then we smoked, coughed, and turned green. Our very wise mom said that was punishment enough. Bob reminded me that we only broke one window playing Anti I Over, and we only teased our little sister, Arlys, once in a while. Oh! We almost forgot about when Mom and Dad were doing the milking, and I was in charge of babysitting. Bob pumped the kitchen sink dull of water and kept on pumping until the kitchen was flooded. Mom always said we did not need to live by the Red River to have a flood in our house! I vaguely remembered someone at Sunday school mentioning forgiveness… that must have been for us.

Christmas finally came and we gathered around the dining room table and gave thanks for our many gifts of family and food. The oil lamp cast a soft glow on our faces as we prayed together and even Bob and I looked angelic. It took forever to do the dishes and the old stove was crackling as our dad put in some more coal and then lit the candles on the tree. We sat around our mother as she read the story about Baby Jesus being born in Bethlehem so long ago, and our dad went outside to check on the animals in the warm barn filled with hay.

All of the sudden, WHOOSH! The door opened and there they were- a pair of brown skis for Bob and a pair of shiny black skis for me. We were speechless. Dad said they had been hidden in the manger in the dry hay. Bob leaned over and whispered to me that our skis were blessed and special like the Baby Jesus born in the manger so long ago. And so it was then, and so it is now.

May your hearts be filled with the true meaning of Christmas as you spend the holidays with your family, and enjoy God's gifts of faith, hope, joy, and love.

The Woman Who Brought Changes
By J. Sharon Hertle of Talmoon, Minnesota
Born 1938

The time of our story takes place in the 1940s in a small, sleepy little town in the upper Midwest of our country. A place where everyone knows everyone and most people nod greeting people on the streets with a smile or a handshake. It was wartime years, making people thrifty; saving on everything including gas for cars and tires, food was rationed. Girls wore rayon stockings, saving nylon for parachutes for the soldiers, which didn't make the girls legs look very attractive. It was a substitute that everyone had to deal with because going without stockings was not acceptable or stylish. Also, cotton flour sacks were used by women to make clothes and dresses for young girls. All of these ways our country and our town practiced so that

Sharon's parents, Agnes and Clarence Johnson

Yvonne was 8 years, and Gloria was 6 years when Sharon, the last child, was born in 1938.

Our father was the local creamery manager, better known as the butter maker, because he made butter and pasteurized milk and cream for the local community, winning many blue ribbons at the Steele County Fair. Once, his prize-winning butter was sent to Washington, D.C., to the White House to President Franklin Delano Roosevelt's table for dinner. We were very proud of Dad. The creamery was only two blocks away from our house, making it easy for Dad to come home for lunch and take a quick nap in the rocker in the sunroom, but if he was too busy, Mother would make a three course meal, putting it in a picnic basket and making the trip to deliver it; no brown bag lunches at our house. Sometimes as children, we would run down to the creamery to play games around the metal milk cans that were stacked in the lot next to the creamery building. Often times we would stop inside to say hello to Dad or to spend time with Dad's secretary, Signey Pelinka. She was a fun lady with strawberry blonde hair with a pleasing personality to go with it. She would give us pencil and paper to keep us busy, literally out of her hair. Maybe this was the beginning of Gloria's drawing talent.

Agnes, our mother, was a devoted wife and mother to her family. She was very clever in sewing, making most of our clothes when we were children. She was an excellent cook, making homemade bread every day, baking pies, cakes, and Norwegian krumkake, lefse, and fattigman. Monday was washday, using the Maytag wringer washer and hanging the clothes out to dry on the clothesline. Tuesday

our soldier boys had supplies that they needed to fight the war overseas. It was a patriotic community that honored each other's privacy, that respected the rights of one another, and a handshake was as good as your word when it came to agreements. I'm sure you get the picture of what the town was like.

In this town a family by the name of Johnson lived in a two story Victorian home just one block off Main Street, two blocks from church, and three blocks from the elementary and high schools, a convenient location allowing the family to walk wherever they needed to go. Clarence, more commonly known as C.O., and Agnes Johnson lived with their five children. We were a typical family except for the age span between the children. Clair was 17 years, Marlys was 14 years,

The Johnson family

and Sunday school where we learned the Ten Commandments and the Golden Rule. When we heard the church bells ringing, we knew it was time to go to church to hear God's word proclaimed. How fortunate we were to have loving parents who taught us right from wrong and took us to church. We were definitely a Norwegian family that played together and stayed together; the all American family, proud and thankful to live in this country, pledging allegiance to the good old USA.

Yes, Agnes sewed and altered clothes for the community, earning a little extra money by being a good neighbor and friend. She was skilled in her crafty ways, which in later years became an opportunity to be an alterations lady at Harriet's Dres-Wel in Blooming Prairie. She also reached out to her community by serving in the Ladies Aid at the Lutheran Church. She volunteered with the Red Cross, making blankets, bandages, and other things needed for the war effort.

Dad also volunteered as air raid warden for readiness in case of an enemy attack. Whenever we had an air raid drill, the house had to be totally dark black without lights, and everyone would find a safe place. I found underneath the heavy wooden dining room table to be the safest place for me.

It all began in this town, in this house, and in this family. It is at this location our story begins. Agnes was a thrifty woman who heard of a woman from Minneapolis who was a corsetiere who represented the Nubone Company. As a young girl, Agnes had always worn a corset to keep a small waist and a girlish figure, a shape that was so fashionable. She contacted this woman to come to our community to offer her services and her product, which meant Agnes would get a free custom made with a custom fit corset. Now, these corsets were very expensive and not locally available in the dry goods store or the Sears or Montgomery Ward catalogs. These garments were made of fine brocaded satin fabrics with Nubone stays that would bend

was ironing day, which included sprinkling the clothes, rolling them up, and putting them in the clothesbasket. When the cotton clothes were damp, they were perfect for ironing. Mother's laundry and linens were crisp, white, and smooth after ironing. Wednesday was baking and cooking, maybe vegetable soup with dumplings. Thursday was more laundry, because we had a big family. Friday was more cooking, canning, and baking. Saturday was cleaning day from top to bottom of the house to get ready for company on Sunday or just because it was the Sabbath day. Sunday was a day to go to church and a day of much deserved rest. No work on Sundays, not even sewing on a button. Sunday meal would often be roast beef, potatoes with gravy, corn, jello salad or tossed salad, and dessert of apple pie or chocolate cake with white frosting and chocolate splotches. What a treat it was with plenty of Dad's dairy products. It might have been Depression for some folks, but it was always good eating at the Johnson's.

On Sunday, we always attended church

with movement, giving a comfortable fit and that girlish figure that most women wanted to look fashionable.

This family was so excited to have this person come to visit. All bundled up in coats, mittens, and head scarves, the family made their way to the train depot, which was only a couple of blocks from home. In the distance, we could hear the steam engine of the train coming. The roaring clanging noise with the choo-choo sounded in the crisp air and the steam poured out of this black engine train. The brakes sounded loud and clear as the train came to a screeching halt, proceeding slowly to the depot. We could hear the conductor say, "All aboard, the train stops here in Blooming Prairie." The long awaited time had come on this cool autumn day. The lady from Minneapolis was finally here. After much preparation had been done by our mother for this person to arrive, we now stood with bated breath, as we saw the conductor of the train call out and step off the train. Then we saw the lady from Minneapolis come to the door and step down off the train with the conductor assisting her hand. She was an attractive middle age woman wearing a suit, hat, gloves, purse, and high heeled shoes, all matching, with of course, jewelry to make me thing she was rich and looked like a movie star that we had seen at the local Rex theatre. We greeted her with handshakes and hugs. Mame Bardsley was her name, with a bubbling energetic personality, and at once, we all loved her and welcomed her to our home.

After this formal greeting, we waited for the big trunks to come from the baggage car. As a child, I wondered what could be in those big black trucks, but found out later the contents were the custom made corsets that were so special to so many women. Getting these trunks home and inside the house and up the stairs was no easy task. The word was out that Mrs. Bardsley the corsetiere was in town at the Johnson residence just off Main Street with Agnes acting as hostess.

Well, the telephone started ringing with women wanting to make appointments to see Mrs. Bardsley. The party telephone line was busy as the receivers on the party line picked up on the conversations. This action was called rubber necking. One by one, the ladies came to our house. Most of the ladies were out of shape, overweight, and needing a garment for an uplift tummy flattener and basically put into a fashionable shape again.

After the last appointment and the last lady would leave, it was time for a great supper with Mother preparing a wonderful meal entertaining our guest at the dining room table. Then it was our time to have fun with Mrs. Bardsley. She was a delight, showing much attention to the sisters. We would sing, dance, and put on a show for her. Even though we weren't exactly talented in performing, she still clapped, laughing at our attempts at showmanship. What a sport she was to let us try on her beautiful jewelry, listening to the jingle jangle of her bracelets and necklaces, trying on her rings and earrings, and of course, her high heeled shoes. She even allowed us to comb her hair, making new hairdos.

This stranger became a real friend to the family, bonding with each one of us. Mrs. Bardsley's yearly visit was something to look forward to. She was definitely a lady of change. She influenced the lives of all of us and her customers by her friendliness and outgoing personality. She changed the lives and figures of the women she sold her garments to. In turn, we changed the life of this woman by showing her hospitality, friendship, and love. We filled a void in her life because she had

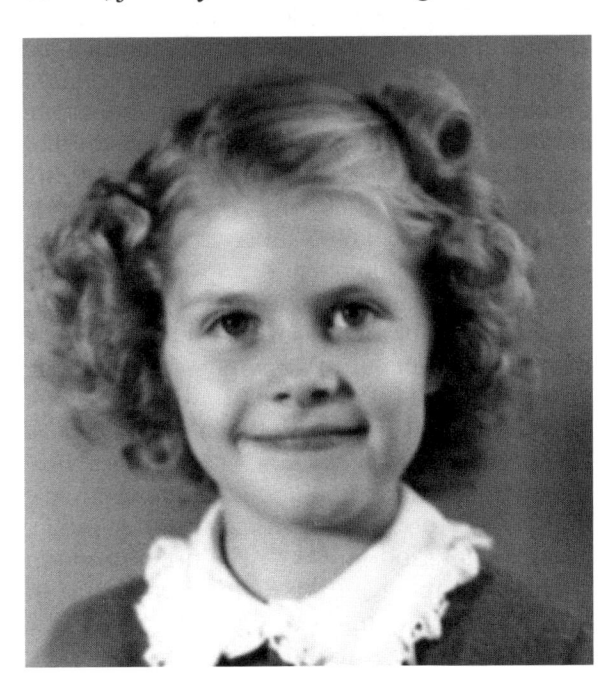

Sharon Johnson

one daughter and the situation in her family was not a happy one. In a small way, we made a difference in her life by making her feel wanted and special.

Yes, there was a change in the community too; by her very presence, she made news in our local newspaper, *The Blooming Prairie Times*. It was big news for a little town to have such a special person come to visit from Minneapolis making the ladies of our town happy with their new garments and new shapes. Some of the men took notice of this attractive lady staying at the Johnson household too. Also, the women in town definitely took on a new appearance that was quite fashionable.

No longer do women wear such garments of yesteryear, as uncomfortable that they must have been, but some people wore these garments all their lives. Our mother wore them because she was used to this type of undergarment that provided the feeling and posture she was used to.

The story of Mame Bardsley will always be a fun memory and experience for the Johnson sisters as we remember the visits she made to our home and to our town. She was quite a lady, making a lasting impression on all of us. Thanks for the memories, Mrs. Bardsley; you are a legend to us.

Lovely Laura: a Grave in the Woods
By James L. Swanson of Omaha, Nebraska
Born 1939

Spontaneously, we decided to go on a search for Laura Briggs. All we knew was that she was buried in the woods by a fast moving stream, east of Kelliher, Minnesota. This, and the name of a neighbor were all my octogenarian brother and cousin could remember – 70-year-old memories.

Driving west of Kelliher, all the way to Red Lake and back, crisscrossing county roads, we have no luck. It's a Sunday and we come upon a country church just letting out service. The drizzle has increased, so churchgoers are hustling to their cars. Jamie, my son, says, "Let me out. I'll ask if anyone recognizes that neighbor's name." Pay dirt! We now have directions to a house we can call on.

Approaching, we spot a blackened building in the middle of a field. Sonny, my cousin, says, "That's where they lived. I remember that building." It now sits alone in a field, and Sonny points out a concrete foundation, remnants of the house, long gone.

Which one of us will go to the door? Jamie volunteers and we watch him, engaged, as he poses our question. We're looking to see if anyone has recollection of the Briggs family who used to live up the road? Soon he's back to the van with news. A very old lady in the back room has shouted out, "That's the lady who killed herself!" They knew the spot where she has lain for decades; no casket, no formal service, just a blanket to shroud the body of the woman known as Lovely Laura.

The grandson of the voice said, "I'd like to help you find her. I know the spot. I hung a violet ribbon a long time back at the place where we'll enter the woods. I've got an old four-wheel jeep, and even though it's a murky mess, there's an old lumber road that I think we can get through on. I know we'll have to stop and remove logs and branches from the trail, and my jeep has no top, so we're going to get wet."

We go south, into the woods behind their house. Driving a couple of miles, we come upon a fast moving stream. Alongside, old wagon ruts are still visible in the grass, going on west. We go another 1,000 feet, and we've spotted the ribbon. It is no longer colorful but still fluttering in the wind. Out we clamber and into the woods.

Within 150 feet or so, we know we've arrived. Depressions in the ground indicate where less than a dozen have been buried; fieldstones are their grave markers. The rain has softened to a slight drizzle. The woods around us are so still. Brother Dick has thought to bring flowers. We select a spot and join hands. Dick kneels reverently to place our offering upon the ground. We thank God for allowing us to find her grave. We ask that God look kindly on her. We just stand, unmoving, in this natural cathedral in the woods, enjoying the silence, ignoring the rain, in full appreciation of the beauty of the moment. Later, we will all concur that we also had been thinking about those first travelers who lost their family members and picked this beautiful spot to lay them down.

Lovely Laura Briggs: we only know the stories of her life that involved such extreme sacrifice, and love, and determination. She was our maternal grandmother and great-grandmother. She married Judson Briggs, a good "catch" in the day, but within a few short years, he fell victim to the Irish curse. In his darker, drunken days, he became a belligerent and abusive lumberjack. He was described by his lumber foreman as the best ax man he ever saw "when he was sober."

After three babies, Laura was cooking for over 30 men in a north woods lumber camp when she decided she could take the work and abuse no more. She returned to Little Falls, where she had grown up. The children were placed for a time with the Franciscan nuns in St. Otto's orphanage. With little education, Laura found work as best she could as cook and housekeeper. Soon she was able to find a spot where the children could be with her. By hard work and occasional help from Judd, she raised them through their teen years and each into marriage.

Once again, she went back to Judd and tried to make a go of it. We can only imagine what then transpired. We do know she desperately needed an operation. The doctor in Little Falls demanded cash up front. Cash was scarce for everyone, but daughters Hattie and Mae had decided they would sell a young heifer calf and send Laura the money she needed. It was too late; she had violently taken her life. Hattie could never speak her name without tears of love, and yes, some remorse, that they could not have, somehow, saved her life.

Laura, while living, had spent her every waking, working hour dreaming about her children's futures. Her indomitable spirit has carried through to her descendants. Today they have achieved, and have become lawyers, successful entrepreneurs, artists, politicians, beauty queens, academics, professors, nurses, teachers, musicians, singers, composers, programmers, corporate executives, accountants, and career military figures. As a family, we ask ourselves, where has this desire and perseverance come from? The answer, most assuredly, has been instilled in us by the example of our forebears. Indeed, Lovely Laura Briggs played a remarkable historical role in determining who we are. She lies in an unmarked grave, but we are vowed to recognize her courage and life of sacrifice.

The Briggs family story is an American story. Briggs men and women carved out cities from the wilderness and fought in every war from the time of their landing in America. They were on the second boat to arrive in the colonies after the Mayflower. Laura is but one of so many people who lived and sacrificed so we may have what we have today.

A Dream Come True
By Shirley Worth of Bemidji, Minnesota
Born 1932

1949 found me starting my senior year in high school at the Bemidji High school, located on 15th Street, first home of the Bemidji Lumberjacks, as far as I know. Even though I was born in the big little town of Nymore, I had spent my whole school life in the Bemidji School District.

That was also the year I was chosen to participate in Mr. Jake Outwin's Occupational Relations Class offering "on the job training." My emphasis was Health Occupations, which is how I became one of Lutheran Hospital's very first Pinkies.

Every Monday through Thursday from 8:00 to 10:00 a.m., Ona Mae, June, Ruth, and I would walk seven blocks from school to Lutheran Hospital on Bemidji Avenue and 8th Street. On Saturdays and Sundays, we worked full eight-hour shifts and for the first three months, got paid a whole 35 cents an hour. That was a lot of money back then! I could buy a whole bag of groceries with those 35 pennies.

I can still remember Bemidji Avenue being two small lanes back then. No matter what kind of weather – rainstorms, snowstorms, or blues skies – we never missed a shift. That paid off as the next three months, our hourly wage was raised to 50 cents. We were really making some big bucks now! The fact that our trainers were some of Lutheran Hospital's finest nurses had much to do with our success.

I remember Mrs. Towley being our very first instructor. She taught us patient relations, which included serving water, making beds, and seeing to their comfort. Mrs. Brenning replaced Mrs. Towley, and she was one of my

Bemidji High School's first Occupational Relations Class

favorites because she actually became part of my family! Her home was under repair for a season, and she was able to room with me and Mom. Mrs. Nelson, Mrs. Wild, and Mrs. Burns were also a large part of the Pinkies' success over the years. Miss Skooge, our supervisor, was efficient at seeing that everything ran smoothly.

After our first six months of training were completed, our wage jumped to $1.00 an hour! Now I was able to buy about two full bags of groceries for only one-hour's wage.

I mostly loved working in the nursery with all the babies. Chances are, if you were born in Bemidji before 1996, we might have met in the nursery. There's one delivery I'll never forget. Dr. Dan McCann had been wishing to deliver triplets and in 1950, his dream came true! The first baby was a boy who was named after Dr. McCann. And the second boy, baby Dan's brother, was named Dave. Just when Dr. McCann thought he was done, along came their little sister, Jean. She was the smallest of the three but the feistiest! (And she later outdid her adult brothers by having her own set of twins!)

At the time of their birth, the hospital had only one old incubator so we put the all three in it together. "Womb mates" became "roommates." The boys were placed on the outsides with little sister Jean upside down in the center. When we heard her cry, we knew the boys must be chomping on her toes!

In 2010, I had the pleasure of attending the triplet's 60th birthday party in the basement of the American Legion right here in Bemidji. I have our photo that was taken together at that party hanging on my kitchen wall even today. Last year they celebrated their 65th together.

I was a happy nurse's aide for 20 years when Lutheran changed to Bemidji Hospital. That's when we were required to have our licensure. Good thing Mr. Jake Outwin had the inclination to start our local Northwest Technical College just shortly before this. Good thing too, that Mom and I lived only five short blocks from the college. One year later I had L.P.N. after my name and by 1980, Bemidji Hospital made the big move to Anne Street and became North Country Regional Hospital.

I've been retired for 20 years now and really miss the babies, but not so much the work! To top it all off, who would have guessed that the original Lutheran Hospital building where my nursing career started and is now known as Baker Park, has become my wonderful home where I am surrounded by good friends!

Loving My Minnesota Life
By Karen Ann Rhen Duczeminskyj of Bend, Oregon
Born 1948

I grew up in the town of Leonard in northern Minnesota. It is a very small town with a population of less than 50 people. I was born in Bagley, Minnesota, a town 14 miles south of Leonard, in 1948. My early years were in Leonard, going to grade school there, and later attending high school in Clearbrook, Minnesota, located about 12 miles north of Leonard. Our family moved to Oregon in 1966 but my formative years were in the Leonard area.

My mom, Adeline, and dad, Yngve, were the best parents a child could ever ask for. They were kind, loving, considerate, and thoughtful. They were married for 57 years before my dad's death in 2004; Mom passed in 2012.

My mom was a homemaker all of her life. She helped with teaching Sunday school, was a member of the Leonard Woman's Auxiliary, a member of the Church's Ladies Aide, and sang with the church choir. I remember my mom always had a schedule for the week. Monday was washday. Tuesday was ironing. Wednesday was usually a day of visiting with friends and relatives. Thursday was baking. Friday was cleaning the house. Saturday we spent time with Dad (he usually worked away from home) sometimes going to a movie in Bagley or a drive-in in Bemidji. Sunday was church and family dinner, and going for rides in the country. Like the families of the time, I remember Mom hanging the laundry outside on the clothesline in winter and them freezing on the line and being brought in solid like boards. There was gardening and canning, freezing fruits and vegetables, and baking homemade bread, cookies, donuts, etc. In rural Minnesota, there was no mass transit; all travel was by personal vehicle. During grade school, Mom had to drive us to and from school and Sunday school. This was especially hard on Mom during the wintertime when the snows came.

My mom's family, the Johnsons, consisted of three girls (including my mom) and two boys. She and her sisters, Bonnie and Joann, all sang in the church choir. Her brothers both served in the Armed Forces; Larry in the US Navy for 20 years, and Arthur in the US Army touring in Vietnam. Her mom and dad, Annie and Lewis, lived in the Leonard area for many years until moving to Oregon in the early '50s.

Frederick and Augusta Rhen

Grandpa Johnson was a farmer and Grandma a homemaker. For extra money (or barter), Grandpa was a barber. He would cut hair for the local residents. One time he had cut hair for a child and, unbeknown to him, the child had head lice. When he realized that the child had lice, he meant to clean his cutting tools but forgot. He later cut my mom's and Aunt Bonnie's hair, and they got head lice. His remedy to kill the lice was to rinse the hair

Karen and Douglas Rhen

with kerosene and wrap it in a towel. Because the head was wrapped tight, the kerosene caused their ears to swell to twice their size. That was a lesson learned! Grandpa and Grandma had chickens. One day my uncle Art and I, we were about 3 years old at the time (he's three months older than me), got into the chicken coop and had a great time throwing eggs at the wall and scared the chickens. We both got a spanking!

My dad was a bricklayer and worked with my uncles, Emil, Vern, and George, and my cousins, Merlin (Punk), Roger, and Rodney. They had to travel to cities and towns away from home and most times would be gone for the week. My dad prided himself in his work, as did my uncles and cousins.

My dad's family, the Rhens, consisted of eight children including my father. There were two girls and six boys, Mollie was the oldest followed by Hugo, Vern, and Tony. They were born in Sweden. The next four were born in Minnesota; they were Ann, Emil, my dad Yngve, and George.

My dad served in the United States Army during World War II in Africa and Italy; fighting in five battle campaigns. He received the Bronze Star for merit and awarded the Good Conduct Medal, European-African-Middle Eastern Medal, American Campaign Medal, World War II Medal, and Sharpshooter Medal. He was commended for outstanding performance of duty. When he came home, he never wanted to talk about his time during the war. Only my dad and Uncle George served in the military during World War II.

There was a story of how Dad and uncles Vern and George would be laying brick and would pick the best bricks to lay, throwing the damaged or not so good bricks onto a pile to be thrown away. My uncle Emil would take those bad bricks and use them. Dad, Vern, and George would just shake their heads and laugh. Four of the boys, Vern, Emil, George, and my dad, were bricklayers; Hugo worked for Edward Hines Lumber Company in Hines, Oregon, and Tony worked in Iowa. His sister, Mollie, was a homemaker and his younger sister, Ann, was a teacher. My dad's mother and father, Frederick and Augusta Rhen, immigrated to the United States from Dortea, Sweden. Medicine in the Rhen house sometimes consisted of Grandma putting kerosene on the wound to clean it, then a pat on the butt, and sending the child out to play. All of the boys in my dad's family were pranksters and LOVED to play jokes on each other, nothing harmful, just enough to get Grandma to get after them. There was the time my dad, about 10 years old, shot an oriole with a slingshot and killed it. Emil went home singing, "Yngve killed an oriole! Yngve killed an oriole!" Needless to say, Grandma threw the slingshot into the stove. There was also the time one of my uncles shot Grandma in the butt with a BB gun. Grandma got a hold of the gun and that was the end of that! One time Grandma, Grandpa, and Mollie were away from the house and left Vern in charge (all of the kids were young). Vern wanted to go hunting so he tied Dad and Emil to a tree, put Ann under the sink with the "slop bucket," and left George running around the yard with a swinging dirty diaper. Again, Grandma wasn't happy and Vern paid a price. There's also the time when my dad and Emil were sick in bed and untied the yarn in the quilt to keep busy; again, Grandma was not happy. There are too many stories to tell and I could probably write a book with those stories. There were many hunting and bricklayer stories too. This may seem like Grandma had her hands full, but it wasn't. The boys were just boys, and Grandma loved each and every one.

I had a brother, Doug, who served in the US Army in Vietnam and Germany; he passed in 2010 at the age of 59. For the most part, he was my playmate when we lived in Leonard. Like most children living in area, we had our chores to do. Chores like mowing the lawn, chopping and hauling wood, cleaning the outhouse with Pine Sol, washing clothes with a wringer washing machine, and hanging them on a clothesline. Doug had a horse that he had to take care of and it was up to us to feed our dog. Doug and I played Cowboys and Indians; we made mud pies, mud cakes, and cookies, which we decorated with stones and twigs. Yum! I remember listening to the Lone Ranger and Fibber McGee and Mollie on the radio. It was a long time before we bought a TV. I remember Daddy watching boxing and Mom watching the soap operas. We all watched Bonanza, The Ed Sullivan Show, Death Valley Days with Ronald Reagan, and the Alfred Hitchcock Hour. Doug and I watched Heckle and Jeckel, Howdy Doody, Ruff n' Ready, Mickey Mouse Club, and American Bandstand with Dick Clark. Mom and Dad would take us to town to grocery shop, sometimes buying a chocolate bar at Strand's Store in Leonard and cutting it into four pieces for all to share (times were hard in those days). I remember buying a comic book for 10cents. Saturday bath time was completed in the kitchen sink; everyone stayed in another room until the bather was done with their bath. I attended a two-room school; one room housed grades 1-4, the other grades 5-8. My eighth grade graduation class consisted of three classmates including myself. During the school years, I made many friends. Some I've seen when visiting the Leonard area and have kept in touch with a few; Sharon, Carol, and Ricky from high school, and I see Carol (CJ) who lives in Denver, once a year. All of my friends are special.

Childhood memories: popcorn on Saturday nights. When we were sick, Mom would rub us down with mentholatem or Vicks. I remember when Doug and I had mumps and whooping cough. Picking wild raspberries, blueberries, choke cherries, and rhubarb. Comfort foods, like homemade bread, tomato soup with grilled cheese and Spam sandwiches. Christmas gifts! No electronic gifts in those days. One year Doug and I got a phonograph. Gifts in those days were Tonka trucks, toy cap guns, dolls, paper dolls, and knitted mittens and scarves made by Grandma Rhen. I remember taking accordion lessons with my cousin Emilie in Bemidji. After the lessons, we would have lunch and then shop at Woolworth's and other stores in Bemidji. Don't forget S&H Green stamps. Growing up in Minnesota, everyone would have stories about the winters. We would ski (really be towed) behind a car while Dad drove, very slowly, of course. Skiing on the hills, tobogganing, ice skating, and hay rides. Afterwards, we would get together for hot chocolate and treats. We had party lines and rotary dial telephone service. I had pictures taped on my bedroom walls of teen idols Fabian, Frankie Avalon, Elvis, Bobby Darrin, and Sandra Dee. I remember the school plays and the carnivals we held at school. All of the schools in the area would have a program and everyone from the different schools would attend to support them.

Growing up in Leonard, there were the outdoor privies. Who can ever forget those?

Family gatherings were a very important time in our lives. Holidays, birthday parties, and picnics with friends and family were a

Karen Rhen in 1949

special time in my life. Grandma Rhen would always bring Jell-O with fruit.

Then there's the Minnesota weather! Tornados and tornado warnings were a common thing growing up. While celebrating my 9th birthday with the family, a tornado hit the Leonard area and we lost electricity. There was much damage in the Leonard area and I believe that was the year my Uncle Emil's barn went down.

Church going was an important part of our lives. There was Sunday school, confirmation, Luther League, and in the summer, Vacation Bible School. I especially remember the Christmas programs, both at church and our local school. At the conclusion of the programs, we received a little brown bag filled with treats of candy, nuts, and always an orange or apple. I am very appreciative of the fact that these religious programs taught us the true meaning of Christmas and how to live our lives.

We moved to Oregon in 1966 after I graduated high school but I am proud of being born in Minnesota and the time I lived there. I have only the best memories of those times with the most loving, caring, understanding, and giving parents. And of my brother, Doug being my best friend and playmate when we were young in Leonard. Minnesota was honest and simple living with the most loving family and friends that last a lifetime.

The Lewis and Clark Expedition
By Harvey Dahline of Grand Rapids, Minnesota
Born 1933

A few days ago a man who I considered a friend of mine asked me if I would like to go with him and another friend blueberry picking up past Orr, about a hundred miles from here.

Now, to be honest, I had gone blueberry picking a few years ago, spending several hours going to the northern part of the state. Then, after a fierce battle with deer flies and mosquitos, we had escaped. I, with a whole quarter bucket of blueberries, him with a half bucket. We still had our long drive home. I still have a taste for wild blueberries but not as much as I used to.

Now this. I have considered this person a wonderful close friend. What to do? How could I turn him down? A man always has his one resource he can turn to. Turning to my wife, I said, "Harold wants me to go blueberry picking with him on Monday up north. We would be gone all day." (I emphasized all day.) She said, "What a wonderful idea! You'll have so much fun." That took care of that!

So, I told Harold, "Great, what time will we leave?" The answer was 6:00am, so I proceeded to get things ready, my clothes, and setting my alarm clock, which I didn't need to do as I always wake up on time. And I always have my backup, my wife, for an alarm clock as she thinks it's a reflection of her if I'm late or not dressed well.

It was no surprise to me when she started to shake me, not too gently, at 5:45am. My alarm had not gone off, bad batteries. I did manage to dress and eat breakfast and was ready at 6:00am, not thinking anyone would notice my not shaving as we were headed for the wild.

We were on the road by 6:10. Harold introduced his friend who was quite likeable. It turned out he was a lumberjack, a very spry young man at 71. We had a nice drive on a beautiful morning and seemed to get along quite well. I did notice a few barbs from Harold that I might miss my donuts this morning. (This really hurt, as I used to be a police officer.)

Along the way, the subject turned to politics which didn't last too long as we found that everyone doesn't think the way we do. But it was easy to understand, as he was only 71 and still in his formative years.

Eventually we did enter the forest about seven miles past Orr, and both men seemed confident in knowing the area. Our next turn-off onto a road should have been around eight miles farther.

At this time, we were heading down a dirt logging road, and after 10 to 12 miles figured, we might have missed our turn-off, so we started backtracking. Do you know how many turn-offs there can be in 12 miles? There were a lot of them. Each one we came to, Harold would say he was quite confident that this was it.

After about an hour, I started to think about the Lewis and Clark expedition and the fact that I had not brought my compass with me. Many times Harold said that there may be a crossroad up ahead. Harold must have a GPS in his head because he always got us back to the main road.

I might say I'm a "naysayer" because after some time, I was having some doubts.

On the way back out, we did come to a clearing. We were always looking for an area that had been logged or burned a few years ago. These areas are the best for blueberry picking.

Thinking we would get out and look the area over, the friend went to the far side, Harold and I to the near side. We did find some low bush berries but not a great number. On the friend's side, it was somewhat better. After about an hour, we drove down the main road. We talked to a road grader operator; he did not know the road we were looking for.

So, we continued our exploration. Soon we came to a grown-over side road. Harold once again said with confidence, "This is it!" He was right again. We drove the road for two miles through many overhanging tree limbs and potholes, up and down steep hills, then a big rock, our destination. Getting out of the pick-up, we talked to a man by the road with his dog. He pointed to a tall pine a quarter of a mile away, atop a steep hill. This was to be our rendezvous point.

In a short time, we were close to the big, tall pine. There were many blueberry plants throughout the area but it soon became apparent the area had been picked recently. But if you looked really well, there were berries to be had. I spent the next several hours either on my knees or lying down, going from plant to plant, crawling on my hands and knees- never walking. I could see Harold on his knees much of the time.

The friend, younger and maybe a little smarter, had brought with him a homemade scoop about six inches wide with prongs on it, and as we would reach for a few berries at a time, he would scoop through several plants.

I must admit after several hours of crawling on my hands and knees, over logs, plants, and bushes, I was starting to tire somewhat, but, as you know, I could say nothing. The last half hour I was on my back a few times admiring the blue sky.

At 5:15pm, the words were spoken. The friend said, "I think it's time to go." We had to find our buckets. The friend was showing the way and I was close behind. I had no idea where we were and the brush was thick. It was about this time that I stepped on a rock that wasn't there, falling to my left with a bucket in my right hand. Grabbing a small sapling with my left hand, I kept control, landing on my face in the brush, but with the bucket of berries still upright. I never lost one berry. Harold and the friend looked amazed that I had such control every time I fell down.

Fifteen minutes later, we came out where the truck was parked. It didn't take much to see who had the most berries. I had close to a gallon and a half, Harold had two gallons or more, and the friend had at least six gallons. His family was going to be very happy.

Harold drove the bad part of the road going out to the highway; I then drove the rest of the way home. Along the way, we stopped in Orr to get an ice cream cone. We had to buy six to a pack, so we each had two.

I got home about 8:30pm and then spent almost an hour cleaning berries. You know the old saying, "You catch 'em, you clean 'em!" I had spent a good day with good friends.

Now, this should be the end to the story. Going to bed, I slept very well but when I woke in the morning, there was this 90-year-old guy in bed. I tried to turn over and get my feet to the floor, but nothing wanted to move, and if it did, it was not pleasant. After some time, I had my feet on the floor and my rear was still on the bed. Reaching over to the bureau, I helped myself stand, taking a few three inch steps. Someone laughed behind me. Then she said, "I'm sorry!"

Making it to the living room, I started walking it off. After a time, I headed to the biff. The only thing saving me there was that I had a new toilet, which was three or four, inches higher than the older ones. Also, the vanity is next to it, which would help me get up. For the next day and a half, every time I would sit down for a while, I would have to walk it off.

I write this not to tell you of my pain or the wonderful pie my wife made. Just to say that I had two friends out there that I hoped were sharing in my pain!

It's been almost a year now. The other day I ran into my 71-year-old friend. He said it looked like the blueberries are going to be plentiful this year.

I haven't been sleeping well.

Our Cabin—Our Beautiful Slice of God's Country
By Mary Lou Meers Schwagerl of Bovey, Minnesota
Born 1951

What wonderful blessings - growing up in the beautiful state of Minnesota with five siblings, and being raised by two parents who were educators! It was just the right combination for making some mighty incredible memories.

While my family was growing up, our mother didn't work outside of the home. Our father had a job allowing him freedom during the summer months. We spent many summers camping at McCarthy Beach Campgrounds on Side Lake (St. Louis County) in northern Minnesota. Some camping trips lasted three weeks- some even longer. Mom and Dad said they wouldn't plan to go home until one of the kids asked about going home. Camping was a wonderful experience for us growing up. Our folks had very little extra money, but they had time to spend with us fishing, swimming, hiking, and any other outdoor activities we were interested in.

We camped in a tent trailer our folks had fashioned out of an old two-wheel, open-topped trailer. Dad improvised the trailer some by attaching two plywood flags on hinges that folded onto the trailer for travel. When parked, those flags would fold out to create platforms to sleep on. Dad didn't want his family sleeping on the ground. Our mother sewed the tent out of canvas - 34 yards of canvas! She sewed the tent with an old electric Singer sewing machine. Mom spent countless hours sitting in the trailer in our garage at home, surrounded by canvas, while she created this masterpiece. Our family spent many nights sleeping in that tent trailer, and many days outdoors enjoying our summer camping trips.

During the summer of 1962, our folks decided to look for a piece of land in northern Minnesota where we could build a cabin in the woods. They didn't have much money, but Dad had heard about some lake lots the State of Minnesota was leasing, and decided that we should check out the prospects.

We spent that summer traveling many dirt roads in northern Minnesota - first up the north shore of Lake Superior, across to the Ely area, and then on to Hibbing and Grand Rapids. The forester in Hibbing had suggested that Dad check with the Forestry Department in St. Paul, where he found maps and more information about leasing lake lots in northern Minnesota.

The next trip up north, we traveled to Grand Rapids, and out Scenic Highway 7. At the intersection of Itasca County Road 8 and the Scenic Highway, was the old "Snaptail Store." Dad had been trying to figure out where some of those roads on the maps were, and he stopped at the old store to ask. He then found out that many of the roads printed on the maps were proposed roads- they didn't exist yet. When Dad asked about using their restroom, the owner told him he didn't have a restroom inside the

The original Meers cabin

store, but he had "a half bath with a path" out back that we could use. That crazy name for an outdoor biffy was used by Dad for many years whenever he told this story.

That same night, we stayed at a resort called Paradise Point on Sand Lake. The next day, our folks discovered Burnt Shanty Lake, where there were many unleased lake lots, and only three existing cabins. I don't know how Dad found that road into the lake because there were no signs on most of the roads in that area. There was a public access on Burnt Shanty Lake. The dead-end road went around the lake about a mile farther, and ended just after the Little Island Lake public access. Dad drove the car in as far as he could, and then he and our mother walked through many lots on the far side of the lake, looking at the terrain, the trees, and the view each lot offered. They chose Lot #1, which was on the other side of Burnt Shanty Lake from the public access and only accessible by boat. It was the farthest lot from the public access, it had southern exposure, and the east side of the lot was bordered by federal land, which made the area more private. In the fall of 1962, our folks leased Lot #1 on Burnt Shanty Lake from the State of Minnesota for $25.00 a year, and they signed a ten-year lease.

Our Aunt Betty and Uncle Kenny were also interested in finding a lake lot in northern Minnesota where they could build a cabin. They took a look at the lots on Burnt Shanty Lake, and they decided to lease Lot #2. Uncle Kenny had some experience with carpentry, and he was going to take two weeks off the next summer so our families could start building the two cabins. Our father, who had no experience with carpentry, was somewhat concerned about how all of this was going to happen; but my very practical younger sister, Becky, put the whole thing into perspective for him. She said, "Dad, you know how to

Kathy, Mary Lou, Auntie Ruth, and Becky in 1965

build a birdhouse, just make it bigger!"

The fall and winter months that year were spent planning, saving money, and looking forward to June when school would be out, and we could spend the summer up north. Also, several weekends that winter, Dad and Uncle Kenny and a few of us kids made some trips up to the newly leased lots to clear brush. We would leave the Twin Cities in the early morning hours on those Saturdays. Uncle Kenny would drive his pick-up as far as he could into the woods. He would park at the "bus stop," and then we would walk the rest of the way in. It was still about a half-mile to the public access on Burnt Shanty Lake from the "bus stop." We would then walk around the lake to our lots. There was deep and drifted snow that winter, and at times, we would be walking though snow up to our waists and deeper. We would spend all day clearing brush by hand with hatchets, and then burning the brush in a bonfire. When we were finished for the day, we would walk back to the truck, and then drive home to the Twin Cities again.

After the brushing was done, and spring weather was on its way, Dad and Uncle Kenny went up a few weekends to dig holes in the newly thawed ground, and poured the footings for both cabins. They used water from the lake to hand-mix cement in a wheelbarrow for those footings.

Also, that winter, Dad collected windows from an apartment building being remodeled near our home in the Twin Cities. He bought the sashes, and then had one of his friends in town build the window frames he was going to use for our cabin.

Early in the spring of 1963, Dad and Uncle Kenny bought a used big-barreled pontoon on a trailer, and a 7.5- horse Wizard outboard motor for $150.00. Aunt Betty and Uncle Kenny hauled the pontoon up to the lake, and left it at the public access. Because there was no road around the lake to our lots, the plan was to have all of the building materials delivered to the public access and then pontoon the materials over to our lots on the other side of the lake. This labor-intense job was completed by our family because of the limited amount of time our aunt and uncle and their family could be there to work on the cabins that summer.

Our family got up to Burnt Shanty Lake ahead of time, and we camped at the public access in our tent trailer. Dad backed the tent trailer as far as he could into the woods, so other folks could still use the public access. We camped at the public access for about three weeks with no running water or electricity- just a small green Coleman cooler to keep a few things cold, and a kerosene stove and lantern.

Cohasset Lumber Company delivered the lumber and other materials for both cabins, and dumped it near the water's edge at the Burnt Shanty Lake public access. For the next week, we spent every day loading the materials onto the pontoon, riding across the lake, and unloading at the other side. We couldn't take full loads because of the weight and what the barrels could keep afloat, so we made many trips. For safety reasons, we were supposed to ride inside the gates on the pontoon; but when we got closer to shore; Dad would let us ride on the front two barrels and drag our feet in the water. The lake water was so clear and cold. While we were moving, we could see fish swimming and many beautiful rocks on the lake's bottom.

By the time our aunt and uncle and their family got up to the lake, we had all the lumber and materials pontooned across the lake, ready to start building. There was no electricity or running water. Dad and Uncle Kenny set cement blocks on top of the footings, hand-mixing cement for fill. They also had to cut the lumber by hand, using handsaws. Somehow, with everyone helping, we got both cabins started. Both floors for the 24' x 24' cabins were nailed in place by the end of the two weeks. Dad pitched a tent on our cabin's wood floor then. We closed up our tent trailer at the public access, and we stayed in the tent at our cabin site while we continued to build.

After we had our cabin's floor in place, we went home to the Twin Cities for a short time. The next trip up north, we worked building the outside walls for our cabin's main floor. A weight-bearing log was skinned and set in place for the second floor loft to rest on. Dad bought a huge 26 - foot white pine log with just the branches trimmed off for this. He bought the log from Charlie and Laddie Pearson, some new friends who lived

Beck and Kathy Meers in 1964

in a year-round home on Sand Lake. Laddie showed us how to skin the bark off the tree trunk with a drawknife while straddling the log. The blade on the drawknife was very sharp, and had handles at both ends to hang onto and to pull back on. This was very time consuming and exhausting. Everyone took turns skinning. When the bark was removed from the log, the log was raised and set on the main floor cabin walls, in the center of the cabin, so the loft could be built above. There were also two weight-bearing tree trunks that we skinned to hold up the weight of the loft in the center of the cabin.

The walls for the second floor loft were then put up, the rafters were set in place, and the roof boards were nailed on. Tarpaper and shingles were added onto the roof right away, so at least we had some protection from the elements. The siding for the cabin had to wait a few years because of dwindling funds. Instead, Dad nailed tarpaper on the outside walls of the cabin to give us some protection from bad weather. By the end of the summer in 1963, we had the cabin completely enclosed.

Our family worked hard that summer building our cabin. We kids never received an allowance for work we did, but because we had all pitched in and helped, Dad gave us each one dollar that we could spend however, we wanted. I had my eye on a tackle box full of hooks, fishing line, and bobbers.

At the age of eleven years, I had no idea how blessed we were to have our cabin, and what terrific experiences and memories we would make together in our little slice of what folks call "God's country!"

My First Friend
By Sharon Jackson of San Jose, California
Born 1946

"Okay. Line up. Oldest to youngest." It was Labor Day, 1949, in Staples, Minnesota, and my brother-in-law, Donald, was about to take one of the rare precious pictures of our young family.

The eight of us got in a row with Eileen, six, and me, three, on the end holding hands and grinning from ear to ear. We couldn't know that the next day would forever change

Marilyn, Eileen, and Shary

our lives. Eileen would go off to school, and I would have to adjust to being an only child for six or seven hours a day.

I'd hero-worshipped all of my sisters, but Eileen and I were the best of buddies. I remember the two of us snuggled together in a wooden rocker throwing our heads back, pumping with all our might. How we sailed that chair up and down the linoleum floored living room singing at the top of our lungs. "A-B-C-D-E-F-G…" or "Mares eat oats and does eat oats…" Though Mom cautioned us about tipping over, I don't remember any complaints about noise or messing up the house.

Mom was a saint; there was no doubt about that. Our older siblings were appalled when they came home from school to our tiny house and found that we had made forts under the dining room table or put up "whole houses," each taking part of a bedroom to mother our baby dolls. Eileen's house was always better than mine and try as I might, including whining to get her to switch places, I was never able to discover her secret. As we played, Mom provided little snacks in measuring cups or jar lids. Raisins, chocolate chips, or shredded coconut were just a few.

Sometimes in warmer weather, we had picnics on a blanket out in the yard. We had peanut butter or bologna sandwiches and jars of room temperature milk. That milk had what I came to think of as a "picnicky" taste.

We weren't allowed to stray far but there was a little park just a short block away and when our older sister, Marilyn, was with

Sharon's siblings with their dog, Star

us, we played there. Marilyn was more adventurous and with her, we climbed trees, explored the creek looking for interesting critters, and chased each other around playing cowboys and Indians, or Tarzan. Although Marilyn was lots of fun, Eileen was more predictable and I always felt safe with her. We felt so comfortable together it was almost as if we were connected by some invisible tie. I was more brave when I was with her because I just believed that nothing bad could happen with her nearby. The park reminds me of another picture taken of the three of us as we returned from an adventure. I smiled at the photographer as I clutched an empty little blanket, not yet realizing that my baby doll had slipped from my grip and was forever lost.

I missed my buddy, Eileen. The house was so quiet. All alone, I played with Mom's button box, sorting buttons by size and color. Occasionally, I had the thrill of finding a penny, which I was allowed to keep. I looked at picture books, built things with clothespins, made animals out of clay, or colored the last remaining pages in my Christmas coloring book. If the radio was on, I sang along. Like the time Dean Martin was singing, "That's Amore" and I joined in. "When the moon hits your eye like a big piece of pie…" Mom burst out laughing. I had no idea what a pizza was but I enjoyed making her laugh.

Mom didn't play with me that I remember. In those days, adults expected children to entertain themselves. Maybe if I had shown an interest in what she was doing in the kitchen she would have let me help her cook. Years later, she entertained her grandchildren by involving them in bread making and baking cookies but her life was much different and less hectic by then.

At lunchtime, Dad would come home from his job at the hospital, just two short blocks from our house. He was the all-around maintenance man there, which among many other tasks included caring for a large garden used by the hospital kitchen. It was hard work but steady and it came with health insurance.

Sitting together at our kitchen table, my most vivid memory is of hard-boiled eggs or chicken noodle soup, along with discussions about the day's news and political talk. Dad was a staunch Democrat and I'm sure Mom followed his lead. She had great respect for his intelligence. Later when Stephenson and Eisenhower were running for president, I just assumed Stephenson would be elected. It was quite a shock when I went to school and found out that most people "like Ike." I would soon grow bored at the table with all that grown up conversation. I tried bringing my doll to the table for entertainment but that just wasn't the same.

That year I made up two imaginary friends named Ordy and Glory. "Ordy, ordy, ordy," was the sound a neighbor's Model T car made. Our doctor, Dr. Lund, another neighbor, had a daughter named Gloria. Interesting that in my hometown we had people in a converted boxcar living across the street and the fanciest house in town right next door to us. Our house was extremely modest in comparison. Ordy and Glory looked exactly like me but Ordy was very poor and Glory was rich. They both liked me very much and would talk to me about their problems. I guess I talked with them when someone overheard because soon my older sisters began questioning me about them, asking to meet them, for example. If I said I was Ordy, they would ask me where Shary and Glory were and I had to make up an explanation. Somehow I knew I wasn't convincing. Funny, I don't remember Eileen being involved. Eventually, I gave them up.

Soon, I was lonely even when Eileen was home because when we weren't playing outside, she wanted to read all the time. She would read to me sometimes, but other times I just wanted to play and would resort to trying to knock the book out of her hands to get her attention. If I bugged her enough, she would hit me and then I would run tell Mom, which got her in trouble. How I mistreated my normally gentle sister. Eventually, Eileen and I went off to school together and I too learned to read.

Although we now live 1500 miles apart, Eileen and I remain very close even though she married and had children, and then grandchildren, while I remained single. Her oldest child is named Sharon. Through frequent phone conversations and less frequent visits back and forth, we keep up with each other's lives and interests. In recent years, we found we had one more thing in common as we both joined book clubs. But this time I was first!

What Fun to Ride in the Bob Sled!
By Marie Schildt of Alexandria, Minnesota
Born 1923

As a young girl growing up, I lived on a farm in Otsego Township. I was the second child in a family of eleven children. We had no electricity and no running water. The neighborhood was all two-story houses. In the family my father came from, when someone got married their father would give them a down payment on a farm. The new farm was often neighboring property. We were mostly related and Catholic. Matter of fact, my grandpa gave land to have a school built. It was named the Greeninger School, named after my grandfather.

I remember as a child, one family lived across the road. They had no car. On Sunday, those kids and parents would come out to the road, and anyone going by who had room would take as many of them as possible to church. When a big snowstorm would close the roads, that father worked all Saturday getting his big bob sled ready, like straw on the floor and stumps of wood and planks across for seats. Then he would pick up all the neighbors for church. What fun! Our mothers would make sure there were blankets for everyone to cover our laps. It was three miles to town.

The man with the sled was Schumacher, in case he has great-grandchildren to read this.

Outhouse in the Barn
By Darlene Davidson of Thief River Falls, Minnesota

I am 83 years old and have lived in this small town all my life. What I am writing about you may have never heard of. It is cold in Minnesota. My grandfather was from Germany. He was a great old man. He had one cow and her name was Bonnie. In the winter, it is very cold, so he made an outhouse in the barn so she would keep it warm. He lived to be 93 and never had a car. He worked with the railroad and never used a car to get to work; he walked. He also never learned to read or write English.

Snakes! Oh, My!
By Shelia R. L. Olson of Roseau, Minnesota
Born 1933

Snakes! You don't have to tell me the tiny Minnesota garter snakes are harmless (I know that), but that doesn't stop me from getting the heebie-jeebies anytime one gets too close. Maybe it goes back to the time when I was a barefooted four-year-old and stepped on one!

In 1960, we lived on a farm south of Swift, Minnesota. The house was ground level. One hot summer afternoon, I walked into the kitchen just as a snake slithered out from under the refrigerator! I stifled a scream so as to not scare my kids, Sheldan (4), Bruce (3), and Jodi (1). My first mistake was in calling my husband, who was working at the neighbor's house. After sharing my predicament with the other men and much laughing and suggestions, his solution was that I could use his deer rifle! I hung up the phone!

I couldn't stay in the house, so I told the kids, "Let's go for the mail." As they ran to the car, I propped open the door, thinking the snake would find its way out...my second mistake.

We got the mail from the post office three miles away. As we got closer to home, I wondered where that snake might be. Before we went inside, I told the boys about the snake. I told them that they would have to be good little hunters. Boy, were they excited about that!

As I stood in the kitchen peering under and around things, Bruce yelled from the front room, "Here it is, Mommy!" Sure enough, in the corner behind the rocker lay the snake!

Now, how was I to get it out of there? I decided an empty cereal box would work to scoop it up and carry it outside, but no way was I going to crawl behind the chair and get it! My brave three-year-old volunteered to do the job, which he did. Of course, being boys, they both begged to keep it for a pet.

In my most compassionate mommy voice, I explained how the poor little snake was lost from its mommy. They could help it by bringing it far from the house and letting it go.

I watched from the window as they emptied the box and sadly waved as the snake hurried away. I sighed a big sigh of relief and sank down onto a chair!

History of Blackberry, Minnesota
By Gordon Greniger of Grand Rapids, Minnesota
Born 1935

I grew up as a young child in a log house in Blackberry. I started school at age five in 1940. We had a ride in a 1939 Chevrolet car as our school bus. The first school was by the cemetery and was later moved by several horses east a couple of miles. Later years in 1911, a new school was built with two rooms and a library in between. Grades one through four were in one room and grades five through eight were in the other room.

In 1946 during the Christmas vacation, the schoolhouse burned down and we had to go to Grand Rapids, Minnesota. In 1912, a teacher's cottage was built with walls only two inches thick and a half basement for wood and a furnace. In 1963, I purchased the cottage and two acres of land. In 1969, I built a new house as we had children to separate and only had bunk beds.

In the late 1890s, a store was built and then a post office north of the railroad tracks. There also was a potato warehouse, pavilion, and section house. Later, the store and the post office were moved south of the tracks. Twice, the store burned down and was rebuilt each time. The first highway (#8) was from Duluth to Bemis. After the war, Highway 2 was built and then tar was added.

In 1911, a bridge was built across the Mississippi River as high as the trees so the riverboats could pass under. In 1938, the bridge was lowered to road level. The one-lane bridge was later unsafe for trucks and busses. In 1978, a new concrete bridge was built a half mile to the west.

After the new school was built, the old

one was used for town hall, dances, meetings, etc. Later years, the old school was sold and moved across the road to the Blackberry antique and tractor grounds where they have yearly shows. Later on, the old school was put back as it was first built. A new town hall and community center was built in 1982 and used very much. We have a large park, skating rink, ball field, tennis court, basketball court, etc. After a lumber company cut off all the red pine, it was stumps and dirt. A lot of volunteer work was done throughout the years to make the park. Highway 2 goes right by the park and new store.

Run for Your Life!
By James R. Thompson, M.D. of Bemidji, Minnesota
Born 1933

Roger and I have been friends since junior high school. We are now both 82 years old, and we both grew up in Bemidji, in northwest Minnesota. Bemidji is about 100 miles from the Canadian border.

About 30 years ago, we were duck and goose hunting just over the international border, in Manitoba. We were driving down a rural road and saw a bunch of snow geese in a pond in a pasture. The farmer said we could hunt there.

Our strategy was for Roger to walk across the pasture and scare up the geese to fly over me. I was hidden on the other side of the pond. This strategy was flawless, and the geese flew right over the top of me.

I dropped two geese and was admiring them when I saw Roger running full speed across the pasture toward the fence. I had never seen Roger run full speed before, because he was held out of physical education because of having rheumatic fever. A large herd of cows had emerged from a small patch of trees and were chasing him out of their home. He dove under the fence and got away from them just as they were right on his heels.

The whole scene struck me as incredibly funny, and I couldn't stop laughing. I drove back to get him, with all the cattle on the other side of the fence.

I will never forget it, and the scene is vivid in my memory.

Mud Vacation in Blackduck, Minnesota
By Thomas H. Gilmore of Hines, Minnesota
Born 1931

In the 1940s and 1950s, many of Beltrami County roads and all of the township roads were gravel. Some of them might better be described as dirt roads. In the spring of the year, we had what we called "spring breakup." That was when the roads were hard to negotiate. After the school busses got stuck a couple of times and had to be pulled out of the mud hole by a team of horses from the nearest farm, the school board decided it was time for two weeks of "mud vacation." The school board actually planned for it by cutting short other vacation days, such as around Christmas and New Year's, or at other times taking a one day break when it should have been three days. So, at the end of the school year, we still ended at a reasonable time in early June.

Back to the muddy roads—you don't know bad roads until you come to a mud hole 20 or 30 feet long, half-filled with water. Two deep ruts lead into it and you don't know which one is the deepest. Maybe there is a high spot you think you can stay on—WRONG! Your front wheels slide off in one rut and the back wheels into the other. Now, you are not crosswise in the road, however you are not parallel with the road either. Now that nice high spot you took is what the frame of your car is sitting on. If you are lucky, the nearby farmer sees you and he's on his way with a horse dragging a singletree (a type of towing bar) and a chain. Fortunately, the car bumpers are strong enough to hook onto!

Some businesses made special accommodations for the muddy season. The roads tended to freeze overnight and the Blackduck Creamery would open up at 6:00 AM so the farmers could bring the cream into town on the frozen roads. I would sometimes be at my neighbor Leonard's house very early to hitch a ride into town since we didn't have a car. Our mail carrier, Elmer, had a surplus, four-wheel drive Army hearse. He could go through anything and he never missed a day. That was a good thing, because at that time of year everyone was ordering baby chicks, and they came through the mail. Can you imagine a couple of hundred baby chicks in the Hines Post Office overnight or for a couple of days?

There was also an advantage to mud vacation. The walleye was not legal during this time of the year however the Blackduck River was running full from the spring thaw, and so were the walleyes suckers!

The Parkers Prairie Schoolhouse Fire
By Donovan Diekow of Miltona, Minnesota
Born 1934

This is a real story that happened to me when I was eight years old. It happened in a two-room schoolhouse ten miles southwest of Parkers Prairie. There was two rooms with two teachers and 53 kids. When I started, there was one teacher and 26 kids.

It was in November of 1942. We were having class, and it started to get warmer and warmer all the time. Then all at once, someone said there are flames coming out of the wall. I guess the teacher put a little too much wood in the furnace. Well, the first thing the teacher done was send someone over to the neighbor's to call for the fire department from Parkers Prairie. The next thing she done was get all us young kids out of the schoolhouse. The next thing she done was have the older kids carry books and throw them out of the windows. Then the younger kids carried them away from the schoolhouse. It took too long, and they had to quit carrying books and get out of the schoolhouse. By that time there were flames coming out of the schoolhouse all over.

Then the fire department got there, but in those days, there wasn't much they could do. They only had a 100-gallon tank. So that was not much use at that time. The schoolhouse burned down to nothing.

Well, you can guess what us kids were doing by this time. We were jumping up and down saying, "No more school! No more school!"

Well, guess what. In two weeks, we were in school again. A mile and a half from where the school burned down was a little old schoolhouse. So they fixed that up and in school we were again. It was a little crowded, but we made it work.

That is something I will never forget. I am 81 years old now. The next year we had a new schoolhouse. Was that ever nice.

Donovan Diekow in 1938

A Lesson Learned by Heart
By Clifton Melby of Oklee, Minnesota

My story takes place in a nice little town of Oklee. Oklee is located up in Northwestern Minnesota. Founded in 1910, a relatively young town, it was named for Mr. O. K. Lee. This is where I spent my early years growing up and is still my home.

After World War II and my father's discharge from the navy, my parents moved back to Oklee to start their lives together. After some difficulty, they were finally able to buy the then closed lumberyard. They named their new business Oklee Lumber. That was in 1946 and it is still going at the time of this writing.

As it was with most small businesses at the time, the whole family worked at the lumberyard. Family recruitment was a common practice. My older brother was born in 1947 and myself in 1949. By the late 1950s, we were actually able to be of some help. We started earlier, but I know that we were often just in the way. I can remember how much I liked the smell of wood. When I was much younger, I would wait for my dad to come home for dinner and upon seeing him, I would run to him and bury my face in his striped bib overalls. They always smelled like fresh pine. I still liked the wood and its smell when I was loading it years later. I also look back at how nice it was to come home good hungry, good dirty, and good tired. The late 1950s is the time setting for my story. Not every day was one of the good old days.

All of the lumber was brought to the yard from the railroad cars by the dray line. Tom Toulouse was the owner and operator of the Oklee Dray-line service. He was born at the turn of the century. By the time I was old enough to be of help, he had been at it for many years. He was a critical part of Oklee, a burgeoning town of over 500 people. He graded the alleys and many of the streets. He hauled away the garbage. He graveled the streets. During the shearing season, he hauled all the wool to the tracks to be shipped east. He dug the basements for the new houses coming up on Oklee. I do not know what else he did, but what I do know is that he was the one and only Steve-a-dor for Oklee Lumber. His two big Belgian mares would pull the loaded drays over to the lumberyard and haul the empty ones back. Many of the kids in town would run alongside and sometimes catch a free ride.

I became a very close friend to these big horses. While I was about 12 years old, they were in their early twenties. They had been diligent workers longer than I had been alive—big, strong, powerful, honest, and noble animals. I liked everything about them, including their smell. Kit and Nel were some no-nonsense horses that took their work very seriously, a curiosity for a 12-year-old boy.

As I remember it, Kit was on the left and Nel on the right. Nel was the slightly older and bigger of the two. Still, I remember that they were close in both age and size. All of Oklee Lumber's bulk trade articles had to be delivered by the dray-line. Local cattle trucking companies were starting to pick up backhaul items after unloading at the Fargo and St. Paul stockyards, but the great bulk of our needs were supplied by rail—all of our lumber, all of our cement, and all of our sheetrock. Redi-mix cement was not around at the time, so we got many carloads of Portland cement. I was a skinny 12 year old and barely outweighed the 94-pound bags.

Needless to say, I spent a lot of time with Kit and Nel. I liked them very much. They would not respond to commands from my youthful voice, but were always nice to me. I used to rub their muzzles and tell them little stories. I remember that sometimes they would suddenly jerk their heads up and look at me. I couldn't even get away with a fib to them. Even though they were serious about their work, one of them would sometimes give me a good push with their massive head. I would go flying away and come back to the guilty party. I'd get this look from her big eyes as if she was saying, "Sorry, didn't see you there. You know, blinders and all." I remember thinking I could see a small telltale smirk along her muzzle. They weighed around 2,200 pounds each. Somehow, I understood this to be the equal of two horsepower. Nonsense. We all know these two gals could drag a 300 horsepower car backwards while it was spinning. I still do not understand this.

Then the day arrived when I had to grow up way too much, way too fast. It was a hot day in July. Tom reined Kit and Nel up into the inlet of the driveway with a big load of Portland cement. Something he had done and I had witnessed many times, but when they were just past my dad's office window, my eyes froze on Nel. What my brain registered I did not know. Something on a primal level told me that Nel was having trouble. Instinctively, I looked at her intently. Her hide began to ripple all the way down both of her flanks as though she was covered with flies, but she wasn't. Though I was concerned, there still was very little that seemed obviously wrong with her. Then it started. She raised up slightly as all four of her legs came up towards her belly. Her front legs were so tightly bent at the knees that they were into her stomach. Her teeth stuck out well past her lips. She dropped to the earth on her side and started convulsing. I was thinking, "Oh God, please make this stop." God stopped it. Her legs became still and slowly relaxed their way back to their full length. Now I prayed, "Please God make it start up again.

But it didn't. Maybe she will just shake

that big head and stand up? I knew better. This was bad. I looked up to Tom sitting on the trailer. He would know what was going on. Tom stepped down to the wagon pole and walked around to the side of Nel. He knelt down beside her. He patted her shoulder and rubbed her cheek. He lifted his head looking away and I could see tears on his cheek. "She's gone."

I replied, "What? No way. What is going on?" Tom unhooked her harness. He then unhooked Kit from the eveners and walked her up in front of her old friend, then backed her up, hooked her up to Nel, and Kit then pulled Nel off her harness. Just like that, she was without her work clothes. I was still working on what in the world was going on.

The next thing I know, she is being hoisted up on the back of a wrecker truck. She was drug across the street and with the winch and hauled up off the ground by the first crossbar of the water tower. That's right, she was butchered and washed up right on top of the city's water supply. I think this was years before global warming.

I was to become one of the butchers. Easy with the hide; it could bring as much as four or five dollars. As they cut the red meat away from this noble beast, I was given a knife and told to begin cleaning all the tripe. Tripe is very high in protein. I sliced open foot after foot of intestine and washed it up. Meanwhile, many tubs were being filled with dark red meat. This is wonderful mink food. It will serve to put a shine on their fur so that the high society ladies will pay a little extra for such a glistening fur coat. I'm sure they would rather not know where the shine actually comes from.

So that's it. I was standing among many tubs of meat and tripe, a good-sized pile of the folded hide, and just behind me the heavy skeletal framework already being eyed already by many of Oklee's dogs. I like dogs, too, but this is not the time. It is all over in less than two hours. There was no text to go with the lesson. Maybe that's why I was having such a hard time comprehending it. Tom looked at us and said, "That's all we can do. I'll take what's left of her on my next trip to the dump." I just couldn't get this worked out. I was raised to believe that when we die our spirit or soul is released and rises to heaven. Well, Nel most definitely had lots of spirit and a giant soul, but it seemed to me at the time that this all happened so fast that they might both have landed in the tubs with the meat. I guess I was supposed to save my grieving for when there was enough time.

Tom kept the dray-line going. He had to use his old pickup for a while and this really proved to show me the true value of horses. In the heat, Tom would have to open the door, slide behind the wheel, turn the key, depress the starter button, step on the clutch, put the transmission in gear, release the clutch, and press on the gas pedal just to move the pickup a few feet. Then the process was repeated in reverse. All this to move the loaded dray a few feet so it wouldn't be such hard work to unload it. With Kit and Nel in harness, the same task was accomplished by walking up to the dray, grabbing the reins, saying, "Kit, Nel, giddup a little bit," followed by, "Whoa." In not too long, Tom found a replacement to work beside Kit. They seemed to get along just fine. The dray-line stayed in business until 1971 or '72. It was not until 1974 that Oklee Lumber got its first forklift. That will always be the most dramatic change to ever happen for me at Oklee Lumber. No, not the computer, just plain old simple hydraulics.

This is one of my memories that is truly indelible. It is etched in my brain and will be with me as long as I live. Where exactly do these old film reels go after you die, I do not know. I still don't even get the two horsepower thing! What I do know is that I had to grow up a lot that day.

As for Oklee Lumber, it is still going. After my mother and father ran it, I took over. My two boys both worked there as soon as they were old enough. Now since 2004, my son runs it. And guess what? His oldest daughter is working there, too.

A Hardworking Girl Doing a Boy's Jobs
By Dorthy Hartel of McIntosh, Minnesota
Born 1941

On June 19, 1941, I was born. I weighed almost 11 pounds, very fat. I was the third girl and three were yet to come later.

My dad was not happy when another girl was born. He really wanted a son, so I became his "boy." I helped with the chores. At the age

Dorothy Hartel and her calf in 1969

of seven, Dad got me started to milk the cows. Since I had taken the jobs that a boy should do, I got strong and Dad was good to me. If a little pig got stepped on and hurt, Dad would give the pig to me to help recover. Sometimes it would be a dog, calf, or cat—whatever needed help.

I started school at the age of seven. There was a country school that had a woodstove, but the cold wind and snow took over. My dad had a van and he took us to school and unloaded kids on the way home. In the spring, we sat on the sunny side of the school where I learned to read from an older boy.

Conveniences were non-existent. We had an outhouse behind the house. An Alden's Catalog was used for toilet paper. In the summer, the leaves on the tree would do.

One summer day, a cow came home alone. I could see she had given birth. When the cow saw me, she started walking up a hill and into the woods. She would stop and look back to see if I was following her. I followed her into the woods. She stopped and I saw a very tiny calf between logs of wood. I picked the calf up and carried her all the way home. I may have been eight years old at the time. The calf was so very tiny. I kept her warm and tried to give her milk. She did at last suck on my finger and soon drank from a nipple pail. The calf got to be around 600 pounds. I sold her and Dad let me keep the money.

I also had a pet pig. His name was Sam. When called, he would come running, roll over on his side, and wanted his belly scratched.

One very sad day, Sam was on the loose and he ran to the barn because the milkman came to take our milk in a big milk truck. The milkman didn't know Sam was under the truck and neither did I. Well, Sam wasn't being careful and he got run over by the large truck. I cried for days!

Working with my dad husking corn and other chores helped at threshing time, so I quit school altogether in the ninth grade. This hardworking girl had no time for school. I did get my GED and missed one question (about cooking). I don't look back and wish for anything missing. Besides working on the farm, I worked in a grocery store, two different banks, and worked as a nurse in a nursing home for 13 years. I have two children and two grandchildren. Life is good.

The Old Church Across the Road
By Scott Cameron of Kent, England
Formerly of Red Lake Falls, Minnesota
Born 1964

I found a color photograph recently from 1969 featuring my older brothers and I trying to teach my younger brother Kevin how to ride a bicycle. His cheeks are flush red but he has a big smile on his face with us holding the bike upright on what appears to be a very crisp autumn day. In the background, I can see an old church across the road.

Staring at the photo, a flood of memories came rushing back to me of the old church with its white paint peeling from rotting wood siding and panes of glass from its arched windows broken from rocks slung from mischievous neighborhood kids. Closing my eyes, I could easily visualize the overgrown lilacs clambering the walls to nearly the roofline and the tall cement steps leading to the padlocked wooden entrance doors.

How did the old church end up in such a state and for goodness sake what was its name again? Finding the answer to those questions should have been a relatively easy process. Uncovering the name of the old church across the road was not too difficult based on local knowledge and with the assistance of the Red Lake County Recorder Joyce Paquin.

As older residents will remember, the church was none other than the former St. John's Lutheran Church that merged with the congregation of Immanuel Lutheran Church in 1957, resulting in the building of the new St. John's Lutheran Church on the Southside completed in December of 1958.

More compelling research was needed to answer the question as to how and why the old St. John's Lutheran Church came to be in such a state and how countless other churches, including St. Mary's Church on the Northside in the early 1950s and more recently St. Anthony's Church of Padua in Terrebonne met a similar fate.

Few things in life are capable of grabbing your emotions like watching an old church being demolished. The image shared on social media of the crossed spire of St. Anthony's being lowered to the ground from its rooftop perch late last autumn is one that will stay with me for a long time.

Similarly, the haunting memories of the old church across the road from my childhood home are surely matched by residents who remember St. Mary's Catholic Church on the Northside and its closure in 1952 and subsequent demolition.

Before my visit to the County Recorder's Office, I visited with an old family friend and a former member of St. Mary's who has been a long-time member of St. Joseph's. We discussed his recollections of St. Mary's and St. Joseph's and their combination in 1952. The conversation started with me trying to find out the identity of the old church across the road in the photograph, which I had incorrectly assumed was St. Mary's rather than St. John's.

The former member shared with me an old photo of Father Henry Pelger, St. Mary's pastor for 29 years until his retirement in 1951, with his dog Jack at his side. In the end, we drove together down Seventh Street N.E. on the Northside to try to more precisely locate where St. Mary's and St. John's had been situated. According to the former member, the area had changed significantly as most of the houses aligning the street and adjoining roads did not exist at the time the church buildings of St. Mary's and St. John's were in use.

We first drove by the lot where he pointed out the "old Lutheran" church was located. This was along Seventh Street NE just before Marshall Avenue NE and right across the road from where my house had been. Where St. John's old church once stood is now a vacant lot with a small playground. He then drove to the end of the street and described to me, as I imagined, the white clad church of St. Mary's in its heyday, with its tall steeple adorned with a cross.

St. Mary's was originally established in 1883 when it separated from St. Joseph's which was predominantly of French Catholic origin. The congregation of the church consisted of a significant percentage of German immigrants although the congregation included many other European immigrants as well. As the former member recalled, Father Pelger would kid about St. Mary's being the "Catholic" church in town as opposed to the "French" church (St. Joseph's) on the other side of town.

Here it is worth noting that St. Mary's Church could not have been located at a more beautiful and scenic location. A painting from the 1880s published in A History of Red Lake County (1976) shows the view from "Kretzschmar Avenue," a vantage point above the clay cliffs looking across the Clearwater River at Red Lake Falls, as it existed at that time. Today, the cliffs of the Clearwater River have claimed substantial land from the Kretzschmar Addition on the Northside.

St. Joseph's was founded in 1879 by Father Pierre Champagne although its origins go back to the first French-Canadian immigrants to arrive in and around what would become Red Lake Falls. By the turn of the century, St. Joseph's had a thriving congregation supported by the continued growth of the town through immigration and, in particular, the increase in the number of Catholic immigrants in the area.

The winds of change, however, were sweeping across America. The industrial revolution progressively moved the population from the countryside to urban areas between 1860 and 1950 according to US census data. In addition, new immigration from Europe from the 1920s onward was greatly reduced, shutting off the spigot that fed the small towns across rural America with new inhabitants. Immigration was halted by a series of federal laws, culminating in the Immigration Act of 1924. Such laws established a restrictive quota system designed to preserve the homogeneity of American society and restrict immigration, in particular, from southern and eastern European countries.

The trend towards a more homogenous and less multi-cultural society also had an impact. This was reflected in attempts to "Americanize" immigrant populations quickly as opposed to preserving national language and faith customs as long as possible. According to an article published by a professor in the Department of Religion at Duke University, the consequence of this philosophy was to discourage the preservation of ethnic religious congregation across America.

By 1950, the Diocese had determined, for a variety of reasons, to merge together the congregations of St. Mary's and St. Joseph's. On March 1, 1952, the combination officially took place with Father William Keefe, who had succeeded Father Pelger as the pastor of St. Mary's in 1951, taking over as the pastor of the combined congregations. At that point, the old St. Mary's church building on the Northside became redundant and was deconstructed shortly thereafter.

The old St. John's Lutheran Church building on the Northside was originally built in 1904 shortly after a group of Lutheran families created a congregation separate from St. Immanuel's Lutheran Church in Wylie Township. The church building was deemed too small when the congregations of St. John's and St. Immanuel's determined to merge in 1957 under the name St. John's and to relocate to the Southside. The result was, once again, an empty old wooden church on the Northside, awaiting deconstruction.

Red Lake County, like most of America, has been struggling with the changing demographics of America and the spiritual needs of its residents. The former members of congregations such as St. Anthony's (Terrebonne), St. Dorothy's (Dorothy) and St. Vincent de Paul (Plummer), among others, can certainly attest to that phenomenon.

As it turns out, the old church across the road was inextricably linked to my childhood home. In fact, my parents purchased the land we built our home on from a couple who had purchased it a few years previously from St. John's. Thanks to the County Recorder, I now know that the lots where our house was situated in the Kretzschmar Addition were in fact part of the land originally owned by St. John's prior to its move to the Southside.

I don't recall whether my brother Kevin ever did learn to ride the bike that day in 1969. He was still very young and from the photo, I can see his feet barely reached the pedals. Nevertheless, my search to identify the old church in that photo turned out to lead down a circuitous path leading back to my own doorstep.

Winning a Camera for Selling Seeds
By Shirley Gillan of Sauk Centre, Minnesota
Born 1925

When I was young, I lived on a farm eight miles north of Osakis, Minnesota, with Pa and Ma and three brothers. We went to country school District #57 until eighth grade.

When we had a snowstorm during the day, Pa would come to get us home in the bobsled and team of horses. There were no tractors, snowmobiles, or computers or phones that took pictures and talked to you, or TVs.

We had horses, pigs, chickens, and a wall phone with a ringer by hand, two shorts and one long ring, and a dog named Buster.

I liked riding horseback, and one year in the 1930s I read on a cereal box if you sold so many packages of seeds, you could win a camera. So I went for it. I rode my favorite horse, Polly, all over the neighborhood. There was still snow on the ground, and I sold seeds to all the neighbors and succeeded to win a camera.

When I started high school, it was the first

Shirley's Pa and Ma in 1957

year that school buses started picking up kids from the country. We were called hayseeds by the town kids.

When I was a senior in Osakis High, Pa had an auction sale and sold out of the farm. He had a beautiful pair of black horses that were hard for him to part with.

We moved to Osakis in an apartment above the Review Office. Then pa bought the pool hall and a house by the lake. He ran the pool hall for years and then his son ran it with him.

Shirley and Harry riding Polly

Pa and Ma bought the only rooming house in town from McNaun. After Pa died in 1959, Ma ran it till she died in 2000. She lived to be 100 years old. A grandson has the rooming house now. I hear it has been condemned.

After our 50th class reunion from Osakis High, we got together every year with the help of Ron and Bob until 2014, which was our 72nd reunion. We all turned 90 years old, so we decided not to have any more planned reunions.

The Blizzard with a Present
By Thomas Huebsch of Lake Elmo,
Minnesota
Born 1949

We called it the St. Patrick's Day Blizzard of 1965. My father and mother were building our home on the prairie about a mile south of Perham, Minnesota, off Highway 78. Highway 10 was only a single lane paved road going through downtown, and it did not exist as it currently skirts south of Perham. There was not a tree around us, only a soil-bank flatland, where the tumbleweeds of North Dakota tumbled across carelessly with the constant northwesterly winds. But, this was March, when winter winds turned falling snow into whiteout conditions, and snowdrifts grew as high as the fences and any structures that lay in their paths, similar to the dustbowls of the 1930s.

My mom and dad, my six brothers, and two sisters lived in the basement of our new, yellow house, while dad and some of us older boys helped him finish the upstairs with the framing, sheetrock, woodwork, and cabinets. My father owned "Huebsch Woodcraft," a cabinet shop on the north side of the railroad tracks in Perham, and then located across from the Perham Railroad Depot, and currently where Tuffy's Pet Foods is now sited. Dad was very good at his cabinetry work, so to build our family house was characteristic of him.

As the snow settled over the prairie, and the winds began to blow the day and night before Wednesday, March 17th, it wasn't long before a full-fledged blizzard began to bury us. Mom called Dad to come home early from the shop that afternoon as the storm revved up. She said, "If you want to get the car in the garage you better leave now." Perham schools had already closed and the busses struggled in straggling fashion as they finished their student deliveries.

Dad took Mom's advice that afternoon and drove his Chevy car home. The snow drifted and blinded, but he made it. As he closed the garage door, he said, "Let it snow." He thought he would now have a few extra hours to work on the house. That was a good plan, but with one miscalculation. Dad was a thirty year, two Pall Mall pack-a-day smoker! When the snowstorm began, he only had a few cigarettes left.

Next morning, St. Patrick's Day, all roads were blocked. There was absolutely no plows, cars, or trucks to be seen on Highway 78. Not even the milk trucks could pick up the milk cans from the farmers. On some farms, every container available was used to store milk, and word was that one farmer innovatively filled his bathtub with milk. Our driveway was entirely plugged with blown, packed snow. Dad wasn't driving anywhere.

By mid-morning and after a frantic search through his dresser drawers, jackets, and coveralls pockets, there was not a cigarette to be found in the house. Since driving was not an option, and in full onslaught of a nicotine fit, Dad told Mom that, he was going to walk to Perham to buy some cigarettes. Mom laid the law down, "No, you're not." For sure the whiteout conditions would blind him and he would be lost, and Mom was not about to be a single mom with nine kids living in the basement in an unfinished house.

So, Dad went back upstairs to sweep up all the cigarette butts that he had flicked on the unfinished plywood floors. He figured he would peel away the cigarette paper and collect the remaining tobacco from the butts for enough to roll a few cigarettes. However, the day before the snowstorm began; my mother and one of my younger brothers had swept all the rooms of the upstairs, and burned all the debris in the outdoor garbage burn barrel. In 1965, we could still burn our trash outdoors. Not a cigarette butt was to be found. But, not to be foiled, Dad had yet one more idea.

Just less than three months before, I had given Dad a cellophane wrapped, "Heap Big Smoke," about 1 ¼-inch diameter, ten-inch long (like a jumbo bratwurst) cigar as a Christmas present. What was I thinking? Back then, it was not a wrong doing for me, at 15 years old, to walk into a filling station and buy a pack of cigarettes for Dad, or purchase a cigar at a drug store as a Christmas present. It was all I could afford. Dad smugly dug into the top drawer of his dresser to snare the stogy, then seized a kitchen knife, where on the end of the kitchen table, he cut off one-fourth chunk of that brown, tubular foliage. He smoked it, and didn't say a word.

Two days later, on the fourth day, the snowstorm subsided; and Dad was near panic exasperation. After breakfast, every shovel we had was employed. First, we had to dig the snow away from the garage door in order to open it. We did not have a tractor or snowblower (a what?), so Mom, Dad, and all of us older boys were outside pushing and heaving the snow off the nearly 150 foot driveway. The snowdrift that crossed the east side of the house and garage had to be tunneled through. On the west side of the garage, the snow had drifted as high as the roof. It was a surreal scene to see our dog on the roof of the house peering and sniffing curiously into the furnace chimney smoke. Mom warned us, as we stood atop the drift, not to touch the highline wire that was strung from the electric pole to the house.

Most all morning we shoveled. Dad continuously rammed and slammed the Chevy through our car wide, shoveled path, spinning tires as we pushed and shoveled snow. By late morning the snowplow had come by to clear a lane on the highway, but as snowplows do, we now had a hard packed three foot wave of chunky, iced snow spread over ten feet wide at the end of the driveway. We shoveled and shoveled some more. Finally, with tires whizzing ferociously and all of us pushing, Dad backed the car through onto the road. Oh, what an exhausted relief that was to my mother, brothers, and me. Dad finally could get to town and get his cigarettes.

As my mother, brothers, and I walked back to the house, we watched Dad, as speedily as a snow-veneered road would allow, head north to Perham. He drove a long block, then stopped. I remember mom uttering, "Oh no, what's the matter now?" Dad's car stayed still as the exhaust spewed into the cold air. We waited. Then, very slowly, Dad backed up the Chevy on the highway and stopped at the end of our driveway. A few more minutes passed and we continued to fear car trouble, a lost wallet, or an unknown worst, as we gawked out the windows. Finally, Dad opened the door of the car and slowly, with head humbled, walked the length of the driveway and came into the house. We were all silent. He was silent. Then, he quietly spoke, "Well, if I can make it this long, I guess I don't need them anymore."

From that time forward, Dad never smoked another cigarette. And, he has told all my six brothers and me, "If you fellows ever want to smoke, I'll cut you off a chunk of that cigar, and if you can smoke it in front of me, I'll never say a word to you about smoking." My father is still alive at 95. Both my parents live at Perham Living Nursing Home. None of my brothers nor I smoke. I have three-fourths of that cigar in my top dresser drawer at home today; and my wife, two sons, and daughter do not smoke. Truly, we were all blessed with an unexpected, priceless present in that 1965 St. Patrick's Day Blizzard.

Parade of the Pachyderms
By Frances Paul Prussner of Park Rapids, Minnesota
Born 1930

The date was sometime around 1935, when I was only five years old, and the Barnum and Bailey Circus was coming to Bemidji, Minnesota. That was exciting news, but what made it especially exciting was that the whole assembly of performers, from clowns to elephants, was arriving at the Great Northern Depot, which was directly south of our home on Minnesota Avenue, and which had to pass our home to get to the county fairgrounds way out at the other end of town.

Brother Kenny and I were up early, gulping down our usual breakfast of oatmeal, toast, jam, and mugs of hot Ovaltine, a chocolate drink for children laced with all the vitamins needed by growing children. "You can't go out to play until you eat your breakfast," was Mama's mantra as long as we lived at home.

Parade of the Pachyderms in the 1930s

As soon as we had filled our bellies and gone to the bathroom to brush our teeth and heard the first sounds of the parade coming, Kenny and I bounded out the door and took our places on the curb in front of our house. Soon, all the children on both sides of the street followed suit, and we called back and forth in excited voices about what we were about to see.

First, there was the sound of the train pulling into the station, then the squeaks and squeals of the circus wagons carrying all the circus paraphernalia being unloaded. Clowns in bright colors and funny hats accompanied the procession, gaily dancing and summersaulting down the streets while throwing cellophane covered candy to the children along the way. And then there was a band in brightly colored uniforms playing the familiar circus music that stirred our hearts.

My favorite attraction was the string of massive elephants slowly plodding along the way. It was a glorious, unforgettable moment that resonates every time I hear that famous music by French composer, Camille Saint-Saens called "Carnival of the Animals," especially when the elephants are depicted.

When all that excitement was subdued, one of our older siblings would escort us out to the fairgrounds to once more see those wonderful beasts perform their dances to the familiar parade of music of the day. It wasn't until I was older that I grieved for those huge beasts being forced into unnatural positions, such as bowing, by a man with a long spiked rod who prodded them on.

The Captain Midnight Radio Series
By Duane Lysne of Perham, Minnesota
Born 1935

The Captain Midnight radio show was a five day a week adventure series for youth beginning in October 1938. The main thrust of the show was aviation and characters who were involved with aviation. The first shows were a radio program based in Kansas City. They were broadcast in this region only. These programs were sponsored by the Skelly Oil Company and promoted gasoline and other automobile products aimed at the children's parents. Later, in 1940, the program became so popular that it was taken over by the Mutual Broadcasting Network and was sponsored by The Wander Company of Chicago, which made a chocolate flavored drink called Ovaltine.

The main "friendly" character of the show was Captain Midnight who was described as a daring pilot in World War I that had won recognition for himself by penetrating deep into enemy territory to complete a mission against 100 to 1 odds. His real name was Jim "Red" Albright, but when he returned from the daring mission exactly at the stroke of midnight, he became known as Captain Midnight. His primary assistant was Chuck Ramsey, another aviator with exceptional flying skills. During the Kelly years, there was a female character named Patsy Donovan. Later, during the Ovaltine years, she was replaced by Joyce Ryan. Their roles were to attract female listeners. There were several other lesser characters who didn't appear in each episode.

The primary "enemy" character was a ruthless and evil man named Ivan Shark. He could be identified by his familiar but sinister laugh, which he used whenever he was pleased with his evil plans and even more so when he thought he had outwitted Captain Midnight. He had a daughter named "Fury" who was just as ruthless and diabolical as her father was. Shark also had a henchman named "Gardo" whose job was to carry out Shark's evil schemes. Gardo was a bumbling fool who often mismanaged Shark's orders, which infuriated Shark to no end. Finally, there was "Fang," an oriental servant of Ivan Shark's who was ever present in a nearby room ready to heed his master's call that was always signaled by a single gong.

The show was fifteen minutes in length and centered around the evil plotting of Ivan Shark and his notorious gang. Captain Midnight and his crew were constantly kept busy trying to disrupt the efforts of Shark and his evil regimes. Although the show often referred to the killing or hurting of people, not one person, either friendly or enemy, was actually killed as part of the show. Shows usually ended with a person, again either friendly or enemy, in dire peril with no hope of escape only to show up on the next day's episode safe and sound.

Due to the fact that the country was involved in World War II during these years, the program lended itself to much of the national news, which also was by way of a radio broadcast. Security and secrecy were paramount in those days and thus were reflected in the show's format as well. This is where the Captain Midnight "decoders" became significant. During the show, almost all messages were encrypted using a special decoder called a "Code-O-Graph." This had a fair amount of intrigue to young listeners who listened, intently trying to determine what was in these messages. In an effort to involve listeners, coded messages were sometimes given at the end of the show, often a clue of the next day's adventure. Of course, the listener would have to own one of these decoders in order to decode the message. It could be ordered by simply sending in an Ovaltine wrapper and "one thin dime" to the Wander Company of Chicago. After an eternity of three or four weeks, a brown envelope arrived in the mail. Inside was the decoder, a secret squadron manual, and a "letter to Mom." In the letter, Mom was praised because she valued the virtues of good health and suggested that if she thought anything at all about her son or daughter she would surely go back to the grocery store and buy more Ovaltine. Such was the power of advertising in the forties.

These decoders were the most fascinating part of this radio series to most young listeners. They were nothing more than a circular dial riveted to a metal plate similar to a badge. It had numbers around the outside of the dial and letters on the face of the decoder itself. One would turn the dial to the "master" code setting and then match letters from the code numbers. It was very intriguing for a young boy or girl to listen to the descriptions of the new decoders. And, even more so, to actually decode the messages at the end of each episode. There were other novelties connected with some of the decoders such as mirrors, secret compartments, magnifying glasses, etc. And of course each came with a manual to show how they worked. Some of the early decoders had a pin on the back so the owner could wear it like a badge. And, of course, all came with a certificate making the owner a member of the "Secret Squadron."

It was common procedure for the decoder to "fall into enemy hands" during the show. Captain Midnight and his crew would now have to begin designing a new decoder inasmuch as the old one had been compromised. Of course, this meant that listeners should start bugging Mom for more Ovaltine because it was time to order a new decoder. This happened seven times during the Ovaltine years of the radio series. There were decoders for the years 1941 through 1949 with the exception of 1943 and 1944. Due to the shortage of war materials, decoders were not made during these years. In 1950, a television series was started and ran for five or six years. Two more decoders were introduced during those years prior to the end of the series. During the final episode, Ivan Shark was apparently dropped onto the frozen Artic ice and was eaten by a polar bear. However, if the series were to start up again tomorrow the episode would surely start out with his diabolical laugh and he would be bragging about how he was able to distract the bear long enough for him to escape.

There was a large number of non-decoder type premiums offered by the Ovaltine Company during these years as well. Some came about through the radio programs and some were offered in the manual accompanying the decoder. Some were even advertised in newspaper ads. Many had wartime connotations such as service medals, secret compartment rings, detector scopes and a host of other novelties meant to be attractive to young listeners.

Many of these decoders and premiums are now being auctioned on eBay for rather large sums of money. I have seen a "Mystic Aztec Sun God Ring" purchased on eBay in 1999 for nearly $2000. Of course, this ring had a red plastic "ruby" that slid off to reveal a hollow secret compartment. The problem (and the reason it is so rare) was that the ruby slid off rather easily and soon became lost. Hence, if a person reading this article should happen to discover a Mystic Aztec Sun God Ring among their childhood possessions and the little red ruby is still intact, one may be in for a pleasant windfall.

The Little Pig of Eagle Lake
By Dave Fastenow of Hot Springs, Arkansas
Born 1950

It was 4:30 in the afternoon when I suggested we have fish for supper. Of course, that meant I had to go catch a fish, as our "fresh fish is best" rule is we only keep fish that we will eat that night; everything else is catch and release. So Hercules, my trusty fish-licking black lab mix, and I set out to fish. When we got to the boat, I noticed a trumpeter swan out on the water, so I texted my wife, Jackie Jo, to come down and see it. We watched it until it flew away. Now I had only one hour to catch supper!

We hadn't gone but 200 yards when I had a good bite, but it hit just shy of the hook. I was hungry and not patient enough before I reacted, so I missed him. We went 50 minutes with no luck except one small northern. I determined it was too small to feed the three of us (Jackie Jo, Hercules, and me), so Hercules took a lick and we let him go. We were heading back slowly to our dock when Jackie Jo texted she was watching not only our loon family but an otter frolicking out from our dock. By the time we got there two minutes later, the otter was gone. I told Jackie Jo that we were going to fish out to where I had the first bite and back. And if I didn't catch anything, we would have to resort to Plan B, which to Jackie Jo meant going out.

We went 200 yards and started turning around when I had a nibble. I gave it some line and then set the hook. I had him this time! After a good fight, the fish finally tired out. I netted him and Hercules licked him. It was a nice 2 ½ pound northern pike. That would feed us tonight! One of our favorite dinners is grilled northern filets (coated with a little olive oil, seasoned with garlic powder, pepper, a little salt, and a dash of hot Mrs. Dash, and tossed on a hot bar-b-q grill) with some fresh grilled asparagus and a glass of white wine.

David Fastenow with his dog, Hercules in 2015

I decided to weigh the fish and to my surprise my 2 ½ pound northern weighed in at 3 pounds. That really puzzled me, how it could weigh more than what it was. But nevertheless, Hercules and I took him up the hill to my fileting station. As my knife started going down the backbone, something was in the way. There was a strange bulge in the fish's abdomen. On investigation, it was a walleye – a whole walleye, over 8 inches long! Heaven only knows how he got inside the northern, but the mystery of why my 2 ½ pound northern weighed 3 pounds was solved: the walleye provided the difference in weight!

And if it wasn't for that northern being a little pig and wanting dessert too, we wouldn't have had our fresh fish dinner!

Stump Sock Mittens
By Keith H. Winger of Bemidji, Minnesota
Born 1949

My father was a World War II veteran who fought in the Philippines. He was wounded in combat, sent to an Army Hospital for recovery, and then back into combat after his wounds healed. A short time later, he lost his right leg to enemy fire. He told me how he had been sitting with a buddy when they called his name, stating he had mail. As he stood up, an incoming shell took his leg and killed his friend. He said a letter from his sister saved his life.

What does this have to do with mittens? Well, I'll get there.

After his recovery, Dad was fitted with a prosthesis, which consisted of a hard leather foot, hard fiber lower leg, steel knee hinges, and leather from his knee to hip. Over his stump, he wore a thick wool sock, which was provided by the United States Veteran's Service. It is difficult to find any good from war, getting shot up and losing a limb, but sometimes if you look you can find a silver lining. First of all, I remember Dad said when he lost his leg, his first thought was, "They have to send me home now, and I am going home alive!" That was the first good thing.

Now, on to the mittens. After the war, Dad married, had three children, and made a beautiful home for us on Balm Lake in Northern, Minnesota. He built a small resort, worked as an auto mechanic, and spent many winters logging. Winters in Northern Minnesota are cold. Many days in the woods, it was 20, 30, or 40 degrees below zero. Work continued regardless of the temperature.

Money was scarce and logging was cold and hard on gloves and mittens. Mother was inspired to sew a pair of mittens from old stump socks for Dad. The socks were heavy, dense wool that would wear out at the knee first, leaving the upper sock in very good condition. She patterned the mittens from a chopper-type mitten with elastic sewn across the back to keep the snow out. Dad said they were the best mittens he ever had. They kept his hands warm and dry all day. That was the beginning of Mother's mitten business.

She soon was sewing mittens for Dad's cousin Edwin and neighbor Ingvald who worked in the woods with Dad. Next, she was sewing mittens for my sister Sheila and me. We attended a country school and our recess was always spent sledding on the big hill in our schoolyard. At the time, there were 50-60 students in eight grades. All of our neighbors were in the same boat financially— not wealthy. Soon Mom was sewing mittens for our cousins. There were plenty of cousins; we were related to about half the kids in the community. Soon, Mom had mitten patterns of many sizes and was sewing mittens for lots of people in our community. To add something special to her mittens, Mother would sometimes sew a colored piece of felt on the back in the shape of a heart or Christmas tree or put some decorative trim on the mittens. The mittens became popular at school and several parents contacted Mom to see if she could sew mittens for their children.

One time close to Christmas, Mom made several pairs of mittens for a large family in our community that was quite poor. She left them anonymously at their mailbox. I'm sure they knew where they came from, but nothing was ever said. Another time she made a pair for an old bachelor who lived near us. Dad delivered them and I remember old George making a special trip to our house to thank Mother personally. He did so with tears of gratitude in his eyes.

The Veteran's Administration kept Dad with a good supply of stump socks, not knowing they were also keeping many fingers warm! I expect many kids and adults who grew up in the Debs, Minnesota community in the '50s and '60s still remember those warm wool mittens that were better than any you could buy in a store.

I wonder if anyone ever thought of the price Dad paid for those mittens? Dad passed away in 1976 and that ended Mom's stump sock mitten business. She never charged anyone for the mittens. It was Mom and Dad's contribution to all our friends and neighbors.

Delores's sister with the pet raccoon in 1935

Our Pet Raccoon
By Delores M. Richter of Evansville, Minnesota
Born 1923

In 1933 or 1934, our family had a pet raccoon. We lived on a farm, and our hired man lived one mile away in town. One morning when he came out, he was carrying a cornflakes box, and inside was a newborn baby raccoon, left by his mother. He was scared and so were we five children, as he hissed and wanted to scratch and bite us. My mother made a bowl of milk with bread and scraps.

He soon learned we would not hurt him. We named him Mickey, and he grew rapidly and allowed us to pick him up, and he also played with our dog. When he was very small, he would climb a tree close to our house. Grandma was afraid he would fall, so she would stand below the tree and spread her long apron, but the little guy never fell.

By summer, he seemed to be full grown. When we picked him up, he would put his front legs around our neck and back legs around our waist. When we would walk to the mailbox or garden, he always went along. Sometimes when my father would drive to town, he would put Mickey in the car, and when he came out of the store he would see people looking at Mickey in the car, and they were so surprised to see a raccoon there.

In the fall, he disappeared, and my brother found him at the end of a long tunnel in a straw stack. The tunnel had a bed Mickey had made near the end where he was protected from the rain, wind, or snow. Twice during the winter, we heard a commotion on the back screened in porch. We found Mickey looking for something to eat. We had no electricity, so my mother used shelves on the porch as her refrigerator. Mickey could open the screen door by using his claws on his front feet. We would pet him, feed him, and then he would leave.

In the spring, he was gone. We guessed he either found a mate or the neighbor's dog got him. I remember Mickey after all these years, as I am now 92 years old. He was a wonderful pet, and we all enjoyed him, even Grandma.

I *Am* and *Was* Blessed
By Darlene Leonard of Wadena, Minnesota
Born 1932

My paternal grandparents emigrated from Sweden to the Red River Valley in Minnesota to homestead land in Clay County. They passed away when my dad was nine (mother – scarlet fever) and seventeen (father – heart trouble). Dad's brother died in the trenches in France in World War I. This left Pa, as we called him, to do the farming. He married Ma, a neighbor girl whose parents were also immigrants. I was born at home in Spring Prairie Township, Clay County, on August 15, 1932. When the doctor got back to town, he registered my birth.

The Great Depression was just winding down. Pa lost the farm, so the following spring my family (Pa, Ma, my two older sisters, my brother, and I) moved to Aldrich Township 1, Section 18, Building site 3, (1-18-3) in Wadena County. Ma drove the Model A Ford with us kids. Pa drove the team of horses on a wagon with our possessions. Our dog would not ride on the wagon with Pa. He ran and walked the 90 miles to our new home, a 120-acre farm. When he got there, the pads on his feet were worn off. He died shortly thereafter.

The driveway was long, a half mile off County Road #161, on the west side of the farm. Half of the farm was covered with trees; how different from the flat Red River Valley skyline. A house, barn, woodshed, chicken coop, granary, and outhouse constituted the buildings. There were no electric power lines. A well with a hand pump was between the house and the barn. The northeast corner of the farm went down to the Leaf River. Here was the ford where the ox carts laden with wheat from the Hubbard Prairie crossed the river to get to the Verndale Grist Mill, which was located near the dam on the river. To the north, east, and south were neighboring farms.

Soon we had milk cows, chickens, and a large garden. Sometimes we'd have a flock of turkeys or geese, and occasionally a pig was raised for meat. Wild berries, vegetables, and meat were canned. Canning was done in a boiler, which held 21-quart jars. A wood burning cook stove heated the water to boiling. Depending on what was being canned, it had to boil for an hour or more. We had no pressure canner and of course, home freezers weren't available yet. Anyway, we didn't have electricity.

Prices for farm produce were low. Farm income had to be supplemented somehow. So Pa worked for the City Dray

Darlene's grandparents, George and Phoebe (Gage) Johnson

171

in Verndale. He delivered coal, bottled milk, and ice to private homes, did repair work in Stang's Garage, and did other odd jobs. Ma did a lot to help the financial situation. She sewed our clothes, baked bread, churned butter, helped milk the cows (done by hand), raised chickens for meat, eggs, and extra money, canned a lot of our food, and tended a large garden and strawberry patch. Each of us kids, when old enough, did our share of these jobs. I remember when Pa got his first tractor. It was a steel-wheeled Fordson. I thought it was so noisy compared to a team of horses.

Darlene Leonard, the teacher with her students at School District #15 in Wadena County

It was 2 ½ miles to Verndale to the church, school, newspaper office, grocery store, gas station, restaurant, garage, a grain elevator, and some homes.

In the early '30s, Verndale Public School needed some improvements. Works Progress Admiration (started during FDR's presidency) workers supplied some of the labor. Pa and our team of horses worked there at one time. They were paid in "commodities," usually foodstuffs, which was standard at that time.

When I started first grade in 1938 there was no school bus. We walked all the time. In the winter when the river was frozen over, we would cut across the field, the river, and the woods to Highway 10 and then east to Verndale. In warm weather we would walk east through the cow pasture, across the Mill Dam Bridge, and up the hill to County Road 23, then south into town to school.

In the water near the bridge lay the mill wheel from the gristmill (1880-1912) that once stood on the hill above the dam. The wheat grown in the surrounding areas was hauled to the mill to be ground into flour. The flour went by rail to Minneapolis. Some years later the mill wheel was pulled out and hauled off for scrap iron.

The day the Armistice Storm of 1940 started, Pa wouldn't let my brother and me go to school, but my two older sisters could. They didn't get home that night. Somehow my parents found out they were staying overnight at the owners of the newspaper, *The Verndale Sun*.

Life on the farm was pleasant. We had a lot of family time. Pa played his violin, Ma the piano, and we girls played chords on the guitar. We sang a lot. We and the neighbors took turns having house parties. The neighbors brought an accordion and a banjo. On Saturday night the living room furniture was pushed aside, the linoleum rolled up, and we sang and danced. We usually also had a lunch. We learned to dance when we were four or five years old.

We didn't have electricity until I was about 13 years old. Kerosene lamps and a gas lantern gave us light. The chimneys on the lamps needed to be cleaned regularly, as they smoked up a lot. Also the wicks had to be trimmed so the flame would burn evenly. The mantle of the gas lantern was very fragile, so care had to be taken when filling the lantern or pumping up the pressure.

All the water was pumped by hand. There was a crock for drinking water with a dipper. We all used the same dipper when taking a drink. The crock stood on a washstand. Beside it was a wash dish for washing hands and faces. There was a reservoir on the side of the cook stove, which held heated water for various uses. A teakettle on the stove provided hot water too. Washtubs of melted snow supplied soft water in the winter. In the summer the rain barrel caught soft water.

Saturday night was bath night. The little ones were first. We got our baths beside the front room heater in the winter. In the summer we sometimes went down to the river to bathe.

On washdays Ma used a clothes washer that had a long lever handle to push and pull back and forth which agitated the dolly. There was a wringer turned by hand on the washer to wring the clothes into the rinse tub. She used a "wash stick" to pick up the cloths out of the hot water. A similar wringer clamped onto the rinse tub to wring out the clothes to be hung out to dry. Sometimes two rinses were done. This meant the winger had to be moved to the second rinse tub. The clothes were hung out on the clothesline. This was done until it was so cold the clothes froze – sometimes they froze dry. Otherwise we had a clothes bar. It was a wooden structure about five or six feet high with twelve or so bars to hang the clothes over. It folded up when not in use. Ma made the laundry soap. Lye and some sort of tallow or lard was mixed together to make a rather harsh cleaning agent.

Our house was heated with wood. We had a parlor or front room heater and a cook stove. Getting up wood for winter was quite a job! Pa used a crosscut saw, a Swede saw, and an ax. Sometimes neighbors would team together to get it done. Also, a crosscut saw required two people to cut wood. When I was seven or eight it was my job to go to the brush pile and get a basket of kindling wood for starting fires. In later years, once in a while coal was bought to supplement wood. In the summer we sometimes used a two-burner kerosene stove to cook on, as the cook stove made the kitchen so hot. There was a register in the ceiling of the living room to allow heat to rise to the bedrooms upstairs. The chimney went through one of the bedrooms for heat. Footstones were heated, then wrapped in cloths and taken to bed with us to keep our feet warm in bed.

With no electricity, we had no refrigerator. We had an icebox. It looked like a refrigerator on the outside, having two doors. The top compartment held a block of ice about 18 x 18 x 12 inches. The cold temperature of the ice cooled the lower compartment, which had three or four shelves on which to store food. The water from the melting ice ran down a tube to a tray underneath the box. This tray had to be emptied whenever it got full. The ice had been cut in blocks from the river in the winter. The blocks were kept frozen by packing them in sawdust for insulation and storing them in an icehouse – in our case, the woodshed. In the summer when the ice was all gone, to cool the milk and anything else that needed cooling, it was put in a gallon syrup pail or a metal cream cooling can and lowered down into the well housing on a rope. The temperature would be about 55 or so degrees there.

We moved several different times during my school days, but were always in the Verndale School District. I really liked school days. School was my "thing." Outside the classes of the curriculum, I was involved in many activities: class plays, chorus, cheerleading, speech contests, triple trio, library helper, annual staff, yearbook editor, hot lunch program worker, class secretary, and class treasurer.

I graduated from VHS in 1950 as one of the honor students. I wanted to go to college, but my parents couldn't afford that. There were no scholarships available at that time. But the State Department of Education in St. Paul was offering a one year low cost program called Normal Teacher Training. Upon completing

Darlene Thompson with her high school sweetheart, Les Leonard in 1948

this program I received a Limited Elementary Teaching Certificate, which allowed me to teach grades one through eight in the rural unincorporated school districts of Minnesota. This license had to be renewed every two years by getting eight college credits from any state college. I started teaching in a two room rural school, grades five through eight.

I also got married in 1951 to my high school sweetheart whom I'd met as a sophomore. He was a dairy farmer. My life on the farm was still a good life: pleasant, busy teaching, being a farm wife, and over the years, raising four children.

I taught school and my husband farmed. Things went well for us. We rented a farm for two years and then bought a farm and more land. We had electricity but no indoor plumbing. After several years we built on to have a pressure pump system, a septic tank, and a bathroom. No more chamber pot or outhouse! As years went by other improvements were made. The farms are now operated by our son and a grandson.

After 61 years of marriage cancer took my husband from me. I stayed on the farm a year after that but then decided to buy a house in town. Of course, I have a garden and a large lawn here. My granddaughter and her family have the home place building site. She is a teacher. She had said as a young girl that she wanted to be a teacher like Grandma.

Now at 84 years old, I look back over the years and know that I *am* and *was* blessed.

A Story of a Little Boy in Euclid
By Robert Weiland of East Grand Forks, Minnesota
Born 1947

Once there was a little boy who grew up in the town of Euclid, Minnesota, and these are his stories. Euclid is a small town of about 82 on a good day, including the cats and dogs. Despite growing up in a small town, the size of the families was not such. His dad was from a family of eight and his mom was from a family of fourteen, so this led to many people attending a family reunion once a year.

He was a little boy who would walk to his two-room schoolhouse each day. One room for grades 1-4 and the other for grades 5-6. He would go home for lunch every day to have a sandwich on his mom's homemade bread, which to this day is his favorite food and makes his mouth water just talking about it. A close second was her homemade caramel rolls. On a rare occasion, there would be toast dipped in thick cream, sprinkled with salt when his dad would bring home a pint of fresh, thick cream from the dairy farmer down the road.

The town of Euclid back then consisted of three churches, a general store, the Legion Dance Hall, two gas stations, a bar called the Windy Corner, Weiland Maintenance Garage (which his dad owned), and the post office where his mom worked for 20 years. The post office was attached to what was once a bank, which they now called home. That where most of these memories are made.

As a little boy, he remembers many trips to the general store. He was known to walk right past the tempting bubble gum, and much like this day, head straight for the nuts and bolts section of the store. While working on occasion in the garage with his dad, he heard stories such as how they had to walk a mile and a half to school, and after the 6th grade, he had to quit school to work on the family farm. When they got the chance to ride horse, it was with no saddle, so he thought to himself, "Well, things are not so tough after all."

Growing up was never easy, especially in the winter, with the outhouse a little ways from the warm comforts of home back then. The black and white pages of the Montgomery Ward and Sears catalogs were little comfort to the cold bottoms when they would wipe. These were known to be far better than the color catalog pages.

The end of the week brought a routine all of its own, with bath night on Saturday and church on Sunday morning. On Saturday night, they would fill a portable metal tub and take turns bathing in the same water, of which he was number three of the four, with his dad being last. When he was younger, the tub was roomy and playful, but as time went on, he had to become more limber relax while taking his bath. Sunday morning it was off to church early, and it paid off one day when he told his mom his head hurt, and she asked him where, he stated, "On my our father."

When not in school, he would play

Cowboys and Indians with the other kids in the neighborhood. On a good day, they would go water skiing or sledding in the culverts that were full of water or snow for a real adrenalin rush. The trips to the big town of Crookston, Minnesota were few and far between, but everyone was always relieved to make it when they would ride with "Hawk Eye Marv." He was known for his hawk eye judgement with reading a low fuel tank that had once again proved to be accurate. Some of the evenings were spent collecting empty beer bottles for a two-cent return after a big dance the night before at the Legion, or they would go out hunting for stripped gopher tails, which would bring them five cents a tail.

During the fall and winter, a time for deer hunting, the Weiland team of 18 would band together to walk the woods that were so big some of the deer themselves would die of old age before they found their way out. They walked through brush, over rocks, and around trees until they found their meat for the winter. Once winter weather settled in, they would take the icehouse that his dad made from scratch up to the lake and go dark house fishing. This was like looking into a goldfish bowl below the ice.

His dad was handy in many ways, especially when it came to building and fixing things up. He was known to hold his wooden screwdriver up to the motor to help diagnose the ticks. He also built a homemade snow cat from a car motor and stretched out tractor tires, which proved to be a powerhouse when his son tried it out.

One day going down Main Street, after a double dog dare, he peeled out and burnt rubber the whole way. This drew a crowd from the Windy Corner Bar that came out to see what was going on. Although the salami and bologna you could get from the bar were smoked in a difference sense, all the cigarette smoke made the meats taste and smell like the butts themselves, which made the memories last forever.

The Legion was the place for many dances. Despite all the loud music and partying, when word spread that someone "had the trunk up," it cleared out like wildfire and everyone was outside for refreshments.

He grew up and joined the U.S. Army out of high school, where he met his wife from St. Louis, Missouri. Her brother, his army buddy, introduced them. They were pen pals for two years before they would later marry. Together they bought their rings from Rocks Jewelers in Crookston, with S & H Green Stamp Rewards. This led to making memories of their own.

Fifi and the Girdle
By Alice Bergeron of Owatonna, Minnesota
Born 1930

It was the early 1960s. We were living near Oklee, Minnesota. I was sorting laundry in the bathroom when the doorbell rang. The caller was an insurance agent who had made an appointment with me earlier to discuss a policy.

He and I stood in the dining area, which had a hard surface floor covering. I did not offer him a chair at the table.

We had a small poodle, Fifi, who was part of the family, or at least she thought so. Fifi was probably a bit jealous, because I usually picked her up. When I didn't, she disappeared momentarily and went into the bathroom where I had been sorting laundry and where dirty clothes were spread all over the floor.

Lo and behold, she came back out to join the salesman and me with, would you believe, my girdle! As many of you from that era may remember, pantyhose had not been on the market as yet, at least not in our part of the country. Our nylon stockings were held up by a garter belt or a girdle with garters, usually a total of four. However, I had been fortunate enough to find a girdle with not only four garters, but SIX; two in front, two in back, and one on each side. I had purchased this garment knowing I would never again find another like it with such powerhouse support. So when necessary, I even patched it.

Fifi was persistent in getting my attention. She positioned herself between me and the salesman, still with the girdle in her mouth, vigorously shaking it. I was embarrassed by the dog's method of getting attention. All six garters were banging against the hard surfaced floor. I knew it was the girdle, and I wouldn't be surprised if the salesman knew it, too. Fifi kept right on slamming the girdle and growling.

Fifi

I tried to get the girdle from Fifi's mouth. This was a challenge for her, and a tug-of-war began. She held on to one end and started backing up and growling. I finally got it away from her and, instead of putting it in a secure place out of her reach; I stepped into the living room and stuffed it between the cushion and armrest of our Naugahyde recliner. I shoved it down as far as possible, all the while trying to keep the conversation going with the salesman.

I thought I had outwitted the dog and could continue with the salesman and his attempt to sell me some insurance. But then I heard a scratching sound and growling coming from the living room. Here came the dog, carrying her trophy. Again, a tug-of-war ensued, and I finally got it from her. In my frustration, I opened the door closest to me, the broom closet, and threw it in. Of course, the dog started scratching on that door.

At this point, the salesman knew it was hopeless trying to convince me to buy a policy. He left, and I'm sure he had a smile on his face.

As the Story Goes Around Here
By Richard Allen Julseth of Brandon, Minnesota
Born 1942

Yes, I find my life with many journeys and mysteries in it, along with many stories.

First of all, I was born to parents who truly loved one another, and I was taken away from them because of World War II in which my father served in Europe and my mother worked in a hospital on the West Coast during the war. And I was dropped off as a baby at my grandparents' to be raised till I was about five years old, till my parents were released from war duties.

The day I started country school I couldn't speak any English, only Norwegian, because that's what my grandparents spoke. So I had to learn how to speak English at five years old. Also, I walked home from school each school day at about a mile. My parents took me to school in the mornings to make sure I got there. Due to consolidation of the country schools I went to a town school, where I was taken to school in the mornings and walked home, about two and a half miles. This went on till halfway through the third grade. Then I switched to another town school where I rode the school bus to and from school each day, which I thought was great. My favorite subject in school was history, and my favorite thing I liked to do in school was to run the school's movie projector. I would show noon

Richard with his mother in 1942

Richard with his Grandma Julseth and Grandpa Julseth

hour movies during the winter months in the gym. I was also asked to run the school projector for after school community events at times.

As the story goes, I grew up on a farm, which turned out to be a dairy farm with cows and stock and chickens. We had no running water in the house to start with so carried water from a water pump and put it on the stove for hot water for washing up for day was an order. The chamber pot and the outhouse were the waste stations of the day.

To start with, my father had a team of horses he got from Grandpa, but soon they were replaced with a tractor and plow he also got from Grandpa. Milking cows by hand was a chore I learned a little about, but my favorite job on the farm as a very young child was to feed the chickens and pick the eggs. Mother took care of the candling the eggs for to sell. The grocery man in town bought the eggs.

My father would haul either milk or cream to town almost every day, and on clothes washing day Father would drop off the milk at the creamery and drain off about two eight gallon milk cans of boiling hot water off the boiler that run the can washer and bring it home and put it in Mother's clothes washer and washing clothes was started. Hanging clothes on the clothesline was the way the clothes got dry. In the summer time, we tried to keep the dust down around here so as not to get too much dust in the clean clothes. In the winter, we hung the washed clothes on drying racks in the living room in the house.

We kept the house warm with a coal wood stove to start with but later changed to an oil-burning stove with an outside tank of oil. My younger brother and I slept on floor mats next to the stove till we finally got a bed to sleep in upstairs in the house. Every evening my younger brother would bring up a glass of water and put it by his bed and in the morning it would be froze to ice, and he would be mad. Ha! Didn't say anything about the frost on the bedpost. Ha!

I got to be blessed with three younger brothers and sisters.

We got running water in the barn before we got running water in the house. The cows had drinking cups to drink out of, and we carried feed to the cows in the barn during the winter. We got enough water pressure out of the water pump to put water up in a water tank in the hay barn so gravity pressure was used.

My father took very good care of the cattle and stock around here. When I turned thirteen or fourteen years old, my father got me out of bed at 0345 in the morning to help him milk the cows with a milking machine at 0400 hours

Richard and his father in 1945

starting time, and when the milking was done, Father went off to drive a school bus and my younger brother would feed the cows silage and Mother and I would clean the barn with a wheelbarrow and fork and shovel and feed all the young stock and calves. All before going to school in the mornings. I got on the school bus about 7:00 a.m. On Sunday morning, it was the same routine, because we had to go to church and Sunday school. Over the years we averaged around 50 to 70 head of cattle or stock per year. The most stock we ever had was about 150 head, many feeders and young stock. We always milked around 20 head of milk cows, less in the summer. I spent a lot of time taking naps in school during fourth hour study hall.

When my first sister was born into our family, Mother was going to walk off the place if running water was not installed in the house, so a bathroom was built onto it and a drain field was laid out. A hot water heater was installed. We also got our first black and white TV, a Zenith, and were blessed with one channel to watch. We also got a new kitchen stove for cooking and baking.

My younger brothers and I found our first baby sister a real novelty around here. After she got out of diapers we would take her with us wherever we went. We gave her so much attention she thought she was a queen. Ha!

For entertainment around here in the summer we would take out our rifles and go gopher hunting in the pastureland and along road ditches. Also in the hot summer time some of us boys in the community would get on our bicycles and ride down to our private swimming hole and without bathing suits on take a little dip to cool off. As the story goes, one time two car loads of girls showed up with their mothers driving the cars at our very private swimming hole, and the girls of various sizes and ages didn't have any bathing suits on either, and the frolicking began with great excitement, gaiety, and laughter. Everybody got really checked out at that meet. Ha! There was even more excitement when the girls started to run off with our street clothes, so us boys chased the girls around in the nearby woods with more laughter from the mothers watching the action. This was in the days before modesty and swimming suits were invented. Ha! One mother commented that she had never seen kids have so much fun without their clothes on. Ha!

In the fall between different farming operations, we would take our shotguns down and go pheasant hunting, and we had a lot of them birds to shoot, and they were good to eat. In the winter, I would take down my rifle and put on my skis and go rabbit hunting. We had a lot of rabbits at that time.

This is a mystery that happened to me while out hunting rabbits one very dark, overcast afternoon. I came upon a circular object about 40 feet through the center and about 8 feet thick, like a saucer. It sat up off the ground on four legs and had a ladder that came down to the ground from the center of the thing. The ladder was like a staircase, and it looked like short steps. All of a sudden the ladder went up into the object like a hatch, and I heard locking sounds, and the object lifted off the ground with no sound of any kind. While it was lifting off the ground I saw the landing pods being pulled into the object, and I got a tingling sensation all over my body, which lasted about a minute or so. I was about 13 years old at the time and suffered no after effects. I never told anybody.

When I turned 16 years old, my neighbor came over and talked to my father about taking me with him south to go custom combining. So I went with my neighbor south to Oklahoma, where we started cutting wheat for a very large farmer, and when we got done with him we moved up to the state of Kansas, where we combined more wheat for different farmers. When we were in Kansas my neighbor boss got sick from the grain dust running the combine, so I had to learn how to run the combine at 16 years old on a Kansas wheat field. My boss drove the grain truck to town with loads of wheat. When we got done combining in Kansas, we moved up to western Nebraska, where we combined more wheat. When we got done there we went home, for I had to get ready for school.

I graduated from high school at 17 years old and stayed on the family farm till I was 18 years old, when I joined the US Navy. That's another chapter in my life.

Over the years, I learned to believe in a hidden power or force, and Jesus Christ, and UFOs.

This brief is between the years of 1945 to 1960.

So You Took Those Eggs!
By Roger H. Majesk of Freeport, Minnesota

I well remember driving west on I-94, heading home from Northeast Minneapolis that fall evening more than 20 years ago, I kept thinking, is that really possible—after 80 years—can't be, well maybe, just maybe!

To shed a little light on the subject, I was thinking about my two elderly aunts, whose house in Northeast Minneapolis, (or as Katherine, would say nordeast!) I had left from earlier that evening. Now both of these gals, although getting up there in age, were still sharp as a whip. Celia was the eldest at 93, and Katherine, or (Auntie Katy) as we called her, was six years younger at 87.

Memory, or in my case, the lack there of, was the topic for thought that evening as I was driving down the freeway. It's kind of reassuring to hear that a lot of people, my age, and also younger, occasionally have a short term memory lapse, such as, walking into the garage, and then standing there, not being able to remember what one came there for, been there, done that! Long-term memory I find quite amazing. Personally, I don't remember a lot about my early childhood, but the one event that I can vividly recall is the afternoon, as a young boy back on the farm with my Daisy bb gun.

There was this rooster, (a big rooster) that just happened to be in the wrong place at the wrong time, now, I surely didn't mean to hurt him, but I just had to see how close I could get to his head without hitting him. (Anyone that has ever owned a bb gun knows that you can see the bb fly) Well, he must have done something terribly wrong, head probably went up when it should have went down, or zigged when he should have zagged, regardless of the cause, the result left one big rooster flopping like a crappie on the ice. If my mother would have happened to glance out the kitchen window about then, she would have seen one very frightened eight-year-old heading for the woods on a dead run, rooster in one hand, shovel in the other. The mystery of the missing rooster remained a secret throughout my childhood, only God and I knew about it, and neither one of us was talking. Now that was over 50 years ago, but my aunts, 80 years.

Roger's Aunt Celia in 1993

A little bit about these two sisters, Katherine was a very intelligent, but also a very outspoken, headstrong, red haired spitfire of a lady. She never had any problem telling anyone, anywhere, anytime, exactly what she thought, and believe me, she didn't stutter while doing it either. More than once as I was waiting, not so patiently for her to finish her grocery shopping, I would observe someone accidently bump into her. If they didn't say, "Excuse me" Katy would stare at them until they made eye contact, then she would say, "WELL, EXCUSE ME!" as she was burning a hole through them with those piercing eyes. Oh yes, Auntie Katy was a very spunky gal, but a very thoughtful and honest person also. She would spend countless hours at nursing homes in her area, visiting people that she didn't even know. As she said, "Wanted to make darn sure that they were being taken care of." Honesty, whenever I would ask her a question she didn't feel the need to answer, such as. About teenagers growing up in her era, where they went, or what they did for excitement, I always got the same answer. "Ask me no questions, I will tell you no lies!" Well, I didn't get much information on that subject, but I didn't get any lies either.

Now Ceil, on the other hand, was much more laid back. Not the argumentative type, she was a tall slender lady with beautiful silver grey hair that she always kept in a bun on the back of her head. Although also very bright, whenever it would come to a confrontation with her younger sister, she would say, "Let her talk, in one ear, out the other!" The one thing that the two of them definitely did have in common though, were there memories, both long term, which is quite common with the elderly, but also short term, which seems to erode with age. I can surely attest to that.

So, getting back to the story, I had just returned from McDonalds, (burgers and fries had become somewhat of a Thursday night ritual with the two aunts) this meal was much the same as most, Auntie Katy did most of the talking, while Ceil busied herself with the meal at hand. Although listening intently, at times nodding in agreement, or adding a bit of pertinent info to the story that Katherine might have missed, also occasionally rolling her eyes when her younger sister would say something that she didn't quite agree with. This particular session, Katherine started reminiscing about their childhood days on the farm. This was a popular topic, and I loved hearing their stories, as much as they loved telling them. There was no shortage of laughter on those occasions and that was for sure. This Thursday evening auntie Katy started talking about how, from time to time, unknown by anyone else in the family; she would sneak around the farm, and pilfer one egg from each nest that she found. After a few days, when she had a dozen eggs, she would take them to the little general store in St Wendel, a tiny town about a mile from the farm, and trade them in for candy. Well, on this particular day, "while on an egg hunting mission" Katherine explained, "I found a paper bag, covered with straw, hidden under some old boards. Inside the bag were six eggs! I knew darn well this was no work of the hens. Had to be one of my four brothers or three sisters that were up to the same thing as me, so I took their eggs too." Katherine exclaims, laughing with pride, at the recollection of foiling the plot of one of her siblings. Now Ceil, who had been quietly eating, although apparently listening intently, abruptly looked up from her burger, and with a look of total surprise, exclaimed with as loud a voice as I have ever heard come out of her mouth, "SO YOU TOOK THOSE EGGS!"

Those two aunts have long passed away, along with their two sisters, and four brothers, one of them being my dad. From time to time, I still think about that evening. Eighty years! That's how long it would have taken for the case of the missing eggs to be solved, is that really possible? Could it be that after close to a century the mystery of the missing eggs was finally solved?

The Heaven Sent Buck
By Mic and Deborah "Blanche" Buschette of
Detroit Lakes, Minnesota
Born 1954

My Father, Ray Buschette, started hunting deer in 1953, the year I was born. His family was growing and he needed extra food for the table. He had 11 children; I am fifth in line. My dad hunted with his family. Most of them farmed and they also had large families.

Mic, Blanche, and Ray

In those days, the bigger the deer, the more meat; trophies weren't the priority. Deer was the only thing he hunted; he was too busy working several jobs to hunt anything else.

As his family grew up, we continued the family tradition of hunting together. Our hunting style was deer drives. We rarely sat in stands and we hunted on the prairie. My Dad was considered a "crack shot." He usually posted, and being from the depression era, he didn't waste bullets. In later years, he told us he had probably shot over 120 deer in his life…and he was never one to exaggerate.

In early 2000, my brothers and I built him a permanent stand. It is a beauty, with slider windows, propane heat, safe stairs, and handrails. He was in his mid-seventies then and he hunted until he was 87. During those years, we all took turns sitting with him and posting with him, precious time spent for all of us. In 2012 when he was 87, he shot his last deer, a spike buck. He was forced to quit after that, due to his failing eyesight, but he still went with us. He sat with his sons, his grandkids, his daughter in law, and his nephews in that stand.

With the passing of our mother in July after 68 years of marriage, he was feeling blue and giving up, wanting "to be with her." A week before deer hunting opened; I asked him if he wanted to spend an afternoon in his deer stand for old time sake. He said yes, and dug out his old hunting coat, his lunch box, and his two thermoses. He even asked if he should bring his gun!

On Veterans Day this year, my wife and I picked him up and headed "Up North" to Norman County and his stand. We talked about deer hunting and the old times on the ride up, he was excited.

We got settled in the stand around 2:30 PM. We didn't see anything but a rooster pheasant until about 4:45. I then told Dad, "You better wake Mom up from her nap and have her send us one over." He smiled, chuckled, and said, "OK."

A very short time later, I heard a rifle shot from my wife's direction. After grabbing the binoculars, I saw a very nice buck heading our way. He was just walking. Turns out, he was hit by my wife, but still very much alive. I waited for a good shot and he fell. I left Dad in the stand and went down to the buck. By that time, my wife came over with the truck. She had loaded Dad and brought him into the field. All three of us were so excited. We had this buck on camera and had seen him before. He was the buck we had wanted to harvest. Mom had indeed "sent us one over."

We called for help to load him and several of the young men in our group came running. We took lots of pictures and then went to the "shop" where we hang our deer. The word was out and most of our hunting party showed up to admire the deer and say hi to Dad. We measured him and he green scored 156.5. My mother had indeed "sent a GOOD one over." My Dad enjoyed seeing everyone so much and loved being a part of something he had so many years ago created for us. It was a very special night for all of us.

As we headed for home, we again talked about deer hunting and how Mom had "sent us one over." When we got home, we ate a pheasant dinner and I put him to bed. He was still excited, but tired. I spent the night with him and sometime during the night, he joined his wife, my mother. He had passed away peacefully in his sleep, with a loving smile on his face.

What a way to end a life well lived, with family and doing something he loved.

My Bemidji, Minnesota Memories
By Tina Siems of Bemidji, Minnesota
Born 1957

The Hi-2 Drive-in Theatre owned by Bud and Gloria Woodard was open. Dad and Mom would get us dressed in our pajamas and go to the drive-in. We would pull into our spot, hang the speaker on the edge of the window, and turn up the volume. They were wise to the fact that we would fall asleep before the movie was over. That was such a fun time! My brothers talked about going to the drive-in and they would have a couple kids in the trunk because they didn't have enough money to get everyone in. I remember the old tractor that would come along during the movie to spray for mosquitoes. That was a very special time in the summer.

The old National Guard Armory was located at the waterfront next to Paul and Babe the blue ox. On Friday nights, we were able to roller skate there. We danced on our roller skates to old 45 records being spun on the turntable. Later in the evening, the fellas would play basketball on roller skates. Oh, what fun it was to watch! We would also go over to the waterfront rides. We rode the Tilt-a-Whirl, Ferris wheel, and swings, just to name a few, on our roller skates. There was a time when they tore the old National Guard Armory down because the building interfered with vehicles being able to see the "one and only stoplight" as the drivers rounded the corner. Therefore, that was a very sad day, ending the fun of roller-skating.

Back when I was a child in the 1960s, we would drive down Irvine Avenue, and over the old "Vi-docks." They were made of wood planking. Travelling over them, as they would shake made me feel like we were going to fall through. That was when there were many trains travelled through Bemidji. On the way home, we would go down Irvine Avenue, passing by the outdoor skating rink located on Sixth Street where Northland Apartments is located today. It made it very special to see the rink light up at night and the Lord's touch of falling snow as they skated to music. Oh, so

Ed Mickalko manager of roller skating at the National Guard Armory in 1977

Tina's house covered in snow

romantic!

My brothers would bundle up in the wintertime as they went out to walk their paper route to earn a little spending money. They delivered the *Star Tribune* newspaper. We even had delivered to our house the "Oakgrove" dairy products by Karsten "Kart" Verke. Kart was a very kind and special man who loved to share his stories. My Mom didn't drive a vehicle, so it helped out a great deal for it to be delivered to our house.

My most favorite time of year was around Christmastime when the streets were draped across with evergreen garland with a beautiful wreath in the middle as they were all lit up. These decorations encompassed from Second to Sixth Street and Beltrami Avenue. To top it off was when it would snow on the garland and wreath; that to me was God's touch. That was when J. C. Penney, Woolworth's, Ken K. Thompson Jewelers, Ben Franklin, The Corner Drug Store, Omara's, S & L Clothing, Patterson's, the Burger House, and the Chief Theatre would all be decorated. Just before Christmas, there would be a very long line of people lined up outside the Chief Theatre to see the special movie for all the children to see. Afterward, Santa Claus would hand out a little paper bag of treats with popcorn balls, candy canes and peanuts in the shell. Carolers would be singing Christmas carols on the streets too! The carolers would be dressed in floor-length, red or green velvet dresses with velvet hats to match and white fluffy mufflers to keep their hands warm. The Salvation Army Church would be ringing their bells along with their collection buckets on the street corners. That certainly was the most special time of year! That meant parents sacrificing to be able to give their children a present or two under the Christmas tree. Churches even helped out families in need. I was about ten years old when a pastor came by our house with presents. When I opened my present, it was a rabbit-fur earmuffs and a silver, coin-like plastic piggy bank, which I still have today. I will never forget that time because it meant so much to my family and me.

Although it was a time of destitution for some people, they did what they could with what they had. Our family of five kids and both parents lived in a two-bedroom house. We kids slept upstairs where there was a single and full-size bed. The oldest brother slept in the single bed while the rest of us slept horizontal in the full-size bed. My family referred to it as "we slept all lined up like cord wood." That way we were able to keep each other warm. To think there were even bigger families than that! In the mid to late '60s, my dad built an addition onto our house, which consisted of an "indoor" bathroom, girls' bedroom, and a big kitchen/dining room. It was so nice to have more room. In the wintertime, we used to bank the snow all the way up to the windowsills to help insulate the house.

The Flood of '89
By Maynard Embretson of Wahpeton, North Dakota
Born 1946

In a flash, "It's here, and coming fast."
Taking things that couldn't last!
Its destructive path, its rolling force,
Slashing waters, making its own course.
Volunteers came, even men in green,
To battle the Red, ugly and mean!
Working together, without rest,
From 9 to 90, people at their best!
Strange faces, working hand in hand,
Fighting the clock with bags of sand!
Sweat and tears rolled down those faces,
Placing dams in all those places!
People sandbagging on the line,
Fighting Mother Nature and Father Time!

The river crested, people cried in cheer,
The river, "Now," has no fear.
New faces among the crowd,
The ages of 9-90 standing proud.
They are the heroes against
Mother Nature and Father Time
And they save the town in the flood of '89.

The Wicked Wild Washing Machine
By Doris Selzler of Bemidji, Minnesota
Born 1933

My mother-in-law, Kathryn, had 13 children and that meant a lot of things to wash.

She was a heavily built lady with large "boobies" (breasts). One day when she was washing, she got too close to the wringer and her boobies got caught. She shouted for help and one of the children came to press the release button on the wringer.

She was a terror with her machine. It seemed like they were fighting each other. It seemed like one thing after another would happen to her, not the least of which was when her arm got caught and the result was a very bruised appendage.

The family teased her for years, and sad to say, I was guilty myself. My payback came one day when I was washing clothes and my mind was somewhere else. As I bent over to put a piece of clothing into the wringer, my long hair wrapped around the wringer. Boy did I scream for help! Luckily, my sister-in-law was sleeping upstairs. When she heard my cries for help, she came running to me, and helped me unwind my hair from the wringer by reversing the direction of the roller. It was painful and embarrassing, but my hair came out intact.

Needless to say, I became much more humble about teasing my mother-in-law. I wish I hadn't been so quick to laugh at her situation. It is said that what goes around comes around, and I found that out the hard way.

The second lesson I learned was that I never washed clothes again with my wicked, wild washing machine unless someone was at home, and even then, I was very careful to pay attention to what I was doing.

The Armistice Day Blizzard
By Alexander Kovach of Akeley, Minnesota
Born 1934

November 11, 1940, the Armistice Day Blizzard (it's called Veteran's Day now) was one of the worst blizzards on record in Minnesota. We had school that day. The morning started out as a beautiful day but around noon, it started snowing. In a very short time, it turned into a blizzard.

School closed early and the buses arrived to take the kids home, except the bus I rode with six or more students aboard. Our bus driver was a farmer and we were told he was late because he had to finish a chore. Needless to say, by the time he did arrive, the blizzard had worsened. From the beginning, the going was hard. The visibility was very bad and the drifts were already getting big in some places. With just a few of us left on the bus and only about a mile from home, the bus got stuck. He had to turn off County road 33 to turn on County road 49 (the road we lived on) which started out as an incline.

We had no choice but to walk to my dad's farm. At just 6 years old, I was the youngest of the bus and was poorly clothed. We were very poor and our parents couldn't afford good winter clothing for the children.

I can recall our bus driver was a very large man. Being small for my age, the bus driver placed me under his coat and had the other kids follow him, taking some of their hands, and he walked the mile to our farm.

Fortunately, we made it. Back in those days there was no such thing as cell phones, and most farms never even had a telephone. I suppose the other parents worried and called the sheriff. After the blizzard, the sheriff found the bus and the other kids and the driver.

Memories of Flag Island
By David McKeever of Warroad, Minnesota
Born 1923

In 1922, my parents came from Belfast, Northern Ireland, to Minnesota to make their new home on Flag Island, Minnesota, on Lake of the Woods. They had two boys, George, age 7, and Joe, age 9. I was born there in 1923.

There was a grade school on Flag Island

(in Lake of the Woods County) at the time, but the county decided to change the location of the school to Oak Island because they had more kids. It was about 3 ½ miles away from Flag, with water between.

I was seven years old when I started school, and my brother, George, took me to school. Sometimes, we went by boat, and when there was ice on the water, we went by horse and sleigh. There are a couple of weeks in the fall before the water in the lake freezes over enough to travel on. This is called "freeze up time." There are also a couple of weeks in the spring before the ice melts. This is called "break up time." Sometimes it was hard to be on the lake during these times. One time, the ice was so bad that the pony pulling the sleigh fell through seven times. We had a couple of men riding with us and we were all able to help pull the pony out of the lake each time.

During one of the spring break ups, I had to stay with a family who had two boys, on Oak Island. One weekend, the boys and I decided we were going for a hike in the woods to look around the island. We went to the Bay Store, the only store on Oak Island, to buy something for lunch. We bought some cans of sardines, and some sugar cookies. We put the sardines between the cookies to make sardine sandwiches. Then, we used the sardine cans to dip water from the lake to drink. This was a special treat for us.

Our school was 45 miles by water to the nearest town. We had to have five kids to get a teacher. There were 6-9 kids most years. The teacher stayed with a family on Oak who had an extra room. There were no men teachers. The teacher had to be a single woman, and if she got married, she could not teach anymore. The families on the island were good to them. Everyone tried to invite the teachers to their homes. That was always a special time.

The teacher had to take care of the schoolhouse. There was a woodstove for heating the building. She made the fire each morning and had to see that there was water in the schoolroom. There were no wells, and we always used water from the lake for school, and home. The school kids had to carry water from the lake. For drinking, we had one bucket and one dipper. Each kid drank from the same dipper, and then put it back in the bucket for the next kid.

I went to Oak Island School from the time I was seven years old through the 8th grade. In the spring of each year, it was always special when the Lake of the Woods County Board and the Superintendent would come to our school to check on how we were doing.

Older Brothers
By Marie Marte of Browerville, Minnesota
Born 1942

Hi, my name is Marie Marte. I was born in Bertha, Minnesota on September 25, 1942. My father was Raymond N. Koppes, Sr. My mother was Clara (Etzler) Koppes.

I was the last of six children. I had five brothers. They watched over me like a hawk. I never had to worry when I went to the local dance hall called BINKS. They were there if I needed protection. I wouldn't trade them for the anything in the whole wide world.

My mother died from pneumonia when I was eight. My oldest brother Raymond Jr. was in the Army stationed in Korea. Brother Lawrence was married and lived in Michigan. Gerald and Harold, the twins, and youngest brother Richard were all at home yet. Brother Gerald did a lot of cooking before Mom died, so he kept his job. Harold did a lot of the ironing especially the white shirts that was worn for Sunday mass. I followed my brother Richard all around the farm asking him "why Mom had to die." He kept telling me he didn't know and he shouted, "I don't know why, stop

Marie and Richard with their pet raccoons

asking."

Being we lived on a farm, we had cats, dogs, and two pet raccoons. We fed them, held them and they came when we called them.

I remember them curling their paws around the porch door bottom and coming into the kitchen where my mother was canning blue plums. She caught them with their paws in the jars trying to pull out some plums. Needless to say, she chased them out of the kitchen and locked the porch door. They eventually grew up and stop coming to the house.

We were the only kids in the neighborhood that had pet raccoons. We sure did enjoy them.

Northwestern Minnesota
By Tim Gust of Los Angeles, California
Born 1939

Growing up during post World War II was a wonderful advantage for me; as compared with my six older siblings who were born before my birthday in 1939. My younger brother, Philip, and I grew up in a different situation compared to the "older six." After enduring the Depression, my parents were finally able to have some little money to buy things. We slowly progressed from using horses for farming to having a tractor. A threshing machine was eventually replaced with a combine. Labor saving machines came along, but I recall milking cows by hand from age 8 until age 18.

At age six, we finally got electricity on our farm and we were actually able to plug in the refrigerator that we initially used as an icebox! And what an unbelievable experience to pull a string and have a light come on! We no longer needed the kerosene lamps in the house and the kerosene lanterns in the barn. We eventually got a water pump powered by electricity; no more hard work pumping at the well for those thirsty cows.

Our farm was located 6 miles north, 4 miles east and ½ mile north of East Grand Forks, Minnesota (EGF). Like many of our neighbors, our small farm (160 acres) included 300 chickens, 6 to 8 milking cows and a couple of pigs that gave their life for our nourishment. Butchering a cow each winter and keeping the cut up meat in the freezer/locker at Sweet Clover Dairy made it possible for us to have good and sufficient food even if we had little spending money. With a productive garden throughout the summer and my Mother canning vegetables and fruits, we always ate well; in spite of initially having the ration tokens required for sugar. My mother and sisters were happy to be able to make cakes with sugar instead of syrup, after World War II was over.

Before television there was always music and singing in our home. Prior to my birth, Dad played in the Tabor, Minnesota band. Without formal music training, he played the trumpet, piano, and violin. I still remember when his brothers, Ernest, and Amos came to our house and all three played the violin together. Mother also played the organ that we later purchased and placed in the living room.

George and Julia (Pribula) Gust had schooling up to the 8th grade, with self-education up to college level. The Library truck from EGF came out to the farm on a regular basis and Mother and Dad were voracious readers. As they approached retirement and had more time, they also took continuing education courses in town; including Spanish language as well as other classes they enjoyed.

Mother was a fantastic cook and baker. Fresh bread rolled out of her wood stove oven, sometimes on a daily basis. Homemade cinnamon rolls were a favorite and I recall my brother, Bob, one time eating almost ½ dozen fresh rolls washed down with cold fresh milk from our own cows. Mother's bread was so sought after that when Holy Trinity Catholic Church in Tabor, Minnesota, sponsored a bake sale, her bread never made it to the sale table. The other ladies working the sale purchased it before others could see it! When I was 12 years of age, Mother taught me to bake and cook, using Betty Crocker's recipes, and always measuring everything very accurately.

Mother listened to the radio for new recipes, cut out recipes from the Farm Journal and any other periodical she could find. Her collections of recipes formed the basis of the excellent baking and cooking that my sisters demonstrated over the years. I still love to visit my sister, Betty, in San Diego, at Christmastime, to enjoy poppy seed kolace, a Czechoslovakian treat.

Many great memories circle around Sunnyside District #46, our one-room school for eight grades with one teacher; located just one mile north of our farm. When the weather was good, we walked to and from school. We played softball at lunch break and recess; along with tag and "police." Police was a game where about 3 kids (police) tagged you and put you in a jail (a corner of the building with a piece of wood on the ground to identify the jail limit). If you were caught and put in jail, your friends could help you escape if they could touch you without being caught by one of the police. It was great fun and provided wonderful exercise.

Being in a one-room school was a terrific advantage for learning. The younger grades always heard the older grades recite, read, or see arithmetic problems solved on the blackboard in front; giving all an opportunity to look to the future. Our holiday celebrations were always fun, with the Christmas plays the epitome of excitement for our young thespians. Current events time, on Fridays, was a time to review the little newspaper that came to the school on Thursdays, just in time for our class. Although we were growing up in the Northland of Minnesota, we were able to project ourselves by virtue of the study of geography along with current events towards the possibility of living somewhere else in the world at large.

When winter weather brought us blizzards, preventing the use of cars to get us to school, Jim Holy (who lived on the farm next to ours) hitched his horses to a large sleigh, and with bales of straw for seats, blankets on our legs and a blanket over the top for some protection, brought his sons, Donald and Lloyd, picked up Larry Kovar, then me, and then my cousin, Grace. The horses took us on the road, over the drifts of snow and got us to school where we were greeted by our friends, our teacher, and the warmth of a great stove. The stove had a ledge all around it and we would take potatoes, wrapped in aluminum foil (we called it tin foil); place them on the ledge in the morning and by lunchtime we would eat our nicely baked potato along with whatever else our parents packed in our Karo Syrup lunch pails.

Sunnyside District #46 had a little library where along with a variety of books we had a hectograph and later a mimeograph machine, used to make copies of papers. Encouraged by my parents to read at an early age, I still remember the time in the 3rd grade when I read a kid's book about Hawaii, with black and white illustrations of a boy sliding down a waterfall on a large leaf. I recall longing to be that little boy, living in a land of warmth and natural beauty; instead of the cold harsh snow covered prairie with no mountains and not even a hill. Wanting to live in Hawaii at age 8, I was pleased to finally get there 22 years later when I accepted a position as Associate Professor of Educational Psychology at the University of Hawaii in Honolulu.

Sunnyside District #46 was a great "prep" school, verified by the fact that most of us who matriculated to Sacred Heart High or Central High in EGF were at or above average in our high school classes. In later years, I came across research indicating that the one-room school was indeed, one of the best methods for ensuring excellent education of children. Unfortunately, school consolidation became the norm and Sunnyside met its demise in the 1960s.

East Grand Forks gave me my first opportunity to work "off the farm." Butch Martin at Zejdlik and Martin grocery store accepted my request to work at age 15, when I was a 10th grader at Sacred Heart High. I worked after school during the week while living in a rented room in EGF; but went home on weekends to work on the farm. My next job, the next year was with Brownie Cleaners, where Chuck and Johnnie Scheving gave me an opportunity to learn every aspect of the dry cleaning process and business.

Delivering and picking up clothes for Brownie Cleaners got me around EGF as well as Grand Forks; providing me with a knowledge of the Forks that made it possible for me to drive for Rocket Cab (across from Brownie Cleaners) during two years while attending the University of North Dakota (UND). Eventually I found employment at UND during semesters, and worked for Hover Vigen building grain elevators during summers. I even worked for the Amen brothers one summer, building a couple of homes in EGF. The growing economy in the '50s and '60s made getting a part-time job for a poor but motivated student, almost easy. I graduated UND with no debt.

Growing up in Northwestern MN was a

great preparation for a poor kid who became a University Professor and later a Clinical Neuropsychologist. I appreciate all my parents did for me; especially the admonishment to "get an education—no one can take that away from you." All of us 8 children listened to them with the result that all of us achieved advanced degrees beyond the bachelor's level! "Pretty good for poor dirt farmers." By the way, my cousins did the same and just think they got their educational foundation at Sunnyside District #46; a one-room school with one teacher for eight grades.

Loss
By Lana Violette of Red Lake Falls, Minnesota
Born 1947

My great-grandparents, Sigrid Annette von Moltzer and Andrew Sanders (his name was changed from Sjolstrom at Ellis Island.) Both came from Sweden in 1900. They did not know each other until they came to Bird Island, Minnesota where they met and married. Then they moved to Mavie Township near Thief River Falls where they homesteaded and farmed.

They had four children, all born at home, Emil, Julia, Clarence, (also known as Kelly,) and Leonard.

Life was very hard on the farm. When Julia was six, she was in charge of the baby all day while her mother worked on the farm. She peeled potatoes and started supper.

When Kelly was 16, he got polio. The country doctor was trying to put a tube down his throat into his stomach to feed him. He got it into his lungs instead and drowned him.

When Leonard was six his father, Andrew, died of pernicious anemia at the age of 54. It was the dead of winter; there was no way for the undertaker to get out to the farm. What was there to do?! 14-year-old Emil and Sigrid carried Andrew's body out to the granary where he would be cold/frozen until the roads could be cleared and the undertaker could get out to take the body. Leonard cried for his dad and wanted to see him. So 12-year-old Julia dressed Leonard warmly and took his little hand and they trudged through the snow to the granary so Leonard could see his dad.

Emil and his mother continued to farm together until Emil was an adult and was able to take over the farm. His son and family live there still. Julia continued to take care of the house until her marriage at age 16. Leonard was killed in battle in World War II.

Lana's great-grandparents, Andrew Sanders and Sigrid Annette (von Moltzer) Sanders

St. Patrick's Day Storm
By Angeline Sande of Bemidji, Minnesota
Born 1929

I don't remember the Armistice Day storm because it didn't hit Northern Minnesota like it hit the rest of the state. But I do remember the St. Patrick's Day storms that came the following spring. There was a dance in the Nebish town hall and it was a Catholic community so they were exempt from lent as we knew it at the time. Anyway, a storm came up and the people weren't aware of the storm and it was lambing time. I was to get my brother up to check the ewes. My brother was 15 months older than me; I was 9 at the time.

My father came home ahead of my mother. He told her to stay in the hall to let it get light before she came home. Then it got cold so she froze her legs and it dripped from those legs and there was dripping from legs for a good month before they healed. A lady did not wear long pants in those days – heaven

Pete, Angie, Joe, Paul, and Ramona in 1939

forbid. I remember the neighbors that lived beyond us came and spent the night and they couldn't go any farther. There were no county plows or road graders so there was no way to get through. I was in high school before we got plows out there and we were muddied in the spring. We had the Red Lake railroad that went right by our house so we ran the railroad to Nebish and the cattle sweep in front of the rails kept our walk clean for us. By then we were four kids going to school as we had twin brothers. They were identical and people couldn't tell them apart. We had a good time with them.

Our family was pretty close. When my husband and I were married, we bought land in Nebish. My husband died of lymes disease after 56 years of married bliss and I had to move to town. Among my three living sons, my oldest son died in his sleep in August 1997.

Drowning in One's Own Sweat?
By Jill J. Holm of Sauk Centre, Minnesota
Born 1949

Remember when there were threshing crews? We had seven in our ring that threshed together north of Sauk Centre, Minnesota. The monstrous machines moving slowly on its steel wheels along the gravel road waiting to be set up in the farmer's field to do its separating of oats, straw, and chaff. Times were slower then.

When the oats were ripe in the field, the farmer hooked up to the tractor to the binder, which needed a rider, that made the bundles, as the children, wives, and/or hired help shocked the oats bundles. A shock was made by putting two bundles head-to-head, and then added two more on each side of the first two so the bundles would stand. Then one bundle was placed on each side. It was like three teepees standing in a row. Then there was a bundle placed on each side for additional support. This allowed the oats to dry under the scorching sun. The blazing sun made sweat drip from the one's nose, face, and whole body thus saturating all of one's clothes. Sometimes it was too hot to shock in the afternoon so we would wait until after the evening milking and shock until dark. A shower felt so good after shocking. For drinking water, we used either a glass jar or a thermos with ice that was placed in the midst of a shock to keep it cool and out of the heat of the sun. It was important to remember which shock it was in. Sometimes finding the water jar was like finding a needle in a straw pile.

While the oats were drying, preparing the threshing machine was very important. Everything needed to work when threshing began. One day Dad and a neighbor were doing repairs on our threshing machine. The neighbor had his hand inside a small hole trying to replace a nut on a bolt when his hand was scratched. He paid little attention to it because working around metal these things happen. However, after a couple more times he pulled his hand out revealing long, stinging scratches. This did not happen when they disassembled the parts. When he looked back at the hole, there was our playful kitten, Fred that had crawled inside the machine, from the front end, making its way to the back end, and saw the neighbor hand thinking it was something to play with. Fred was not appreciated at this time. Later its name was changed to Fredrica; she, not he, had kittens.

Threshing was an exciting time for us kids because we usually drove the tractors while the men pitched the bundles on to the wagon. When the wagon was full, we would walk over to another rig that did not have a driver or ride up to the threshing machine and wait for the first one who unloaded to go back out into the field.

There was a big dinner (noon), 3:00 pm lunches. Supper was when the evening dew fell. Some of us kids had to go home for the evening milking and then return to the place we were threshing to eat. At our farm, Mom served chicken salad sandwiches, cake, and other goodies at the 3:00 lunch. Everybody loved those chicken salad sandwiches.

One time at the neighbors, I was driving a rig in a field next to the driveway when a car stopped at the end of the road. A young man in an Army uniform got out of the passenger side, walked over to our rig, took off his service coat, and helped pitch bundles. He was returning home from the service to his country, decided to see all the neighbors, and serve them with some help. He had not even seen his parents yet.

Threshing was a lot of work and toil but it also had its fun moments. There was one neighbor who was always joking or pulling pranks on the others. One did not want to sit by him at the table because if you were not there, he would hugely dish up your plate, especially with mashed potatoes and told you that there was no dessert until the plate was cleaned. If one placed jelly on the bread and left it opened-faced, it was an invitation for a jellied face.

Many a visiting child learned to drive a tractor. One time about an eight-ten year old neighbor girl was on a tractor when it slowly kept on rolling when she put in the clutch. Instead of pressing on the brake, she was yelling, "Whoa, whoa" to the tractor. Our cousin from Florida would sit on a tractor for hours. So one season he drove, however, one of the neighbors was not impressed with his driving skills and asked him where he got his license, out of a Cracker Jack box. The cousin replied that my brother had taught him. Some of the teenage boys wrapped a garter snake around Dad's steering of the diesel tractor empowering the threshing machine. Dad stepped on the draw bar, reached for the steering, when he froze. He did not like snakes.

In the fall, it was the same crew that sawed firewood together. The kids were in school so it was only the men who worked around the huge circular saw and handled the wood.

Currently, there is only one alive in our threshing and wood cutting crew who will be 98 in June (2016.) Times have changed. There are only a few threshing bees and farming has changed. From horses to combines, from family farms to corporate farms, from milking machines to parlors, from binders, shockers, and threshing machines to self-propelled combines. Back then, there was community within the farm folks and social functions. One of those social functions was that whoever had the greatest oats production had to provide a party for everybody in the ring. It was also potluck. Now there is less community and more of an individual operation on the farms. Change is good but good memories are forever. It also proves that no one ever drowned in one's own sweat!

Farm Life
By Pauline Wilcowski of Pennington, Minnesota
Born 1946

In the good old days of northwest Minnesota, my dad was born in Nebraska, he lived on a farm with his parents. He couldn't speak English until he was 8 years old and he only went to the 8th grade in school. Then he had to help on the farm where he grew up. He met my mother in Bemidji, Minnesota, they went together for a while, and got married in

Pauline's parents

Pauline's grandparents, Oscar and Mary Olson with their children

July 1934.

They had 7 boys and 3 girls plus Mom had 4 sets of twins. The oldest set was fraternal boys, then me and my brother fraternal twins, a set of identical twin boys, lived only 6 weeks and died, and a set of identical twin girls that were still born.

My dad built a house on Irvine Avenue in Bemidji. That's where my brother and I were born. On our first birthday, we moved 3 miles west of town to a 40-acre farm. It had a big house with a basement and upstairs so we had plenty of room.

We had no electricity so Dad bought some gaslights to hang up in the living room. They were very bright when they were light. And we had a pump in the corner of the living room so we had a water bucket with a dipper in it in the kitchen.

Mom cooked on a wooden stove in the kitchen year round. She canned many many quarts of vegetables, berries, and fruits in the summer.

We all helped in the big garden throughout the summer. It took a lot of food to feed our big family. Dad built a small barn and bought some nice milk cows. They would make butter out of the cream and cottage cheese out of the milk; it was very good.

My mom made homemade bread, cinnamon rolls, and fry bread that was very tasty.

Mom also washed clothes every week in a washing machine that had a gas engine on it to make it work. We had lots of clotheslines outside to hang clothes on to dry. They smelled really good being dried outside.

My dad was a mechanic and worked at the Ford garage in town until he bought and built a garage out on the farm and then he worked out of his own garage.

I remember us kids picking lots of radishes and washing them clean. Then we would put 12 in a bundle, take them to town, and sell them for 10¢ a bundle to city folks. They would buy them all every time we went to town to sell them.

We picked lots of wild berries in the summer for pies, jams, and jellies throughout

Jerome, Arlene, Paul, and Pauline

the winter. By fall, my mom had many many quarts of food in the basement for winter.

In these days about all we bought in a store was coffee, flour, yeast, and sugar. We never went to the store everyday like people do now.

We had chickens for eggs and meat. My Dad bought in pigs for meat in the winter. Also, we raised bull for meat.

Mom had jobs for everyone to do on the farm. We didn't sit around and watch TV. It wasn't allowed back then. We didn't talk back to our elders either like kids do today.

We also had an outdoor toilet until I was 18 years old. I had a chamber pot for years in my bedroom for years that I dumped and washed every day.

We didn't go anywhere very often, but we were happy and had things to do.

We still have the famous statue of Paul Bunyan and Babe the blue ox down by Lake Bemidji.

My brother and I graduated from the same high school that my mom graduated. Our farm is still being lived in. Yet my niece bought it but is trying to sell it to my great nephew. She has lots of health problems.

I'm 69 years old, will be 70 in May. I can't believe the changes that have taken place in such a short time.

More next time.

Farm Animals
By Cindy (Pesola) Fox of New York Mills, Minnesota
Born 1950

Back when I was growing up in northwestern Minnesota, animals ruled our lives from sunup to sundown. No one in our farmhouse overslept. How could you with that darn Bantam rooster crowing at the crack of dawn? After breakfast, I jumped off the house steps and the rooster darted at me as I hightailed to the barn. I looked back and saw him strutting with his neck feathers fluffed out like a greasy dude flexing his muscles. His wives flocked together, rolling their eyes and clucking they never got any rest either.

The hen party encircled a bachelorette, protecting the pullet from the rooster's amorous intentions. Fulfilling their roles as mother hens, they cackled their worldly advice, forewarning the young chicken she'd be laying eggs for the rest of her life, never enjoying a day of rest, if she hooked up with this cocky man.

Alongside my siblings, we cared for our farm animals while they tended to our education. Sex education, that is. I don't recall ever having a conversation with my parents about the birds and the bees. No words were necessary when Dad told me to chase the bull and the cow into the barn from the barnyard. I'd holler and wave my arms at the pair, but the bull was having too much fun playing piggyback on the cow.

The life cycle of farm animals began with mating and by springtime, the birth of farm animals was a joyful world of chicks peeping, piglets squealing, and calves bawling. Though I enjoyed calves sucking my hand and cuddling baby pigs, they grew up fast and so did we.

Like any new mother, I thought a sow would love her adorable little piglets. But she'd flop on the pen floor, ignoring muffled screams from her offspring that lay crushed beneath her. When the ones that survived were old enough to eat on their own, we moved them away from their crabby mother to the pigpen outside.

You didn't forget a drive past our pig farm. You could tromp on the gas, but you couldn't get away from the stench that filled the car. Your hair, your clothes, even your spit tasted rancid. In late spring of 1962, our family had a hundred hogs. The suffocating odor in our farmyard was a hundred times worse than people could smell driving past in their cars. But Dad said hogs were a cash crop, just like planting corn or oats, and that was why we raised them.

One day we castrated the boy pigs. Dad said after we castrated them, they would leave the girl pigs alone and get big and fat over the summer months. Our neighbor, Gust, came over and did this thankless job. His knife was sharp and he set up his operating station in a tiny pen on the south side of the pig house. The boys and I were in charge of herding the pigs, one at a time, into the small pen.

The pigs whirled around in a rabid frenzy when we tried to grab their hind legs. Our hands, slick with mud, slipped over their hooves. The pigs came back to tempt us. They thought we were playing—goofy pigs. We put on our thinking caps and used cobs of corn to lure them into their torture chamber. Gust dowsed kerosene over the incision, which supposedly prevented infection. The pigs squealed and I bit my top lip so I wouldn't cry. I remember thinking if I was ever to be a pig, I wouldn't want to be a boy pig.

Cindy's grandfather, Charles with his workhorses

By late summer, we butchered some of the pigs and sold the rest. My little brother, Mike, loved the pigs so much I often found him sleeping with them on a bed of straw in the pig house. When it was slaughter time, Mike was nowhere to be found.

I tried to get lost, too, when it was time to clean out the calf pens in the barn—my least favorite job on the farm. Opening the gate, I hoisted myself up to get into the pen. The manure and straw were compacted after the heifers walked and slept on it over the winter months—sometimes over half a year here in northwestern Minnesota. I tried to lift a layer of the mire with my pitchfork, but it was intertwined with the rest of the pen. I tugged, lifted, pulled and finally a chunk released its hold. I heaved it towards the manure spreader parked beside the pen, but it splat on the barn floor along with my patience.

I was breathing methane gas from the fermenting muck, but I didn't know it. The pungent fumes intensified with each forkful, and steam rose in the sunlight that tried to peek through the smeared barn window. My arms screeched in pain, and a whiff of resentment needled me as the cattle kicked up their heels in the barnyard while I cleaned up their mess. I used to feel sorry for them being penned up all winter, but I wasn't feeling sorry anymore.

But, for some reason, fresh manure didn't seem to bother me. In the warm summer months, I walked barefoot to the pasture to usher the cows back to the barn for evening milking. I stepped on every cow pie I could find and loved feeling the goo squishing around my toes.

Cows might be females, but

Cindy's brother, Mike Pesola with Frisky the dog in 1966

The chicken coop on Cindy's parents' farm in 1949

that didn't mean they weren't bull-headed. As our cows entered the barn, they headed for the nearest stanchion, unlike my uncle's cows who religiously claimed their own stalls. Cows come in different sizes, as did the length of the stalls in our barn. When one of our long cows chose a short stall, she stood with her hind legs in the gutter. Milking her became a challenge, but was one I'd rather endure than switching cows around like musical chairs.

A strap, much like a belt, was slung around the cow's midriff to hold the milking machine off the floor while four suction cups drew milk from her teats. But with "Miss Daddy Long Legs," the strap wasn't necessary, so the milking machine sat on the stall floor beneath her. With so many flies on the farm, and even more on the cows, she swatted me with her tail that had been soaking in the gutter. Angry, I returned the favor with a jab to her back. Her tail retracted between her legs. She thought she was the queen of the castle, but I was her master that day.

Occasionally, the cows broke through the fenced-in pasture where they were supposed to be grazing. True to the expression "looking for greener pastures," they followed the leader, the least docile cow in the herd, to the alfalfa hayfield. Alfalfa was intended to be cut and baled two to three times each summer and then stored in the hayloft for their winter feeding. They wolfed down the luscious, purple flower clusters like a kid licking frosting off a cupcake. If we couldn't get them out of the alfalfa quickly, the cows would bloat. This wasn't an easy task as they headed in the opposite direction you wanted them to go. Everyone was on high alert, as the death of a cow was serious and costly.

When a cow was bloating, a huge balloon-type swelling rose right above her hip. Using a sharp knife, Dad stabbed the swollen area to release the gas. Otherwise, the cow died a death by explosion. Thankfully, we never saw that happen.

Greenhouse gas emissions from cattle are a hot topic today. Back in the 1960s, we never knew the methane saturation was at deadly levels cleaning calf pens, or on our farmyard where pigs wallowed in muddy cesspools. We were never alarmed at the cows belching and passing gas in the close quarters of the barn while we milked them. Their splashes into the fermenting barn gutters added to the brew, but we grew up with no bad side effects other than getting on the school bus smelling like a barn. Recent news concludes to reduce our personal carbon footprint we need to eat less meat and dairy products, the very livelihood of my upbringing, which injures my pride.

Our farm dogs were also prone to injuries. Frisky, our playful black lab, tagged along with Dad while he cut hay in the field, stopping occasionally to sniff out a gopher hole, or paw a garter snake that had slithered onto his path. Frisky had free reign on the farm and never attended obedience school. His rampant spirit and natural instinct to hound prey soon escalated to chasing cars. He ignored our pleas to stop and, sadly, he encountered a fatal accident running alongside a passing car. After the dust settled, Frisky was a motionless heap on the side of the road. His legs were broken and Dad had to put him down.

My brother, John, had a hard time facing the death of our beloved Frisky. He stayed at his friend's house for a week and wouldn't come home. I didn't know if he was sad or mad; maybe he was both.

Farm animals needed daily care, so we never went on a summer vacation. But one

Sunday afternoon we drove 50 miles north to Itasca State Park. Mom packed a picnic lunch with liverwurst sandwiches, rhubarb pie and three quart jars of strawberry Kool-Aid. We sat on a picnic table under the towering pines, the guys on one side and the gals on the other. John ate his sandwich in two bites and asked if he could go exploring. But Dad looked at his watch and said it was time to head back home for milking. Sad but true, my family was probably the only one within an hour of the park that hadn't splashed their toes in the Headwaters of the Mississippi, a famous landmark in the middle of nowhere that didn't have much else to brag about.

The philosophy of "keeping up with the Joneses" was evident in town, even in our church, but it crept into the countryside, too. For my father, it was not how rich he was, but how his crops compared to other farmers. His lopsided grin broadened into a smile when his corn grew taller and greener than our neighbor's, even though they had a new-fangled irrigator. His chest puffed out when he cut and baled our hay before the rain fell while the neighbors' hay swaths soaked up rainwater, green alfalfa fading into an unsavory brown.

Dad's world was the farm, the only life he had ever known. But I yearned to see what the world held outside a twenty-mile radius of the farm, the boundary of my young life. With Dad's interests in mind, it wasn't hard to convince him to venture out if the plan was to look at other people's crops.

So, on another Sunday afternoon we drove away from the farmstead in our black and white 1955 Ford Fairlane with kids stacked like cord wood in the backseat. Out the windows of the car, Dad and the boys marveled at the farmer who had two blue Harvestore silos, while Mom and I drooled over a new house, a rambler snuggled amid flowerbeds bursting with a riot of colors. The car actually stopped if a particular field warranted a more rigorous assessment. Then we'd mosey on, swerving from lane to lane as Dad surveyed the fields and Mom would grab the steering wheel to keep the car from diving into the ditch.

As the sun grazed the top of a grove of trees, we were getting closer to home. A stray dog chased our tires, and the boys' chatter began to evaporate with the daylight, their conversations fading with fatigue. But there was no time for rest when Dad turned onto our driveway. I could hear the cows bellowing. Our mini vacation was over.

These Good Times Built Strong People
By Elmer Maciejewski of Avon, Minnesota
Born 1934

I am an 82-year-old guy, born in 1934. As a kid, I grew up on a farm. It was a rough life, especially in the wintertime.

We had a wood heater in the house. When getting up on a cold morning, the only warm place was in the barn. There was no electricity. We had kerosene lanterns for light. Our water well was a quarter of a mile from the yard. We had to haul the water for the pigs with barrels on a stone boat to the yard. Maybe a quarter of it splashed out and froze on the side of the barrels.

I was the oldest in the family so my dad used me as a hired man. He had me doing a man's job at 10 years of age. At that age, I was plowing with farm horses. I was always with

Elmer Maciejewski the milk truck driver in 1954

him and learned how he did things. When he told me to go do something, he didn't explain how it was to be done. I ran a threshing machine for custom threshing at the ae of 16. People would look at me when I pulled in the yard and would ask, "Where's your dad?" Well, he was working in town to make farm payments. They watched me pretty closely at first but then decided that I knew what I was doing.

When I was a kid, my dad planted 10 acres of potatoes. At that time, it was quite an undertaking. They were planted with a horse drawn planter. They were rows were dug with a horse drawn digger. But we sprayed them by hand with a 3-gallon sprayer, and Paris Green Bug poison.

They were picked by hand with neighbors and relatives doing the work for weeks.

Some were sold, and others were fed to the cows and pigs during the winter. The basement under the house was full of them. Then, in the spring, we started cutting them up for new seed.

I drove a milk truck for one year, picking up cans of milk from the farmers. At age 18, I started working at Woodcraft Millwork and Windows in a five state area. I have been doing this for what will be 64 years in April. I do not have a single moving violation on my record and have never had an accident. Maybe some I should have gotten, but I've never been caught.

I am now driving for Trinper of Sauk Rapids, Minnesota. I have driven millions of miles. Nowadays, people's driving habits have gotten terrible.

I believe I have lived in the good times. They were not easy but they built strong people with common sense. My dad was one of them and he was a good teacher.

"Central" Heating
By LaRayne Johnson of Osakis, Minnesota
Born 1923

The wood-burning, heating stove sat proudly in a chimney corner of our living room on the farm, clearly dominating that room. It was black, of course, with gleaming metal, we thought they were silver, guardrails surrounding the fire chamber to keep little bodies from accidentally bumping the hot are of the stove. Another shiny metal "dome" covered the top. This could be lifted off and a container of water set on the flat surface directly over the fire chamber, to provide humidity. Of course, on washdays, quantities of humidity coursed down frosty windowpanes, when frozen overalls, long johns, and bath towels were brought from outside lines, hung over chairs and sometimes over temporary lines strung from doorway to doorway, to finish drying by the heat from the stove.

Round, black pipes from the stove went through the ceiling into a bedroom I shared with my grandmother. The pipes entered the chimney in that room and a small amount of heat warmed the bedroom…sort of. At least, water in a glass did not freeze there, as it did in other rooms upstairs with no pipes going through them.

It was pleasant to sit in the rocker in the living room and dreamily watch the blue, white, and orange flames dancing behind the ising glass panes of the stove door. These were clear and bright when the heating season began, but as the winter wore on, the light became dimmer as the windows sooted up. The stove never cooled down enough to allow for cleaning of the mica panes until spring.

A cleaning that had to be done daily was carrying the accumulation of ash that gathered in a tray under the stove. This was usually accomplished without incident, but occasionally a wandering child would bump the ash bearer, or when opening the outside door, a sudden gust of wind would swirl the top layer of ash back into the house, necessitating another cleanup.

On nights, when temperatures were severely cold, or there was a lot of wind, Dad would stay up late and get up during the night to take care of the fires. A fire in the kitchen range was also kept burning in extremely cold weather. My Dad was deathly afraid of chimney fires – we never had one, but I recall seeing the belly of the stove and the lower pipes glowing red hot.

On Saturday night, the round, galvanized tub was placed in front of the stove and the bath ritual began – starting with the youngest and on up to the eldest. Pajamas were hung on chairs near the stove, as were towels. Shivering bodies were dried quickly, popped into warm night clothes and after turning 'round and 'round close to the stove to soak up more heat, we would dash into bed and snuggle under mountains of woolen quilts, to sleep without moving until morning.

My recollection of the heating stove in the corner always brings up a Sunday morning routine. Of course, after the Saturday night bath, we would have clean underwear to put on, on Sunday. These were long-legged, button up the front with a drop-down seat and fleece lined. It was the fleece lining I couldn't stand. When dried indoors, that fleecy stuff dried into hard, scratchy little lumps. How I <u>hated</u> getting into those clean ones! I would stand behind the stove, in the chimney corner, turning this way and that, trying to escape the inevitable. I would see how many words I could make out of KALAMAZOO, which was printed in two-inch letters across the base of the stove. I would scratch my legs and try to rub down the goose pimples that kept coming on my arms at the very thought of my skin coming in contact with the sandpaper inside my underwear. <u>Finally</u>, my mother's ever-patient voice would carry just a subtle hint that I better cut out the dilly-dallying, get dressed, and get out to breakfast. So, I would hold my breath, grit my teeth, and with great haste, I would struggle into those detested, tight, shriveled up, bristly, long johns. The rest was easy. In less than five minutes, the whole business was forgotten until the next Sunday when the entire ordeal would be repeated. (There are some brands of pantyhose that conjure up the very same reaction and emotions!)

Central heating, as we know it today, it was not, but the black heating stove, was certainly of central importance in our homes, our lives, and my memories of days gone by.

And It Shall Come To Pass
By Mabel Tesch of Long Prairie, Minnesota
Born 1920

We got a letter from our son, Bob, today. He is happy with his work and family. Hearing from him made me think of other letters. One morning we got one I'll never forget. After reading it, I opened my Bible and found this

Mabel's son, Robert with his wife, Patty Tesch in 1976

verse, "And it shall come to pass, that before they call I will answer, and while they are yet speaking, I will hear." I know my prayer had been answered!

Bob was just out of high school in the spring of 1963. That fall he joined the Air Force and was sent to Lockland Air Base in Texas. He liked his work, made new friends, and was so proud when he came home for furlough. After his training there, he applied for duty overseas, but was sent to Ellsworth Air Base in South Dakota instead. His job was cooking; he liked that about the new salads he made up. Soon his letters showed his restlessness and disappointment. He had his church membership transferred to the church in Rapid City and tried to find a place for himself there. That didn't help either. It wasn't as though he were homesick or even tired of his work. It was more than just plain boredom of nothing to do to keep his mind and hands busy. One day a letter came full of discouragement, he said it was enough to make a guy go A.W.O.L., to be caught in such a place! What could I do to help him? He was in the service of his country; I couldn't go to him.

God was the only one to help us. Petitions for him had been in my prayers everyday, it was my only comfort. In our church, right

Mabel's husband, Reinhard Tesch with his children Bob, Karen, and Betty

after the benediction, we have a time of silent prayers. Every Sunday as I stand beside my husband and two daughters, it is a very special time of prayer for me. A special time to ask God for a strong healthy baby and he blessed us with four of them. Then as they grew older, a special time to pray for help when they were sick or help in any of our problems. Karen was only two years old when she had pneumonia and Betty has had surgery twice. Bob had polio when he was eight. We asked for help and then gave thanks for their complete recovery. How well I remember that particular Sunday morning?

I prayed for Bob, that God would find some way to help him, to get him interested in something, to get his mind occupied in some way.

The very next week, we got another letter and that's when I found this verse. I knew that while I was asking, He was already answering.

Bob was bubbling over with news; he had found a new interest! One of the men on the base, Tech Sgt. Hall, had invited Bob to visit his church on Sunday. After services, Mr. Hall's daughters had invited him home with them for dinner. Besides the two daughters of the Hall's, they were caring for four little foster children and two of them were Sioux Indian boys. How much fun he had to be included in a family group, to have dinner with them, and have little children around. After that, his letters were full of what he had done at the Hall's. They were building an addition to the house, fixing on cars or helping the girls with the housework. He wrote that the Hall's never complained of him being there and soon Patty's name was mentioned most often. He joined the church Patty and her folks went to and then he wrote that he hoped we didn't care.

A year later, Bob and Patty were married, on August 9, 1976. He had been in the Air Force for nearly three years and then in November he got his orders to go to Vietnam. After serving overseas, the Air Force discharged him in November of '67. Now they are still making their home near Rapid City and his letters, few and far between, I'll admit are filled with news of his work, his wife, and his little ones. How many times I've thanked God for all his blessings and then turned to Isaiah 65 Verse 24 and read it again!

Ancestors
By Kay Keller of Virginia, Minnesota
Born 1938

The first thing your hear when you step out of the car is the wind whistling over the prairie. Tall grass bends in the breeze shimmering from silver to gold and then green again. Red-winged blackbirds perch on swaying cattails rooted in a necklace of stagnant water strung along the fence line. Meadowlarks sing, happy to see you. Then it is quiet while the prairie inhales and the wind stirs again.

More than a half-century ago the cemetery that lies beyond, within the twisted rusty black fence, was lost and abandoned to dry grass and tumbleweeds. It was difficult to find unless you knew about the cottonwood that cast its cool shadow over the graves.

My grandparents, their brothers and sisters, cousins, and neighbors are all buried in this desolate place along the lake that separates the vast grasslands of western Minnesota from the Dakota hills.

The wrought iron gate is a tangle with vines winning out. There are not more than a handful of bleached white headstones that bear a name or year. Names and dates carved so deeply into the marble have all but vanished, worn smooth by the relentless wind, exposed to more than a hundred years of the elements. Kick a toe into a pure white stone but it does not move. It is the corner of a headstone that has slowly sunk into the earth. No one has ever bothered to set it upright again.

The scent of roses hangs in the air. Strong and brave enough to endure, the beautiful yellow blossoms are everywhere. The ancient bushes are gnarled and thick, full of protective thorns. Planted with love, they remain a gentle reminder of whom they have been watching over all these years.

At some point in time, the church began taking care of this small cemetery. Headstones were groomed and grass kept mowed down, once again paying respect to our forefathers, the pioneers who came from Sweden to turn rich prairie into farmland. Buried in the deep black soil lie the men and women who built homes and churches, granaries, and elevators, brought in the railroad, and sent money home so the next in line could sail for America.

This place is all I have of my grandparents. There are precious few photographs or stories handed down. The only heirloom I have from them is love of yellow roses, my connection to where I come from.

Mischievous Girls
By Judy Drewes of Frazee, Minnesota
Born 1938

My sister and I are two and a half years apart. We grew up together on a farm in west central Minnesota in the 1940s and 1950s. We had two older sisters who were ten years older than we were, then when I was eleven years old, my mom and dad gave us a little sister. A year and a half later, they gave us a little brother (finally.) Our Dad always referred to all of us kids as their "three teams."

My sister Dee and I loved to play house, so we would clear out patches in the woods near the house and pretend that they were rooms. We had a very big imagination, making mud pies and even using some of our Mom's chicken eggs that we would sneak from the chicken house. We would decorate the mud cakes with the apple blossoms from the trees in the grove.

During the winter months we were left in the house (Mom and Dad's big mistake) while they were out in the barn milking cows. That was the beginning of our experimental cooking careers. Needless to say, I don't remember using a cookbook so we just used our memories when we watched our mom make candy. We usually got found out, as the candy never wanted to set up so we had to use a spoon to eat it and the dirty dishes gave us away. Mom usually was very upset it was a "waste of sugar" in those days, when it was hard to come by. I remember one night after Mom and Dad went out milking we were going to stir up a batch of candy. We went to get a cookie sheet out of the cupboard, we opened up the door, and there was a Santa Claus mask staring at us. It scared the living daylights out of us. Little did we know that our Mom was standing outside the window watching us and having a good laugh. She told us some years later.

There is one memory thought that stands out above all the rest of them and that was our "try at making divinity candy" (it takes a grown up to make that stuff, and they don't always succeed at it either.) This time it was in the summer while Mom and Dad were out milking in the evening. We had watched Mom make it different times, so we thought we knew how to. Needless to say, it just would not set up so we poured it on a dinner plate and decided it needed a cool place to get hard. We didn't have a refrigerator in those days, so the coolest place we could think of was under the gas barrel stand on the north side of the milk house. Oh boy, mistake number two! That was the place the chickens liked to bathe in the dirt to cool off. You guessed it, Mom's great big leghorn rooster stepped into our plate of candy with both feet and he was

Judy's sister, Dee and Judy

stuck, like he had stepped in cement glue. All the poor thing could to do was try to fly to get rid of this plate of candy stuck to his feet. So there he is flying a little ways and stopping, flying a little ways and stopping, he just couldn't get rid of it. My sister and I hid behind our car not knowing what to do. And then who should come out of the barn but Mom! She came stomping down the hill with this angry look on her face and the closer she got to the rooster, the less angry she looked and finally broke out laughing so hard at the pitiful sight she saw. Believe it not we never got a spanking for it, only a good talking to about wasting all that sugar. I don't think we ever tried making divinity candy again. I bet our parents were wishing they would have had four boys instead of four girls, as maybe the boys wouldn't have been so mischievous as I and my sister was. (This all happened before our only brother was born.) I won't go into the time we baptized the cats in the stock tank (holy cats.) And then another time taking our older sister's nice prom formals and getting them all dirty and then hiding them in the culvert under the driveway, forgetting to bring them in right before a good rain came and washed them out the other side. I wondered if our older sister ever wondered what ever happened to those dresses. I don't recall what we ever did with them either. We still felt loved by our parents despite all the naughty things we did when we were young.

Was It Bigfoot?
By Tom R. Kovach of Nevis, Minnesota
Born 1945

When I was growing up on a farm in north central Minnesota in the 1950s, we never heard any stories about Bigfoot, but the UFO craze was getting started by then and like most places around the country, we had our legends and monster sightings. But, the Bigfoot thing was not in the news as it is now.

However, I remember in the late 1950s we had reports of the sighting of a strange, man-like creature with reddish hair. Some of the newspapers referred to this so-called Wildman as the "Red-Headed Gory Man." The gory part referred to this creature's habit of ripping up some livestock like calves and sheep and eating part of the poor animal and leaving the rest for the upset farmers to find. Now bears were not as numerous as they are in the area now, but we did have some wolves and coyotes. Apparently, there were some witnesses who claimed to have seen this wild, red-headed creature. How reliable these sources were, I'm not sure. But for me, in my early teens, these stories were frightening, yet very interesting. I have always been curious of the unknown and this redheaded Wildman was about as interesting as one can get.

What made it even scarier for me was that we had a couple hundred acres of woodland and during the spring, summer, and fall, our dairy cattle roamed this vast forest and I had to round them up for milking both at morning and in the afternoon. I had my trusty dog Rusty with me and I usually carried a .22 rifle so I felt somewhat secure. But, a couple of incidents happened that made my hair stand on end and crumbled some of my courage.

I remember one time, I believe it was in the summer of 1958, we had finished the morning milking and the cows had ambled off into the woods to feed at the various meadows we had scattered among the groves of oak, pine, birch, and aspen. I was working in the garden when all of a sudden I heard a lot of bellowing, bells clanking (to make it easier to find the cows in the woods several of them had cow bells around their necks,) snorting, and all sorts of noise as our cattle herd came rumbling out of the woods. When they got into the area next to the barn, they turned around and looked into the forest they had just vacated. Cows have big eyes, but now those eyes looked especially large… and very frightened. I had never seen these animals spooked like this before. Just looking at how scared they were, made a shiver run through my body even though the temperature was in the 80s.

What scared them? A bear? Possibly. Although as I mentioned before, bears were very scarce in our area back then. Even our big Holstein bull looked like he'd just seen a ghost. My dad and I were very puzzled. He (my dad) shook his head and said, "You know, maybe there is something to those crazy stories about some sort of Wildman."

After the cattle finally settled down, my father did caution me and my older brother John to be a little more careful the next time we ventured out into the woods again. He didn't have to tell me twice. I was already having some nightmares about this Redheaded Gory Man. But, there was one more scare in store for me shortly after the scared cows incident.

After chores one evening, my brother and I went to visit some neighbor kids who lived about a mile or so away from us. Of course, the conversation turned to these rumors of a Wildman on our woods. As teenage boys, we naturally boasted that we weren't afraid of anything…especially if we had our faithful dogs with us or a rifle of some kind. At any rate, when we were heading home from the neighbors that evening, we took a shortcut through the woods of thick pine trees. This wasn't pasture so it was extra brushy and rather difficult to walk through. We had no guns with us but our dog Rusty was at our side so we felt pretty comfortable. It was just getting dark and there was a big moon on the Eastern horizon. Suddenly we heard this awful crashing in the brush like something huge was making its way toward us. Rusty's ears pricked up and the hair on my arms and neck shot straight up. But what really scared

Mary Kovach, Joseph Kovach, John, Martha, and Tom with Rusty the faithful dog

me was the way Rusty reacted. Here was this wonderful mongrel dog who up to now was afraid of absolutely nothing. I'd seen him go after snakes, bees, and even large male raccoons and badgers. But now he woofed, then moaned, and then took off with his tail between his legs, making a bee line for the farm. My brother and I were right behind him!

When we got back to the farm, puffing and panting, we found Rusty under the porch, still shaking and whining softly. Boy was he scared! We were out of breath and extremely relived to be safely back home. We finally turned around but there was no creature behind us…Thank Goodness! We laughed a little sheepishly, but we couldn't hide the fact that we'd just been scared out of our pants.

Things were pretty spooky for the rest of the summer and autumn. But then things got back to normal. Like a lot of unexplained things like wild men and such, stories of the Redheaded Gory Man faded into local legend. By the following summer, there were no more sightings, no more missing calves and sheep. If the Wildman did indeed exist, he was either bumped off by someone or something more powerful than he was or he'd moved on to greener pastures. Later, when stories about Bigfoot started appearing around the country, all the way from the bayous of Louisiana to the forests of the Northwest, I began to place our local Wildman into the Bigfoot category. But I never did find out what the creature that scared our cattle, my brother and I and our dog, really was. Was it Bigfoot?

Winter Vibrant
By James Evans of Southern Pines, North Carolina
Born 1955

Cold air, blowing winds, cloudy skies, white. It's wintertime.
As December rolls around, you'll being to hear bells chime.
I think of quivering. Always think of icy snowing days.
As you look out your window you might see the birds at play.
I can see people dancing to a song for the New Year.
Four whole months, the winter-vibrant is here.
A winter that can chill my soul, but will chill with joy
When winter-vibrant hits, I think of happy girls and boys.
This sixteen degree weather, love is beginning to make life,
Some people in winter will begin to take them a wife.
From a very cold winter we need a love to keep warm
So we won't be alone when there comes a cold windstorm.
All loves that are apart will all soon come together
To prepare themselves for the winter-vibrant weather.
For a together winter warmth will grow like lightning
When you're in your lover's arms, there won't be fighting.
Though the sky is in a thing called a winter-vibrant storm,
People don't have fighting on their minds, they're keeping warm.
Inner love is growing strong, they love winter at night.
Winter-vibrant makes us put the coldness outta sight.
Nothing but warming energy will be coming straight across,
They don't think or care how many lives are lost.
The cloudy sky, with snow white cotton, soft balls.
They don't worry about freezing when winter-vibrant calls.
Snow is floating in the cold air, wind is making its pass,
Winter-vibrant kills almost all things. Things that grow. Grass.
It'll be renewed in the springtime, in summer prepare
For the winter-vibrant that will almost now be here.
Rain dropping with sleet, snow, and freezing ice
When winter-vibrant strikes, we'll be in paradise.
Mother Nature is winter-vibrant, a life of your destiny.
She can't stay hot for you, and can't stay cold for me.

Happy Easter
Flora, my mother-in-law
Knew what times I was in
Jesus though her, my wife
Brought me out of a spin.
On that avenue, by now
I could be there still
Betty on this happy
Easter, to reach you, I will
I know I can't be a father
Husband as most can be
On a happy Easter, Betty
I hope you will answer me.
For a marriage, Jesus
Did have me to surrender
Jesus loves us on Easter
Jesus is so sweet and tender.
I'm guessing you say
This is a happy Easter for you
If this touches you, It'll
Be a happy Easter for me too.
We have a once in a lifetime
Thing and it is real
I know Jesus gave it to us
Because of the way that we feel
We have something to love
We have something to gain
Only Jesus can tell you
For me it's hard to explain
Tell kids, our kids, the truth
Certain things have to be
That one this happy Easter
Jesus will bring you to me

Visiting the Farm
By Betty Flora of Sun City Center, Florida
Born 1929

We were "town kids." Our mother and father grew up on farms near Cyrus, Minnesota and Sacred Heart, Minnesota, but their destiny was not the farm business; it was in the retail business in Breckenridge (which was "our town"). As we were growing up in the metropolis of Breckenridge/Whapeton, Grandma and Grandpa lived on their farm near Cyrus. To get away from the Monday through Saturday business of running The Sagness Variety Store, on Sundays out parents often piled us in our Buick and drove to the country—to the farm.

My earliest memories of the farm are of Carlo and Tippy. I was very leery of the fiercely protective collie farm dog named Carlo. He barked, wildly ran around, and eyed everyone with suspicion. When we arrived, Daddy was the calming person to win over Carlo before we climbed out of the car. Carlo knew it was his duty to guard the farm complex- barns, sheds, fields, and livestock. I kept my eyes on, and stayed clear of Carlo the entire time we spent visiting. Tippy was the housedog. He was totally dippy, with flies buzzing around his head as he lounged on the cement door stoop leading into the house. In order to enter the kitchen, it was always necessary to step over Dippy-Tippy who would happily wag his tail, and would never budge from his spot by the screen door. I found it very important to watch Carlo, but I could ignore Tippy.

There were other hazards on Grandpa's farm. In the eyes of a little "town girl," the turkeys that roamed freely were huge, tall, black formidable creatures. They were not aggressive, but as they proudly strutted around, their size and height indicated, "Stay away!"

The big barn holding Grandpa's herd of milk cows was out of bounds to children. I do recall jumping into and romping in heaps of hay. I don't think at that time parents considered allergies an important issue, nor did they fear for our safety while we floundered around in the hay.

Then there were the pigs, which were huge, penned-in, and smelly. We avoided getting near or looking at the pigs, considering them ugly and dirty. The sheep that roamed the field near the house were more appealing, especially when they had cuddly little lambs. Once again, it was look but don't go near.

The women were usually busy cooking in the kitchen with the big black iron cook stove and big round table. I was delighted to skip over Tippy and open the screen door to enter the dark kitchen full of busy women. The prize was edging one's way into the small pump room where a very large water pump sat by a big sink. There was always a long handled dipper for anyone to use hanging on the wall by the sink. It was a challenge and a fun effort to grab the handle of the big pump, strain and pull to bring forth the ice cold water, and then, drink from the big dipper. On those hot summer days, it was the "nectar of the Gods."

While the women chatted and visited in the house, one could hear the clank of the horseshoes hitting the stakes in the game that entertained the men. There were two strategically placed stakes about 15-20 feet apart, the goal being to throw a horseshoe to ring the stake. From the house and yard, we couldn't see the horseshoe court but we could hear the laughter of the men, and the horseshoes hitting the stakes. There was probably a bit of betting going on.

If I was lucky, I got to sit on Grandpa's lap as he sat by the big round table in the kitchen. He was a very big man with a thick shock of gray hair and parts of fingers missing from accidents while working with his farm machines. I think his proudest day was leading the families to the big barn to demonstrate the new electric milking machine. Not having been near the cattle, the whole operation of milking a cow was a revelation to me. I soon discovered that "milking the cows" was like having a time clock and never, ever miss job.

Sometimes when we visited Grandma, she had a big flat metal container in her living room holding cute little yellow peeping and squeaking chicks. It was a brooder container, which kept the chicks fed and warm until they were big enough to go to the chicken house. Chickens were Grandma's business and her source of spending money. We town kids didn't consider the fact that those cute cuddly chicks would grow up to be eaten.

For me, the most fun of going to the farm was joining up with cousins. My favorite cousin and I found that sometimes jumping on the beds on the second floor was much more fun than looking at the animals.

We rarely stayed overnight. The ride home in the dark of night, squished into the backseat with my sisters, was a cozy sleepy finale to a day visiting the farm.

Grandma Goldie
By Nancy Zondlo of Wadena, Minnesota
Born 1956

I have only one grandparent who I remember well, and who was alive for the first 24 years of my life. As my own children were growing up, they often heard mention of my Grandma Goldie and her one-room house.

Nancy with her Grandma Goldie in 1958

By the time I was born, my Grandma Goldie was a widow and already 68 years old. She was mother to eight children and grandmother to 23 grandchildren. To this day, if I have trouble falling asleep at night I think back to Grandma Goldie and the times I spent with her. She would have already been in her mid-70s when I remember spending the night with her now and then. Her little house, which she had shared with my grandpa for many years, lacked modern conveniences. She had no electricity or running water, and by this time in her life, was just spending the warmer months in her house and spending the winter months alternating between some of her children. She would be so happy when spring and nice weather arrived so she could return to her own place.

Her house was located in the country right across the road from my aunt and uncle (her son). Whenever, I would go visit Grandma with my mom and dad, it was almost certain that it would be my job to take the water pail (sometimes two pails) and go across the road to my Uncle Sven's to get water for her. Another "kid" job was emptying the slop pail.

Canning sauce was very common back then and, without doubt, my grandma would serve us sauce and bread. I especially remember raspberry sauce. My grandma spent the summer working in her vegetable garden which included a strawberry patch and

Nancy Gallard Zondlo in 1962

raspberry patch, and she always had lovely flowers growing in the garden and up around her house. The hollyhocks particularly stand out in my memory.

When I would stay overnight, I slept with her in the trundle bed, which was in one corner of the house. This was her only bed, and would simply be like a twin bed for her each night but when I would stay, she would pull out the second bed that was stored underneath that was a little smaller than twin size.

She had a treadle sewing machine, and a buffet/dresser, as well as a rocking chair, all at one end of the house, accented by a round, braided rug on the floor. In the middle of her house was a round, white table with a kerosene lamp in the center of it, where we would sit and eat. I would often see her big, black Bible nearby with a magnifying glass on top of it. The other end of the house had a few cupboards (not built-ins), as well as a trash burner and a small gas stove. There was a sink with a cabinet around it where the dishes were done after heating the water to a desired temperature. Of course, there was an outhouse, and also a couple other sheds on her property. Security consisted of hooks on the screen doors, and a butcher knife slid above the doorknob, and into the casing on the inside doors.

There were two doors, one on each side of the house, and on hot days, she would have both the inside doors open so she could get a cross draft through the screens.

I remember her praying out loud at times and naming each grandchild in her prayers.

Some terms common to that era were, "remember to blow out the light," and "look in the icebox." My grandma always made good sport about being an April Fool's Day baby, being born on April 1, 1888.

On a more personal note, in the 1960s, I remember girls did not wear slacks to school. We always wore dresses but could wear slacks under our dresses on Fridays or cold days in the winter. Teachers always wore dresses, too. I was in the 7th grade at Mentor Public School in Mentor, Minnesota, and it was the 1968-1969 school year when teachers were first allowed to wear pants. It couldn't just be pants and a shirt but had to be what was referred to as pantsuits (pants with a matching jacket or blazer). I remember us kids were so excited to see what certain teachers would look like in pants.

Minnesota Farming Memories
By Martha Wilkowski Barclay of Perham, Minnesota
Born 1933

I was born in 1933 and have some memories of what my parents and grandparents told me about what happened before I was born.

My parents got married around 1928 in a country church, St. Hubert, northeast of Wadena. Times were hard but they bought a small farm. It had sandy soil and then drought set in. The house was small with four rooms, and had a small barn with enough space to milk about 10 cows. In the summer, we would go to the outhouse; a building 6 feet by 4 feet. It had a seat with two holes to go to the bathroom and a Sears or Wards catalog to use. During canning season, we were in heaven when we had peach wrapping paper to use. In the winter, we had chamber pots under our beds to use, then the next day we had to take turns dumping them outside in the outhouse.

We didn't have phones then, but we had a battery radio. Communication was slow. We got news from neighbors.

We went to visit our grandparents 6 miles away. There were six uncles and five aunts in a four-room house. The aunts slept in one room, and the uncles in the other room, except one or two uncles slept in the attic. There were little peepholes in the ceiling. They could see the stars shine, and in the winter, they could see snowflakes coming though the holes. They just hated to get up in the morning because it was so cold.

When I was about three years old, my six-year-old sister and five-year-old brother and our parents wanted to move from the poor sandy farm. They bought a farm 9 miles north of Wadena near Hwy 71. The soil was nice clay. My mother cleaned the yard because it was cluttered with old diapers and garbage from the people that lived there before us.

We still didn't have electricity or running water. We didn't go to the outhouse at night because it was scary near the woods so Mom would give us castor oil- then we would HAVE to go.

A few more years went by and farming was so much better. I got two more sisters, Cathy and Caroline.

We got chicken pox and Mom would rub Vicks salve on our chest and put cold washcloths on our foreheads to keep the fevers down. We hardly ever saw a doctor. There were no vaccinations. We all got measles; the remedy for that was wet, cool washcloths on the forehead, and coffee and toast to eat. A few years before this, my older sister had whooping cough. She was lucky she made it through that. Then later on came the rheumatoid fever. Years later, the doctor said her heart was enlarged from the fever. We made it through all the illnesses.

When we were a little older, we all had chores to do. We had to take turns pumping water for the cattle. There was a huge tank outside the pump house; it was about a 300-gallon tank that had to be filled with water. We hated that job. There was a long, 40-foot pipe that ran from the pump to the cattle tank. It took about an hour and a half to pump the water and fill the large tank.

Another job was to milk the cows by hand. I had to milk one cow. I sat on a stool close to the cow's teats with my head against the cow, and pull on the teats. I was about 8 years old then. When I was done milking, my older sister, Willa, 11, brother, Isidor, 10, and sister, Cathy, had to walk 3 miles to a one-room school, sometimes barefooted.

One winter, halfway to school, I got really cold. I turned around and went back home. My dad decided to drive me to school. On the way home from school, we hurried home to listen to the Lone Ranger on the radio, and then do our chores. We had to carry wood in for the woodstove, and carry water in from the pump to fill the stove reservoir and for the drinking pail with a dipper to drink out of.

One evening when our parents were gone, we had a kerosene lamp lit on the table close to the stairs. My younger sister, Cathy, 7 years old, slid down the stair rail and fell on the burning lamp. Her clothes caught fire. My older sister, Willa, grabbed Cathy and rolled her in the grass and put the fire out. Cathy only got small burns. We were always lucky that we didn't get seriously hurt.

Another time when our parents were gone, my older sister, Willa, took our younger sister Agnes, 3 years old, to the outhouse. My little sister slipped into the hole. She was sitting on whatta-mess. Willa had a hard time trying to get Agnes out. When she finally did, there was a lot of cleaning and watering down to do.

For fun, is kids would play ball in pastures with the neighbors, or our aunts and uncles would come and play cowboys and Indians, and other games. In the spring when the hay mount was empty, our parents would clean the upstairs in the barn and have a barn dance. We would dance all night.

We finally got electricity in the 1940s. That changed everything. Farming was easier.

My mother was a hard worker. She had a large garden and lots of cabbage to make sauerkraut. She had a large barrel in the basement that she used to make it. She also canned corn, beans, and pickles all on the wood cook stove. It got awfully hot in the house during canning.

We would have hay and harvest with horses. Our enjoyment was listening to stories on the radio, and lots of games outdoors.

My kin are still around, except for our younger sister, Agnes, who died when she was 42.

Spike
By Francis Seifert of Perham, Minnesota
Born 1939

Our dog, Buster, was killed in the fall of 1949 when he tried to cross the road ahead of an on-coming car. It had rained the night before and the temps dropped to below freezing causing everything to be covered with a sheet of ice. Buster slipped on the icy road, the on-coming car could not stop in time, and Buster was killed instantly. He had been my companion since we got him as a puppy two and a half years earlier. I really missed him.

We were without a don on the Saturday morning in February when Spike came to stay with us for a while. He was without a collar so we had no idea what his name was so we called him Spike. He was black and white, showing some signs of Border collie, but by all appearances, he was a true mongrel. He was in the middle of dog anatomy as far as size was concerned, and looked somewhat scruffy, as though he had been abandoned to fend for himself for a few days.

I came out of the house after breakfast that morning, and the Minnesota cold reminded me it was indeed mid-February. Starting for the barn to do chores, I saw Spike slowly walking up the driveway toward the house. At first sight, I thought him to be the Border collie belonging to a neighbor. When I realized it wasn't their dog, I got excited. He stopped when I looked at him, sat down, and intently watched me. I approached him slowly, and he lay down on his stomach in a submissive position and started crawling toward me. I extended one hand toward him which he licked cautiously, so I placed my other hand on the top of his head which was covered with frost from his own breath. I felt comfortable with him right away, thinking he was a dog I could trust.

I turned to go to the house, and Spike jumped to his feet and gingerly followed me. Figuring he could be hungry, I asked my mother for something to feed him. She gave me some leftover chicken soup which he ate heartily. He stayed by me most of the day, followed me closely as I did my chores, and sat by the door whenever I went into the house. There was a rule of no dogs or cats in the house, so he had to stay outside.

He slept in the barn with the livestock on cold winter nights, and then started to sleep in the doghouse by the garage in the spring.

Spike

It wasn't long before he fit into his new surroundings. Maybe it was because I made friends with him and fed him firs that made him become "my dog."

Summer came, school was out, and Spike and I spent a lot of time together. He ran along as I went for bike rides, and was my companion every time I went to the waterhole where he and I would try to catch frogs. He barked at turtles and looked at them in dismay when they pulled in their extremities. I think he wondered where everything went.

It was toward fall when Dad, my older brother, and I were harvesting grain that I saw a behavior I had never seen before in a dog. I maned it "the rabbit chase game." One no less than three occasions, I witnessed Spike as he trotted along the fence line, sniffing the tall grass until he flushed out a jackrabbit. As the rabbit ran at its full speed, Spike stayed about 20 feet behind, paying close attention to the rabbits every move. When the rabbit started to get tired it invariably would angle off to the right or left. After three or four times of this pattern, Spike would anticipate the direction the rabbit would go. He would angle off first, causing dog and rabbit to collide. The rabbit usually rolled a couple of times, got up and dizzily hopped off. Spike watched for a bit, then came to where we were working and laid down in a shady spot until it was time to go do barn chores.

One cow, I think her name was Hilda, had given birth to a calf one night in October. Even though the calf was taken away soon after birth, Hilda remained unusually protective for a couple of days She had horns which extended out the side of her head about six inches, then curved at a gentle 90 degree angle forward to come to a point 8 inches from her forehead, with about 18 inches between points.

The morning after calving, Hilda was let out of the barn and on her way to the water tank when my six-year-old brother happened to be going to the barn to feed the cats. When Hilda spotted him, she charged, lifted him off the ground between her horns, and pinned him against a shed wall. He was suspended off the ground, between her horns, as she pawed the ground, bellowing loudly. Fortunately, she was unable to crush him because her horns were on either side of his stomach, below his ribcage, and above his hips.

When Spike saw and heard what was happening, he charged Hilda, throwing himself onto her neck, biting at her ears. Startled, Hilda backed off and ran away 30 feet allowing my brother to fall to the ground. She turned, looked at Spike, continued to paw at the ground, and then walked away. Spike stood growling between my brother and her until Dad took my brother to the house. Because of Spike's bravery, my brother was uninjured other than for a badly bruised stomach. Spike was truly our hero that day.

I noticed after Spike saved my brother's life, he seemed to grow more distant. He spent less time following me around. During the winter, he spent long periods of time sitting in the yard, looking out over the frozen fields to the west. Then one day in April, he was gone. We never found out where he came from, and are not sure where he went.

Three weeks after Spike left, a neighbor told us he saw a dog that looked like Spike at another farm about 10 miles away, and that he seemed content there. I watched the driveway many times thinking he may come back but after a while, I quit looking.

He provided companionship for me for over a year. Maybe he was never "my dog" at all but was sent by God to save the life of my brother. I missed him greatly, and I think, "What if he had never come to us?" Young boys are not committed to a dog relationship for long. When Dad came home with a new puppy later that spring, I just knew that young puppy was going to be my best companion.

#9 of 12 Children
By Irene Twist of San Diego, California
Born 1937

As a child, I grew up in Osseo, Minnesota. I was #9 in a family of 12 children. We lived on a farm. My older sister tells me this story.

In the fall, after the wheat was harvested my father would take lots of the wheat to the mills to be made into flour. He would come back with 100lb bags of flour. In those days, flour came in cloth bags. My mother would make us children pajamas and underwear from the bags. The panties she made for the girls were called bloomers.

In the winter, my dad would be the first

Irene and her sister going to skate in 1947

one awake. He would start the fire in the round potbelly stove, then go out to do chores. My mother would then get up to put more wood on the fire. When it got nice and warm, she would get the children up. We would get to sit around the wood stove. I was the little one at the time so I got to sit on mother's lap. One morning I was very wiggly, my mother said Irene sit still. I said it's hot on my bloomers. As mother stirred the fire, a live hot coal had jumped in her apron pocket, and then she discovered the hot coal in her apron pocket. I felt it on my bloomers.

My Memories

Farm Chores: Because the last 5 of the 12 children were girls and me being one and the ninth, I got stuck doing more outside work than housework.

Picking Rocks and Mustard Weed: In the early spring after the soil was prepared, it was time for picking rocks. We walked the field putting the rocks in a pail. When the pail was full, we put them on a wagon to be taken to the dump later. Then the oats, wheat, or corn was planted. As it grew so did the mustard seed. When the growth was about 10 inches high and no longer could be cultivated by tractor, we walked the same fields pulling the yellow mustard. On July 4th we received a box of Cracker Jacks and a sparkler to light up in the evening. That was our reward.

Trashing Crew: In those days, one farmer would have a thrashing. I would drive the tractor while the farmer or helper would load the shocks on the wagon to take to the trashing machine. They would put it on the belt to be thrashed. If I wasn't driving the tractor I was in the granary shoveling oats as it was elevated into the granary bin. Best thing of the day was eating the big noon meals. The farmer's wives were good cooks.

Baling Hay: When bailing machines first were introduced, they used wire. Two people were needed to tie the bales. My brothers did that, but as each bale was used the wire was saved. Before it could be reused, it had to be straightened. My sisters and I did that. We would put one end in a vise and the other in a pull hook and pull until straight. We then put them in a stack to be used again.

Household Amenities

Eating: To get cooking, dishwashing, and drinking water we had to go to the barn area where the windmill was. Water was furnished by the wind and hand pump. Pails of water were carried to the house.

Heating: Wood for stoves was cut from trees in the woods. After sawing and splitting, the wood was put in the basement through the side cellar door. The girls had to stack it by size, small-medium and large. Every day we would have to carry wood upstairs to the wood box. Wood was for the kitchen cooking stove and the living room potbelly stove. We kept count of the armfuls each one carried a day. We marked the count on the basement wall.

Bathing: Water was heated in the boiler on the stove then poured into the washtub in the

The wringer washer used from 1940 to 1947

washroom. Saturday was bath day. Youngest one went first and washed by the older one if necessary. I was the third one in line; same water for all.

Wringer Washer / Wash Day: Monday was washday. Wash machine and a galvanized tub. A cistern was outside the house with the board over the top for cover. Dad would tie a rope on a pail, stand on two boards with space in between, and lower the pail to fill, pull up and put in the boiler on the stove to heat, then put in the machine. The clothes went from washer through a wringer to rinse the tub, through the wringer to the clothesbasket, to the clothesline outside.

Games: Some of the outside games we played during the summer months were hopscotch, horseshoe, croquet, Annie-Annie over the outhouse, and tag. In the winter, we would go sliding, skating, and skiing, making snow angels and snowmen. The girls had a playroom where we played dolls. We had dollhouse furniture my uncle made for our older sisters. It was a bed, table, benches, and dresser. We used an old breadbox for a stove. We would slice raw potatoes in salt water, carrots for lunch. We had big and little dolls.

We also set puzzles, played cards, and did coloring books.

Outhouse: What an appropriate name but a necessity. It was a place you wanted to stay <u>OUT</u> of. In the summer, the smell was obnoxious and a fly trap. In the winter, contents would pile high because it became frozen and one had to take care where they sat. It was a good place to use the Sears and Montgomery Ward catalog pages.

Summer Storms: When it rained, we would put rags on the windowsills and put bread pans to catch the dripping water. If it got real bad we went to the basement northwest corner.

Hiking: In the summertime, we would take hikes into the woods to collect flowers and fruit. The flowers we got in the spring were violets, trillium, lilies, and bloodroot. In the fall, we would get bitter sweets and cattails. We used them for bouquets.

We also picked wild fruit. We would make juice and jams with them. We got grapes, gooseberries, cherries, strawberries, raspberries, chokecherries, and thorn apples.

Drive-In Movies: Our summertime movie was a screen on the side of the town mill. They showed them on Friday nights. We took blankets and sat in the parking lot to watch them. We took snacks and drinks with us. There was a train track on the other side of the mill. When a train went through, they stopped the movie. After all the cars had passed, the movie continued. The movie was free.

Comfort Foods: Mother made a cake or bars every weekend. About once a month Dad or one of my brothers would take us to a one store in town to pick out pints of ice cream. It was smooth Kemp ice cream. When we got back to the house, we cut the pints in half and shared with other siblings.

My mother used to do glass painting. The words were left clear with some glitter. Foil was crushed lightly and put behind the letters. In those days, the only foil available was from Hershey candy bars. She used to give the pictures as wedding gifts. We were happy every time there was a wedding because Dad had to go to town to buy the candy. Mom used the foil and we got the candy.

A Magical Christmas
By Darlene Koropatnicki of Goodridge, Minnesota
Born 1941

The year 1948 was one of my favorite. Two weeks before Christmas my parents would go pick out a Christmas tree. Dad would put it in the tree stand that he made leaving room for plenty of water to keep it green until New Year's Day. We made many decorations, colored paper to make chain link garland and other items we made in country school. Mom would always buy the tinsel to put on last. It was a slow process hanging them straight. Mom and Dad usually hung most of the tinsel. The tree was so pretty with all the decorations.

Our Christmas program at our country school District #60 (Peppy Inn) was so much fun. We did little skits and lots of singing. Once in a while, my dad would bring his accordion and accompany us. But most of the time the teacher would start us out on a song. We exchanged $1.00 gifts and received a bag of goodies, apples, nuts, peanuts, ribbon candy, mixed candy, and a Hershey bar.

We also had our church Ebenezer Lutheran program. All the Sunday school children had a part to say. We also did the Nativity scene where each child dressed like shepherds, kings, angles, Joseph, and Mary. Baby Jesus was a doll. We also received a bag of treats after the program and lunch in the church basement with delicious Kool-Aid to drink.

Christmas Eve we always stayed home. 5:30AM Dad would light the old Coleman lantern. He and my brothers would go to the barn to milk the cows and feed the other animals. We had cows, horses, pigs, a few sheep, and chickens. Mom and I would make breakfast. We also would get water from the well. No electricity, running water or bathroom back then. After breakfast, Mom and I would make pies, usually apple, pumpkin, and Dad's favorite Graham Cracker Cream Pie. Dad would go to town to get lutefisk at Hartz Supermarket, Thief River Falls, Minnesota. The lutefisk was in big barrels. Dad would pick one out. The man behind the meat counter would wrap it in white butcher paper. Dad also brought us all a treat, pink and white marshmallow cookies with coconut, twelve in a package. They were delicious. We didn't see a bought cookie very often. Mom was a good cook and baker so she made all the bread, buns, rolls, cookies, cakes, and bars.

About 5:30PM Dad and my brothers went back out to the barn to do the chores; while Mom and I made the Christmas Eve meal. I don't think I was much help at 7 years old, but I tried. I remember Mom using the big canner to cook the lutefisk. She would wash it in cold water, wrap in cheesecloth, and drop it in boiling water. By the time the evening chores were done, Christmas Eve supper was ready, lutefisk, lefse and all the trimmings. In 1948, there were five children, four boys, and one daddy's girl. We all liked lutefisk and still do. After supper Mom and I would do dishes, Dad played Christmas carols on the piano and we

Darlene, Grandma Skalet, Larry, Darryl, Grandpa Skalet, Ronnie, and Punky in 1950

Darlene's parents, Alton and Evelyn with their children in 1960

would all join in on the songs we knew. After dishes were done, Mom would mix up a batch of her famous white sugar cookies to make Christmas shape cutouts. Frost and decorate to bring to Grandpa and Grandma Skalets Christmas Day. After the cookies were done, we all hung our stockings. We made sure there were no holes in them. And we went to bed. Santa would come during the night. In the morning, we would run down the stairs and find our favorite toy. I got my first doll that opened and shut her eyes. I couldn't wait to show Dad and Mom.

This year Christmas Day 1948 was a little different. It had snowed. Grandpa and Grandma's driveway was drifted in with the wind overnight and we wouldn't be able to drive in by car. Grandpa Skalet hooked up his team of horses to a hayrack sleigh that he used to haul hay home in the winter. Grandma heated up some bricks, put quilts and heavy sheep lined coats on the sleigh to cover up the small children. Grandpa had bells on the reins. It was so much fun to ride on the sleigh up to the house and hear the bells jingle all the way. As each family came, Grandpa would go pick them up. Each family brought a dish to pass. All of us cousins exchanged gifts. I got a weaving kit, one of my favorite gifts. After a fun day at Grandpa and Grandma's, we all got a sleigh ride back to our vehicles parked on the road. Christmas is magical.

Our family started growing again in 1952. I finally had a sister. I was 11 years old. Two more sisters and one brother followed our family of nine children, 5 boys, and 4 girls. (Donna, Sherry, Susie, Richard, Ronnie, Larry, "Punky" Alton, Jr., and Darryl.) We all enjoyed the Christmas season and still do.

Our First Experience with a Color TV
By Marlene Pedersen of Alexandria, Minnesota
Born 1936

"Here he comes!" Our daughter Sherry, 9, announced. "Dad's carrying a really big box."

We all helped carry it downstairs to our rec room. Surprise, surprise! It was our first colored TV. We decided that in the evening we would all watch our first movie in color and of course, have some popcorn. It will be perfect.

Evening finally arrived and we all settled down in the rec room. Bear in mind that we lived in a very small town and we received only one station. Oh dear, No! I was panicky when I realized the movie was "The Birds." Alfred Hitchcock was definitely not my favorite. Sherry had had some unpleasant experiences with birds. One time a baby King bird fell out of its nest right in front of the lawnmower she was using. Another time a boy at school put a Sparrow in her locker. Again, while mowing the lawn she walked under the clothesline where a dead Sparrow was hanging. It had caught its foot in a knot in the wire.

So we shall see how she handles this movie. I'm so worried…It started at 7:30 and as the movie progressed Sherry and her dad sat comfortably watching and munching on popcorn. But as I said, Alfred and I have very little in common. By 8:00 I was hurrying upstairs and quickly closing the curtains and drawing the drapes. By 8:30 I was nervously pulling the shades behind the curtains. By 8:45 I was turning off the lights in a panic. By 9:00 I was locking the doors. By 9:05 I could no longer go back downstairs. By 9:30 Sherry and her dad came upstairs laughing and chatting carrying popcorn bowls. They found me sitting at the kitchen table, best defined as traumatized.

And so…1) there will be no more worries about Sherry and birds. 2) Alfred is no longer allowed in the house. 3) This is the end of the true experience of our first evening with a color TV.

March Blizzard of 1966
By A. Beth Grandstrand of Karlstad, Minnesota
Born 1936

I was expecting a baby anytime. We lived 5 ½ miles from Karlstad, Minnesota. Our hospital had closed in December of 1965. I doctored in Thief River Falls, Minnesota.

I had some trouble in my pregnancy in the first 3 months but doing fine by this time. My relatives in town were worried about me. My uncle and cousin came late afternoon the first day of the storm to take us to town to my dad's place. We couldn't drive in the driveway because of the snow, so my husband borrowed a snowcat from the neighbor across the street. My husband tipped the snowcat on the way up the driveway. We laughed, I was okay. We were getting ready for bed when another uncle came and said the doctor wanted to see me. The time was 11:00 PM. The state snowplow would lead us. My husband drove our car and followed. My aunt went with. We had called the gal that use to be the head nurse and asked if she would deliver my baby if it came during the storm. She had called the doctor to see if there was anything specific she should know being I had trouble earlier in the pregnancy. That's when the doctor said I had to come. He must never have known of the storm because we got to Thief River Falls at 3:00 a.m. He checked me and sent me out in the storm! The motels were filled. We sat in the lobby till light out and walked a block, in the snow up to our hips, to a café. Then we walked a block and half to my husband's niece and stayed for 2 days. The sun was out and we drove to Karlstad to my dad's. One way on the road, snow to the roof on some buildings that was Saturday. The following Monday it was blowing and blocking the road to town so we went and spent the night at my husband's folks. Wednesday morning, I woke up and my water had broken. We hurried to Thief River Falls and our son was born at 11:15 AM. All was well! We had two daughters 12 and 10 ½ so we were happy to have a son! He was 50 years old on March 9, 2016.

The Garbage Run
By Pat Nelson of Mendota Heights, Minnesota
Born 1940

We are campers. About 45 years ago, we tried a place called Campers Paradise. It is located on an island between Park Rapids and Walker, Minnesota. The town it is in is Nevis, Minnesota. There are between 80-85 campsites, some on the water, and some inland. Beautiful white sand beach, crystal clear lake (20-26 feet out you can see the bottom) and shallow along shore for all the little ones. It is called a recreational lake with a lot of water skiing, tubing, jet skis, and sitting on the lake with your pontoon. There is what you call a "causeway" for a road to get on the island. It is a one-lane dirt and gravel road just above the water line. You have to take turns driving on it.

Anyway, their unique feature was at 7:30 at night they would do "garbage run" with a truck with barrels in the back and two island workers, Mark and Brian, in the back. One boy would be in the truck taking care of the barrels and the other one would jump off the back of the truck and pick up a smaller can at each campsite and dump the garbage into the barrels on the truck or if the campsite bagged the garbage throw it on the truck. When they would finish picking up at a site, they would holler "Go" and the owner, Jean, would drive to the next site. I have two teenage girls, Pam and Sherry, which got along very well with Mark and Brian. Also, have two boys Tim and Terry. The kids started to have fun with the garbage run and they would fill the garbage bags with sand and then Mark and Brian had to pick them up and throw them on the truck. The whole time Jean keeps the truck slowly moving. It made for a whole lot of laughs and sometimes a few words.

Then they started water fights on the garbage run with squirt guns and buckets of water. Pam, Sherry, Terry, and Tim would hide the water buckets and themselves behind trees and bushes, or wherever they could. Mark and Brian never knew what to expect coming by our site. They even used water balloons. Eventually Mark and Brian started carrying water buckets with them. Then the water fights would start and other campers became a part of it. Then the owner Jean had an idea and she took the truck with a fishing boat in the back of it and filled it with water, drove it back across the causeway and the water shifted in the boat and it fell off the truck. I cannot think what would have happened when they got to our campsite with it. There were plenty of laughs though in telling us about it.

The garbage run they do not do anymore but it was so much fun when they had it. The island is so much fun and the owners are fantastic. The original owners, who bought the island, Chris and Jean Swaggert have passed away but the kids have taken over, Loni, Pat, and three grandsons. The whole Swaggert family is awesome. Everyone camping there enjoys the island, as it is just beautiful. We have made so many, many friends there. We are now the Rangers their and love every minute of it.

The Tale of the Tail
By Helen Wagner of Roseau, Minnesota
Born 1937

Dusk had come. Dark would not be far behind. In the small farmhouse kerosene lamps had been lit. After the evening meal, Daddy had settled into his chair in the living room and was already napping. Baby sister was asleep in her crib. My older sister and I were snuggled with Mama on the sofa.

"Tell us what it was like when you were little like we are," my sister said.

"All right," Mama replied. "I'll tell you about the adventure Uncle Hank and I had one winter day. It was sunny, calm, and with a beautiful blue sky. Your grandpa had hitched up the sleigh. He and Grandma went to town for supplies.

Hank and I were playing in the snow when they left. We had the sled that was used to haul firewood to the house and were giving each other rides on it. Well, that got tiring after a while, and we stopped to rest and throw snow chunks at each other. Then Hank had a bright idea. 'Let's get the tame calf from the barn to pull the sled.' I'm not sure how he did it but soon he had the sled tied to the calf's tail. He jumped on the sled, slapped the calf on the rump, and off they went down the road. It wasn't very long before the calf came galloping into the farmyard alone. After a longer wait, Uncle Hank came trudging back, pulling the sled with one hand, and holding the tail in the other hand."

My sister and I sat there speechless. Our eyes were wide open as well as our mouths. Finally, Sister asked, "What happened then?"

"I don't know," said Mama. "Your grandpa never said a word about the missing tail. Now it's bedtime. Give me a kiss, say your prayers, and hop into bed."

Because Mother enjoyed telling stories to us about growing up on a farm, we always believed every word. As we grew older (and wiser), we realized her recollections of her youth, true, or a little exaggerated, are treasures. My sister and I still chuckle and wink when we tell the tale of the tail to our children and grandchildren. They, too, have been highly entertained as in their minds they picture the adventure of long ago. Fact or fiction? Does it matter?

Note: farm kids are very inventive and so are their mothers.

The Weather Changed Fast
By Gerald Lenk of Browerville, Minnesota
Born 1936

I grew up on a farm nine miles south of Staples, where I still live today. I am sure many of the young people growing up on farms today do not realize how good we have it today compared with "the good old days." When I was a small child we had no electricity, plumbing, or central heating, and I am sure if someone would have said television or computer nearly everyone would have said, "What's that?"

Even our weather is much better now than it was when I was a child. The weather is something we cannot take for granted. It can change fast but it changed even faster when I was a child. I am sure everyone has heard of the Armistice Blizzard of November 11, 1940, when many people lost their lives because it came up so suddenly. Few people realize there was another blizzard hit our area later that winter in March that was nearly as bad as the Armistice Blizzard.

My second cousin George and his wife, Helen, decided to visit George's parents who were our neighbors. Helen was pregnant, but it being a nice day and only 91 miles to go they were not concerned. After being on the road a while it started snowing. It was snowing harder and harder, and it started getting colder.

When they were about four miles from their destination, they got stuck and could go no further. They abandoned their car and started walking. After walking two and a half miles, Helen could not go on. Fortunately, there was a farm place there they were able to stop and have shelter. After a brief rest, George decided to keep going. Helen wanted to go, but George insisted that she stay behind, which she did.

George walked about a mile to where my parents lived, and my dad was feeding pigs when George arrived. My dad said you could not see ten feet in front of you, and he heard someone say, "Hello, Joe." In the storm, he could not see the person, but he recognized George by the voice. His answer was, "George, what the hell are you doing here?" George explained his predicament and asked my dad if he would hitch up his team of horses and sled and go to the neighbor's and get Helen and take them to his folks. My dad being a good friend and neighbor did not hesitate to do so.

Marsh Grove Township
By Janice (Olson) Ramsey of Detroit Lakes, Minnesota
Born 1943

I was born at the hospital in Thief River Falls on March 24, 1943. My sister, Elsie, had been born at home weighing 4 lbs. 4 oz. on March 11, 1937. She almost didn't make it. She was blue when she was born. My mother said they put her in a dishpan of warm water until she came to life. She is still doing well now at 79 years old.

As a four or five year old, my parents were definitely convinced they had a strong willed child on their hands. Once I wanted to go to town, Newfolden, with my dad. I was so determined, I held on to the bumper of the car as he was driving away. My dad said, "No, you can't go this time." I guess I threw a conniption fit and cried a long time after he was gone. No spanking was given but a very good talking to.

A few years back I wrote down the memory of our house burning down on Christmas morning of 1949. We lived seven miles west and two miles south of Newfolden, Minnesota when these memories took place. Now I live in Detroit Lakes.

I was six in 1949. We lived on a farm nine miles out of Newfolden. I was six or seven years old when my dad put me behind the wheel of our old car, that was stuck in the snow in the driveway. With no brothers and one sister, who must not have been home that day, my dad had to push by hand to get the old car moving. I could barely see over the steering wheel. The car took a little rocking back and forth to get it to come out but we finally made it. I never forgot being so scared and excited at the same time.

One summer we were staying at my cousin's place and I got the stomach flu during the night. The only choice was to go in the dark to the outhouse. I will never forget the sound of the leaves blowing around on the floor out there. I was so sure it was an animal, a mouse, of heaven forbid a skunk. Somehow, I survived being sick. The outhouse looked pretty harmless the next morning.

I remember the Christmas program in our one room schoolhouse when I was in the first or second grade. My sister, Elsie, was in the seventh grade when I was in first grade in 1949. Each student was coming in to the schoolroom from the coat hall carrying a candle as we were walking. The girl behind me started looking for her parents when she got too close to the back of my hair. My hair started on fire and my sister saw it and came rushing over and put her hand on the back of my head and put out the fire. I hardly knew what happened but we never forgot that incident in Green Valley School, Marsh Grove Township.

Tom with his dog, Abbey

Weather Forecasting Dog
By Tom Twist of San Diego, California
Born 1967

One summer day while visiting my aunt and uncle in Alexandria, Minnesota, there was a quick change in the weather. It started to cloud up and thunder. "Because it is dull and long thunder it is going to be hail," Herb said. Then the sun comes out and light rain starts. Herb tells us if it rains when sun is out it will rain again within three days. But we are still going to get hail now and every time moisture goes back up hail will get larger. When the dog, Abbey, runs to the garage it about to start. Just then, Abbey runs into the garage. Herb says, "Okay, it is going to be a bad one because Abbey wants the door closed." Next thing you know the wind starts blowing, and it starts hailing the size of golf balls. It sounded like a stampede of horses on the roof as we headed to the basement.

Once it stopped, we go back upstairs to survey the damage. The house is okay but leaves and twigs are all over the yard. The garden looks bad. Tomatoes and melons are pelted off their vines. Hail is still on the ground. It took two hours the next day to clean up the mess.

Guess what? The next morning at 3:00, the tornado siren watch went off. But we only had wind and rain. Thank God no tornado, but the within three days proverb came true.

Three years later, I was back in Minnesota. Again, we went to Alexandria. About halfway there the sun disappeared and the clouds set in. We were lucky it didn't rain until we were only a driveway away. I said, "If Abbey is in the garage I am going right to the basement."

When we turned into the driveway, the garage door went up and there was Abbey. I got out of the car and immediately went to the basement.

The Clotho School
By Violet Kramer of Long Prairie, Minnesota
Born 1915

I was fortunate to be born to Christian parents and to be blessed with good health. At age sixteen I graduated from high school. There was no school bus service and as we lived about five miles from town, I either walked to school or worked for my room and board. I rented one room in a private home for $3 per month and somehow got through those four years. The title I chose for my graduation speech was "Perseverance." My motto has been: with God's help you can attain your goal.

I wanted to become a teacher. My brother took me (and hopefully enough food) each Monday morning to the Teacher Training School 24 miles from home. Many weeks the food did not last until getting back home on Friday. No money, no food, no eat!

I prayed that I would obtain a teaching position and I was the first one in my class to be hired. Many of my friends were not as fortunate. I taught grades one through eight in a one room rural school for three years. My salary was $40 a month. This was 1933-1935, during the Great Depression. It was my first opportunity to earn money and I was elated.

In the summer of 1956, there were off-campus college courses being offered in Long Prairie. Education has always been a priority for me and, since our three daughters were helpful at home on our farm, I decided I could take courses. My goal was to somehow accumulate enough credits to earn my degree. Over the years, by going to summer school, attending off-campus courses in the evening, and taking correspondence courses, I did graduate from the University of Minnesota with a Bachelor of Science degree.

While I was in class that summer of 1956, a gentleman I did not know asked me if I would teach the school in Clotho that fall. I had absolutely no intention of working away from home or teaching again. I informed him that my husband and I had a pre-school son and that I really could not consider it. He asked me to think about it, which I did, and realized that my son was out with his dad most of the time and that they could get along without me during the day. And so I agreed to teach the Clotho School.

One afternoon in August of 1956, I decided it was time to go to Clotho and begin to organize my work for grades one through six. I knew which road to take out of Long Prairie and after driving what seemed quite a distance, I thought I would soon have to inquire just where the Clotho School was located. I took one more curve in the road and there it was! Over the bridge and across the river, there sat the neat little while schoolhouse.

As I unlocked the door I never dreamed that I would be going there to teach for ten years. Inside the little entrance was a place to hang outer garments and a bench for lunch pails. A rope came down to reaching distance from the ceiling. It was connected to a large bell on top of the school. I estimate that during those ten years I rang that bell approximately 7,500 times. It called students to the first classes, signaled the end of morning recess, the classes following lunch break, and the end of the physical education period in the afternoon.

The schoolroom, shared by all students, was about 28 feet by 40 feet. It had windows on two walls with a large oil-burning heater in a back corner. The room was very clean and pleasant with good chalkboards. Outside there was ample playground space for softball games and other activities. There was no running water and no bathrooms. Outside on the playground was a hand pump. Water was brought inside in a pail and poured into a water fountain. Behind the schoolhouse were two little outhouses, one for boys and one for girls. It got very cold out there in the winter.

My teaching experience for those ten terms in Clotho was one of the best periods in my life. It was a most rewarding and very happy time. The students and parents have become wonderful friends. The salary proved to be very important and led to good social security.

There is no way I can express the excellent cooperation I received from that super school board. They gave me permission to order anything that I wished to use to enrich the education of the students. Besides material for the basic subjects we had supplies for various art projects, simple musical instruments, and physical education equipment. One day I merely mentioned that it would be great to have a piano. The following Monday morning, there was a piano in the corner!

At Christmas time, we presented a program for the parents and community. The school board would erect a stage and hang up curtains. We had a great time with musical numbers, plays, recitations, etc. Afterwards, of course, the mothers supplied a fine lunch. For Thanksgiving those good cooks would send food to school and we would have a cozy dinner. A student would offer a prayer before we ate.

We took many field trips. We went to Duluth, to the State Capitol in St. Paul, to visit a beaver dam, and to the maple woods when the sap was running. We also took trips on foot to collect things from nature. For another memorable trip, parents transported up all to Sauk Centre, where we boarded the train and rode to Alexandria where they picked us up. They were wonderful people in Clotho! After I would sign my contract to return another term, there would be a Welcome Back picnic.

Once a year we had Pet Day when children brought quite an assortment to school. One kitty went behind the piano. One Halloween we constructed a life-size dummy. Ronald, Leroy, and Joe supplied clothing for it. We named it "Rolejoe."

A lovely lady thoroughly cleaned the school about once a month. She often told me how she enjoyed the displays of the children's work.

There was a creamery in Clotho and we were always invited to attend their annual creamery meeting to partake of the delicious dinner and then to present a program for entertainment. On my way to Clotho each morning I would stop at the Long Prairie Creamery and a man would load into my car enough milk for each child for that day. During the cold winter we often put potatoes on top of the stove to bake for lunch.

Bedsides all the fun, we had very serious hours of classes and study. As early as possible I arrived at the school and covered the back chalkboards with study questions, which kept the older students busy and quiet while I taught the lower grades. Often there was only one student in a grade. Sometimes as many as six. They were all good kids.

Many hours of preparation were necessary to plan each subject for six grades, to check written work, and to grade each student in every subject at report card time. Before putting a book to read in the hands of a first grader, I would make many one-word flashcards to study as well as copy phrases on the chalkboard. How well I remember the big brown eyes of a little girl as she glanced at that first page in her book. She said, "I can read!" That was a wonderful moment for me because I love to read, too.

For about six weeks in the spring I would have a Spring Primary class for little ones about to enter the first grade in the fall.

I detected an unusual quality in a little girl's voice and hoped that someday she would develop that talent and she has! The little girl with beautiful eyes, voice, and personality was Cecile Hansmeyer.

May I be forgiven for many mistakes and poor judgment. I am certain I was not a perfect teacher. Following my years of teaching in Clotho, I taught the second grade at St. Mary's parochial school in Long Prairie for 17 years. Again, the Board of Education was very kind, generous, and cooperative. When I retired from teaching in 1982 the former students, their parents, and the Clotho community held a huge surprise party with a dinner, beautiful gifts, and kind words for me. Indeed, I am very thankful for those friends, my husband Ted Sr., our dear children, and all of God's blessings.

Angels Among Us
By Paul Twist of Henning, Minnesota
Born 1930

The Bible teaches the existence and importance of angels. They are real and God uses them in various ways. They can take on human form when serving a special purpose or protecting a Christian.

Christian missionaries living in dangerous countries have given testimony of personal protection or chastening. I have never, as far as I know, met an angel, although I have often felt they were protecting me on a trip.

I did know a missionary in Mexico who believed he had met an angel. Being tired from a busy day, he turned away a man who came to his door one evening asking for help. Immediately, he felt convicted and opened the door, but the man was not there.

Up and down the streets, he searched, yet he could not find him. The missionary felt God had sent an angel to rebuke him, and never again did he refuse to help someone in his village needing assistance. All of us, if we willingly help someone in need, may be considered angels.

Just about two weeks ago, my wife and I met such a person. We had been gone all day attending a funeral in another city. The highways were clear, and we had a safe trip both ways. But when we drove up the alley to our garage and turned in, there was a hard snowdrift just six feet from the open door, and we were stuck. The car would not budge as the wheels spun in the snow.

As I went to get a shovel from the garage, a lady dressed in a snowmobile suit came walking up the alley and said, "Looks like you need some help."

"Yes, thank you. We do." Even though she was on another errand in the area, she stayed and helped shovel and push and push and rock the car back and forth for about 15 minutes until I was able to back into the alley again and drive safely into the garage.

We had never met the lady before and didn't know who she was. We invited her in for a few minutes, but she had to get up at 4:00 a.m. to go to work, so back down the alley she went in the direction from which she had come.

My wife and I were so grateful for her help and chuckled to ourselves that after safely driving more than 200 miles, we got stuck in a 15-foot driveway six feet from our garage door. Thank, Kris, you are a Henning angel to us.

The Bible teaches that we are to help one another in times of need. "Blessed is he who is kind to the needy" (Proverbs 14:21)

Often it means setting aside what we had planned to do in order to be of help. But we experience inner satisfaction when we give a helping hand to someone in need. It's another key to our happiness.

Brownie, the Notorious Cattle Dog
By Kenneth Raap of Henning, Minnesota
Born 1951

I was born in 1951 in Parkers Prairie, Minnesota, in Doctor Liebold's hospital, which was also his home and is now a part of St. Williams Living Center. I was raised on the family farm and attended first through third grade at Otter Tail County District 1534, which was a one-room schoolhouse on a little hill on the very northeast corner of my father's property.

I remember walking down the gravel road a quarter mile to the schoolhouse with my little metal lunch bucket in hand. The schoolhouse consisted of an entry room where we hung our coats, one room that housed grades one through eight, with a very small library in the corner, and a wood shed in the back. The water was brought in from a long handled hand pump outside, and the restrooms were two little white buildings out back referred to in Alaska as long drops. There was a little pond close to the schoolhouse, and in the winter months, we would play fox and goose and other games on the pond during recess.

My first grade teacher lived close so she drove to school each day. But my second and third grade teacher moved a small mobile home about the size of today's small pull-type travel trailers next to the schoolhouse in which she stayed during the school year. Prior to that, some of the teachers boarded at my parents' house during the school year. After third grade the school districts consolidated, the school was closed, and I caught the bus to Parkers Prairie Elementary School.

Our farm was the typical family farm at that time with dairy cows, a few hogs, some chickens, and even a few sheep.

Let me tell you about our family dog. Brownie was a crossbred dog, sometimes referred to as a mutt, born the same year that I was so it was always easy to remember how old he was. He grew to be a fairly large dog and developed into a notorious cattle dog. He was a proud dog and carried his tail arched high above his back, which sometimes got him in trouble. We pastured our dairy cows and had to bring them down a quarter mile lane from the pasture to the barn for milking every morning and evening. Brownie would

Brownie in 1957

always help round the cows up and convince them to go home for milking. This is when his tail would get him in trouble. Sometimes he would cross under the electric fence in the lane on the way home and his tail would touch. He would yip and then growl in little short segments the rest of the way home. My father said he was grumbling the rest of the way home.

Brownie was also somewhat fearless. I remember one time my father was mending fences and he had to rescue Brownie as he tangled with a raccoon and the raccoon was pulling him under water in the creek that ran through our property.

Brownie also enjoyed the nightlife. He would leave at night and not return home until about ten the next morning at times. I remember going to town with my father one time and meeting Brownie about two miles from home. Needless to say, my father stopped the car and in a very loud voice told Brownie to get home. One of my sister's friends referred to Brownie as a traveling salesman. One would think this would have gotten Brownie in a lot of trouble, but being the notorious cattle dog he was, that wasn't the case. Our neighbors were elated to have puppies sired by Brownie. Brownie passed at the age of thirteen but not without leaving his legacy.

Lara and the Ghost
By Jill A. Torgerson of Bagley, Minnesota
Born 1947

Lara, my Cocker Spaniel dog with silky black fur was totally devoted to her master-me, and was my close companion for five years while working as a parts runner for a pipeline company in northern Minnesota. I was sent to bring parts, welding rods, diesel fuel, oil, and other job related items to the crews spread out over a 100 miles. From my starting point in Bemidji, Minnesota, I could see prairies, pine forest, hilly areas, and lakes abundant in my travels. I loved the duty, working alone gave a sense of freedom and I could bring my buddy Lara along for company. Adventuresome and loving new challenges, I was happy, needing only my dog, pickup, and a place to stay each night.

I did have one challenge, however, finding motels that would accept dogs. Some charged more to accommodate pets, others sneered saying dogs were filthy and left behind fleas and ticks. I respected their wishes and went on to the next one.

One autumn day I was sent to Little Falls, Minnesota. I knew better than to try a hotel, thinking they would balk taking one look at me in dirty overalls reeking of diesel fuel. One look at the dog beside me would clinch the deal. Motels were usually friendlier to construction workers, yet I heard over and over again, "No, we don't allow dogs." Finally, after six attempts, I found a motel accepting Lara- in a separate section of the main motel, which was rarely used. Wondering if it was safe, I banished the fear after viewing the nostalgic park across the road, donned with weeping willows framing the walkways. This seemed a desirable place for us, so we could take our brisk night walk unencumbered by traffic and stoplights.

We were the only ones in the parking lot of the lack-luster building, which looked like it had been deserted for a long time. Although in dire need of fresh paint and general clean up, I still was happy to find a home for the night. I inserted the key and slowly opened the door. Creak, creak. We stepped inside and immediately Lara's fur stood up on her spine. She was agitated. I walked about the cold, clammy room, smelling something like mothballs or sulphur making me wince and my nose to run. As I tiptoed through the two rooms, I felt like someone was watching me. There was no one there, yet I turned around several times to check the area behind me, beyond me, and beside me. The hair on my arms and neck stood on end and my whole body felt like it had been thrown into a refrigerator. I wondered what I would do if I saw a ghost or a spirit with my natural eyes. I had heard somewhere that demons smelled like a just-lit kitchen match. Something was not right, yet I determined to be brave and not complain. Not Lara. She would not move past the multi-colored rag rug laid out in front of the door. When I tried to coax her to come and jump on the bed, she flatly refused. Something was wrong. She began growling in an eerie way. This was not a normal Lara growl. This one was a howl accompanied with a long

Lara

smell, you are my memory friend. I almost forgot about the strange room.

Then I heard a still, small voice, "Get out of that room. There is evil in that room." Evil? You mean ghosts? Or demons? I had read about both and thought they may be one in the same, and I recalled what to do about them. Don't entertain them. Kick them out! That room was my property for the night. I was in charge. I had authority. Still, the still small voice urged me, "Don't stay in that room. Ask for another."

drawl, her head lifting up and pivoting to the side. She resembled a wolf at that moment. I continued to coax her to come and try out the room. No way. She would not budge.

Tired of the howling and now feeling uncomfortable myself, we stepped outside where Lara beat it for the pickup, wanting to get in there and out of this place. I had a decision to make and remembered I did best while walking. The park across the road was the place for such mental deliberation. I could sort this ghost business out and settle the dog down. Trying to convince my mind that everything was normal, I turned to the beautiful works of nature in the park. Passion enveloped me as I watched the trees, birds, squirrels, and striped gophers. They were at peace. Did they have an inkling of what I was feeling? Perhaps not.

It felt good to get away from the room. The weeping willows swayed back and forth in the cool breeze while leaves gently made their way to the cold earth. Wood stove smoke in the houses nearby left a trail leading to the sky and I recalled the house I grew up in. Waking up to the smell of coffee, eggs, and meat frying on the old cook stove, smoke billowing out when Mom would add more dry firewood, a place I felt secure and happy. Musty smoke

Was I afraid of ghosts? Rallying between believing and not believing in them, I thought of Lara's response, who sure didn't like them and sensed something tangible in that room. Could it be that dogs have a sixth sense that humans don't? I decided that Lara was smarter than me, and thought it may not hurt to listen to that unusual voice I heard. I went back to the office of the motel, not liking to complain. It wasn't in my Scandinavian nature. You make do. Well, this time was different. I had my buddy to please.

"Hi, I just went into the room you gave me and my dog is so uncomfortable there that we cannot stay. Do you happen to have another room we could try?" I asked the office lady. The lady said, "Why sure, we'll have you stay in number nine. I hope that will work out for you."

Whew, relief. I just hated to trouble people. I would have rather stayed in the ghost room than bother the motel staff, but relieved she didn't tell me to hit the road and find another place. She could have thought I was a weirdo who listened to dogs. Not at all fitting for a Scandinavian. I had been taught to be nice and not fussy. It is good enough. Not this time.

With new key in hand, we entered the

next room, two doors down from the first one. No creak, creak, this door was all oiled up. Sun brilliantly shown through the window in this one, sky blue filmy curtains framed the white cottage style windows. The bed covering was delightful, in colors of cobalt blue with peach and yellow flowers rising above the background fabric of pale blue- almost white. The rugs were in the same pale blue and a little white rocking chair sat by the bed, adorned with back and seat covers in the same fabric with the blue, peach and yellow flowers. Throw pillows of similar shades were upon the bed. The room seemed heavenly in comparison with the other one. The atmosphere was warm, refreshing, and I could faintly smell lavender. I felt cozy in the warm bathroom, filled with colors of pale yellow and white. I liked this place. It felt like home.

"Lara, where are you?" I looked around and found her snuggled under the many throw pillows on the bed. Snoozing peacefully, I couldn't believe the difference in her temperament. In this room, Lara was totally at peace. We slept well that night, both of us dreaming sweet things. I could tell Lara was dreaming because she whimpered and moved her legs as if swimming in the lake near our house. Lara loved to swim; it was her enjoyment, reward for a good day's work and way to cool off. Knowing her so well, I knew this was a good dream.

The next morning we brought the key back to the motel office and I couldn't wait to tell the staff person what a lovely night Lara and I had experienced. "Good morning, I want to comment on the good time we had in room number nine last night. I suppose you heard that we swapped rooms. We were amazed at the difference between them," I said to the office man with Sam on his nametag. Before I could explain my dog's behavior, he looked me straight in the eyes and smiled. I halted my story. "Lady, I have heard this before. I have worked here many years and always hear the same. We felt such love, warmth, and peace. We slept better than we had in years. Lady, I feel the same way when I clean that room. I even had one response, I saw an angel in room number nine- a guardian angel." I smiled and went on my way, knowing who my guardian angel was the night before, a little black Cocker Spaniel named Lara.

Childhood Christmas Memories
By Norma Sims of Gonvick, Minnesota
Born 1938

The best and most important holiday of the year to us was Christmas. We never had a lot of money since this time was during the Depression. So my mother would sit and sew at night after we, the children, had all gone to bed. She would make us "sock dolls" from men's stockings and when finished they looked like monkeys. We loved them! Also, she would sew us a new dress or blouse that we could wear for the Christmas programs coming up soon. She did have a Singer sewing machine that she had bought from a salesman that came to the house pedaling his belongings. She made a deal with him to pay $1.00 a month until it was paid for. She also purchased a Maytag wringer washing machine from him paying him the same way. They were both real necessities for a family of 10, which is what ours ended up at.

We would have a lot of fun during the Christmas programs in our country school and church. All the students took part in the program. There would be different plays, some would sing, etc. We would practice for weeks before Christmas and have the program just before school was let out for Christmas vacation. My little brother, who was only 3, was also given a poem to learn and told he could perform that. He was very excited so he came up on the stage. We pulled the curtain open; he looked out in the audience and spotted our folks. He slapped his knee and looked at them and said loudly, "I forgot!" Everyone laughed and we helped him get started and he did fine. It was a two-room schoolhouse so when done with the program everyone had lots of goodies to eat. Then time for games. The older ones went into the other room and started the circle games where you have to sing along like, "Go In and Out the Window" and "Farmer in the Dell," and many more. All enjoyable!

There were 6 girls and 2 boys in our family. My two oldest sisters were both married but they would all come home for Christmas Eve. This year we finally got electricity so it was somewhat different than other years. After a big meal that evening of lutefisk and lefse, plus many other things, we younger girls had to go into the kitchen and do dishes. My 2 oldest sisters went into the living room and closed the sliding door that was between the living and dining rooms so we couldn't see what was going on. My dad had just cut the fresh spruce tree, never before the 24th, so we hadn't even trimmed it yet. We always had candles on our tree Christmas Eve and we would light them while we were all in the room opening gifts. Finally, they opened the sliding doors for us and the tree was all lit up with bubble lights. It was so pretty and something we had never had or seen before. It was a nice surprise and we enjoyed those lights for years. Then we got our gifts, nothing big but lots of little things. We had a great evening but never a Santa Clause.

Then Christmas day after church and a nice dinner, our dad would take a little nap then go to the barn and harness the horses, put bells and red tassels on them, and we would all go with the horses and sleigh to our grandfather's farm about 5 miles away from ours. This was a fun sleigh ride. Every once in a while one of us would get pushed off the sleigh, then my dad would make the horses run, then whoever was pushed off would run to catch up and as soon as he or she got close enough to jump on the sleigh, dad would make the horses run and that one was left behind again. He would let us get on after about 3 or 4 tries.

We would spend the afternoon over at their place then another trip home. By this time, we were all tired out from playing outside and eating goodies all afternoon. So we were happy to get home again. This was a lot of fun and only done at Christmas. So it made the day special and another good memory.

The Cabin on Leech Lake
By Catherine Fieldseth of Cohasset, Minnesota

Ah! The cabin. Where do I put all those memories? Never dreamed we'd have one. Those were for rich people. My dad was the high school band director and my mom was a stay-at-home mom. My childhood memories are, for the most part, all good.

Then mom got Multiple Sclerosis and pregnant by surprise with child number 4. I believe Dad wanted to be near water, so we moved from town out to the river. But, I get ahead of myself. Dad wanted a cabin. He loved hunting and fishing. So, he scavenged bits and scraps of wood, windows, flooring, and whatever else he needed to build that cabin. Back then. It was down a rough dirt road that was barely (if at all) maintained. Michael, my brother, and I went along a lot during building. It was so fun! When we turned off Highway 2, Dad had us lay down on the floor of the back seat and tough it out. What an adventure!

Once, when my relatives from California were visiting, the kids were at a neighbor's cabin dancing and enjoying ourselves playing music and goofing off. The adults were having a few beers and enjoying themselves in our cabin. Of course, there was no inside plumbing so I was using the outhouse. I opened the door when I was finished and right there was a skunk. I immediately shut the door and tried to call for help. No one came. I have no idea how long I stayed in there but eventually got the nerve to open the door and look. Apparently, the woods' gods heard me and the skunk was gone. I ran very quickly to the safety of the cabin much to the laughter of all the adults.

Another time, our dog Corky, a lab mix, got into it with a porcupine. She came looking for Dad. This is a story of the love and trust between a man and his dog. Corky had quills all over her muzzle. She sat by my father and allowed him to extract the quills one by one with a pair of pliers. Not one cry emerged from her nor did she flinch. It was amazing!

The final story I'll share is when the California folks were visiting and we had a horrific storm. As happens frequently on Leech Lake. Dad had a homemade pontoon boat and he and my Uncle Joe decided they needed to save the motor. The wind was howling, rain was pouring, and the waves were monstrous. The boat had busted loose from the dock and was smashing into the rocks by the shoreline. The water there was only 2-3 feet deep but it was very hazardous that day due to the waves from the storm. Dad and Uncle Joe donned rain gear and off they went for the rescue. We four kids lined up on the hill above to watch the action. At one point, Uncle Joe went under to loosen the bolts on the motor to remove it. He was under the water for a very long time. We all were watching in amazement and discussing how long he was holding his breath. Finally, Uncle Joe resurfaced looking terrified and gasping for air. As it turns out, a string from his rain hood had hooked itself around the motor and he couldn't get free. He could have drowned that day while we all stood there watching. Thank the Lord he lived and ended up retrieving the motor!

So many more stories but these are just some of the most memorable. I hope someone out there will read this and enjoy a laugh or two. The times and trials of our little piece of Heaven growing up, our cabin.

Saving Duke
By Daniel R. Vandergon of Maple Lake, Minnesota
Born 1955

When I was about 7 years old, we lost our family dog, Blackie to an accident with the milk truck. Sometime later we got another dog, Snooper but he didn't last long due to his habit of killing young chickens (our future Sunday dinners). One spring day we picked up a puppy from a couple that rented the second house on my Uncle Hank's farm. He was a shy stocky Collie/Golden Retriever mix, we named him Duke.

I was thrilled as any young boy would be to have a new dog. I was a middle child being younger than my two brothers and older than my two sisters. I spent a lot of my free time with Duke, he and I wandered about the farm or down by the lake (Milestone) across the road from our farm.

On Saturday mornings in November and December, we had Christmas program practices at our church. During one Friday night, we had a cold front move in and the lake had new ice along the shore. Before we went to practice that morning, I had enough time to take Duke down to the lake to check out the newly formed ice and whatever else may be down there.

The ice was strong enough to support my weight maybe a yard or three from shore. I was walking along the shore chasing the minnows swimming under the ice. I was having fun and not watching where Duke was. He was a lot lighter than me and was able to go out father on the ice as he spreads his weight among his four feet. He was walking about 30 yards from shore, way too far out on the thin ice. I saw him out there and started to call him to me. The next thing I knew is that he had fallen thru the ice and was swimming and trying futilely to climb back on the ice. He could not manage to climb on top of it as it would break off in front of him. I had no way of getting him to shore so I ran up to the barn to where my dad and brothers, Rick and Dean, were working. I let them know what had happened so hopefully that could rescue Duke. I reluctantly had to leave to go to church. I had tears in my eyes, a lump in my throat and a knot in my stomach all morning at practice thinking that my dog was going to drown. Duke would be dead the next time I would see him.

Being at program practice that day was miserable; my mind was only focused on my dog, Duke. A short time before the practice was over I learned that my dad had called my mom at church letting her know that Duke had been saved and all was well. I was so relieved; I couldn't wait to get home.

When I came home that day I heard the story of what had happened. Rick and my dad carried a ladder down to the lake; they laid the ladder out on the ice to distribute the weight out more evenly. Being that Rick was lighter than dad he crawled out on the ladder, as he came close to Duke he broke through the ice allowing Duke to be able to swim to shore. Rick then had to fish the ladder out of the lake and help carry it back home while being soaking wet in ice-cold water on a cold, November day.

When we arrived back home both Rick and Duke were in the house warming up. I was one very happy boy who had his buddy Duke back alive. I was very thankful to have a big brother who was willing to risk a lot (he could not swim) to save a dog and make his younger brother very happy.

Our Neighbors
By Patricia Peterson of Lancaster, Minnesota
Born 1939

We lived in the northwest corner of Kittson County in Minnesota. My parents farmed 640 acres, raising small grains and milk cows, pigs, chickens, two horses, some bottle lambs, and some years turkeys. Our buildings and house were on a hill with the north branch of the Two River winding its way in front of the house and around towards the back. The house was small and very cold in the winter. Our heat was on oil burner in the living room and a wood cook stove in the kitchen. We had no bathroom, no electricity, no running water, and no phone. Dad hauled water from Hallock and filled a cistern in the spring and fall. Our baths were in an oval galvanized rub. Water for baths was heated on the wood stove, also for washing clothes. The wash machine had a gas motor so exhaust pipe had to run outside. It made a loud putt putt sound and could be heard by the neighbors, a mile away. So they knew when Mom washed clothes. The clothes were hung on the line outside even in the winter. I don't know how my mother stood to hang clothes with bare hands in the cold. The clothes would be frozen like boards when they were brought inside. They would thaw and be hung upstairs to dry. It made moisture in the house and the freezing killed germs.

The soil where we lived was called gumbo. When real wet it would get like grease. When it started to dry it would stick together and ball up. The lumps would get like cement when dry. Our road was not graveled so in spring or when it rained we had to stay home. In the winter, the road would be blocked with snow. One spring the roads were bad and the river was high. Our neighbor walked through the woods to our place. He stood on one side and dad on the other side of the river and visited all afternoon talking, farming, and solving world problems. Don't know if they agreed on things but enjoyed the company after a long winter.

When I got old enough to start school, I was to walk a mile and a half to meet the bus or walk through the woods to the neighbor's to catch the bus. But then I had to cross the river on a fallen tree. Dad made a bridge for me but when the river got high, it took the bridge. Dad used to walk with me until I got old enough to go myself. In the winter, he'd bring me to the bus with horses and stone boat. One time he decided to take me with the car. The road was blocked with snowdrifts that were so hard he could drive over the top of them. What a bumpy ride that was.

One year the house needed to be shingled. Dad had the truck parked by the house and had 2x4's with rope on the roof tied to the truck. It was on a Saturday and we went to town in Hallock to take cream in and the high school band played. Mom bought groceries and visited neighbors. Anyway, we were ready to go and got into the car and it wouldn't start. So Dad said, "We'll take the truck." Forgetting the ropes tied to the side, when we came home that night the chimney laid on the ground.

In 1948, we got electricity. What a treat that was. We also got a phone. Dad had a good crop that year so he also got a new tractor, truck, and car. I was pretty proud when Mom and Dad picked me up from school in a brand new car.

Around 1949 we got caught in a bad snowstorm after Christmas shopping in Crookston. We got as far as Donaldson, Minnesota and spent the night at The Tavern. The owner kept the place open and people were coming in all night out of the storm. Next morning we had to wait for the plows to open the road. We got as far as Hallock. Mom and I stayed with friends and Dad and my brother got home somehow to care for the animals that had been left outside.

In 1950, we had a flood. Our house was on a hill but the river got so high it came within three feet of our front porch. Water backed up around the back of the house too so we were on a peninsula. I stayed in Hallock so I wouldn't miss school. There has been many more storms, floods, and tornadoes but we have been lucky to survive them and able to tell about them.

A Frog in the Hand Pump and Pepsi in the Sky
By Marilyn Kern (Robert) Swanson of
Wadena, Minnesota
Born 1936

We had root cellars underground, where potatoes, squash, turnips, carrots, etc., were stored.

We had cisterns in basements where rainwater was stored, as water softeners were non-existent in the early years. Rain barrels outdoors also collected rainwater.

A large water pump was on our back steps, and a smaller pump was on a sink in our kitchen. Water had to be pumped by hand; there were no faucets or running water. The smaller pumps had to be primed sometimes to get the water up. One time Mother was priming it and couldn't get the water to come up. When it finally did, it shot straight up in the air! She said, "Something must be plugging it," so she put her finger in it and poked it right into a frog's belly.

In World War II we had what was called black outs. At 8:00 p.m. or 9:00 p.m., all the lights in town had to be out. If not, there would be a fine. During the drills, sirens would blare! It often was a moonlit night, so hopefully the German bombers wouldn't see our towns. There were air raid wardens to check on every house to see if the lights were out.

Children saved foil wrappers and rolled them into balls for the war effort. We brought them to school, where they were collected and delivered to the OPC, Office of Price Controls. We also collected milkweed pods to make life jackets for our soldiers.

There also were chips or tokens made of a hard cardboard type of material of different colors to make some purchases at grocery stores. Due to the scarcities, many things were unavailable or rationed. Some tokens were red for meat; some were blue for sugar; etc. There were numbers indented in the tokens.

If we had a dry year, airplanes seeded the clouds. Airplanes also flew up and advertised, spelling out Pepsi-Cola in the sky!

Some of the games we played were pump, pump, pull away; king on a hill; fox and goose; tick tock double lock; tag; hide and seek; marbles; hopscotch; Annie I over; drop the hankie; kick the can; button, button, who's got the button?; I draw the frying pan; red light, green light; captain, may I?; and I spy.

We made igloos in snow banks and laid gunnysacks on the floors to keep dry.

Flour was purchased in large cotton cloth sacks (bags), which were many designs. Ladies sewed new dresses of the material when the flour sacks were emptied.

Icehouses and iceboxes preceded refrigerators and freezers. Huge blocks of ice were cut from rivers and lakes, etc., and were stored in icehouses. In there they were stacked up very high and were covered with sawdust. The iceboxes in homes were lined with tin in which milk, butter, etc., was then stored. Some people stored perishables in their farm pump house or milk house. They placed the items in the water tank, which contained cold water.

In towns, milkmen delivered milk to homes. The milk, cream, etc., came in glass bottles.

Later in the 1950s and 1960s, there were great comedians: Flip Wilson, Artie Shaw, Victor Borge, Bob Newhart, Red Skelton, Johnathon Winters, Ruth Buzzi, Art Carney, and Lily Tomlin. News reporters on the radio were Cedric Adams, Fulton J. Lewis Jr., Gabriel Heater, etc.

Mushroom Picking and Fishing in the Rain
By Bette Peterson of Wadena, Minnesota
Born 1933

Life began in 1933, the Depression era. When I was born, my family was Ma, Pa, and my 1 ½ year old brother. I was born at home on a farm near Bluffton. I was born on my grandma's birthday. I wore cloth diapers that were hand washable.

Wild Morrel Mushrooms
The yearly search for picking the

Bette and Bob Kempe in 1972

Bette's grandmother, Jessie Tranby

mushrooms, normally in May after a nice warm rain. Find the right spots. Pick carefully (some are not edible) then clean them and cook them sautéed in butter after coating them in flour with salt and pepper. We all loved them. We all thought this was fun in the woods, and it was too early for mosquitos, but we did have to be checked as we left the woods for wood ticks. We didn't want them to get attached to our skin. I still love to go mushroom picking 75 years later.

The Garden

Most families grew large gardens with a variety of vegetables, berries, and flowers. Planting started after the last frost. The soil was readied by hand or maybe horse drawn plows. Animal manure was the fertilizer. Seeds were planted in hand hoed rows, weeded until ready to pick, and provided fresh produce all summer. All the rest was canned or stored for the winter's supply. Extra produce was normally shared with the neighbors.

The old dead plants were raked off the garden and burned. We often found a few potatoes and threw them into the fire and then dug them out of the ashes and ate them. Now the garden was ready for the next year.

Farming

Most farms were of small acreage – 40 to 60 acres. Crops were diversified: corn, oats, wheat, etc., and were planted and cultivated by horse drawn plows, cultivators, and hay mowers. Most crops were fed to the animals (cows, horses, pigs, sheep, chickens, etc.). Cows were milked by hand, and a milk separator separated the milk from the cream. The cream, except for some kept to be used for ice cream and butter, was sold to the creameries. Milk was fed to the pigs.

Rainy Days

We couldn't work outside because everything was too wet. So it was time to go fishing. We would get out the cane poles and hooks and dig a bucket of worms and drive to a nearby lake. We would rent a rowboat and just have fun and hope to catch supper. I used to think that the fish only bit on rainy days.

Evenings

The work done, cows milked, chickens and pigs fed, and supper over, it was time for fun. Either the neighbors would drop in or we would go to their place. Everyone visited and the kids played. There was a lot of card playing and then a nice lunch of cake, sandwiches, and whatever was available. Saturday night was go to town time. Mostly the men went to the card room and the women and kids to the movie theater where we watched Westerns, Tarzan, and many others. Then we went to the café for ice cream.

Disasters

You or a neighbor got sick or had a bad

Betty Peterson

accident and were unable to do the work or a storm destroyed something and you could lose everything. But here came the neighbors. They would harvest your crops, milk the cows, feed the pigs, etc. They would help rebuild and clean up. These were caring friends.

All the Blessings of My 93 Years
By Alta Mandt of Perham, Minnesota
Born 1922

I am 93 years old. I live in an apartment and still take care of myself. I was born October 1, 1922, and was delivered by my paternal grandmother. This was in her Knute township farm home 4 miles southeast of McIntosh, Minnesota. My grandma delivered many babies in the neighborhood.

I walked to country school a mile away. The school was on Foot Lake right across the road from Grandma's home. I can't understand how they knew to name it Foot Lake because it was in the shape of a foot. Now I have a picture of it from the air. It is definitely a foot! Perhaps they walked around it with a surveying type of instrument.

Little girls only wore dresses, and we also wore hats both summer and winter, especially to church. We wore caps and mittens in winter. I started school at age 5 and then skipped two grades, so I went to high school at age 13. In winter, I would get a sleigh ride to Foot Lake School if my dad or uncle would be going to town. When I was going to high school, I would walk to the corner a mile away and get a ride with a neighbor. However, in winter we would have to stay in town, as there wasn't any personal snow removal equipment. Only the county road was kept open. I graduated from high school at age 16.

My father died when I was 13 years old. My mother, Agnes Ostenson Svalen, received help from all the neighbors. My Uncle Ernest came to live with us to do the farm work, including milking cows morning and evening, so I grew up with cooperation in many areas of my life.

We had no indoor plumbing so we had an outdoor toilet. Our toilet was better than many others because whoever built it had a small hole with a step below it for children. All 3 hole edges had been sanded so no rough edges! My grandma and I often sat together. At night, we had a pot near the bed. It was emptied outside, several yards from the house.

I milked a cow at 5 years of age (one which was so old she couldn't kick the pail over). Later, I helped milk cows in evenings as well as feeding chickens, keeping water troughs filled, picking eggs, and feeding pigs. We had a cream separator to separate the cream out of the milk. We had to take maybe a half gallon of sour cream to churn to make butter. I turned the crank to make butter many evenings for a lot of butter. The butter solidified and the liquid was buttermilk, which most everyone drank except me. Buttermilk was used in many baking recipes.

We had 4 or 5 turkeys with one gobbler. Mother had leaves or some type of compost for them to build their nests on the edge of the woods, and every spring for a few years we would have little turkeys running around with their mother. I was scared of the gobbler, as he would fly at me.

The chickens had their own chicken coop. They would be let out in the morning and would be pecking for whatever in the grass. They would be locked in at night, as there

Alta with her doll and dog

228

Alta Mandt in 1927

were wild animals that would eat them. They were fed oats, spread by hand in the yard.

The 1930's Depression was bad, but we had a good life even with the dust storms. We had no money, but we had plenty to eat with Mother canning peas and corn (scraped off the cob) from the garden. Cucumbers were planted and Mom canned many quarts of pickles. Every fall a pig was butchered so we had meat all winter. I can still see my mother standing by the well house wringing a chicken's neck for some of our meals. She sometimes canned beef too.

In 1935, I was a freshman when a salesman on a truck came by with a secondhand piano, and Mom bought it. Right away, Mom paid for lessons, and I walked about 3 blocks after school (3:30) once a week the 9 months to take lessons. My cousin Stanley lived a mile away and played violin. He came over maybe once a week and I would chord on the piano to old time waltzes, schottisches, polkas, fox trots, and two steps. We usually had company, and we all enjoyed tapping our feet.

Back then, we always had 3 big meals a day. Breakfast was bacon and eggs fried, cooked, or poached or pancakes or waffles with homemade syrup. The noon meal was potatoes either cooked whole or mashed. Supper was usually leftovers from noon, like fried potatoes.

A lot of baking, including cookies, cakes, pies and sweetbreads was done. Someone usually stopped in to visit, and Mom had to have something to serve with coffee. Neighbors, uncles, or Ostenson and Carlson cousins often stopped by to visit. Every summer Mom would buy a crate of peaches and pears. They would be canned in quart jars and used in winter. We had an ice cream freezer. Mom would mix up the liquids, and my uncle would chop up ice and turn the handle until it was frozen. We enjoyed it and made it often in the winter because there was no ice in the summer.

Along with the baking above, I want to add that when potatoes were dug in September,

Alta's high school graduation

229

Mom could make lefsa through the spring. A machine would dig them up row by row, and my uncle would get some young boys to pick them. They carried gunny sacks attached to their backs and would pick them into bags about three fourths full so they could be lifted onto (in earlier days) a horse drawn wagon. Most people had basement storage. Mom only had a dirt cellar with a small window. The potatoes would be thrown down into a bin. Lefsa was mainly potatoes. At Christmas time, Mom made rosettes and fattigman (Swedish meaning poor man.) Both of those were fried in a big kettle of boiling liquid lard. A rosette iron was shaped like a six-pointed star. Fattigman was fried with a long handled fork. Fruitcake (same ingredients as now) was also baked. Lefsa was rolled thin on a breadboard. Knackebrod was rolled thin (about a foot in diameter) and baked in the oven. It was turned over with a baking stick. Out of the oven, it was cut HOT in pie shaped pieces.

Grandma Ostenson had a strip of land between fields, which had wild cranberries. I picked many pails of cranberries. These were cooked till they were into thick sauce. Sugar was added. Delicious! She also made jelly from pin cherries that I had picked.

We were the only farmer that had a granary with steps to upstairs with a full smooth floor. The builder must have liked to dance! When Dad was living all the neighbors came over around 8:00 pm and there was dancing to the violin and button accordion. Maybe when I was 6 years old I was allowed to watch the dancing until 9:00 pm. However, one night my dad had to take me, kicking and screaming, to put me to bed upstairs. I later bought a second hand piano accordion.

There was an old country school about a mile and a half from our home. I was around 17 years when area neighbors got together for music games like "There is Somebody Waiting for You," "Four in the Boat" and "Steal." That led to moving to McIntosh and learning to dance up above the Fire Department.

Every Saturday night (except in winter), my mother and neighborhood farmers would milk cows early in order to get to McIntosh in time to park in front of Wichern Store. There would be a lot of visiting, and we kids would run the sidewalk and get an occasional one scoop ice cream cone from an uncle.

There was no electricity for our home till 1950. I remember having a special gasoline to fill the hanging ceiling lamp over the dining room table. It had 2 mantels and a special little tube pump to put air into the gasoline. When that no longer worked, we had an Aladdin lamp on the dining room table. We had a lamp in the corner of the kitchen wall in a fancy holder. Winter evenings the lamp had to be put on top of the piano when 3 neighborhood guys came to play whist with my uncle. That's when I learned to play whist at 9 years of age. We kids learned how to play rummy too.

My Mom made laundry soap. The only ingredient I recall is lye. She melted the ingredients and poured them into a long pan only 3" wide. When it was solid, she cut into bars. Laundry was done in a tin tub of water with bar soap and rubbed on a washboard. The tubs were stored on the outside of the hallway. Washing was done first with a foot paddle to start the Maytag motor. Grandma Ostenson was given the Maytag by her sons. When she died in 1930, the Maytag was given to my mother. It was stored in the unheated entrance hall and used there in both summer and winter. In winter, we had a wooden clothes rack that Mom would put the wet clothes on and put it outside to first freeze dry and then brought in to finish drying. The family helped her hang it on the line. After electricity came, the Maytag was plugged in. Clothes were always washed on a sunny day, as they were hung on the line between two trees.

Mom's house had water pipes stored around the roof to run rain water into the huge clay cistern in front of the kitchen window. This water was brought into the kitchen sink by a hand pump. It was then pumped into a big pail and carried over to fill the kitchen range reservoir. This water was used for laundry and cleaning. Water for drinking and cooking was carried in pails from the well house engine or hand pumped. In summer, the pail was stored in the unheated hallway on top of the wood box. In winter, it was on a shelf in the kitchen. Everyone drank from the same dipper!

At Christmas time every year when I was a child, Reese's Drug Store in McIntosh had a contest, giving away 20 dolls in which customers were given a vote for every purchase made. All neighbors, relatives, and friends voted. These dear people got me the 2nd place: a big beautiful doll, of which I have a picture.

At age 93 now, I realize how much farmers worked together: working with horses for planting, cultivating and harvesting. Grain was cut with a binder, bundled, and hauled in to be threshed by my father with his Rumely tractor and separator. My dad threshed for 5 neighbors, who picked up bundles in the field, took turns hauling them in, and pitching them into the separator. The grain would then be blown into sacks to be hauled for storage in the granary right on the farm or hauled in to the Farmers Elevator, McIntosh, to be sold.

My Uncle Martin cut hair for all the neighborhood guys. He also cut my hair until I entered freshman in high school. Then I had to have a permanent. Back then that took almost 3 hours. I chose a curly croquignol. There was also a less curly one entitled spiral. I have the two haircutting scissors made by Solingen Scissors, Solingen, Germany. They are still making scissors.

I thank God every day for all the blessings of my 93 years.

Spear the Suckers, Not Your Toe!
By Robert Ronning of Auburn, Washington
Born 1945

Excitement runs high when the warm temperatures of spring arrive around Dent, in west central Minnesota. Snow and bitter cold winter weather gives way to warming spring temperatures and calls people to get outside and enjoy the action. Spring also brings thawing ice on the lakes and streams. The gentle rains, greening grass, budding trees, and returning birds bring that wonder of renewed life. For some, however, the pull to check out the streams for spawning suckers is an adventure to anticipate.

Suckers are rough fish that overpopulate the lakes and damage game fish habitat, so it was good to keep them under control. Spearing suckers was great sport and provided a great deal of live action. It also provided a tasty dish of fish once they were soaked in a salt brine and smoked with apple tree wood in a cinderblock smoker at the local creamery. The smoker was used regularly to smoke many different kinds of meat. The suckers are typically about two to four pounds, with some even bigger, and spearing a limit was a lot of fun. Cleaning a sucker is also pretty easy. Some people slice down the back and others slice down the stomach then cut the head and tail off. A quick wash to clean the guts was all it took to prepare them for the brine.

During the mid-1960s, my younger brother, Jerry Ronning, was about fourteen years old. It was a very memorable year. He had a few years of sucker spearing experience under his belt, so when the neighbor, Bob Johnson, asked him if he wanted to spear some suckers, he was excited to get his gear together. The five-tine spear with sharp barbs belonged to our dad and hung in the shed since icehouse spearing ended a short time before. It was a hefty spear. Five-tines with sharp barbs would easily go through a sucker when the spear was forcefully driven. Hip waders were hauled out and checked to be sure there were no leaks. The water was cold but not very deep, so the hip waders were adequate in most creeks. Gunnysacks were plentiful and would easily hold a limit of suckers. While collecting the gear to go sucker spearing there was no way for Jerry to know how important the gunnysacks would become.

Bob was the local creamery manager, and in that position he knew many of the surrounding farmers who had creeks running through their property. Charles Peach's creek ran south under Highway 108 into the west arm of Star Lake, and that was the choice for this spearing trip. Spring typically brought many suckers up this creek, and Bob and Jerry were very optimistic. Bob had already checked the creek for suckers and knew they were running.

The trip began on a beautiful warm spring day, and it was only a short drive from Dent to Star Lake. Once the car was parked on the side of the road, Jerry was quick to get his spear and gunnysacks. He was confident the limit would be speared. He walked quickly ahead of Bob through the road ditch and up to the fence. Once over the fence, he waited for Bob to catch up. From the fence to the creek was a short distance, but it was important to slow down and walk as quietly as possible to the creek so that the fish would not be startled. They both had planned for Jerry to walk in the creek while Bob went ahead. Bob would walk about twenty feet ahead along the bank of the small creek, as Jerry walked along in the water and pushed the fish upstream. Bob had a great opportunity to spear fish as he saw them swimming upstream, and Jerry would be able to spear fish that were not immediately startled by the disturbed water.

The plan was working well, as Jerry walked slowly through the water while kicking under the banks and around brush, where the suckers typically had room to remain stationary for a time. Bob had speared a few fish and shook them off his spear, as they slowly walked up the creek. The speared fish were left on the banks to be picked up and put in the gunnysack on the walk back. Jerry was having a great time because he was kicking up plenty of fish and spearing was good. Most of the time the fish would sprint upstream before Jerry could get a spear in them, but his spear also found its mark in a few suckers, and the fish were good size. Very few suckers turned downstream between his feet, but that was going to change soon, and it would not be a good change.

Within an instant, a fairly big sucker turned in the water and quickly swam downstream between Jerry's feet. Jerry quickly reacted and drove the spear at the sucker, but one tine of the spear went through his boot and his big toe instead of the sucker. Two other tines nicked two other toes. The severe pain was immediate! Jerry cried out for help, and Bob quickly came back to see what had happened. Between the two of them, they managed to awkwardly hold the spear and climb out of the creek.

Bob decided they needed help so they agreed that he would go up to Peach's house and get Charles to help. He was quick to reach the car; it was less than a mile to the house. Charles was home and they both hurried back to the creek. Bob and Charles first tried to pull the spear out of Jerry's toe, but it proved too painful and impossible with the barb on the end of the tine. All three of them decided they would have to cut the tine off in order to get Jerry to the doctor. Charles decided they needed to get Cliff Amundson from a nearby farm. Cliff had an acetylene torch in his pickup that they could bring down to the stream. Charles and Cliff moved fast, but it seemed like an eternity to Jerry and Bob.

It didn't actually take long for Cliff and Charles to return with Cliff's pickup and torch. The gunnysacks were soaked in the cold stream water and wrapped around the tine and toe. As Cliff began to cut with the torch, the tine became very hot through the toe. The doctor would later tell them that the heat actually cauterized the wound and stopped most of the bleeding, but it did not stop the pain. When the tine was finally cut off, they picked Jerry up and put him in the pickup. Cliff drove them to Bob's car and helped switch Jerry to Bob's car to take him to the Perham Clinic.

The best Jerry could remember was that Dr. Schoenberger administered Novocain to the wound. The doctor admitted he had not seen a situation quite like this before. Dr. Schoenberger and Bob tried again to pull the tine out of the toe through the same path it went in, but decided it would be best to shorten the tine more and pull it through the toe. Bob went to the local hardware store and brought back a hacksaw, but the steel spear proved too strong to cut, and the movement was very painful despite the Novocain. A second attempt to remove the tine was to smooth the tine out with a file, cut a hole in the bottom of the toe, and pull the tine through the toe. The filing helped narrow the tine, and the doctor cut a hole in the bottom of the toe. Slowly Dr. Schoenberger pulled the tine through Jerry's toe. He cleaned the wound as best he could, wrapped the wound in gauze, and released Jerry to go home.

Bob was a little squeamish as a result of the whole episode, but he had found time to call his daughter, Bonnie, who was home from college. He asked Bonnie to drive to Perham and give Jerry a ride home. Bonnie picked up Jerry in her new Camaro and took Jerry to Dairy Queen for an ice cream cone before heading back to Dent. About a quarter of the way home and before the cone was gone; the Novocain began to wear off. Fifty years later, Jerry's best recollection through painful memories was that Dr. Schoenberger had prescribed strong aspirin for the pain.

Bonnie later became my wife and Jerry's sister-in-law, which makes the adventure an interesting story that is often recanted during family reunions. The toe comes out, the scars are noted, and the wrinkled toenail brings some laughter as Jerry retells the story. The spear is still used for icehouse spearing and for suckers in the spring.

The Button Box Finds a Home
By Mavis Winger of Bemidji, Minnesota
Born 1929

I grew up on a small farm near Debs, Minnesota, and when I was six years old, a family of eight moved into an abandoned house about one fourth mile away. We went to school together, swam together, and played together. One day the mother, Mary, showed me a rather beat up "button accordion." I had fun trying to play it. She told me she had it since she was a small girl. She didn't know where it originated from, but she brought it through Canada in a covered wagon sometime in the early 1900s.

One late afternoon she told one of her kids to run over and get the neighbor kids and we'll have a dance. She wasn't real adept at playing the accordion, but she kept the beat. We had a ball over the next five years. Often we would get together and dance to the "button box."

We grew up and all went to school, the war, or to work somewhere. The Mary McMaster family moved to Longview, Washington. My sister and two of my brothers moved there eventually. We saw the McMaster family from time to time.

Mrs. McMaster died and her son, Robert, got the button box. He lived in a remote area out of Longview and during a torrential rainfall, his house was inundated by a sand landslide, and they lost almost everything then owned. My sister, Opal, heard of the disaster and went to their place to see if she could help. As they were digging, he pulled out this box wrapped in plastic. He tossed it to my sister and said, "Here, you take this. It belonged to Ma." She cleaned it up and put it in a new bag and stored it in her garage.

About 20 years later, I spent a week with my sister, who had just moved in to an assisted living home. She told her daughter to dig it out and give it to me. I was on a plane, so I did not really want it.

I then visited a niece in Portland, Oregon, and a cousin of my husband. I told them the button box story. My husband's cousin said, "We are taking a motor home trip to Minnesota. We will take it with us. You may pick it up in Fosston, Minnesota." So the button box made a complete round trip over nearly 70 years.

Okay, so…I had it in my closet for five years and was showing it to my granddaughter, Sara, who was engaged to be married. Her eyes opened wide and she said, "Grandma, I looove it!" There was a wedding shower for her. I wrapped the button box up with a short story and gave it to her. I played a tune for the group, and so it has found a home. She lives in Williston, North Dakota, and has the button box and the little story on a shelf in her living room.

The Model T
My dad, Albert Thompson, was in World War I. He came home, married my mom, and

Mavis Winger, Opal, Leroy, Mavis's mom, Grandma Bertha, and Gordy Thompson

started a small farm. We lived off the land for a lot of years.

In 1938, Dad received a $300.00 payment for being in service. He bought this Model T Ford for $17.00 from a neighbor. We all got new clothes and our first drive was to Bemidji, our nearest big town, the next July 4th. We all got ice cream cones from David Parks' ice cream window and our first glimpse of Paul Bunyan and his blue ox, Bemidji's big attraction on the waterfront. I believe it was built in 1939.

The Model T was the only car my dad ever drove. We all got to drive it at times, as we grew older. I remember someone said, "I see you got yourself a convertible."

Simpler Times in the One-room School
By Lorraine Trout of Browerville, Minnesota
Born 1929

The bell rings! We all rush inside. It's the first day of school, September 1935. I've walked two miles with my two brothers and my best friend to get here to our one room school.

The teacher says, "Welcome; my name is Mr. Comstock." From that moment, I was hooked! After school, I went home and told my parents, "I'm going to be a teacher when I grow up." Fourteen years later, I too was saying, "Welcome, my name is Mrs. Trout."

I loved that one room school with all eight grades. We had a wood stove in the back of the room. It had a metal jacket around it so no one would get burned. Our coats hung behind it. In the winter we'd put our mittens around the bottom of the jacket to keep them warm and dry.

We had a duty list, and almost all the students had a duty. The older children had to carry in wood and water. The others had to wash blackboards, clap erasers, pass out papers, etc. Our drinking fountain held two pails of water in the top section. The bottom part caught the water that dripped when we drank or when someone pushed our head down when we drank.

Our desks were screwed onto slats and were put in straight rows. When one desk was moved, the rows were crooked. The big boys loved to move their desks. Then everyone in the row had to stand up and get the row straight again. A good time waster!

We had eight grades and usually around 25 students. Some of our eighth graders were 15 or 16 years old. If you didn't pass the state's eighth grade exams, you stayed in eighth grade another year. At age 16 you could legally quit school, which some did. Those state exams weren't easy. We had booklets of previous exams, which we really studied. The exams covered English, math, social studies, and science. Our library consisted of three bookcases of an assortment of books for grades one through eight. For every five books, we read and made a report on, we got a certificate.

Each morning after the bell rang we stood and recited the flag pledge. After the pledge, there was a health check. We had to put our hands on our desks, and the health monitor for that week would check if we had clean hands and fingernails. If we did, we'd get a star on the health chart. We were also asked if we had brushed our teeth for another star. On the first day of school, we were given a toothbrush and a tube of toothpaste. A week of stars was rewarded with a treat. A month of stars merited a small gift.

We had a morning, noon, and afternoon recess. School started at 9:00 and was out at 4:00. When the weather was nice, we would play bat and ball. Even the first graders could play if they chose to. We played other games also, like ante over the woodshed, prisoner's base, fox and goose, Captain, may I?, and tag. We jumped rope and had little rhymes that went with the jumping. No teacher supervised recess. We didn't worry about bullying. The older students watched over the younger ones. At recess, if we saw a gopher on the playground we found his hole, got pails of water, and drowned him out. Sometimes we'd go in the woods that bordered the school and look for flowers.

Although some of the school families were more affluent than others, and some students dressed nicer, I can't remember anyone making fun of that. I was one of the students who wore hand-me-downs and flour sack dresses, and no one laughed at me.

Christmas was so exciting! The school always had a Christmas program for the parents and anyone else. This was really a community happening. There was always standing room only. The students memorized their parts in plays, poems, and songs. We used bed sheets for backdrops. From the time the curtain opened and the welcome poem was read, until the last song was sung, the audience applauded everyone. The final performance was the Nativity. Whoever was chosen to be Mary and Joseph always felt honored. If there was a new baby in the school family, he or she was chosen to be the Baby Jesus. Everyone sang the carols with the children, ending with "Silent Night." At the end, the children would all take a bow. Hark! What's that? Bells would jingle. Ho! Ho! Ho! Santa would come in the door. He had a sack of candy and nuts for each student and extras for the little ones in the audience. Sometimes apples were given to all the grownups (all courtesy of the teacher).

I had five teachers during my eight years. I liked them all. As I think back, they each had a different style of teaching, but we learned. I remember when I was in the sixth grade. We all arrived at school, but no teacher was there. We waited a while and then someone said, "Let's go in the school through the window. We'll all take our seats and surprise our teacher." We thought about it a while and then in through the window we went. We took our seats and one of the boys said, "Take out your books, and Lorraine can be the teacher." Oh, glory! I was getting my chance to teach! I called the first grade to the front and was teaching them some of their new words, when the door opened and a school board member walked in. He asked what was going on and we explained. "You're a bunch of good kids. However, there will be no school today because your teacher's brother died." We were all shocked. Not too many of us were familiar with death, unlike today when the television has death in the news and in its programming.

Airplanes were not a common occurrence in the '30s. At school, when we'd hear an airplane, the teacher would let us go outside and watch it. We almost always walked to school. The only time I remember getting a ride was if it was raining hard or a blizzard. If a snowstorm developed while we were at school, my dad or older brother would pick us up with a sled pulled by a team of horses.

At the end of the school year, a school potluck picnic was held for parents, students, and anyone in the district. Games were played, races were run, and a lot of food was consumed.

Those were simpler times. Times when students got hugs from the teacher. Times when children learned you weren't always a winner, so you tried harder.

Know Who to Trust
By Constance Hinnenkamp of Alexandria, Minnesota

Well, I am supposed to tell all of you readers about a certain type of story, so I'll explain to all of you how I see it through my eyes over the years. Most of my life I grew up on a farm and as many know it's hard work even if it is just a small hobby farm. There is always work to be done, from dawn until dusk, whether it's feeding them, tending to their health, and on the occasion, helping them with birth. This is just a small amount of what we all do in a day. Everybody these days should learn that you have to work hard to earn a living; it's not given to you on a silver platter and never should be. In the small towns like Osakis and Nelson, where everybody knows everybody and people who lived in the country always helped each other out in so many different ways. Neighbors cared but nowadays many people do not even know their neighbors, and it's sad to hear about. Life in my opinion in many ways should go back to the way it used to be. To me it's full of too much technology. Seems like it has taken over many generations to the point where their only means of conversation is through texting. Sad to see life turn out this way.

Now during the times I lived or visited the various towns in Minnesota, I could see that not much changes from town to town. So much is the same, yet there are differences, from the reckless, impatient drivers to the people just trying to get by in life with the little money they have to survive off of from day to day. From quiet and discreet to the everybody knows towns, nothing really changes.

For me, I learned all about the dangers of people. Like who and who not to trust and who to stay away from. Truth is, I believe all females should know how to tell if a man is a potential threat or not, so they know to stay away.

Rather not have things that happened to me happen to them. Better to avoid all the pain and suffering and stop it before it even begins. Women these days should not have to be scared to speak up about what is happening to them. I know it hurts and are truly afraid. I have been there before and reporting it will be the biggest step for you to take. Things like that is no laughing matter. It can really traumatize you and scar you for life. You may never ever be able to fully get over it. Life for this person will forever be changed and the past will be hard to put behind them. Like myself, I became a stronger woman for it and taken many precautions but tend to fall back into a similar relationship because of how it has affected them. This is not the case for all, but it is for so many out there. You go into an unhealthy relationship where they always seem like a great person, yet over time, you find out who they really are.

Some men take longer than others to show their true colors, unless they do not change at all and is truly who they are. For me there was the controlling one and also the player who never talked much at all. Then there was the one who for years seemed like the best thing in my life, yet could not let the past go, had to always be right, and said they never had. Got to the point where it felt like he was being verbally abusive, controlling, and nothing I ever did or said was good enough. You have to be able to let the past go in order to have a future together in any way shape or form. I found out the hard way about so much in my life. May have chosen this, but that' the best way I learn things. No one ever said life was going to be easy, because if it was I do not want to know what the world would be like. Nor do I or like the way it is now corrupt.

To end my very simplified story I'll leave you with a couple sayings I have heard and believe. One is life is not about the destination but the journey on which you take and live one day at a time. Also stick with the golden rule too, and it will be okay. So keep your head up and keep on keeping on. Best of luck to y'all.

The Life and Times of a Car Salesman
Submitted by Gaylord H. Solem of Oslo, Minnesota
Born 1939

When you have a job you love and are able to meet, help, and just plain visit with thousands of people, you have had the opportunity of a lifetime. Add to that, you have attended a small school, raised a family and have worked in that same area all your life. In a nutshell, those two statements describe the life experience of 1955 Oslo High School graduate Gaylord Solem, who has been employed at Dahlstrom Motors in Oslo for just a few months short of 60 years. What follows is a more detailed description of the life and times of Gaylord Solem, record-breaking car salesman.

He was born into the William and Esther (Olson) Solem family at St. Michael's Hospital in Grand Forks, North Dakota. As the youngest child, he joined brothers Donald, Elton, and Ralph, and sister Ila. They lived on a farm one mile east and six miles south of Oslo. All attended the Lakeside School, seven miles south of Oslo. Lakeside was a one-room country school, which had first through eighth grades with 36 students, which he attended for six years. Some of his country school memories are when he was in the sixth grade, their teacher would have them take the first graders to the back of the room and work with them on numbers and speaking. "It was something for us to do and a way to help out the teacher." The school was a mile and a half from their home. "In the winter, if it was 25 degrees below zero or colder, our dad would hook up the horses and give us a ride to school, otherwise we walked every day."

His most enjoyable memory from country school was once a year in the spring, three country schools – Lakeside, Esther Township School, and Tabor Township School – would get together and have a play day. They would all enjoy softball, track, running, and jumping. "That was the really high point of the year."

"When we were in sixth grade, our Lakeside school district decided to send the seventh and eighth graders to a new school. It would be either Alvarado or Oslo. My father fought against sending us kids to Alvarado, because we all wanted to go to Oslo. But my best friends lived on the other side of the line so they went to Alvarado; about five of us went to Oslo. So from seventh grade to our senior year, we were in completion with each other."

When asked what his favorite junior high story from Oslo was, he replied with a big grin, "The day I scored every point for Oslo in a basketball game in the seventh grade! I'd never seen a basketball before. I'd never held a basketball or shot one until that day when the superintendent came to the classroom and pointed to me and six other boys in the seventh grade and said, 'You are dressing for the B basketball game.' At halftime, Minto led us 21-0. I scored two free throws in the second half. And I tell all my kids how great I was to score all the points in the game! But I don't tell them the final score."

Another favorite memory for Gaylord was meeting his future wife, Patricia Michalski or Patty, in eighth grade. They were in many of the same classes, and when Gaylord was a sophomore he and Patty started dating. They dated all through high school and got married on June 23, 1956, after Patty graduated.

Gaylord liked geometry and bookkeeping, and has always been good with numbers. Mrs. Feste, the bookkeeping teacher, was one of his favorite teachers. He was the only boy among 20 girls and according to his wife, Patty; he was the teacher's pet! She was in the same class.

"I played basketball and baseball in high school. After the split of the country school, my best friends played baseball for Alvarado and, of course, I played for Oslo, so we ended up being competitors and neighbors all through junior and senior high. During one of those years, Alvarado had a very good baseball team; they were 10-1 for the year. But we didn't have a very good team that year; we were 2-10. We ended up playing them in the tournament and beat them 26-7! That caused some hard feelings with some of the neighbors, but we all worked through it."

Gaylord graduated from Oslo High School in 1955 with 17 in his graduating class. At that time, the kids from the North Dakota side of the river were attending school in Oslo, too. Patty graduated the next year in 1956. After Patty graduated, they got married in Oslo and have lived there ever since. Patty laughs saying, "We didn't go too far!"

When asked, "What are some experiences from your youth that helped prepare you for life?" they each had a story to tell.

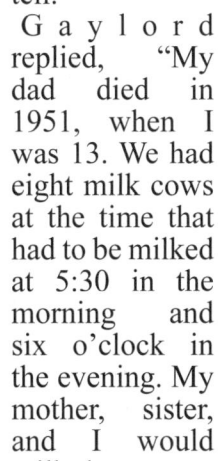

Gaylord replied, "My dad died in 1951, when I was 13. We had eight milk cows at the time that had to be milked at 5:30 in the morning and six o'clock in the evening. My mother, sister, and I would milk those cows in the morning. I'd go to the barn at 5:30 and go straight from the barn to the bus at 7:30 and off to school. We never even got a chance to go back into the house and clean up before getting on the bus." If you've ever been involved in milking cows, you know what he's talking about when he says straight from the barn to the bus. "My mother told me that in 1947 the farm's gross income was $900.00. That's why I moved off the farm and started working in town after graduating from high school."

Patty's reply to that question was, "I lost my mother in my teens; she passed away when I was 15. My mother would fix my favorite food, which was chili, every day for my lunch. We lived right behind the school, so I always went home for lunch. The day after my mother's funeral, I was walking home from

Gaylord H. Solem and his wife, Patty Solem in 2014

school for lunch and could see a figure sitting on the back step of my house. I knew that it couldn't be my mother, but I could not figure out who it was. As I got closer and closer, I realized it was my Auntie Maude. She had made a pot of chili for me and came to visit so I didn't have to go home to an empty house." That loving experience in life has clearly made Patty a very caring and compassionate person. Patty has sung in the choir and played the piano and organ for St. Joseph Church for many years. She volunteers and plays for many senior organizations and enjoys getting out and being with others. Patty taught piano lessons for over 42 years with approximately 42 students a year.

Gaylord's first paying job was during his sophomore, junior, and senior summers working in Oslo. "Halbert Lofthus, a carpenter, hired me to be his helper. I started my first full time job for Dahlstrom Motors May 10, 1956." He's still working there full time today. "I was the bookkeeper, parts man, shop foreman, and some sales. There were a total of four employees at that time. My total wages were $175.00 a month. I would go to work at 5:30 a.m. to do the bookwork, then go to the shop and write up all of the shop orders. The crew back then was Bobby Jamieson, Ray Durkin, Bob Dahlstrom, and me, all Oslo residents. Now the business has grown, we currently have 35 employees. When Dahlstrom Motors first opened, it was located where it is now, though they have expanded and added buildings and lots. There was a filling station there also, but it closed in 1955." Gaylord had been a part of the Dahlstrom Motors team for nearly 60 years!

The '60s and '80s were the toughest years for car dealerships. Many of the surrounding area dealerships closed, some in Warren, Argyle, Stephen, Drayton, and Minto, and other small towns in the area. In those years, the car dealerships started to lose financially. DMC was lucky to hang on through those tough years, and is the only new car dealer in Marshall County.

When asked what changes he's seen in the car industry, he mentioned a few. The biggest changes would be the prices. "Back in 1957, I heard people comment that they would never buy a new car if it cost over $2,000.00. Now many of the new vehicles cost up to $40,000.00 to $50,000.00 with an option to take out a seven year car loan. People tell me they are paying more for their new vehicle than they paid for their house with a 40-year mortgage. And they are still paying on their house!"

The integration of computers is another thing that affects the industry greatly. "There are so many computerized systems that run the cars now, and I just love computers!" he said with a smile.

"On May 20, 2015 a couple came into the garage and wanted to buy a pickup. I showed them the pickup, and they said they would take it. When I asked where they were from, they replied 'the North Pole, Alaska,' so Dahlstrom Motors' selling territory runs 2,800 miles north. Another day I sold a car to a person from Montana and a person form Two Harbors, Minnesota. That's about 800 miles apart!" He never knows who he will have a chance to visit and get to know when his day starts. "I've sold over 26,000 cars and had the opportunity to meet over 100,000 people. All people are great. Just about everywhere we go, there's someone that knows me, and it's tough remembering all of those names!" He has sold more Chevrolets than any other Chevrolet salesman in the world.

The Solems love the small town atmosphere in Oslo. You get to know all of the kids and parents, plus you get to know all of the kids and parents from the surrounding towns. "We used to go to basketball games in Oslo and Alvarado and the gyms would be packed. And we'd get to visit with everyone. It was so much fun to be a part of a small community." Patty and Gaylord raised five children in Oslo that attended Oslo Schools: Tony, Billy, Kathy, Sally Gowan, and Larry. Larry is also a DMC employee; he has been there for 22 years. They have 12 grandchildren (two of them work at DMC) and seven great-grandchildren.

Their most memorable trips include going to see their grandson Casey play semi-pro baseball. "We went to his games in St. Louis, Kansas City, and Topeka, Kansas. We'd leave Friday after work, watch the game on Saturday, and turn around and be back at work on Monday morning."

Some of the pastimes Gaylord has enjoyed are deer, duck, and pheasant hunting; fishing at Lake of the Woods; and he golfed in a Warren League for 27 years. He enjoys watching his favorite teams play, the Vikings and the Twins.

And now for the last bit of information – the final score of that seventh grade Minto-Oslo basketball game that he usually never tells. "We got beat 37-2."

By Nice, Janet (2015, Fall) Gaylord Solem – The Life and Times of a Car Salesman. Warren/Alvarado/Oslo Public School Education Foundation, *Connections* newsletter

Playing with the Scoop and Commodities at School
By RuBelle (Hanson) Towne of Baudette, Minnesota
Born 1930

Here are some of my memories of the past while living in northern Minnesota. When I was very young, I was taken outside for fresh air nearly every day, regardless of how cold it was. I didn't say small because I weighed 10 ½ pounds when I was born and was about 8 months old when winter arrived. My face was not covered by a blanket when my mother took me outside. On very cold days there was cheesecloth placed over my face so I still got plenty of fresh air. They told me I had very few colds until I started school.

One lesson I learned early in life came from the broken scoop. Kids will tend to find something to play with in the kitchen cabinet instead of in their toy boxes. It was not different when I was a child. I found a long handled scoop, which looked like it, was made of aluminum. It was a favorite for me to play with until one day something came about that didn't suit me, and I became very angry, so I threw the long handled scoop. When it landed the handle broke, and it became a very short handled scoop, which did not interest me at all. At our house, broken items became part of my mother's recycling program. Seems like there had always been a shortage of funds in our home so instead of replacing it with a new one we continued to use the old one. My mother decided that the short handled scoop could be used to measure the coffee that went into our white enamel coffee pot each morning on our wood stove. That is how I made my coffee this morning, using the same short handled scoop. Today, I use a Swedish decorated coffee pot for my boiled coffee. My mother had to start a wood fire in the kitchen stove, but I only need to turn on a burner on my glass top electric stove that I purchased in 1966. My favorite toy went in to the dry coffee grounds, and this same story was told many times when she made coffee for our friends. At first, I didn't want our friends to hear about what I had done. I learned early in life that it doesn't pay to get angry, and it doesn't bother me to tell the story now.

My dad got sick when I was about a year

RuBelle Hanson in 1933

and a half old and did not recover. He passed away twelve years later. Since he was not able to care for me in the house while my mother was doing the chores in the barn, I had to go with her. We had two milk cows, a couple of calves, a few cats, and some chickens all in the same room in the barn, so it was warm. I sat in a wooden apple box and ate soda crackers while my mother did the milking. This was fine until the chickens found out that they liked my crackers too. My mother gave me a short wooden stick so I had full control of the chickens after that. Where were the movie cameras then?

All the teachers that I had while going to grade school stayed at our house. Board and room for a month was $16.00, and my mother never changed that amount all the years that I attended grade school. We lived half a mile from the school, so the teacher and I walked mornings and evenings in order to be there to heat the school before the rest of the students arrived by bus. The teacher that I had in the first grade wasn't very interested in making a fire in a wood stove, so I got the job. My mother fixed a paper bag with birch bark, paper, and kindling in it, and I carried the bag under my arm each morning. After putting the bag in the stove, we would carry frozen chunks of wood from the entryway. The wood had been carried in from the woodpile the previous day by the older students. With no heat in the entryway, they would still be covered with snow and ice. It was not an ideal way of making a good fire. We had many winter mornings when the thermometer reached 30 to 40 degrees below zero. We had an old building with a birch bark roof, and it had been torn down. That gave us an endless supply of birch bark, which we used to start fires. I really believe it was that birch bark that saved us from freezing. There was a boy in the upper grades who was asked to build the fire to heat the school, but it seemed like his alarm clock didn't work very well on such cold mornings, so I continued with my new job at the age of six years old.

Our water supply at our farm came from two wells, one close to the house and the other by the barn. They were hand dug by using a big auger. They were about 12 to 15 feet deep and had a wooden wall casing at the top with a wooden cover with a flat rock placed on top to keep the water supply clean. A gallon bucket nailed to a pole was used to dip the water out. Since there has usually been plenty of rain in our area, the water supply was plentiful until once in a while the well by the barn did not produce enough water during the winter months for our two cows. It then became my job to bring pail after pail full of snow from a snowdrift close to our house and put it in a galvanized washtub on the wood stove. I dug out snow and made a cave so I could crawl into it and scoop out the snow closest to the ground. That snow had the most ice crystals in it and produced the most water

ReBelle Hanson with her calf in 1938

when melted. One doesn't realize how much water two cows can drink until you melt snow for them. We were always glad during the winters when the well did not go dry. When these memories come to me now, I really appreciate my deep well and faucets.

School lunches in our one room school came from home in our lunch bucket and were kept in the schoolroom near the heating stove because if we kept them in the entryway in the wintertime they would be frozen by noon. In the fall, surplus commodities were given to the country schools, and they were delivered by a farmer who raised goats. He delivered them to our school by using a team of horses and a wagon. Grapefruit, apples, rutabagas, and shelled walnuts were some of the commodities that I can remember.

One cup of shelled walnuts was emptied on each child's desk every day until the box was empty. How many days in a row can children eat that many walnuts without getting their fill? It wasn't long before my walnuts got dumped into my lunch bucket and taken home. My mother made nut bread and sent it back to school with me, and the walnuts tasted really good then. The walnuts came in 50-pound boxes to our school. At the time, walnuts were being sold in our grocery store at ninety cents a pound. That gave us $45.00 worth of walnuts, which was a lot of money then. We enjoyed these commodities, especially the fresh fruit, which we didn't have a lot of at home. Our main fruit from the store was oranges, which were sent to school with us in our lunch buckets.

The rutabagas that came in the surplus commodities turned out to be the beginning of our hot lunch program. An older boy and I became the cooks. We peeled and cut up rutabagas and boiled them in a kettle of water on the wood heating stove. One of us brought a potato masher from home so we had warm mashed rutabagas with our cold sandwiches at noon. Now we were living like kings, or at least we thought we were.

Soon we expanded the menu and added hot cocoa, which is called hot chocolate now. We used the large size white coffee cup to stir the cocoa and sugar together and then added milk from the pail in the refrigerated entryway before it froze. This we added to the hot milk in the kettle, which had been made into a double boiler by placing it into water in a large blue enameled roaster. We couldn't have both mashed rutabagas and hot cocoa on the same day because the opening on the wood stove was not large enough to accommodate two kettles. We used that roaster with hot water in to also place our small glass fruit jars that we brought filled from home. The menu that day might consist of leftover mashed potatoes and gravy that our mothers served to us the previous evening for supper. In those days, dinner was served at noon, and supper was the evening meal.

My thoughts go to refrigeration and how it has changed during my lifetime. The land that we lived on had been developed into farmland by burning off the muskeg or peat, but the corner of the farm where our home was had not been burned. Muskeg is light and quite easy to dig into. Since we did not have an icebox or ice in the summer, we asked a neighbor to dig a rectangular hole about 2x4 feet and 3 feet deep in the shade on the north side of our house. We put gravel on the bottom and made walls and a cover out of boards. Tarpaper and a heavy rock were placed on top. Several bricks and flat rocks were placed on the gravel. Our kettles and other containers with food were placed there. If we got a lot of rain then the kettles would be floating when we went to our fridge. Bringing in food from our fridge seemed to be my job quite often when I was a kid since that needed a trip to the other side of the house. Just think of how many times the cook in the kitchen opens the fridge door in a day, and it was not much different then. It was breakfast, morning coffee, dinner, afternoon coffee, supper, and evening lunch. Butter, cream, or milk was usually needed when we set the table or when we carried lunch to the people who were working in the fields. Most of our meats were canned venison and chicken. We used a lot of smoked meats such as bacon and sausage. Macaroni hot dishes were made with bacon rather than hamburger at our house, which was probably because of lack of good refrigeration for raw meats. Let us all be thankful for the refrigeration we have today.

My grandparents moved to this area from Alvarado, Minnesota, which is in the northwestern part of the state. They arrived in Baudette by train on November 6, 1907, and they survived the fire of 1910. My grandfather had chosen this area because of the timber, which was not available on the prairie where they had lived. When they arrived by train they were met by a relative who carried a lantern so they could see where to walk on the board sidewalk. They stayed in town till morning and then walked about five miles following the river to the cousin's home before going another two miles to the homestead where some sort of shelter had been built. Both of my grandparents died before I was born. I would have like to have known these hard working pioneers of this area.

The Blizzard of March 15, 1941
By Mark Edman of Alvarado, Minnesota
Born 1933

The weather had been mild, unusually warm. People were dressed in lighter clothes and lighter coats. I was seven years old then, but I remember it like it was yesterday.

My sister Carol, her husband, and son Charles were visiting on that Saturday afternoon. When they were getting ready to leave, my brother John took their son Charles out the car.

Then, the storm struck. It was like a solid white wall of snow, John had trouble with Charles, who wanted to get away, but John was able to get him back to the house, which was around 120 feet away. The thing that kept them from getting out in the storm was Carol's love of talking and visiting with Dad. This probably saved their lives.

There were many who died in that storm. Some were not found till the snow melted.

Playing Hooky
By Lavonne Smith of Silverdale,
Pennsylvania
Born 1938

This story happened in Menahga, Minnesota sometime between the years of 1926 and 1929. My mother was sixth in a family of eleven children.

My mother, Rose, was quite a handful in school especially when she was with her friend, Annie. They could think up all sorts of mischief to get into. They heard about playing hooky from the older kids and it sounded so adventurous. Rose asked her mom if she could play hooky. Her mom had never heard about it, but it sounded like a game. She said, "Yes, it sounds like fun!"

So, the next day, while walking to school with the other kids, they slipped away. They walked to the river just north of the school and played in the water—skipping stones, watching the animals, and taking off their shoes to walk in the water. When they got hungry, they ate lunch from their lunch pails. Then they walked to the fire tower on a hill and climbed it. They could see so far and could see the school. The day got a little boring and Rose was wishing she was back in school.

When they thought it must be time for school to be over, they realized they were on the wrong side of the school to join the rest of the kids for the walk home. They decided to crawl in the ditch next to the school, thinking no one would notice. One of the students had gotten up to sharpen his pencil at the pencil sharpener, which was by the large windows on the side of the room. Teacher noticed the student intently looking at something, so she got up to look as well. She saw the absent girls crawling in the ditch. She said to the rest of the students "Everyone might as well come to the window and watch this!"

The girls were teased on the way home and I'm sure they got punished when they got there. They played hooky about once a year after that—a new tradition for them!

The Imperfect Christmas Tree
By Marilyn Hansel of Dalton, Minnesota
Born 1954

I grew up on a farm in North-Central Minnesota. One of my fondest memories was going out to the swamp each year to cut a Christmas tree. Dad would hook up the 1941 Minneapolis Moline tractor to the hay wagon and the entire family would ride out to the swamp at the north end of the farm. Dad never considered cutting a young tree that was just the right size. He left those for future growth since he wanted young trees to replace the

Harry and Dorothy Witt with six of their children in 1965

old trees. Instead, we wandered among the evergreens, studying the tops of each tree. Usually Dad would finally see just the right treetop. Then he would tie a handsaw to his belt and up the tree he would climb.

Pretty soon, the top of the tree tumbled down. We would load the tree onto the wagon along with all of the family and eagerly head home. Each of us anticipating decorating the tree and smelling the fresh evergreen scent in the house for the next few days. Each year the tree was totally different from the prior year tree. Some were much better than others were.

One year didn't go as smoothly as usual. That year it had rained a day or two before and then froze hard. When we went on our tree-hunting excursion that year, everything was coated in ice. When Dad cut a treetop and it tumbled down, several of the tree branches broke. It would have been a perfect Christmas tree except for the breakage. We all accepted Dad's statement that we would have to be satisfied with the damaged tree. He didn't want to waste another beautiful treetop since they were all covered in ice.

Bundling up and going out in the icy winter temps back then was a lot more fun than the current process of going to the storeroom and pulling out the artificial tree. Even changing decorations, the artificial tree looks the same every year. And there isn't any adventure in the trip to the storeroom. It is warmer though.

Choosing to Serve My Country
By Henry Wieland of Red Lake Falls, Minnesota
Born 1931

My name is Henry Wieland and my wife is Marilyn. We've been married for 54 years. We have four children—Deb, Todd, Kristi and Casey Jo. We live in Wylie Township located in Red Lake County, in the State of Minnesota.

Everyone has a good reason why they do things, and that is why I ended up in the Korean War. My dad served in the army in the First World War from 1918-1919. He always said he enjoyed it (Maybe yes—Maybe no). My sister's husband, Blackie Casavan, served in the Second World War from 1942-1946 in Africa and Italy. He said it was hell. My oldest brother Kenneth served in the Second World War from 1945-1946. He also hated it. Then my next brother Alvis and I joined the National Guard in June of 1948, in Thief River Falls, MN. I joined because my brother Alvis was joining and some of my good friends were joining. I was just going to turn 17 years old and I figured I would look pretty important if I joined. Then you would get to go to Camp Ripley for two weeks in the summer, and that would be like a two-week vacation. Another thing was that the veterans that came home from the Second World War were really looked up to. It was not the same with the Korean War Veterans.

I was born in 1931, so being raised in the depression years was quite tough, as there was very little money around. Then came the Second World War and it went from 1941-1945. The government had to ration so many things like tires, gas, sugar, coffee, etc. I have a few gas rationing stamps yet just to look at them. New machinery or cars couldn't be bought, as they didn't make any due to the War efforts.

The kids had to all pitch in and help with the chores and the fieldwork. Everybody had to help with shocking the grain and hauling bundles to the threshing machine. The guys that were 18 to 40 years old were mostly in the service, so there was very little help around.

Then came June 1950 and the North Koreans attacked the South Koreans. Around December 18th, President Harry S. Truman called in the 47th infantry Division that was the Minnesota/North Dakota National Guard to active duty (What a Christmas present). He gave us 30 days to get our affairs in order. Not too bad for a single person, but had to be horrible for a married guy with a family.

About January 18, 1951, we started training in Thief River Falls for about ten days. Then they had a troop train lined up to take us to Camp Rucker, Alabama (Fort Rucker now). They had a big gathering at the city auditorium the night we were leaving. They had some people give speeches, we did close order marching, and they served a big lunch. At 12:00 midnight, we were supposed to start loading on the train. There were about 81 men in our company. We marched with our rifles the six blocks to the Soo Line Depot. The temperature was -30 degrees below zero (what a parade). There were many tears shed that night. We also picked up two more companies that night. It took us three days to get to Camp Rucker.

After we got to Camp Rucker, they started to send men that had enlisted to our company. Uncle Sam was also drafting men and sending them to our company to get us up to a division strength, which was about 16,000 men. When we got overseas, they wanted your Division at 22,000 men, which they called a Combat Ready Division. Then we had to train them to be combat ready.

About the last week of July, our company got orders to send the names of three men from our company that had come from Thief River Falls to ship overseas, which they called FECOM (Far Eastern Command). I am not very lucky when it comes to drawing for a prize, but I hit the jackpot here because my name was one of the three. I happened to be in the hospital at the time with poison ivy in both eyes. They were swelled completely shut, so that I couldn't see at all. I was a pretty picky eater when I was young, so they had to feed me and I never knew what they were putting in my mouth. So they then decided to take me off of the list.

I was in a ward at the hospital with 42 other men who had poison ivy. I think I was better off than some, as they had blisters that were one to two inches long, one inch high, and an inch wide. They had the blisters all over their bodies. Blisters were from their feet to their groin area, chest, and back.

About two weeks later, our company got orders to draw ten more names from our original company to send overseas. My brother Alvis and 4-5 good friends of mine were on the list. Sol asked if I could get out of the hospital and go also. (I never told my mother this, as I don't think she would have understood my decision.) The head of the hospital was a woman that was full colonel and she said she would grant me my wish (another wrong decision).

They sent us by troop train to Minneapolis, and gave us seven days of leave. When we came back to Minneapolis, we were sent to Fort Lawton, Washington. It took us three days to get to Seattle Washington. It took about four days to process us and then they told us where we were going. I think we all knew where we were going. Korea. We weren't that dumb.

We then were loaded on a ship and we left Seattle at about noon. They announced on the loud speaker that they were starting to serve chow and we were to get in line. Alvis and I got in line and it was a long line. By the time we got done eating, it was three o'clock in the afternoon, so we got back in line for supper. We then met up with Maurice Russel who joined the Guard with us in Thief River Falls. Maurice was picked to be a Special Police on the ship. He had to wear a SP band on the ship while on duty. He gave me one to wear when I would go to eat. He then told us that Jerome Horiem was also on the ship and that he was a cook. He also had joined the Guard with us and was a very good friend of ours. We looked him up that night and he gave a white cook's jacket to Alvis and me to wear when we wanted to eat. After that, Alvis and I never had to stand in line again. I don't know if that was the right thing or not, but it sure worked good.

It took us about 18 days to get to Japan. They took us to Camp Drake by Tokyo. They processed us again and in about four days, we were on our way to Inchon, Korea. We had to stay out four miles from the beach at Inchon because the tide over there is one of the highest in the world, which is 30 feet. When we left Japan for Korea, they put Alvis and me on KP. We worked the first day, which was terrible down there where they ate. So many of the guys were seasick and they were puking all over on the tables where the other guys were eating. The smell was horrible. We did not go back for KP the next day. Well, don't you know that they wouldn't give us our chow cards back, so we couldn't eat! So our friend's and buddies had to sneak food for us (I didn't use the word steal). At midnight, we started to crawl over the side of the ship to load into the landing crafts to go ashore. By the time we hit the beach, our landing craft had about seven or eight inches of water in it. The front door didn't fit very tight.

When we got off, they wrote a number on your helmet as to which division you were going to. They gave you a can of soup and put you on a train to Seoul. I went to the 15th Regiment in the Third Division. My brother Alvis went to the 7th Regiment of the Third Division. So, that was where we got split up. I always said I guess we really lucked out, as I think it was the best Division over there. I think some men over there wouldn't agree with me, but everybody has their own opinion.

I was a squad leader in a rifle squad. I thank the Lord many times over for not getting hit over there. Alvis was also a squad leader in a rifle squad, but he got wounded in March. He was discharged six weeks after I got out.

When I joined the Guard back in 1948, I really wanted to stay in the service for 20 to 30 years and make it a career. Funny how some things can change. Yes, if someone give you and offer for a free trip halfway around the world, with free meals, clothing, housing, medical, toothpaste, cigarettes, etc., BEWARE, as it is not really free. Yes, my hearing got bad and also my memory, as I do not remember anything about staying in for 20-30 years.

Mabel Bahr Named Midway Drive
By Debbie (Bahr) Braaten of Bemidji, Minnesota
Born 1951

It was in the late 1940s and my mom, Mabel (Wick) Bahr was working at the Standard Lumber Company. (I remember so well the cute little miniature home that was on the front lawn of the Standard Lumber Company.)

There was a contest in Bemidji to name the street that ran along the west side of Lake Bemidji. My mom always liked contests and was always very creative and clever! Mom

Debbie's mom, Mabel (Wick) Bahr

came up with the idea of naming the street Midway Drive. Such exciting news when my mom received the grand prize!

For naming this beautiful street along Lake Bemidji as Midway Drive, my mom won the prize of $5.00! Being the wonderful

Debbie's dad, Clifford Bahr

Christian woman my mom always was, she gave $3.00 of her winnings to her church and saved $2.00 for herself.

That's my beautiful mom. I love, honor, and respect my mom so much! This giving kindness describes how my mom lived her life.

Clifford Bahr Drove Three Million Miles

My dad, Clifford Bahr, was the hardest working, most ambitious, most reliable man I have ever known. My dad was a lifelong resident of Bemidji, Minnesota.

Dad started his truck driving business as a young man. He owned many trucks over the years, putting in long, hard days. My dear dad drove over 3,000,000 miles in his long trucking career! He did all this for us, his family! He was so dedicated to making a good honest living by hard work and devotion to his family!

I remember Dad bringing me with him to the "Globe" gas station and luncheon bar at the junction of Midway Drive and 2nd Street. Our treat at the Globe was a yummy, big Bismarck! What a treat!

Dad's buddies would say, "Which of your little partners do you have with you today, Cliff?"

Dad would answer, "This is Debbie, my middle girl, my little pal!"

I loved those Saturday mornings that Dad wasn't on the road and I could make these wonderful memories with my dad!

Stoking the One-room Schoolhouse Stove
By Elden Johnson of Hallock, Minnesota
Born 1934

I don't think my story is very unique, not much different than most other kids that grew up on a small farm, except for one thing. We did have a very small farm, about eight milk cows, a team of horses, pigs for our own meat, chickens for eating and egg—nothing unusual. In summertime, once a week a trip would be made to town with eggs and cream to sell, and wait for the check to buy groceries, one dollars' worth of gas, and head back home again. In wintertime, it was every two weeks. We had very few acres of tillable land, enough for my dad to plant some oats for chicken feed and maybe a few acres of corn for cattle feed in winter.

I went to a small one-room country school through the seventh grade, at which time the country schools were consolidating with the town schools and a school bus would pick us up, after walking the same one half mile. I was the only first grader; there was only one second grader and one third grader. At the end of the first year, the third grader did not pass to the next grade, so the second grader went to be in the third grade, making two of them. My teacher did not want me alone in the second grade, so I also jumped up to the third grade. (I was only five when I started school, and by skipping the second grade, I was only 16 when I graduated from high school—too young.)

My unique situation was that the schoolteacher stayed at a home about three miles from the school, and had no way to get to the school in the mornings except to wait for the car that brought the students. So, for about six months of winter weather in northern Minnesota, the old, large, round stove had to be fired up so it would be warmed up some before the others came. Being it was the schoolteacher's job to do that chore and she could not get there until about 8:00 A.M., she hired me to do the job. She paid me $5.00 a month for six months. I had money! However, what I think about now is that I was only ten and eleven years old when I was doing that, walking a half mile in the dark, getting to the school building by 7:00 A.M., entering a dark, cold, unlocked school building, and using matches to light the several kerosene lamps in the building before I could start any of the other work. After that, I began by carrying out the ashes from the stove, carrying in water from the well for the water fountain, and getting a fire going in the large, round woodstove so it could warm up the one-room school before the others came. I was the last one to leave the school at the end of the day because I would carry in enough wood from the wood shed for the next day, empty the water fountain so it wouldn't freeze overnight, and do a little floor sweeping. $5.00!

My parents must have had enough trust and faith that I could do the job at ten years old. I remember it was a long, dark walk, absolutely no light, and sometimes the temperature was well below zero. I am wondering how many parents would let their ten year old son do that nowadays? I am proud I never did burn the building down!

We never had electricity until I was a senior in high school. We never did have running water, always carried it in from the well, and carried the "slop" back out to dump. We never had an indoor toilet; it got mighty cold walking through the snow in the middle of the night if nature called. All the cooking was done on a woodstove, and all the heat was provided by another wood heater. Again, there were ashes to be carried out each day and water to be carried inside.

It was a small house, with two rooms downstairs (we called them kitchen and "other room"), and one room upstairs, with the roof so low you could not walk near to the outside walls. There was no heat upstairs, except for what came up the stairway. There was no insulation, just the pole rafters and roof boards, so in wintertime when you woke up the roof above your head would be all white with frost.

We never did have a telephone; some neighbors did in later years. There was no television until I was a senior in high school, and that was a black and white unit. We had a battery-operated radio (with a dry cell battery) that could only be used for two daily programs for my mother, Ma Perkin's Family and Pepper Young's Family, and the news at suppertime. Then the radio was turned off until the next day. We had rural mail delivery, every Tuesday, Thursday, and Saturday. A postage stamp was three cents.

As previously stated, we raised a pig or two for meat, never to sell. My mother canned much of the meat so it was always ready for a meal or company. We had chickens for an occasional Sunday dinner. However, in wintertime there was no shortage of deer meat, rabbit meat and grouse meat. My dad would never butcher a beef, as he got much needed money for it by shipping it to a slaughterhouse. I did not know what a hamburger was until about 14 years old. We never had pork chops, as Dad would make as much as he could into "roasts." The pork hams would be cured in a stone crock with salt brine in it to cure them.

We picked a lot of wild berries, which my mother canned, such as high bush cranberries, strawberries, raspberries, and ground cherries. Choke cherries were picked and the juice was canned to be used later for pudding and jelly. We had a large garden for producing vegetables to eat fresh as well as for canning.

My mother had an old Maytag wringer washer for washing clothes. In wintertime, we would have a large tub on the kitchen stove that we would keep filled with snow to provide soft water for washing clothes the next day. That same tub was used once a week, Saturday nights, for the bathtub. Being the youngest, I was first!

I can remember one time, maybe around 1940, I went and stayed with my grandparents for a week, my parents were going to pick me up the next Friday. During that week is when we heard on the radio that the "world was coming to an end on Friday." Wow, was I scared. I was so anxious to get home that when my parents did come to pick me up, I didn't even want them to stay long enough to have coffee with Grandma and Grandpa; I wanted them to take me home immediately so we would be there when the "world ended."

I wouldn't want to go back living like that now, but in hindsight and memories, I would not have wanted it any other way. I had a great home.

Drive-ins and Green Stamps
By Carole Hagen of Detroit Lakes, Minnesota
Born 1959

On our vacation, driving to Minnesota, my brother, Doug, stuck his tongue on a window in the winter. Mom poured coffee on it and ripped it off. I stepped on a cactus at the Antelope. Growing up, my sister Kathy (age 6) broke Karin's (age 4) leg giving her a ride on a bike. Karin stuck her leg in the spokes. Boy! We were a bunch of naughty children!

In the 1960s, the only cheap way to see a movie was through the drive-in theatre. The Owens family jumped in the station wagon and went to the movies. Afterwards, Carole, Kathy, Doug, and Karin got an ice cream cone for a dime.

The first color TV was purchased in 1963. I was four. Karin, the youngest child, got the hand-me-down clothing. I was born first, then Kathy, Doug, and Karin. We were born one year apart. Mom was pregnant for five years. Luckily, my mom had diaper service.

My mom and dad had a black lab named "Blackie" which we grew up with. Blackie would protect us. One time, my dad was a little rough and Blackie snarled and almost bit my dad.

One of my dad's favorite pastimes was building and racing jeeps in the sand dunes. He and his buddies built and raced. My dad mostly raced on the west coast. As a kid, I swam in the Pacific Ocean.

In the '60s, my mom collected S&H green stamps. My mom got the stamps and booklets from the grocery store. When the booklets were filled, you chose a prize. My mom and dad used the milkman, too. An empty bottle would be placed outside and a fresh one was there the next morning.

There's one thing we still do today. At Thanksgiving and Christmas, we all get together at Kathy's house and celebrate.

We Made Our Own Fun
By Kathryn Goligowski Motl of Browerville, Minnesota
Born 1952

I grew up one of six children in Todd County during the '50s and '60s. This was a time when Saturday mornings were filled with TV shows like *Sky King*, *Fury*, and, best of all, *Roy Rogers*, the king of the cowboys and his horse, Trigger.

My sister Peggy was two years older than I was. Both of us loved Roy (my favorite) and Gene Autry (Peg's favorite). Because I was the little sister, Peggy was in charge.

Living on a farm gave us plenty to do. There was the haymow where often among the hay bales were new kittens. The straw stack was fun to slide down until we got caught. The old chicken coop became our playhouse. Then we had our horses, just like Roy and Gene—only our horses were really two gas barrels up on a large cement platform.

We would crawl up on our horses and ride like the wind singing cowboy songs. After all, the best cowboys could really sing.

One warm summer day while we were "riding," I noticed my horse had a screw cap, so I unscrewed it and smelled an odor I really liked. I sniffed, and sniffed, and sniffed again. Pretty soon, I was laying on my "horse" with my nose over the hole.

Before I knew what happened, I passed out, rolled off my horse, off the platform, and landed on the ground.

My sister jumped down in a panic and ran to me. She was sure I was dead. The fear she had was not that I died, but that because she was "in charge," she was in big trouble. Needless to say, that put an end to my gas sniffing days.

One of the chores my sister and I did in the summer was to hang clothes on the line. We had four lines, each about 60 feet long. Our younger brother Steve would play outside while we watched him along with our job.

The trouble was that Steve liked to run away. Every time we took our eyes off him, he would disappear. We became very good at finding him before anyone found him missing, but still, he would end up gone on our watch.

We came up with a good idea. Since many of Steve's shorts had straps over his shoulders, Peggy and I tied a thin rope to the clothesline and the other end to his shorts strap. Steve then could run up and down the length of the line without constant supervision. So, now we could do some serious reading while lying in the grass.

What a surprise for Mom when she came outside to find Steve's shorts attached to the clothesline…without Steve in them! He had escaped again! Because we could not contain him, Mom resorted to tie a red bandana on his head so we could spot him in the field or pasture when he was on the run.

I am proud to say my brother, Steve, grew up and followed his wondering foot. He joined the army, served his country for 20+ years, and traveled the world.

Memories as a Child
By Joyce E. Hanson of Herman, Minnesota
Born 1928

Many of my memories as a child were about snow, the problems it caused, and also the fun times. Shovels were a very important tool on the farm. Our family, the Charles Simpsons, lived on a farm on the main road between Herman and Chokio. Many places the road was lower than the fields bordering it, thus much snow would drift onto the road. Snowplows were not very powerful then, so after a storm, farmers would go ahead and break up the hard drifts so the plow could continue on.

The winter of '36 was a bad one. Snowbanks were 6-7 feet high between our place and school. Yet, I never missed a day of school then or other years, as I had perfect attendance for all eight years. In my early years of schooling when it was very cold, my dad would walk halfway with my sister and me; he then would turn to go back home but kept checking on us to see that we made it there. We were dressed very warm, wearing long underwear, long brown stockings, snow pants, heavy coat, buckled overshoes, and a big scarf to cover everything but our eyes. Still we were very cold when we go there. We carried our lunch in syrup pails.

One mild moonlight night, our family dressed up warm and we walked to our neighbor's for a visit. My dad nailed a box to the sled and we put our two-year-old brother in there so we could pull him along. It was fun to visit after being housebound.

The winter of '42 was another snowy time. Because of blocked roads and living nine miles from the post office in Chokio, we did not get mail for 11 days. Finally, my uncle who lived a couple miles west of us found a road open to Collis, about 15 miles further west. He met the Chokio mail carrier and brought home mail for six or seven families. My sister, Mavis, and I walked over to my uncle's place pulling a sled with a box nailed on to get our mail and also for two neighbors. The Sears Roebuck Catalog was part of the load.

Every farm had animals, so that involved shoveling paths, sometimes fences, so cattle couldn't walk out over on snowdrifts. My dad would chop ice from the cattle tank so they could drink. He also had a tank heater in the water to use during daylight hours.

We did have fun times, too. We would play "Fox and Goose" at recess time in school and we had a pond that we did ice-skating on. One family brought a big toboggan to school. Five or six of us would pile on it and, from a snowbank, would ride down the hill to the creek bottom. That was fun! Once we made a big, tall snowman that we had to use the stepladder to put his head on. We also made tunnels through the big drifts.

All my high school days were during World War II. Many things were rationed. Two of the things were gas and tires. The out-of-town basketball games only allowed the team to go. No pep buses were used. Dances were a big thing then. There were dance halls in Donnelly, Herman, and Norcross. Each town had a little orchestra that usually included a fiddle and an accordion. Admission was maybe a quarter or fifty cents.

I was married in 1949 to Neil Hanson and we spent 60 years on a farm five miles east of Herman in Grant County on the west shore of Lake Ulsrud. Much work was done to improve the place and nature abounded. It was a haven for birds and other wild animals. Seeing many rainbows and moonlight on the lake will forever be a memory.

Depression Days, Blizzards, and Troop Trains
By Helen Goldthorpe LeClaire of Bemidji, Minnesota
Born 1925

When I was ten years old, we raised many chickens. Mom would almost fill a five-gallon pail with hand-washed eggs and put the pail in a wagon for me to take to the poultry house about a mile from home. There I would watch a lady candle the eggs (see through egg with a light). We would be paid cash. This was my mom's egg money. We sold eggs and fryers, too. On my way home from the poultry house, I would have to stop at the nearby restaurant and get scraps of lettuce and potato peelings for the chickens. Often when my brother and I wanted to go see an 11-cent movie, we would "steal" eggs from under the hens and sell them to our neighbors.

It was a mild day in St. Cloud, Minnesota when I walked to Technical High School. I was 15 years old, had on a spring coat, and wore anklets. After noon hour, our German history teacher, Mr. Theodor Zeyer, had gone home for lunch and when he came back at about 1:00 P.M., he told the class the weather wasn't fit for "man nor beast." My neighbor,

Mrs Allen, said that I could not walk home; the snow was already knee-deep. We had no telephone and I knew my mother would worry about me, so I left for home two blocks away through a wooded area and had to cross a big dance hall parking lot.

The wind would just take your breath away. I remember stopping by each tree to rest and catch my breath, and figure out where our path was, which we always took. I couldn't see it for the blowing snow. I was worried that I would fall right by our backdoor, no one would know, and I would freeze to death. I got in the house okay, but covered with snow. About two hours later, my older brother Russ came with my sister Doris, who was 12 years old. We had to carry her about two blocks as the snow was so deep.

In my junior year of high school, I took a sheet metal class where we learned to rivet and read blueprints, etc. Many of my classmates went to work at defense plants. I went to work at Northwestern Bell Telephone. Telephone operators were needed in California, and I signed up to be transferred there and five operators went. The war ended, so I wasn't called.

I remember we had scrap and paper drives. Our fifth grade coat closet was almost filled with bundled newspapers. Our room won the prize for collecting the most.

I had scarlet fever when in grade school. We were quarantined with an orange-colored sign nailed near our door. No one could visit us. It was on our siding so long that it left a colored imprint.

During the war, we had blackouts. We had to hang dark curtains over our windows at night so no light could be seen. We had block captains to check on our houses. This was done when we heard air-raid sirens blow.

When I got home from school, I had to fill the wood box with kindling and shelled corncobs so Mom could start the fires in the kitchen range and woodstove in the morning.

In the evening about 7:00 P.M., Mom and I would walk about a mile to watch the troop train come through on the Northern Pacific Railroad. We would wave to the service men and watch the mail being sorted in the mail car. We could see the cook in his tall, white cap in the cook car. It was quite an event.

We were one of the first to own a TV set on our block in 1951. I remember many of our relatives and friends would come over in the evenings to watch the wrestling matches. They were very professional then and not actors like nowadays.

A Great Childhood
By Donald W. Coil of Staples, Minnesota
Born 1937

I am Donald W. Coil, born at Bertha Minnesota Hospital in Todd County on March 17, 1937. I grew up in Thomastown Township, Wadena, Minnesota on a farm. My parents were Virgil B. Coil and Pearl M. Reed. They were both born in Iowa in July of 1897. They were married on March 31, 1935. I am their only child.

We lived on a rented 80-acre farm with dairy cows, chickens, pigs, and workhorses. There was no electricity or running water.

My mother had polio as a child. Sometime around 1940, she fell and broke her hip. Doctors tried to pin it back together, but that did not work. Infection set in, so she had to go to the University of Minnesota Hospital where they amputated her right leg. Around this time, we moved to another rented farm.

Don Coil in 1939

Don Coil with a lamb in 1948

Then, about 1942, my dad bought a 120-acre farm with a very small old house and not much tillable land.

I started first grade in 1943 at District #7, a one-room country school one mile from my home. In 1947, the school closed and I was bussed to Staples for my fifth through twelfth grades. I graduated in 1955.

We got electricity in August of 1948. The cost was $3.00 per month minimum and we had to be sure we didn't go over that. Up to this time, we cooked and heated with wood. After we got electricity, my dad found and bought a used electric refrigerator and a hot plate to make it a little easier for my mother who did everything while in her wheelchair. We still heated entirely with wood and carried water from a hand pump outside. The house remained that way until it was destroyed in the late 1970s.

It seems my parents had more than their share of heartbreaks. My mother died in 1959 of cancer, never having lived in a modern house. They really never had anything. My dad could not leave my mother alone to go to a job, so he tried to make it farming. He was a good man, but could not manage. He worked hard all the time and died in 1979. All in all, I had a good childhood. We were poor, but I thought everyone was poor.

After high school, I enlisted in the army and spent 18 months in Korea. I came home and got married in 1960. I have had a great wife for 56 years. I have two great kids and five wonderful grandkids. My kids, their spouses, and the five grandkids are all college educated. I also have two great-grandkids who are six and four years old. Life is great!

Close to the Courthouse, Ahead of the Curve
By John Sherack of Thief River Falls, Minnesota
Born 1948

Passing the Minnesota driver's license exam (or any state's exam) is a big deal. Maybe not for a farm kid, who probably started driving tractors, trucks, etc. in the first decade of life, but for an 18-year-old city kid who was vertically challenged, obtaining the license to drive could not be undervalued.

The exam took place on Monday, August 7, 1967. The 1955 Chevy Bel-Air, which was to be driven in the exam, was given a quick once-over at the neighborhood service station. A burned-out turn signal flasher was replaced. The examiner could have passed for a Marine drill instructor, or had been one in a previous life. In uniform with dark glasses and a well-tuned gruff demeanor right out of central casting. His inspection of turn signals, brake lights, etc. passed muster. We pulled away from the courthouse and the "joy ride" began.

My strategy was to not put too much emphasis on the parallel parking part of the test. As long as a flag wasn't hit (instant failure of the exam), the points docked would be minimal. The turning procedures/proper lane changes were where many of the points were. In addition, there was the sudden stop that you could figure on being prompted to execute when the examiner gave the command to do so.

When the "stop" order was given, I hit the brakes hard, which was okay. However, as I resumed driving, a bunch of dust (smoke?) came out from under the dash. I tried to ignore it, but the examiner noticed it, said something, and I applied the brakes. To which he said, "Don't stop in the middle of an intersection." Whatever it was, the dust or smoke didn't show up again.

I wasn't overly confident to begin with, and at this point, I was starting to think about when I would be retaking the exam, maybe with a different examiner. The rest of the driving was uneventful and the final park at the courthouse was coming up.

The examiner asked me something like who would be at the courthouse to pick up the car, etc. I was thinking if I had passed, I could drive myself home, so I was pretty certain I had failed the exam and didn't care much about the final park, which had the car maybe three feet from the curb. My older brother was across the street from the courthouse. I thought I saw him shaking his head or slapping his forehead as he watched the final park.

When I shut off the engine, the examiner opened his door and commented something like, "...the reason we have narrow streets is because of people like you parking like this..."

Anyway, when the examiner totaled up the score, it, surprisingly, came to 76, when 70 was a passing grade. My theory is that I beat the curve because the examiner didn't want to give me the test again in that car.

Kathleen's Polio Story
By Kathleen Anderson of Hoffman, Minnesota

In 1952 and 1953, there was another rise in polio cases in Otter Tail Co. and Minnesota. I was nine years old and I would hear of people I knew coming down with polio.

I shared the fear that others spoke of. Who was next?

My younger sister and I attended a small country school a couple miles from our home. We walked home on the gravel road in the fall and spring. One warm October day in 1952, I could only walk the first half-mile home and then my legs would not carry me. My sister carried my lunch bucket and I crawled home on my hands and knees.

That night I could barely get up the stairs to bed and after Mom watched me struggle up the steps, my parents said I had to go to the doctor the next day. It did not take the Henning doctor long to determine that I had polio and he said I had to go to Sister Kenny Hospital that very day.

We got in our '41 Ford car, with me lying in the backseat. I peeked out occasionally to see all the towns and city lights I had not seen before.

When we reached the Twin Cities, my dad stopped at a gas station to ask directions to the Sister Kenny Hospital. A helpful man said he would lead us there. We followed him at a steady pace. I can still hear the clutch and brake working as we wound our way to Sister Kenny.

When we reached Sister Kenny, I was admitted immediately. My parents were told to leave, as I would be placed in isolation for at least two weeks, after the required medical procedures. Our goodbye to each other was a quick wave to each other across the crowded, noisy admission room.

I was immediately placed on a cart in a line with other patients on carts. We were all scared and some of us crying and wondering where our parents were. Each of us had our turn for a very painful spinal tap and other medical procedures.

You never quite knew or understood what was coming next. It seemed like there were people all over. When Dad and Mom left, I had no idea when I would see them again or what things would be occurring in the hospital. I did realize I had polio.

When I was done with the procedures, I was taken to isolation and placed in an iron lung for a short time. After a few days, I was breathing on my own and was placed in a bed in the isolation ward. Once in the ward, I realized there were beds and iron lungs in the halls as well; it was crowded all over. You could hear the iron lungs "pumping" near you.

After two weeks in isolation, I was placed in a general ward with six or seven other girls, 6-10 years old. Each of us had the Sister Kenny hot pack treatment. They were indeed hot, but we seldom blistered from a burn. We also had some physical therapy in bed but it was not daily, due to lack of staff I think.

My parents came to visit me every weekend when I was in that ward and I received a letter nearly every day. They always seemed to find something to write.

They told me that when I was in isolation, they also were. My sister could not go to school and no one else could go anywhere either. Someone would bring groceries to the end of the driveway and leave. No one else in the family was hospitalized for polio.

Quite often survivors of polio were in some way crippled, requiring crutches, braces, wheelchairs, breathing apparatus, etc. For many it was a lifetime challenge. The polio immunization is indeed a blessing.

Memories of Mesabi Iron Range
By Audrey J. Orlando of San Jose, California
Born 1937

I grew up on the Mesabi Iron Range from 1941 to 1959. The house we were living in in 1941 did not have electricity, telephone, or running water. We had the usual chamber pots and outhouse in back and summer or winter, we had to use it.

On Saturday nights, we filled a large tub with warm water, heated on the wood burning range, and one by one, we bathed, starting with the youngest to the eldest. My chore was carrying water from the well and wood for the cooking range and heating stove.

When I was six years old, I attended the one-room schoolhouse, with one teacher, Miss Thomas, teaching first through fourth grade. The school previously had gone to the eighth grade, but there were not enough students, so the administrators decided to have the older students bussed to town.

The janitor of the school was a farm lady, who lived across the street from the school. She started a warm fire every morning during the winter in the wood burning pot-bellied stove. This was very welcome to the students, when we arrived in 30 to 40 degrees below zero weather.

Miss Thomas taught for only one year, and the following year, Miss Bernice White was our teacher. She got married and became Mrs. Bernice Mandich, and she taught for three years. I loved school, especially when the upper grades were being taught, and we could eavesdrop on the lessons.

We had a library with many good books. I especially liked the tales of the kings, queens, and knights of the Middle Ages. When I got to fourth grade, the teacher assigned me to be librarian, because I had read most of the books and could tell the students what the stories were about. I felt this was quite an honor and I took my job seriously, filling out the cards, showing who had checked out books, and collecting fines when they were overdue.

We were driven to school by Frank Deithman, Sr. in his own Model-A. He only drove the students from the country in West Lawrence Lake to the Lawrence Lake School. All of the older students were bussed to town in regular school buses. (We all thought Mr. Deithman was old because he chewed on his six-inch whiskers and drove an old car), but he was probably only 55 or 60.

Whenever we had a blizzard, the school would shut down. We didn't have a telephone so we couldn't call anyone, and we just assumed the school was closed. We were never wrong. Afterward we just went back to school and picked up where we left off.

I don't feel I was at any disadvantage attending a one-room school. When we were finished with fourth grade, we transferred to fifth grade in Bovey and the one-room school was closed. There was nothing in the town school, which was any better than our one-room school.

As we got older, we found we could not participate in school social activities, but eventually school buses were provided so that we could travel to ball games, dances, and other functions in the nearby towns, Bovey, Coleraine, Grand Rapids, Pengilly, Calumet, and Marble. Chaperones were engaged for the teenaged dances on Friday nights and it kept most teenagers out of trouble.

Old Time Farming and Courting
By Edward Pavek of Fertile, Minnesota
Born 1930

I was born February 9, 1930 in a family of six brothers and four sisters. My oldest sister, Patty, is currently living at the Oak Manor in Detroit Lakes, Minnesota. For being 94 years young, she is doing well. After birth, it was the custom to be baptized as soon as possible. We are members of the Catholic Church here in Fertile, Minnesota.

Oh! My first grade teacher was Gwendolyn Fields and she was a wonderful lady. We sat in those little green chairs.

Our farm near Waubun is located on the White Earth Indian Reservation. White Earth is the largest reservation in the state of Minnesota. We always went to Waubun Public School. The school bus went past our farm, close to the main county line.

We had a country school located south of the farm, around the distance of a mile. As a young trapper, I knew that a country school was handy to set traps for weasels, muskrats, mink, raccoons, and skunks. All longhaired fur was in great demand. On December 3, 1943, I broke through the ice while trapping muskrats. The temperature hit close to 70 degrees that day. Muskrat pelts were worth $4.00 apiece for an extra-large.

Like other farm folks, you took a weekly bath on Saturday nights. The cleanest sister took her bath first, and then we boys followed our sisters. Hot water was added from the woodstove's reservoir. We never caught any itch or such!

Yes, we, like others, had a two-holer outhouse that we used. We used the old Sears and Wards catalogs for a wipe. Charmin wasn't invented as of yet.

Those were the days that our favorite radio programs were Dr. IQ, Gang Busters, and Fibber McGee and Molly. Of course, we always tuned into the news at 6:00 P.M. Everyone had to be quiet!

We, as small farmers, had beef, dairy cattle, hogs, chickens, geese, and a large garden. And let's not forget our pet dog and cats. When you had a bad day, your pet dog and cat always welcomed you when you got out of the car!

I remember the bad blizzard of November 11, 1941. It caught many folks off guard. Many people lost their lives and the farmers lost many beef cattle due to the blizzard. In the winter, we went to school in an enclosed sleigh. It had foot warmers. The roads were not passable. When the snow was two feet deep, we went to school cross-country.

In the wintertime, my parents made homemade sausage, ham, and bacon. That farm-cured bacon when being fried with eggs brought an aroma to the whole house. The bacon of today couldn't hold a candle to that good, old-fashioned home bacon.

In 1950, Dad bought a new ten-foot grain drill and a new tractor. That spring I started sowing a field of oats. I started at 8:00 A.M. and finished at midnight. I sowed 65 acres. I was proud that most of the field was sowed. With today's large machinery, they can sow 65 acres in a half hour! I planted corn with a two-row planter. Today, many farmers have a 100-row corn planter. When the grain prices were attractive, land was selling for $7,000 an acre. This was in 2008.

With dating, everything had to be "top notch." Always put your best foot forward. Number one: shoes shined, white shirt (pressed), suit (pressed), and the car washed. The first impression could be your last. Always have a sense of humor. Don't rush into courtship too fast! Always keep in mind what your date's parents think of you. For a novice, these acts are good to ponder!

After three years of courtship with prayer and dedication, she said, "Yes." We are married now for 54 years. Oh, it's not always "Honey" this or that. It is normal to have cloudy days, but the sunshine that follows is warm. Remember the old adage: Murder, yes. Divorce, never. And, too, all sunshine makes a desert.

My prayers have been answered. We are sticking together! Where is the kitchen?

Wild Ricing
By Merlaine Taylor of Grand Rapids,
Minnesota
Born 1939

I remember when we moved our young family up to Grand Rapids, Minnesota. I was raised on a farm near Canby, Minnesota located about ten miles from the South Dakota border. My husband was raised in Dawson, Minnesota only about 15 miles away. I had never been this far north and could hardly believe there could be so many trees and lakes. To say I had a lot to learn was putting it "mildly!"

One of the things I was to learn was wild rice. I didn't know there was such a thing.

People unloading the rice they just harvested off the lake

Our neighbor Ed told us about how it was harvested and that a person could make some pretty good money doing it. We soon learned from Ed the rules and the equipment we would need. We already had a proper canoe and soon made ourselves a duckbill pole and beater sticks from the end of some old pool cue sticks. Next, we learned that everyone knew of a rice lake, but we didn't. Once again, our good neighbor Ed took us under his wing and let us follow him. We were off for our first experience of wild rice harvesting. It was hard work, but we made some money!

After several times gathering rice with Ed, we decided to look for some better lakes. My husband heard from a good friend he worked with about a good rice lake. Not many people knew about it, but it had good rice. However, there wasn't a public access to it. We would have to drag our canoe through the woods, down a hill, and through a bog to reach the lake to get to the rice, but we would get lots of rice!

The next day, we followed the directions, parked our truck, and carried our canoe through the woods. There was the bog. We made our way through the bog, pushing and dragging our canoe out to the open water on a lake "no one was supposed to know about."

Well, there was a public access and people were driving right to the shore and putting in their canoes! They looked at us as if we were crazy when we finally got out to the bog and onto the lake. The one good thing was the ricing was good and we ended up with a canoe full of long, good rice at the end of the ricing hours. But as people went to the public access, we realized that we would have to go through the bog. With the boat full of rice, it was going to be much harder on the way back. Once through the bog, it was a trip back up that hill and through the woods to our truck.

What I learned was to "think twice" when my husband says, "It is a lake no one hardly knows about!"

From Feed Sack Dresses to Mini-skirts
By LoAnn DelGrande of Hibbing, Minnesota
Born 1953

I was born in Mahnomen, Minnesota in 1953. I was the sixth sister born to a farmer who really wanted a boy. We lived on a farm that had a pink house in the Beaulieu area. We were very poor. Everything we had came from the farm we lived on. We lived in a small two-bedroom house, so all the kids were in one room, except me. My crib was in with my parents. I can remember standing up in my crib. I was probably five or six. My nightlight was lavender under my crib.

Being 18 miles from Mahnomen meant an hour bus ride in the morning and an hour bus ride to get home. I was very shy and backward from living such a sheltered life. I was afraid of everything: mice, bats, lightning, electricity, talking to people. We got ready for school by putting the gas oven on high and standing in front of the open door to get dressed. Then we would stand by the window, and when that bus came over the hill and we could see it, we all went running out to the road.

I did well in school even though I had terrible eyesight. I did not get glasses until

7th grade because my parents could not afford them. I remember the first time I put them on and my mom and I went to the grocery store, and I could see the lettering on the boxes. There it all was. A whole new world. Cheerios, Wheaties, Sugar, Charmin…I had no idea. Do you remember when Charmin came in colors? Yellow, pink, and aqua. Then we went outside. It used to be just a solid green. I could see leaves and grass blades, and I was amazed.

All of our food was meat raised on the farm, or garden vegetables or canned fruit, which my mom made when those fruits were in season. One morning, I went outside and there were a couple of chickens, running around with their heads cut off. Mom was butchering. That was a terrifying sight.

We had very few toys, but I had a Barbie doll. I also had patterns for Barbie's clothes. My mother was an excellent seamstress, so I had plenty of scraps to make clothes. I wasn't old enough to use the sewing machine, so I sewed everything by hand. I did this with my sister Cheryl, my best friend, and the closest to me in age. The other thing we did was cut people out of the catalogs, and their clothes and their furniture. Whenever Sears, Penney's, or Spiegel's came, we were ecstatic.

My mother sewed my clothes from material that came from feed sacks. On Easter, Cheryl and I would always get a new outfit from new material. They were very nice. My mom would take us to church three times a week. We had a wonderful spiritual upbringing. My dad did not agree and stayed home, which caused a lot of dissention.

On the farm, I helped feed the cows by putting down their pellets in front of their stanchions. I also fed the younger calves milk replacer. I would mix it up with water in a pail and each calf would come take his/her turn. Some were bullies, so I would have to back them up by hitting them over the head with a stick. We always had a couple of dogs and many, many cats that hung out in the barn hay loft. There were too many to count and they were wild. I would always try to be-friend them, but they were very scared; so I would give them milk until they would come out of hiding.

Cheryl and I were always together. We took long walks on a path out to the fields to a little stream with dogs following behind. We would eat chokecherries along the way. We picked rocks for our dad. He would drive the tractor and trailer and we would walk along and throw rocks in. This was to rid the fields of rocks that were to be planted. We would ride along on the tractor by leaning on the fender. My dad would empty the manure spreader, and after it was emptied, I rode in it. We didn't think anything of it. Farming is not a clean profession. When my parents baled hay, I was too young to help, but I remember riding on top of the pile of bales loaded into the trailer and it was very high. Now, that was fun.

My friend, Ronnie, neighbor and 4H buddy, was driving a full sized tractor down a narrow gravel road near his home. He lost control of it. The tractor rolled over and killed

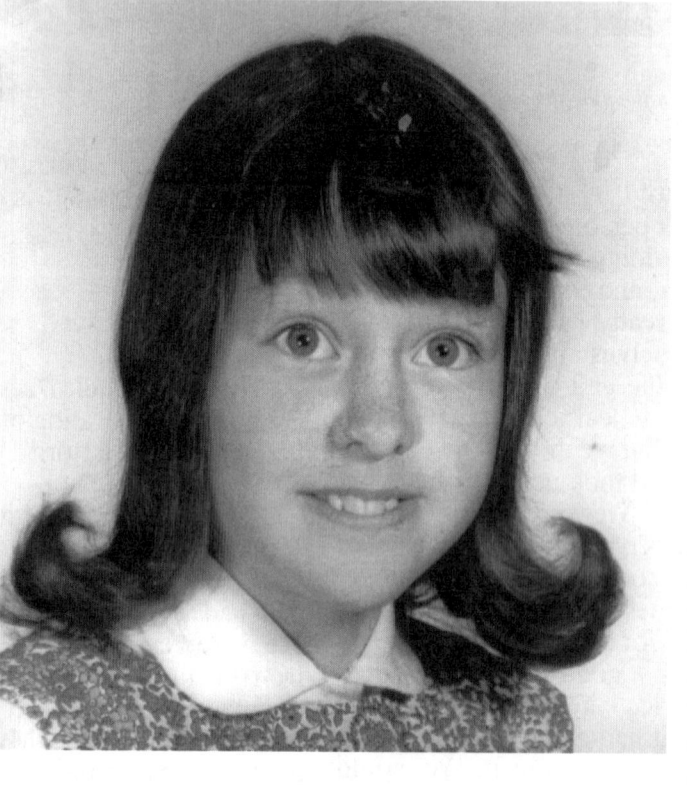

LoAnn DelGrande

him. It was the first funeral I had ever been to. I can still see him lying in the coffin with his favorite blue sweater on. It shocked me to the core. We were both in second grade. Back then, farm parents expected their children to work.

I don't ever remember a time before television. We had one. Of course, it was black and white and kind of oval shape. We had an antenna, so we had three blurry, snowy channels. But it was great! Cheryl and I never usually fought, but we had a knockdown, hair pulling, fight over what to watch on TV. For some reason, the picture went black, so we would just listen to the TV. There was no money to fix it. I don't know how long that went on, but it seemed like six months to a year. Now, whenever something breaks I freak out just a bit, because in the back of my mind, I think it won't ever get fixed.

Everyone in the family liked chocolate cake. The cake pan was never left empty. With a mother and six girls, as soon as it was gone, someone would make another pan. It was made by scratch in a brown ceramic bowl. The frosting was delicious thick fudge. There was always chocolate cake and no rules about when we could eat it.

There weren't many rules in our family, but all the kids had great respect for our father and mother, which is what kept us in line. Our religious training was huge in making us good kids and we did not need a lot of further direction. We knew right from wrong.

When I was thirteen years old, my parents sold the farm, and we moved to Mahnomen with a population of 1,300. I thought I had moved to a big city. It did not take long to make friends and live a more normal life. By this time, my four older sisters were all married and had their own homes. Cheryl got a nice job at the First National Bank, and I went to school.

My mother didn't believe in doctors, and there were several times it could have taken my life. I stepped on a rusty nail that went deep into my heel. I couldn't walk for weeks. Her home remedy was to soak it in a pail of hot sudsy water every day, and the poison would come out. It worked.

Another time, I got impetigo from my nieces. The problem was that it went through my blood stream. I had huge sores everywhere and was too weak to get up. My mother's two sisters came from North Dakota and said, "Take your daughter to the doctor or she's going to die." That spurred my mother to take me to the doctor and I got a penicillin shot in the butt (my mom called it my "hinder"). I missed the first two weeks of sixth grade, but I lived.

The third time I almost died was when I ran out in front of a car on Main Street of Mahnomen. I was with a group of friends and did not see it. All of sudden, the car was right in front of me, and I knew it was going to hit me. No one was behind me. I suddenly felt a fast but gentle push from behind and I was out of the way. A feeling of peace poured over me. I believe with all my heart that my guardian angel was there and saved my life.

After moving to Mahnomen, I had a four-block walk to school. Wearing pants was not yet in style for girls; that came a couple years later. I wore a mini skirt every day with nylons and it didn't matter if it was 40 below, that's the way I walked to school. By the time I got to school, my legs would be red and numb, but I didn't care. I was in style.

This was all a very long time ago, and it may seem sad to some of you, but I wouldn't change a thing. God has been good to me.

Milking Cows and Selling Cream
By Betty (Laznicka) Kelly of Napa, California
Born 1933

I am a former Roseau girl who grew up on a totally self-sufficient farm in the Malung Township. I went through eighth grade at Brandt School District # 3 and then by bus to high school in Roseau. Then, I went to college, taught school, and later became a registered nurse after my family was all in school, worked in a hospital for 16 years, and am now retired.

My father, Virgil Laznicka, grew up as a young man in Czechoslovakia and immigrated to the United States at age 18. His name was Vratislav, but he changed it to Virgil when he came to the United States. He left his home because he was the youngest son and could not inherit his father's mill business, which could only go to the eldest son. Therefore, my father came to the U.S. and loved to tell about the first sighting of the statue of Liberty in the harbor of New York City. He came through Ellis Island and his name is on a granite wall on the island. He then went to Milwaukee, Wisconsin where he worked for International Harvester Co.

He was well educated and spoke several languages, but not English, so with his first earnings he hired a tutor to learn to read, write, and speak English. He did not teach us any other language. He was also an accomplished violinist and gymnast. He also knew chemistry and was an apprentice buyer for a pharmacy and store. Yet, he wanted to be a farmer, purchased 480 acres in Roseau County, and cleared the land with the help of a hired man.

Afterward, he met and married my mom Mabel Fichter, who was born in Southern Minnesota but finished grade school in Malung. She was an excellent cook, baker, and seamstress. Her parents never let her get more education, but required her to be at home to care for her four younger brothers and themselves. Her parents believed that a girl did not need an education because she would just get married and have a family. My philosophy is that if you educate a girl, she will have an educated family and be happier.

Women worked very hard on a farm without electricity or running water. She always had a huge garden, canned beef and chickens and planted flowers in the summer. Our kitchen had a dugout basement under it where we stored our potato crop on the dirt floor and it was surrounded by all the Mason jars of home-canned food around the top. We had our own wood, chopped for heat. Every home had a wood box inside. The woodpile was neat, with the cut wood stacked in a large circle with the extra pieces piled in the middle.

In the winter, we liked to make Jell-O, as it jelled quickly in a large covered bowl set in a snow bank. We whipped cream with vanilla and sugar for the topping. We made ice cream in a wooden churn.

Dad sold cream to the Land O' Lakes creamery and Mom washed crates of eggs to Peterson & Biddick for cash, and we bought what we could not grow on the farm from the Red Owl store, such as coffee, sugar, rice, oranges, etc.

I hated Monday, which was always "wash day." The Maytag washer was in the middle of the kitchen with tubs of rinse water and a then a final "bluing" rinse for the white things. Then, everything was put through the wringer into a basket, to be pinned to a clothesline for drying. In the winter, it all froze stiff and had to be brought in the house and hung on a line over the heating stove or on a wooden clothes rack made of wooden rods. To do this washing, Mom had to carry water from the hand pumped well to a big copper boiler to heat on the stove for the Maytag washer.

On busy washdays, Mom used the heated cook stove oven to make a complete one-dish, hearty farm style meal. In a large pan or roaster, she would layer raw pork chops, add a slice of yellow onion on each chop, and then put a half of a peeled potato on top of the onion. She would then add two cups of rice and a large can of tomatoes, making sure there was enough liquid so that all of the rice would be submerged. She would then add green string beans if desired and salt and pepper to taste. She would cover it tightly and put it into the oven until the meat was tender.

I will never forget one washday when I was eight years old. My dad came home from town with the news that Pearl Harbor had been bombed by the Japanese the morning before. My parents were very upset and I was scared.

In school, Valentine's Day was always special. A large cardboard box was decorated to put the valentines into. At Halloween, we had a party and bobbed for apples. Christmas programs were the year's highlight. The Malung Hall had a nice stage and below it was always the large decorated tree with gifts, as we all had drawn names and every child was also given a bag of Christmas candy. Boxes of red delicious apples were passed to everyone that came.

One year camel was to be pulled on to the stage. A tall eighth grade boy had one end of the rope and several off-stage boys had the other end of "the pretend camel." Everyone pulled too hard and the rope broke. Stanley fell flat on his back. We thought this was hilarious.

We called the time from Christmas Eve through New Year's Day "the holidays." Visiting neighbors and friends was fun, as each homemaker had her own special Christmas goodies to serve.

At Halloween, we would hear kids saying to others, "We're going to tip your 'can' tonight!" Everyone had an outdoor toilet, or "can."

School was from first grade through eighth and then you had to take the Minnesota State Boards. No preschool or kindergarten like my children had, but I had a much better education. We learned phonics and how to read and spell. We also learned how to do cursive writing at the end of first grade. My teacher was Miss Audrienne Peterson. Other favorites were Miss Nelson (Marie Comstock) in the fourth grade and Mrs. Lisell (Thea) for the seventh grade.

I got up early before school to milk cows by hand. I am appreciative of my schooling and growing up on a farm, which in itself was a fantastic learning experience. I loved driving the A-Farmall tractor.

I enjoyed 4-H club, paying a tenor saxophone in the high school band and college band.

We loved our farm animals. We had horses, cattle, geese, chickens, and pigs. I learned to make a smudge fire to keep the smoke going all night to keep the mosquitoes from the barnyard animals. When the horses and cows saw me coming with the materials for the smoky smudge, they gratefully would meet and surround me. In the morning, it would still be smoking.

Mom's Memories and My Experiences
By Pat Twist of San Diego, California
Born 1960

My mother started grade school in 1943. It was a two-story building with a basement. The basement had restrooms and a recreation room. The first floor had two classrooms and the Sisters' living quarters. The second floor had chapel, Sisters' sleeping quarters, and a music room. The two classrooms were the Little Room, which was for grades one through four. The Big Room was for grades five through eight. There was one teacher for each room. There were six students in her grade. Her dad drove them to school in the morning, but they had to walk home after school. It was a two-mile jaunt. They had classmates for the first mile. The second was just them.

Pat's mom's grade school
St. Walburga Grade School

Her high school days were at a boarding school. She had to work after classes and on Saturdays to help pay for tuition. Her job was working in the library. Duties were checking books out, and in, filing clippings for research studies, bookbinding, and other library duties. At the end of each school year, the rooms had to be cleaned thoroughly. All the furniture was moved into the hallway. Then down on the knees scrubbing the floor, waxing, and buffing it with the buffer.

Her family lived on a 160-acre farm. I vacationed there several times and was at my grandparents' 50th wedding celebration. The party was in the grade school building she attended. It was made into a hall where social events could take place. I met all my aunts, uncles, and cousins for the first time. It was in November. It was cold and snowing.

We went there during the summer several

Pat's mom's high school
St. Francis High School

times. We did a lot of sightseeing. We went to Lake Superior, Fort Williams, Canada, and tubing down the Apple River in Wisconsin. I went to my aunt's place in Alexandria. She lives by Lake L'Homme Dieu. We did canoeing, swimming and fishing.

At the farm, my brother and I raced the moped and go-cart up and down the driveway. When the go-cart engine stopped, Uncle Bernard pulled it with the tractor down the driveway to get it started again. That was a funny sight. Uncle Erwin was moving machinery parked in old cow pasture so they could cut the weeds. The pasture was going to be used as softball field on Sunday. He wanted me to use the other tractor and help him, but I didn't know how to drive a tractor, so I told him no.

He told me to go to the house and get your mother to come help. I did and she remembered how to drive it and they got it done. I laughed because to this day she does not have a driver's license and does not drive a car. We had a family reunion at the farm the next day for a goodbye to the old granary. It was going to be knocked down before it fell down. A group picture of all the cousins was taken for old time sake. The total count of family there was 40 people. We did use the pasture for softball game and mucho food and drinks was consumed.

Every weekend in August there is a big Renaissance Fair. I went to three of them. They are much bigger and more fun than the ones in California. I also helped the aunts and uncles move from the farmhouse to a house in town. The old homestead was up for sale. Once everything was boxed up and the furniture loaded to the truck, it took off to the new house. After all was unloaded, we all went out to eat. Reason for the sale was the uncle that owned it was 71 and getting married for the first time the next weekend. All his siblings, nieces, nephews, and friends were there to celebrate with him.

Another year, a cousin got married in Nelson, Minnesota. The next day, we took a trip to Itasca, the headwater of the Mississippi. 1475 ft. above ocean, it begins flow to Gulf of Mexico 2,552 miles. It creates falls on its journey. In Minneapolis, we took a Mississippi Cruise ship down the locks.

Minnesota is called the State of 10,000 Lakes. I believe it and saw many of them. There is much to see in the state. Here are some sites I visited: Itasca State Park, Itasca Kensington Runestone, Big Ole and Chain of Lakes in Alexandria, Lake Superior and ore ships in Duluth, Paul Bunyan & Blue Ox in Bemidji, St. Anthony Falls Dam, Minnehaha Falls & Mall of America in Minneapolis, Museum of Spam in Austin, Pioneer village in Hastings, and Northfield Bank where Jesse James and the Younger gang robbed. These are just some of the ones I remember.

My mother moved from Minnesota to California in 1959. Sometimes I wonder why? Guess it was the winters.

Reminisces of Gary D. Hartel
By Gary D. Hartel of McIntosh, Minnesota
Born 1942

I was born October 24, 1942. I was a honeymoon baby. My name is Gary D. Hartel.

My life from infant to age of remembering was moving three times to the farm Mom and Dad bought in Sec. 7, Brandsvold Township in East Polk County, Minnesota. In the spring of 1946, loans were very hard to get. Dad was one of two farmers to receive a loan of 300 others. One year later, it was much easier for others to receive loans. This is because of World War II and prior to that the, "Dirty '30s." I, with brother, Ron, and sisters, Linda and LeAnn, all lived on this farm in Section 7 to adulthood.

Now back to me, Gary. I was the oldest and I like to be outdoors. At five years old, I was going to walk three miles to Grandpa and Grandma's farm. Too much relief of my parents, Pearly and Eunice, the neighbor stopped me one mile from home (I stopped to look at the pony on John Oak's farm) because in the spring all the road ditches were full of water of four to five feet deep. Therefore, Mom and Dad were glad to have me home again safe. So you see, at five years I was adventurous!

.I walked one and a quarter miles to country school District # 176, Sunny Vale, located in Section 8 in Brandsvold Township. In those days, there were four country schools in one township. We had about 30 children in a one-room school, grades one through six. As I remember, we all got along quite well because our parents were good parents and we all learned respect for others and our elders. To be exact, I never knew a dirty word until I went to McIntosh High School in seventh grade at McIntosh, Minnesota. I later graduated from there in 1960 with a class of 17 boys and 17 girls. (The class of '60 are still friends.)

One problem I had in country school was when I was in second grade. The weather was nice that day in September, so I signed out on the blackboard to go to the outdoor toilet behind the schoolhouse—one for boys and one for girls. Well, I had on a one-piece suit, the kind with a zipper from throat to bottom. Well, the zipper caught. As a result, I wet my pants. I never went back into the schoolhouse, but ran for home. When I walked in the house at home, Mother took one look at me, made a quick change, and took me right back to school and told the teacher, "We will talk later."

While in country school, I had two teachers. One was Mrs. Affeldt. She taught grades one through three. Her husband was Representative Leland Affeldt in the state legislature. The other was Miss Solberg.

One occasion I looked forward to was the fall social. We had a fishpond, grab bags, confetti, good food, an auction for older girls' lunch baskets, to raise money for the school supplies. We also put on a play, us students, for the audience, as well as songs. Well, I couldn't sing, so Miss Solberg had me bark like a dog in the song "How Much is That Doggy in the Window," while George and Charles sang. It went over quite well. We had an encore and the audience clapped even longer the second time. Ma said I stole the show!

In winter, our one-room schoolhouse was heated with wood and cold in the mornings. Also, I carried my books and lunch. My lunch was frozen solid. Later, my dad got on the school board and they got an oil stove, which made the schoolroom warmer. Some parents thought the school district would go broke. I remember Dad asking those people later if they wanted to go back to wood. They didn't.

My how thing have changed!

At country school when weather was cold at noon, we had lunch, did some schoolwork, did some exercises, or pin the tail on the donkey. On nice days, we made snow houses by sawing snow blocks. In nice weather, we raked the school lawn and had a wiener roast. In fall/September in nice weather, we played Anti-I-Over the schoolhouse with a rubber ball, rode stick horses, and also played marbles.

On the farm, I helped my dad. I was driving the tractor by myself in the fourth grade. I had the job of cleaning calf pens and hog pens every Saturday. In high school, I missed about ten days for spring planting and about ten days in fall for harvest, sometimes with zero makeup with one teacher I didn't like, who later was fired. I still came out with a C+ average. Some honest neighbors said me and my brother Ron always worked from an early age!

Dad bought me a pony, a Welch and Shetland cross, unbroken. He bucked me off, so I broke him to ride by taking him in the deep snow. Nevertheless, I could not stop him from turning and biting me. The pony, named Pronto, could really run. I used to ride him to get the cows on the east end of the farm until he stepped in a badger hole at full gallop. I went over his head and it knocked the wind out of me. That ended my riding.

So, in closing, we now live in Section 6 of Brandsvold Township. My wife of 48 years, Dorthy, and I have farmed here all the time since we were married. We farmed through the '80s that were bad and farmed all this time to survive. I have trucked. I drove for 33 ½ years for one company. I was one of 150 people who had worked for over 30 years for said company.

In closing, I love the land! I like working with people! I have most likely lived the best years of this fine country!

Bluebells and Buttercups
By Ginny Davis of Las Vegas, Nevada
Born 1925

"Precious memories, how they linger..." Do you ever catch yourself wistfully daydreaming? I recently heard a doctor telling his television audience that, "A great way to relax and energize your system is to visualize happy moments of days gone by daydream, if you will." So finding myself retired with more than enough time on my hands to daydream, I decided to take the good doctor's advice and energize my system.

I found myself drifting slowly back in time to a small, Midwestern town in the 1930s. My best girlfriend Wilma and I—two carefree, six-year old girls—were on a mission to find a choice location for our playhouse. The vast countryside offered many possibilities.

We had an incredible fear of being out after dark when the hoot owls and bobcats began making their eerie, nocturnal sounds. My girlfriend lived on the outskirts of town, so we thought it only fair to look for a spot halfway between her home and mine. Then, if we played until dusk, we would have the same distance to run to reach the safe haven of our real homes.

Fortified with a couple of peanut butter sandwiches and a thermos of Kool Aid, our search was on. Much to our delight, we soon spotted a maze of low bushes and shrubs under two large, spreading oak trees. We selected this as an ideal place to settle and claimed it as our home site.

Since the imaginary walls were already in place, our first project was to furnish our dwelling. We handcrafted most of our furniture from whatever small pieces of wood and logs we could find—*Little House on the Prairie* style. We salvaged cracked china, mismatched silverware, and whatever old pots and pans our mothers had tossed out. After a fair amount of cleaning and polishing, everything was neatly arranged in our orange-crate cupboards. I must say it was a very eclectic, but serviceable, assortment of housewares.

In the true spirit of the pioneer women, we foraged the nearby countryside for edibles for our make-believe families. We filled old coffee cans with a wide variety of fruit and berries. A bountiful supply of crab apples, plums, Juneberries, and chokecherries graced our pantry. Sometimes, with a bit of luck, we would come across a small patch of wild strawberries—the delicacy of the day!

Now that the necessities of life were in place, we began our home beautification program by turning to nature's botanical garden. The hillside was blanketed in a dazzling array of wildflowers. Much like gifted ballerinas, delicate yellow and white butterflies danced across the flower tops in a slow, mesmerizing performance.

Early each day while the flowers still sparkled with the morning dew, we would gather wild roses, daisies, bluebells, and buttercups for our wildflower bouquets. Our flowers were artistically arranged in our best silver vases, which were of the "tomato-can-with-the-label-scratched-off" vintage. I am sure Martha Stewart would have given her seal of approval to our charming, little bouquets.

We certainly weren't remiss about neglecting our spiritual duties either. You might say we were young evangelists, of sorts. We would venture into the meadow and find an appropriate tree stump for a pulpit. Our small congregation consisted of a few bushy-tailed squirrels and a herd of cud-chewing cows. What a faithful and receptive audience. They were very quiet with just an occasional "Moooo," which we loosely interpreted to be "Amen" in cow language.

As the "days of our youth" are prone to do, they passed by all too quickly. Upon returning to my small, Midwestern town some forty years later, I found it quite unchanged, still very small, and tranquil. With the exception of a new schoolhouse and a new highway running to the side of the village, time had graciously enhanced and preserved the entire countryside.

It was a glorious summer afternoon and I was excited about retracing my steps to where my girlfriend and I had spent so many fun-filled days. By following a familiar bend in the road, I knew I was nearing the exact spot I was looking for. A noisy woodpecker broke the solitude of the day with the cadence of his "rat-a-tat-tatting." Turning to get a better look at the bird, I spotted the two stately oak trees that had sheltered our playhouse years ago. I let out a gasp of delight!

'The bushes beneath the trees were lush and green and, much like me, had matured noticeably. I smiled as I visualized small fragments of our broken china or perhaps an old rusted-out pot or pans nestled safely in the thick undergrowth. Loving thoughts flooded my memory and time seemed to stand still. The countryside had a warmth and personality all its own and I savored every precious moment.

The sun was beginning to cast tall shadows across the grass and it was time for me to go back down the narrow, graveled road. A light breeze rippled through the treetops and a cheerful chorus of songbirds ushered me on my way. Pausing to brush a small teardrop from each cheek, I could smell the lingering fragrance of the roses and, in my mind's eye; I could clearly see two laughing, six-year-old girls gathering bluebells and buttercups for their wildflower bouquets.

My 1947 Log House Christmas
By Vergene L. Routhe of Shoreview, Minnesota
Born 1942

Looking out our farmhouse window, my five-year-old mind worried, "Will we get to Grandpa and Grandma Niemela's for Christmas dinner at noon and the presents Mom said would be waiting for us under the tree?" Mom's nine sisters and one brother always tried to make it home for Christmas, but the thrill for my brothers, Gerald and Milfred, and me was to see all the cousins.

It was bitter cold with a blustery northwest wind blowing snow in drifts across the farmyard. Dad put on his heavy jacket and cap with earflaps and went out to start the old turtle-backed dark blue Ford sitting out in the yard. Earlier he had warmed the block beneath the hood with bricks warmed in the wood cook stove oven and wrapped in an old patchwork quilt. Yay, it started! He came back in to warm up while Mom busily bundled up my two brothers and me in our warm woolen coats, hand knit stocking caps, neck scarves, mittens, and buckle-up black rubber boots. While Mom put on her woolen headscarf and dark green coat with an imitation fur collar and cuffs, she had ordered from the Spiegel catalog, Dad went out to set out the tire chains. He shoveled enough snow to back up and center the rear tires and secure the chains before we climbed into the car and started out with warm blankets over our laps.

It was only three miles on rutted country roads, but would we make it safely with the almost-blinding snow? Dad kept the speed steady, and the car lurched as it hit each finger of crusty, compacted snow drifting over the road. Mom screamed, "Watch it Bill, we're sliding into the ditch!" Dad jerked the steering wheel and we got back on the road. My brothers and I sat wide-eyed with fear that we would get stuck and be stranded, but we finally turned into Grandpa's winding lane with tall pine trees protecting us from the fierce wind.

The old two-room farmhouse, built with hand-hewn logs in the early 1900s, was a welcome sight with smoke curling out the chimney. We were the first to arrive. Would we be the only family to make it? We didn't have telephones in those days.

We stamped our snowy boots on the wooden porch and crowded quickly into the warm kitchen with the wonderful aroma of roasting turkey. We quickly removed our boots and lined them up under the long wooden bench by the door. Coats were laid on the big bed in the corner of the "other" room that served as a living room and bedroom.

The log house

Grandma Selma, her hair pulled back in a bun, wearing her gray Sunday dress with a hand-made fill-length cotton print apron over it, greeted us warmly and gave each of us children a pat on the head. Grandpa Andrew, mustachioed and freshly shaven, was sitting at the round oak kitchen table. He nodded and said, "Païvä," (hello in Finnish). Dad, a man of few words with his clear blue eyes looking stern after the driving ordeal, shook hands with Andrew and sat down with relief. Mom, always happy to come home to her birthplace, was all smiles as she chatted with her still-at-home youngest sisters, Lorraine and Eleanor, both with long braids wound around their heads like crowns. Sister Rose and her three children—Joe, Lavonne, and Eugene—also lived with Grandpa and Grandma, and they were happy that we made it despite the storm.

Other family members were attempting the same trip from points farther away. Some of them got there, but oh, the comments they made as they arrived. Uncle Vic strode in, tall with large-boned features, thick wavy hair and his booming voice, saying, "We're darn fools to be out in this weather." He had driven all the way from St. Paul and had seen many cars in the ditch.

Next to arrive were Walt, Aunt Ida, and their three kids who drove at least eight treacherous miles to join the Christmas celebration. Walt, red and black plaid woolen cap with the ear flaps down, ruddy faced and eyes showing frustration, wasn't in a happy mood. Ida was nervous, saying, "We probably can't stay long." But cousins Delores, Marlene, and Marvin squealed with excited "Hellos." Soon we had hauled out the bushel basket of Lincoln Logs and toys from the cubby beneath the attic stairs and turned it over in the middle of the linoleum floor to begin playing.

Before long we heard a car horn announcing Eddie, Aunt Agnes, and their three girls. Eddie, ever jovial with mischievous twinkling eyes, came in saying, "Ho, ho, ho and a Merry Christmas." Agnes, with her matching deep blue woolen coat and hat, giggled her greetings to everyone...not even mentioning the weather. The girls were jumping with joy to see all the cousins. Twenty-four were crowded into that two-room log house with its attic bedroom for the children.

The unfortunate turkey had been roosting on the barnyard fence early that morning before Grandpa nabbed him and took him to the chopping block and then brought him into the house for Grandma to de-feather and prepare him for roasting. Once he was in the oven, Grandma lifted open the trap door in the middle of the kitchen and sent Aunt Rose down into the earth-lined cellar to bring up potatoes, squash, canned corn and green beans. Finnish flat bread had been baked the day before and butter churned from fresh cream. Mom and the other aunts brought blueberry and apple pies and sponge cake.

When Grandma called out, "Dinner is ready," we came to the table set with chipped Blue Willow plates and mismatched flatware. The little ones sat on their parents' laps around the table extended to its fullest. There wasn't room for everyone to sit, so Rose, Lorraine, Eleanor and the oldest cousins filled their plates and ate in the other room, plates perched on their knees. I don't remember Grandma sitting. She just hovered at the black wood-burning cook stove and made sure everyone got fed. There was enough for all and nobody left the table hungry.

After dinner, we crowded into the other room, kids sitting cross-legged on the floor to open the gifts. Many were hand-made items of clothing or knitted mittens, but we all got toys from Aunt Senia who was a nurse in Denver, Colorado, and always sent a big box of gifts parcel post well before Christmas.

As everyone left at the end of the afternoon, there were cheery goodbyes and promises to be there next year. That Christmas remains vivid in my memory because by the next December, Grandma had died.

However, the tradition of gathering at Grandpa's never ended while he was still living. The children and their families found comfort in carrying on after Grandma went to her heavenly home. One of her favorite hymns, often sung as she worked, was *Bringing in the Sheaves*. Like a sheaf of grain, God gathered her into His fold.

The Importance of Spending Time with Family
By Carol J. Sayres of Henning, Minnesota
Born 1945

Growing up in the 1950s in rural West-Central Minnesota was an experience to be fondly remembered. Of course, hindsight blurs the tough times somewhat but the happy times are the ones we primarily remember the best and would like our children and grandchildren to know about. At the present time, seeing young people who are visiting relatives but sitting with their Game Boys, phones, or computers, we feel they are missing a part of growing up. In the '50s, the socializing was face-to-face and active and we really knew our relatives.

In winters, Friday and/or Saturday nights were spent visiting with grandparents, aunts, uncles and cousins and playing cards and board games at our home or the homes of relatives. The children played checkers, Parcheesi, Michigan rummy, and hearts while the adults played card games such as whist and sometimes crazy Pedro or smear. As we children played the games, we were readying ourselves for the time we would be old enough (and skilled enough) to play whist with the adults. Once we reached that milestone, our biggest fear was being partners with Grampa. He was the best whist player and we didn't want to disappoint him! The pressure was on and we would work hard to remember everyone's invites, which cards had been played and then hope we were right. Grampa never told us you should have done this or that so it wasn't as frightful as we imagined. However, he would say after many hands, "I've never seen a hand like it!" That came whether we won or lost. Now as we are the age of Grampa, we always remember and comment on what his favorite exclamation was. By the way, he and his partner were very often the winners of the game.

The cards and board games were played in the cold winter months. Summer visits were spent playing outside. In the evenings, we kids would play hide 'n seek, kick the can, pump pump pullaway, and red rover. Playing outside under the yard light was not always the smartest thing to do. We would get some bumps and bruises, a bloody nose from running into an unseen clothesline, and once a trip to the doctor for one unlucky kid. My sister ran into a guy wire for a light pole and put a gash in her leg that required 26 stitches. By the next week, we were back at the same activities with warnings to be more careful. I am sure we pretended to heed that advice!

Afternoon visits on warm summer Sundays were spent playing outside. Then the favorite game was softball. We often didn't have enough people for two full teams, but that didn't stop us. First, we would get the bat and ball and next would come choosing the teams. The bat would be tossed handle up to one of the "captains" who would catch it with one hand. Then the other captain would grasp the bat with one hand atop the opponent's hand. The alternate hand placing would keep going until the very end of the bat was reached. Whoever could hang on with just the fingers barely grasping the bat would get to choose the first player for his or her team. Upon finishing choosing teams, the game would progress and inevitably turn into an argument as to the rules, was the ball foul or fair, who was up next, or who might or might not have been out. The game would come to an end, we would all be friends again, and then have lunch. Eating was a big part of the gatherings and lunch would be sandwiches, cake, Jell-O with fruit and whipped cream, nectar (a liquid mix purchased from the Watkins or Raleigh salesman), and ice cream.

Lunch was a big part of every day of the week, just a little more special for company. During the week, lunch would be about 10:00 in the morning and would be perhaps a slice of homemade bread, coffee or water, and a cookie. Afternoon lunch was about 3:30 and would be nectar or water, a sandwich or two, and a piece of cake. Add this to the regular meals of breakfast, dinner (at noon) and supper and sometimes evening lunch, and that was a lot of food preparation and a lot of eating! None of us were overweight though.

Now when I see kids "visiting" family but they are busy with their electronic devices it seems they are missing a part of their growing up. When I see the cousins, with whom I and my sisters and brothers played those games fifty and sixty years ago, we reminisce with laughter and enjoyment. I hope today's young will be able to remember their youth with happiness and feel they know their relatives as well as we did.

Pelican Valley School District 116
By Ethelmae Duenow of Detroit Lakes, Minnesota
Born 1941

Pelican Valley School was built in the year of 1916. Pelican Valley School is located in Richwood Township, Becker County, Detroit Lakes, Minnesota. The first teacher was Helen Heuters. My mother, Minnie Elsie Peterson, and her three siblings attended Pelican Valley as well as my two older sisters.

Bobbie and Ethelmae in 1942

In September 1947, I started school at Pelican Valley School District 116. There were grades one through eight and 16 pupils in our school. Our teacher, Miss Mahlum, stayed at Wayne Wolden's home about ¼ mile from the school. She walked to school every day. In the winter months, she had to start the furnace to get the school warmed up. Sometimes we did exercises and jumping jacks to keep warm. Then each class would sit by a table near the heat vent to keep warm while they did their lessons.

There were three girls in my class: Ethelmae, born on January 30, 1941, Diane, born March 30, 1941, and Bonnie, born June 30, 1941. One day I asked permission to go to the bathroom, which was an outside toilet. I stayed outside and played around. Pretty soon, Diane came out, and then Bonnie. The teacher came out and got us and we each had to stand in a corner. Diane, Bonnie, and I had a playhouse under the porch. We spent many of our recesses making up our pretend lives.

There were different jobs we had to help with: cleaning erasers, bringing water in from the well for the water fountain and to wash our hands, cleaning the blackboards, and putting up and taking down the flag. The older boys had to help put wood in the furnace during the winter months.

Recess was spent outside; weather permitting, playing softball, games, tag and sliding down McCaslin's hill on cardboard. After Christmas, Marcelyn took my new sled down the hill and broke it. When it was really cold outside, we would play games in the basement.

On Halloween, we always had a huge program. A stage was brought up from the basement. Mothers furnished sheets for curtains to pull between acts. We performed plays, sang songs, and recited poems. All of the neighbors and parents would come to

Jimmy and Ethelmae in 1950

watch us to perform, play bingo, and have lunch. There were numerous games for the children to play.

In December 1947, I had my first Christmas program. Our parents were invited for our program. Each one had a poem to recite and we all sang Christmas carols. We exchanged names so we had gifts to open. The teacher served lunch after the program. Everyone got a bag of candy, nuts, and an apple.

My mother had been busy sewing gifts for Christmas. She always kept her sewing machine in the living room so she could sit by the west window for better lighting.

We had a bowl with a large peg in the center to place the nut in and wooden a mallet to crack the nut. I placed a hazelnut on the peg and hit at it with the mallet. I missed the nut and it went flying across the living room floor. We had hardwood floors and they were very slippery. I ran and slid on my knees across the floor and suddenly I felt a terrible pain in my knee. A darning needle had dropped in between the crack of the board and the eye end of the needle had gone into my knee and broken off. I screamed from the pain. Mom and Dad came running into the living room to see what happened. All they could see was the little hole going into my knee. My knee was bent so they straightened my knee out and the needle must have gone in further. Back then, people didn't go the doctor every time something happened, so they laid me on the couch and after a while, it quit hurting.

Several days later, my knee started swelling and I started to run a temperature. My parents took me to Dr. Larson where he did an x-ray under a fluoroscope. He could see the needle inside the kneecap. He gave me a shot and sent me home. Finally, the pain and infection got so bad he admitted me to the hospital on December 26, 1947.

Dr. Larson consulted with a specialist and he said not to operate because I would lose the water on my knee and would have a stiff knee the rest of my life. The specialist said I had to stay off my feet and eventually a callus would grow around the needle and it wouldn't bother me. Every day I got a shot of penicillin in my knee and my temperature taken many times a day.

Finally, the day came when I could go home on January 15, 1948. I still had to be in bed and could not go to school. By the time my birthday came on January 30, I could finally be up for a while. My mother invited the teacher and kids to come after school for lunch and cake. That was the first time that I had seen them since Christmas. Thanks to my mother for tutoring me with my homework, I passed first grade.

When I did go back to school, Mom or Dad had to drive me. When it was really cold, my dad had to use the crank to start the Model A. At school, I still could not play games. It was terrible to have to sit and watch everyone have fun.

I attended Pelican Valley School through seventh grade then started at the Holmes School in Detroit Lakes, Minnesota in eighth grade. I graduated in 1959. My class was the first to graduate from the new high school.

Ethel Johnson Duenow in 2012

The No-School Announcement
By Delores Kading of St. Hilaire, Minnesota
Born 1944

When people talk about long-ago blizzards in Northwestern Minnesota, pictures rush to their thoughts: frigid landscapes, stalled cars, overcoats and long underwear, or even wooden chairs pulled up close to the kitchen cook stove. I can identify with all the above, but one thing stands out far more vividly in my mind: NO-SCHOOL ANNOUNCEMENTS ON THE RADIO. Hearing "There will be no school in Red Lake Falls today," were what happy dreams were made of back in those days. No worries about multiplication tests for another day. Happy decisions (win/win decisions) needed to be made by my brother Larry and me: Do we go back to bed for a while or do we get right to the pinochle or 500 Rummy? Fudge or cookies would have to be made at some point during the day.

The no-school announcement never came without preparation on our part. Weather reports that snow, wind, and bad weather could be a future possibility were noted days ahead. Prayers began to ascend with pleas for a day off from school. We received school assignments from teachers with the private smugness that all this work will have to be postponed because of our coming days off.

School shouldn't have seemed like a jail sentence for Larry and me. We were good students; we had kind teachers and fun friends. Nevertheless, good times in school could not compare with a snow day at home.

Occasionally, a snowstorm came up quickly while we were at school. I would anxiously watch out the large window near my desk as the snow swirled around the corner of the building and the wind swayed the bare branches of the trees on the playground. Surely, the only safe thing was to send all the students home promptly! Ping! The sound of the inter-room loudspeaker being turned on immediately caused all sound to stop in the classroom. If the announcement was something like, "Bucky Schmitz, please come to the office. We have found your lost textbooks," we would groan in disappointment. However, it could be, "Due to the weather, school will be dismissed in 15 minutes. Buses will leave at that time. All students should go directly home." That announcement brought glee to students and teachers alike. Announcements such as, "Due to the weather, all buses will leave in 15 minutes. Bus students will be dismissed from classes immediately. Other students will remain in school and continue on as normal." Perhaps we felt a twinge of compassion for our in-town friends and the teachers, but I can't remember that. We exchanged grins of triumph with our fellow bus companions, as we not too quietly trooped out of the room.

Bus trips home in storms were often adventurous. Roads were not maintained then as they are now. The bus shuddered as it hit large, hard drifts. The snow whipped around the windows of the bus and stuck on the windshield. Cliff, our conscientious driver, kept wiping the windshield with his gloves and checking his mirrors hoping he was keeping the bus on the road. So often, we felt the sudden sagging of the bus and knew we had slipped off the side of the road. The bus would grind to a stop. Attempts at backing up and going forward were fruitless. Of course, there was no way to communicate with the school or the highway department so getting unstuck was solely the bus driver's responsibility. He sent the older boys off the bus with shovels (that were kept under the seats at the back of the bus) to do what they could. The rest of us were instructed to "rock the bus" as he worked the accelerator. Cliff would be in and out of the bus, checking on the shoveling boys and assessing the situation. The normally cold bus became frigid with the opening of the doors. My toes hurt so bad from the cold that I was afraid tears would come—and that would be the ultimate embarrassment! Two older girls who sat right behind Cliff's seat must have noticed my misery. They invited me to sit with them and put my feet right against the heater. "You just come and sit with us any time you get cold," they kindly told me. I felt shy sitting there with those big girls, but I was also thinking they must be some of the kindest people on earth.

If the bus couldn't get out, other considerations had to be made. Was it safe to send one of older kids to a neighboring farm where the farmer would pull us out with his tractor? If the weather was too bad to send out one of the boys, we settled down to wait. Parents would be watching for their children. (The radio had informed them that bus students were on their way home.) If they didn't arrive, phones would be ringing. "Is your Johnny home yet? Since he's already home, and our kids aren't, the bus must be stuck somewhere between our places." The capable farmers would make sure that the bus would be pulled out as soon as possible and the children safely delivered to their homes.

There were times when our bus got stuck on the way *to* school. That changed things.

The older boys still went out to shovel; however, (at least according to their bravado when they privately told the rest of us about their activities) now they shoveled snow *into* the tracks. When Cliff asked them to push as he accelerated, they braced their feet and held back. True or not, more than once Cliff decided it was best to just take us all back home and not try to get to school. We cheered his wise and sensible decision.

Ah, yes, all these memories that come flooding back with the thoughts of childhood blizzards. However, I digress from my original plan to tell about THE ANNOUNCEMENTS and the preparations for them.

When the weather indicated that a storm was looming, Larry and I got busy. Larry is five years older than I am, so, of course, I relied on his good judgment as to our preparations. We would take our old pair of mismatched skis (one five-foot ski and one six-footer) to the end of our driveway and start creating a drift on the corner of our county gravel road. With each of us using a ski, we pushed snow into a ridge across the road, angling it to catch the wind-driven snow. We smiled as the ridge grew with the falling snow and blowing wind. We trudged back up our driveway in the gathering darkness, satisfied that we had done what we could. Then, we settled down to wait.

School cancellations started early in the morning. The Thief River Falls radio announcer on KTRF surely realized that hundred, if not thousands, of schoolchildren and their parents were carrying out morning duties silently, not getting out of earshot of the radio.

"...and we've just received word that the Plummer school has cancelled their classes for today," the announcer importantly intoned. "That's the fourth cancellation of the morning. Stay tuned." (As if we would do anything else!) "And, now a word from our sponsor."

"You better sit down for breakfast, kids," Mom told us. Did that mean she thought we'd soon be leaving the house to catch the bus as usual? Was hope lost?

The announcer was back. "Okay, listening audience, the phone is beginning to ring off the hook. Newfolden, Goodridge, and Middle River have all cancelled for today. And here's the latest one...Thief River Falls!" It seemed that now that the announcer had informed us that the large school of Thief River Falls was closed for the day, he could get on with his routine work. Larry and I dismally pushed the oatmeal around the bowl, nibbled at the toast, and drank the cocoa. My stomach had way too many knots to enjoy the food. Mom laid out my snow pants and heavy winter coat.

"Oh, another cancellation just got called in. No school today in Red Lake Falls!"

Oh, sweet reprieve! Larry and I grinned at each other. A day to call our own! Mom was happy for us. "I was beginning to think I'd have to send you out to the bus on this nasty morning. Maybe I'll play some cards with you today."

"Don't forget to thank God," Larry whispered to me. "Someone from the bus department must have seen the drift we made on the corner and realized it would be no use to send out the buses."

Even as he said it, I wasn't positive that that was the reason for the cancellation, but I smiled happily. Where would we start the drift for tomorrow morning?

My Old Country School
By Gary Bjorstrom of Osakis, Minnesota
Born 1941

The year was 1947. It was the day after Labor Day. That was when school always started back then. I was six years old and it was my very first day of school. Dad drove me down the gravel roads, past Mud Lake, to that one-room school that seemed so big to me that day. It was District 29 and was also called Lakeside School to many. It is in Little Sauk Township. All eight grades were in that one-room school.

In the years I went there, the attendance was around 24 or so. Elsie Witsoe was my teacher and would be my teacher the whole time I went there. Although I had many good teachers in town school later, Elsie was my favorite. To me, she was the best! She also got stuck with me on Sundays, as she was also my Sunday School teacher at the Little Sauk, Long Bridge church another mile or so away.

Most of the kids that attended this school when I did, also went to that church. There was only one family that was Catholic and I

The teacher and students of the old country school in 1951
Gary is right in front of the teacher

remember asking Mom why they could not eat meat on Fridays. Sometimes we would have something special on Fridays, and I remember they would have egg salad sandwiches or something for them.

Like I said, the school seemed so big to me that first day. I remember years later when I came back after being in town school, it seemed so much smaller to me then. But that first day, I especially remember the smell of the place. They always varnished or oiled the floors or something over the summer, and the smell of that plus the smell of all the books, crayons, pencils and even the chalk gave it a real "school" smell.

I remember facing the flag and saying the Pledge of Allegiance every morning. That first year, the Dick and Jane books must have been fun to look at. I remember listening to the teacher up front with the other classes. We learned a lot listening to them, too. I remember Elsie standing up front reading a chapter of a book to us and I think that was part of every day. I remember Black Beauty being one of the many books she read to us.

Our school was modern for its time, as most country schools had outhouses. Ours had indoor toilets and there was a chemical tank in the basement. You could sit and hear the "splash" below. I remember thinking I had better not fall into that.

We had a big coal furnace that was built into the furnace room and next to it was a separate room that was a coal bin. I remember when the truck would come and the guy would open the coal chute and shovel in the coal.

The school at that time did not have running water yet. One of our chores was to run and get it from the old pump in back of the school. We would carry it in and fill the pitchers on a table in the basement where one kid would pour out the water over a basin so we could wash our hands before we ate. The crockery drinking water fountain was also filled by whoever had the chore of carrying in the water for that day. Another chore was to clean off the blackboards and go outside and pound the erasers to clean the chalk off.

Recess was always fun and one of the things that sticks in my mind was when we would build stick houses or forts or whatever. Being the school was on the edge of the woods, it was easy to find lots of sticks to drag together to make something neat We would often use the fence for support and put together these sticks and cover them with leaves. I think we even had a two room once. Thinking about that, I can almost smell those wet leaves. The bell would ring and we would run back inside.

I think at first, I had a syrup pail for a lunch bucket, but I graduated up to a Hopalong Cassidy one year later. Mom always had lots of good cookies or cake in there, and the sandwich of the day was often a peanut butter and banana one. I still eat that a lot today. I guess I was a spoiled kid, as I remember that often I would have a thermos with ice cream in it, too.

We decorated that one-room schoolhouse for Halloween, Easter, or Valentine's Day or just about everything that came along, but the real special effort was of course put into Christmas. We used some of the same patterns every year, and I especially remember making all those red bells with the green holly on the top. We would use colored chalk to draw a border on the top of each blackboard. We would string popcorn and make paper chains out of colored paper to decorate the tree with. To us kids, the place looked fantastic!

There were many fun things going on in our country school, but the Christmas program was definitely the highlight of the year! I remember that night so well! I remember sitting in the backseat of Mom and Dad's gray Plymouth, driving in on a dark winter night and seeing the schoolhouse all lit up and the colored lights of the beautiful spruce tree in the window. I am sure I was saying a prayer asking God that he would not let me forget my piece or screw up in front of all those people. We had practiced for weeks and had put a large stage curtain across the front of the whole room. We would put on a play and we each had our pieces and we would sing songs to a room that was packed full of people. The whole neighborhood was there! After the program, lunch was served and there was even homemade candy to buy and it was only a nickel a bag. Those where the days when everybody took the time for something like that and it was a big deal back then. The memories of those Christmas programs are priceless.

The next big event was the picnic on the last day of school. Everybody brought food, there were games to play, and we had the whole summer to look forward to. We could go through eighth grade in country school, but I was alone in my grade towards the last, so I went to town school for eighth grade. That was a big difference. If I remember right, I was getting almost straight as in country school, and that sure did not happen in town school. Must be one reason I did not like the teachers there nearly as much as I liked Elsie Witsoe.

I feel fortunate to have had the experience of going to a country school! I feel kind of bad for everybody that did not have that chance. It was a neat experience and it was in a time when the world was different and much more carefree. I could walk to school or ride my bike and back then, I don't think my parents had to worry too much about something happening to me on the way.

Actually for me, I never really left country school for very long anyway, as when it closed

The old country school now as Gary Bjorstrom's home

in 1967, I bought the building and remodeled it into my home. Those who know me well would tell you that I have been remodeling it ever since, and that I will never get completely done, as just about the time I get something done, I get another idea and start on something else. That is what makes it FUN! It was the best thing I have ever bought!

Work Hard, Play Hard
By Ronald D. Stork of Grand Rapids, Minnesota
Born 1935

My name is Ronald Duane Stork, the oldest son of Oscar and Vera Stork. I was born April 27, 1935 on a dairy farm in Todd County near Eagle Bend, Minnesota. When I was born, the doctor said that I would not live more than five days. After crying for four days and nights and not eating, my two grandmothers decided it was time to do something, so they had my dad drive me to a chiropractor in Long Prairie, Minnesota. The doctor said that he had never worked on such a small baby, but he massaged my back and neck. Well, they took me home, I slept that night, and I have not stopped eating since.

When I was about four years old, my parents bought my Grandmother Storks farm. I lived there until I was 21 years old, except for the times I worked off and on for different dairy farmers in the Eagle Bend area from the time I was about 15 years old. As I was the oldest of six children, three boys and three girls, if I wanted any money, I had to work. The farm we lived on was just 80 acres. My brothers and I called it an 80-acre rock pile, as we had to pick rocks off the fields every spring.

My parent never had much money, but we never went hungry or without clothing. However, we did have lots of love.

The old farmhouse was heated with two wood burning stoves plus the wood burning kitchen range, until Dad had it insulated in the late 1940s. Before that, if you took a glass of water upstairs in the winter, it would freeze overnight. My mother would heat up the old heavy cast iron bottoms (these were irons that my mother used to iron cloths with at the time) on top of the kitchen range and wrap them in a towel and warm our beds up before we went to bed. After Dad had the house insulated, they heated the house with one oil heater.

I just barely remember the Armistice Day storm of November 11-12, 1940. I do remember another snowstorm that same winter in the month of March. I remember it for two basic reasons. One is because my dad had to take the horses and sled to town to take the cream in to the creamery and I got to go along. I remember all the cars in the ditch along U. S. Highway 71. The second reason is because the snow blew in between our farmhouse and barn so high that my one uncle had to shovel a tunnel large enough to drive a team of horses through it. My mother had a picture of my uncle standing in the tunnel with a shovel in his hand, but I don't know what happened to it for sure. I think one of my sisters may have it.

I went to a one-room country school (121) for the first eight years, the same one my dad went to when he was a boy. In the fall and spring, we had to walk about a mile and a half across the fields and pastures. In the winter when the snow got to deep, we had to walk about four miles around the plowed roads. When it was real cold and snowy, if Dad could get the old Model A started, He would drive us to school and come pick us up. After arriving at the one-room school, the older boys would have to go to a neighboring farm for drinking water to use for the day. In addition, the teacher would have us carry in the coal for the old big round wood, coal-burning stove, which had to be fired up every morning by the teacher. Of course, the school had no electricity, so there were no indoor restrooms. The restrooms were two outdoor toilets, one for the boys and one for the girls. You did not stay in them very long in the winter. Wouldn't the child protective services have a hay day with that nowadays?

As I got older when I got home from school, I had to help with the farm work. I had chores to do like throw down hay and silage to feed the cows. Sometimes my older brother and I had to clean the barn, also, as my dad worked at odd jobs to supplement the income. Then we would go in the house for supper and back to the barn to do the milking and feed the cows again. Then come in the house and do any homework we had to do before going to bed, to start all over again the next day.

My dad still farmed with horses till I was in my teens. I rode many a mile looking at the back end of a team of horses, cutting and racking hay, hauling out the manure after cleaning the barn, or cultivating corn, hauling grain bundles to the threshing machine, corn bundles to fill the silo filler. I am so thankful that I got to do these things—things that boys don't get to do nowadays unless they are Amish.

My dad bought an old Fordson tractor in the early 1940s, and then about 1948 or '49 he bought a "B" Farmall tractor that had a two-row cultivator. Boy were my brothers and I happy! No more sitting behind a team of horses all day.

We did not get electricity till Christmas Eve day of 1942. My oldest Brother and I were walking across the field on our way home from school when we saw the electric lines running from the light pole to the house. We ran the rest of the way home and turn on all the lights, both downstairs and upstairs, and plug in the Christmas tree lights as well. (That was sort of sad, as no more candles on the tree after that year.)

My dad raised a few sheep every year for the wool. In the spring, he would have a man come over to shear them. Then my older brother and I would have to card the wool to loosen it up and get as much dirt and other things out of it. After that, my Grandmother Stork would spin the wool into yarn and then knit it into nice warm sock, mittens, and the like for us to wear as we walked to the one-room country school across the cold frozen ground and snow.

As we arrived home from school, my mother would almost always have something warm just coming out of the oven for us to eat before going out to the barn to do chores. It could be fresh buns, bread, cookies, cake, and such. What a wonderful thing to come home to.

Ronald's Grandma Stork spinning wool

As I said, we did not get electricity till 1942 and even after that we did not get a bathroom in the house till I was about 16 or 17. We took our baths in an old round washtub. In the winter, Mom would get the wood burning kitchen range going good and warm and open the oven door. When you were bathing, you would roast facing the oven and freeze your back, then turn around and roast your back and freeze your front. You went from the youngest child to the oldest. I was the oldest. I always had the most water, as Mom would add more warm water after each child got done. You did this every Saturday evening whether you needed it or not.

I would not change my childhood for anything. We did not always work. Dad and Mom made sure we had fun, too. They would take us to the movies. I always wanted to see Roy Rogers or Gene Autry or any western. We went fishing whenever it rained in the summer

Ronald D. Stork on his way to school

and we could not put up hay or cultivate corn. Sometimes we would just go to the lake to go swimming.

I made many things to hitch the horse to for fun out of old buggy wheels or old wooden wagon wheels. I even made a two-wheeled sulky out of a pair of wagon wheels once. However, the thing I made that I had the most fun doing was a homemade saddle. I took a big old log that was hollowed out, nailed a pair of sweat pads, (you used them between the collars for the horses and the horses shoulders to keep them from becoming sore) on the underside of the log. Then, I made a saddle horn out of a piece of tree branch, took a metal seat and cut it to fit on the back of the log for a back rest, and used pieces of leather straps for the stirrups. Then I used an old wide belt to put around the horses belly to hold the saddle on. It worked real well until a nail work its way through the sweat pad and hit the horse on the back. He sort of let me know that it did not feel good as I hit the dirt. He would never let me get near him again with it.

I wish I had a picture of it, not sure what happened to it, but that was about 66 years ago.

Dad and Mom sold the farm and moved to an apartment in Eagle Bend in 1990. By that time, Dad found out that he had lung cancer. He only got to live in the apartment for a year and four days, as he died on March 20, 1991 at the age of 82. Mom lived another eight years in the apartment before she had a stroke and died May 6, 1999 at the age of 86. How I still miss them.

They sold the farm to a neighbor who only wanted the land. He bulldozed the barn down and is letting the old house go back to the earth.

It is sad to visit the old farm, but yet what wonderful memory of days gone by. We boys would get Dad to sing some of the old cowboy songs while we were doing the milking by hand and then when we got in the house, we would hand him his guitar or his fiddle. Sometimes we would listen to the radio (never heard of TV yet) programs such as, Fibber McGee and Molly, The Squeaky Door, The Lone Ranger, Lux presents Hollywood, and Amos and Andy, just to mention a few.

Like I said, said I would not change my childhood for anything. We worked hard and played hard, too. We had good times and hard times, but what a great time to grow up in!

My Memories

My Memories

Index A
Hometown

Alexander Kovach	Akeley	Minnesota	184
Constance Hinnenkamp	Alexandria	Minnesota	235
Helen Kuester	Alexandria	Minnesota	43
Cindy Pazdernik	Alexandria	Minnesota	74
Marlene Pedersen	Alexandria	Minnesota	212
Marie Schildt	Alexandria	Minnesota	155
Delores D. Smith	Alexandria	Minnesota	127
Joanne Williams	Alexandria	Minnesota	100
Mark Edman	Alvarado	Minnesota	242
Robert Ronning	Auburn	Washington	231
Elmer Maciejewski	Avon	Minnesota	195
Bertina Hanson	Bagley	Minnesota	53
Sandra Renollette	Bagley	Minnesota	107
Tim Renollette	Bagley	Minnesota	111
Connie (Strandlien) Riewer	Bagley	Minnesota	20
Jill A. Torgerson	Bagley	Minnesota	220
Carol Birkeland	Baudette	Minnesota	95
Donna M. Erickson	Baudette	Minnesota	96
Eileen Olson	Baudette	Minnesota	85
Clarence Sindelir	Baudette	Minnesota	54
Grace Sonstegard	Baudette	Minnesota	70
RuBelle Towne	Baudette	Minnesota	239
Debbie (Bahr) Braaten	Bemidji	Minnesota	245
Theresa Kunze	Bemidji	Minnesota	71
Helen Goldthorpe LeClaire	Bemidji	Minnesota	249
Ardell Nyhus Lewis	Bemidji	Minnesota	59
Bernard Lewis	Bemidji	Minnesota	61
Angeline Sande	Bemidji	Minnesota	183
Doris Selzler	Bemidji	Minnesota	184
Tina Siems	Bemidji	Minnesota	182
James R. Thompson, M.D.	Bemidji	Minnesota	157
Keith H. Winger	Bemidji	Minnesota	169
Mavis Winger	Bemidji	Minnesota	233
Shirley Worth	Bemidji	Minnesota	143
Karen A. R. Duczeminskyj	Bend	Oregon	144
Mary Lou Meers Schwagerl	Bovey	Minnesota	150

Richard Allen Julseth	Brandon	Minnesota	176
Mary Lu Stephanie	Bronson	Minnesota	49
Gerald Lenk	Browerville	Minnesota	215
Marie Marte	Browerville	Minnesota	185
Kathryn Goligowski Motl	Browerville	Minnesota	248
Lorraine Trout	Browerville	Minnesota	234
Howard Tyrrell	Browerville	Minnesota	35
Jim Frick	Cass Lake	Minnesota	38
Elsie Olson Lindgren	Cass Lake	Minnesota	132
Violet Hagen	Clearbrook	Minnesota	53
Fern Jackson	Clearbrook	Minnesota	98
Elizabeth Anderson Lindsay	Clearbrook	Minnesota	57
Michelle Bickford	Cohasset	Minnesota	43
Catherine Fieldseth	Cohasset	Minnesota	223
Lynn M. Jeffers	Cohasset	Minnesota	60
Andrea Mackey	Coleraine	Minnesota	107
Doug Maki	Coleraine	Minnesota	101
Dennis O'Gorman	Coleraine	Minnesota	114
Jeanne Roberts	Coleraine	Minnesota	63
Tom Shaughnessy	Coleraine	Minnesota	98
Cecilia Merschman Plante	Crookson	Minnesota	15
Heidi Lamb Castle	Crookston	Minnesota	112
Michael Holst	Crosslake	Minnesota	22
Marilyn Hansel	Dalton	Minnesota	242
Mic and Deborah Buschette	Detroit Lakes	Minnesota	180
Ethelmae Duenow	Detroit Lakes	Minnesota	265
Carole Hagen	Detroit Lakes	Minnesota	247
Jacob Harvala	Detroit Lakes	Minnesota	125
Janice (Olson) Ramsey	Detroit Lakes	Minnesota	215
Andrea Hepola	Duluth	Minnesota	82
Thomas Salomonsen	East Grand Forks	Minnesota	76
Leonard Vonasek	East Grand Forks	Minnesota	120
Robert Weiland	East Grand Forks	Minnesota	174
Melinda K. Taylor	Edina	Minnesota	44
Janice Knight Evensen	Effie	Minnesota	60
Thomas Huebsch	Elmo	Minnesota	164
Lloyd Gran	Erskine	Minnesota	17
Darlene Greendahl	Erskine	Minnesota	77

Name	City	State	Page
Delores M. Richter	Evansville	Minnesota	170
Ethel Mindermann	Fergus Falls	Minnesota	110
Sister Mary Jean Gust	Fertile	Minnesota	116
Edward Pavek	Fertile	Minnesota	253
Daniel Thonn	Fertile	Minnesota	33
Josiah Hoagland, Sr.	Fosston	Minnesota	133
Judy Drewes	Frazee	Minnesota	199
Marlyss Rivard Hernandez	Freeport	Florida	104
Roger H. Majesk	Freeport	Minnesota	179
Norma Sims	Gonvick	Minnesota	222
Janyce Bakken	Goodridge	Minnesota	30
S. James Berg	Goodridge	Minnesota	69
Sandy Henrickson	Goodridge	Minnesota	137
Darlene Koropatnicki	Goodridge	Minnesota	211
George Newton	Grand Forks	North Dakota	126
Richard Bullock	Grand Rapids	Minnesota	97
Marvelyn M. Burtwick	Grand Rapids	Minnesota	129
Harvey Dahline	Grand Rapids	Minnesota	148
Gordon Greniger	Grand Rapids	Minnesota	156
David G. Holmbeck	Grand Rapids	Minnesota	80
Nancy (George) Rudd	Grand Rapids	Minnesota	91
Ronald D. Stork	Grand Rapids	Minnesota	272
Merlaine Taylor	Grand Rapids	Minnesota	254
Allan R. Gustafson	Hallock	Minnesota	50
Elden Johnson	Hallock	Minnesota	246
Joan Johnson	Havre	Montana	45
Arlene Jenkins	Henning	Minnesota	134
Kenneth Raap	Henning	Minnesota	219
Carol J. Sayres	Henning	Minnesota	264
Paul Twist	Henning	Minnesota	218
Gaylan Witt	Henning	Minnesota	131
Joyce E. Hanson	Herman	Minnesota	248
Harold Freyholtz, Jr.	Hewitt	Minnesota	97
LoAnn DelGrande	Hibbing	Minnesota	255
Thomas H. Gilmore	Hines	Minnesota	157
Kathleen Anderson	Hoffman	Minnesota	252
Dave Fastenow	Hot Sprints	Arkansas	168
Jack Burt	Jacobson	Minnesota	131

A. Beth Grandstrand	Karlstad	Minnesota	213
Ruth Johnson	Kensington	Minnesota	102
Scott Cameron	Kent	England	161
Patricia Peterson	Lancaster	Minnesota	224
Ginny Davis	Las Vegas	Nevada	261
Barbara Olson	Litchfield	Minnesota	66
Marilyn Dahl	Loman	Minnesota	136
Violet Kramer	Long Prairie	Minnesota	216
Karl Kuebelbeck	Long Prairie	Minnesota	63
Dennis E. Nordstrom	Long Prairie	Minnesota	64
Mabel Tesch	Long Prairie	Minnesota	197
Tim Gust	Los Angeles	California	186
Daniel R. Vandergon	Maple Lake	Minnesota	224
Nancy Dahlquist Harris	McCall	Idaho	102
Dorthy Hartel	McIntosh	Minnesota	160
Gary D. Hartel	McIntosh	Minnesota	260
Lawrence Torske	McIntosh	Minnesota	63
Rose Niemela Taylor	Menahga	Minnesota	24
Pat Nelson	Mendota Heights	Minnesota	213
Jacob Efta	Middle River	Minnesota	26
Patricia Berg Hanson	Middle River	Minnesota	130
Donovan Diekow	Miltona	Minnesota	158
LaVerne Halverson	Minneapolis	Minnesota	99
Lorraine D. Niemela	Minneapolis	Minnesota	129
David Steinhorst	Mizpah	Minnesota	79
Helen Nemzek	Moorhead	Minnesota	97
Betty (Laznicka) Kelly	Napa	California	257
Tom R. Kovach	Nevis	Minnesota	200
Cindy (Pesola) Fox	New York Mills	Minnesota	192
Joan Sethre	Newfolden	Minnesota	69
Jeffrey D. Sorenson	Newfolden	Minnesota	44
Peter Donald Gravdahl	Northwood	North Dakota	67
Carolee Bruder	Oakdale	Minnesota	80
Clifton Melby	Oklee	Minnesota	158
James L. Swanson	Omaha	Nebraska	142
Gary Bjorstrom	Osakis	Minnesota	269
LaRayne Johnson	Osakis	Minnesota	196
Gaylord H. Solem	Oslo	Minnesota	236

Alice Bergeron	Owatonna	Minnesota	175
Sarah Carson	Park Rapids	Minnesota	126
June E. Gartner	Park Rapids	Minnesota	118
Frances Paul Prussner	Park Rapids	Minnesota	166
Virginia Wilcowski Long	Pennington	Minnesota	103
Pauline Wilcowski	Pennington	Minnesota	190
Martha Wilkowski Barclay	Perham	Minnesota	205
Patrick T. Doll	Perham	Minnesota	117
Jerry Huebsch	Perham	Minnesota	46
Duane Lysne	Perham	Minnesota	167
Alta Mandt	Perham	Minnesota	228
Francis Seifert	Perham	Minnesota	207
Cynthia L. King	Red Lake	Minnesota	93
Hazel Cartier	Red Lake Falls	Minnesota	42
Lana Violette	Red Lake Falls	Minnesota	188
Henry Wieland	Red Lake Falls	Minnesota	243
Lisa A. Lundquist	Rochester	Minnesota	128
Chris Wahlberg Goodson	Roseau	Minnesota	72
Shelia R. L. Olson	Roseau	Minnesota	156
Helen Wagner	Roseau	Minnesota	214
Andrea Searancke	San Diego	California	122
Irene Twist	San Diego	California	208
Pat Twist	San Diego	California	259
Tom Twist	San Diego	California	216
Sharon Jackson	San Jose	California	153
Audrey J. Orlando	San Jose	California	253
Shirley Gillan	Sauk Centre	Minnesota	163
Betty Holm	Sauk Centre	Minnesota	25
Jill J. Holm	Sauk Centre	Minnesota	189
Nancy Pepin Kjeldahl	Sauk Centre	Minnesota	89
Connie Sell	Sauk Centre	Minnesota	86
Irene Bromenshenkel Trisko	Sauk Centre	Minnesota	29
Mary Ann Uselman	Sebeka	Minnesota	123
Vergene L. Routhe	Shoreview	Minnesota	263
Marlene Mattila Stoehr	Shoreview	Minnesota	40
Lavonne Smith	Silverdale	Pennsylvania	242
James Evans	Southern Pines	North Carolina	202
Joyce Flermoen	Spring Lake Park	Minnesota	108

Arlis Bresnahan	St. Anthony	Minnesota	56
Delores Kading	St. Hilaire	Minnesota	267
Sandra Carlson	Staples	Minnesota	128
Donald W. Coil	Staples	Minnesota	250
Jean Koppes	Staples	Minnesota	24
Richard Koppes	Staples	Minnesota	45
LaDelle Neal	Staples	Minnesota	135
Betty Flora	Sun City Center	Florida	203
James B. Allen	Swanville	Minnesota	99
J. Sharon Hertle	Talmoon	Minnesota	138
Dan Bartsch	Thief River Falls	Minnesota	76
Darlene Davidson	Thief River Falls	Minnesota	155
Marie Engen	Thief River Falls	Minnesota	64
John Sherack	Thief River Falls	Minnesota	251
Dennis Gordon	Verndale	Minnesota	47
Clarence Horsager	Verndale	Minnesota	110
Kay Keller	Virginia	Minnesota	198
Darlene Leonard	Wadena	Minnesota	171
Bette Peterson	Wadena	Minnesota	226
Marilyn Kern Swanson	Wadena	Minnesota	225
Nancy Zondlo	Wadena	Minnesota	204
Peggy Rattei Donahe	Wahpeton	N. Dakota	54
Maynard Embretson	Wahpeton	N. Dakota	183
Glennys Medenwaldt	Wahpeton	N. Dakota	127
Carol M. Kofstad	Warroad	Minnesota	66
David McKeever	Warroad	Minnesota	184
Evelyn A. McKeever	Warroad	Minnesota	71
Jinny Foldoe	Waubun	Minnesota	83
Andy Boessel	Wirt	Minnesota	98

Index B
Year of Birth

Violet Kramer	1915	216
Delores D. Smith	1918	127
Rose Niemela Taylor	1918	24
Mabel Tesch	1920	197
Janice Knight Evensen	1922	60
Alta Mandt	1922	228
LaRayne Johnson	1923	196
David McKeever	1923	184
Delores M. Richter	1923	170
Marie Schildt	1923	155
Allan R. Gustafson	1924	50
Howard Tyrrell	1924	35
Ginny Davis	1925	261
Shirley Gillan	1925	163
LaVerne Halverson	1925	99
Betty Holm	1925	25
Helen Goldthorpe LeClaire	1925	249
Evelyn A. McKeever	1925	71
George Newton	1925	126
Helen Nemzek	1926	97
Sister Mary Jean Gust	1927	116
Hazel Cartier	1928	42
Joyce E. Hanson	1928	248
Betty Flora	1929	203
Violet Hagen	1929	53
Clarence Horsager	1929	110
Lorraine D. Niemela	1929	129
Angeline Sande	1929	183
Lorraine Trout	1929	234
Mavis Winger	1929	233
Alice Bergeron	1930	175
Helen Kuester	1930	43
Glennys Medenwaldt	1930	127
Edward Pavek	1930	253
Frances Paul Prussner	1930	166

Joan Sethre	1930	69
RuBelle Towne	1930	239
Paul Twist	1930	218
Joanne Williams	1930	100
Joyce Flermoen	1931	108
Thomas H. Gilmore	1931	157
Cecilia Merschman Plante	1931	15
Irene Bromenshenkel Trisko	1931	29
Henry Wieland	1931	243
Marvelyn M. Burtwick	1932	129
Marie Engen	1932	64
Darlene Leonard	1932	171
LaDelle Neal	1932	135
Marlene Mattila Stoehr	1932	40
Shirley Worth	1932	143
Martha Wilkowski Barclay	1933	205
Marilyn Dahl	1933	136
Harvey Dahline	1933	148
Mark Edman	1933	242
Nancy Dahlquist Harris	1933	102
Betty (Laznicka)Kelly	1933	257
Jean Koppes	1933	24
Shelia R. L. Olson	1933	156
Bette Peterson	1933	226
Doris Selzler	1933	184
Clarence Sindelir	1933	54
James R. Thompson, M.D.	1933	157
Lawrence Torske	1933	63
Donovan Diekow	1934	158
Elden Johnson	1934	246
Joan Johnson	1934	45
Alexander Kovach	1934	184
Bernard Lewis	1934	61
Elmer Maciejewski	1934	195
Mary Ann Uselman	1934	123
Carolee Bruder	1935	80
Sarah Carson	1935	126
Gordon Greniger	1935	156

Fern Jackson	1935	98
Duane Lysne	1935	167
Ronald D. Stork	1935	272
A. Beth Grandstrand	1936	213
Gerald Lenk	1936	215
Barbara Olson	1936	66
Marlene Pedersen	1936	212
Marilyn Kern (Robert) Swanson	1936	225
Janyce Bakken	1937	30
Arlis Bresnahan	1937	56
Donald W. Coil	1937	250
Richard Koppes	1937	45
Elsie Olson Lindgren	1937	132
Audrey J. Orlando	1937	253
Irene Twist	1937	208
Helen Wagner	1937	214
Patrick T. Doll	1938	117
Judy Drewes	1938	199
Bertina Hanson	1938	53
Patricia Berg Hanson	1938	130
J. Sharon Hertle	1938	138
Kay Keller	1938	198
Connie (Strandlien) Riewer	1938	20
Norma Sims	1938	222
Lavonne Smith	1938	242
Tim Gust	1939	186
Patricia Peterson	1939	224
Francis Seifert	1939	207
Gaylord H. Solem	1939	236
James L. Swanson	1939	142
Merlaine Taylor	1939	254
Peggy Rattei Donahe	1940	54
Dennis Gordon	1940	47
Sandy Henrickson	1940	137
Nancy Pepin Kjeldahl	1940	89
Pat Nelson	1940	213
Jeanne Roberts	1940	63
Gary Bjorstrom	1941	269

Name	Year	Page
Ethelmae Duenow	1941	265
Dorthy Hartel	1941	160
Michael Holst	1941	22
Darlene Koropatnicki	1941	211
Ardell Nyhus Lewis	1941	59
S. James Berg	1942	69
Carol Birkeland	1942	95
Donna M. Erickson	1942	96
Gary D. Hartel	1942	260
Richard Allen Julseth	1942	176
Marie Marte	1942	185
Ethel Mindermann	1942	110
Vergene L. Routhe	1942	263
Grace Sonstegard	1942	70
Jim Frick	1943	38
Janice (Olson) Ramsey	1943	215
Tom Shaughnessy	1943	98
Melinda K. Taylor	1943	44
Chris Wahlberg Goodson	1944	72
Marlyss Rivard Hernandez	1944	104
Delores Kading	1944	267
Carol M. Kofstad	1944	66
Tim Renollette	1944	111
James B. Allen	1945	99
Darlene Greendahl	1945	77
Lynn M. Jeffers	1945	60
Tom R. Kovach	1945	200
Dennis O'Gorman	1945	114
Robert Ronning	1945	231
Carol J. Sayres	1945	264
Maynard Embretson	1946	183
Sharon Jackson	1946	153
Pauline Wilcowski	1946	190
Jinny Foldoe	1947	83
Arlene Jenkins	1947	134
Ruth Johnson	1947	102
Theresa Kunze	1947	71
Connie Sell	1947	86

Name	Year	Page
Jill A. Torgerson	1947	220
Lana Violette	1947	188
Robert Weiland	1947	174
Karen Ann Rhen Duczeminskyj	1948	144
Harold Freyholtz, Jr.	1948	97
Lloyd Gran	1948	17
David G. Holmbeck	1948	80
Jerry Huebsch	1948	46
Cindy Pazdernik	1948	74
John Sherack	1948	251
Andy Boessel	1949	98
Sandra Carlson	1949	128
Jill J. Holm	1949	189
Thomas Huebsch	1949	164
Keith H. Winger	1949	169
Dave Fastenow	1950	168
Cindy (Pesola) Fox	1950	192
Sandra Renollette	1950	107
Debbie (Bahr) Braaten	1951	245
Jack Burt	1951	131
Dennis E. Nordstrom	1951	64
Kenneth Raap	1951	219
Mary Lou Meers Schwagerl	1951	150
Kathryn Goligowski Motl	1952	248
Leonard Vonasek	1952	120
LoAnn DelGrande	1953	255
Jacob Harvala	1953	125
Mic and Deborah Buschette	1954	180
Marilyn Hansel	1954	242
Nancy (George) Rudd	1954	91
Daniel Thonn	1954	33
James Evans	1955	202
June E. Gartner	1955	118
Cynthia L. King	1955	93
Daniel R. Vandergon	1955	224
Andrea Hepola	1956	82
Nancy Zondlo	1956	204
Tina Siems	1957	182

Name	Year	Page
Jeffrey D. Sorenson	1957	44
Gaylan Witt	1957	131
Carole Hagen	1959	247
Lisa A. Lundquist	1959	128
Mary Lu Stephanie	1959	49
Pat Twist	1960	259
Karl Kuebelbeck	1961	63
Thomas Salomonsen	1962	76
Scott Cameron	1964	161
Dan Bartsch	1967	76
Tom Twist	1967	216
Andrea Searancke	1970	122
Michelle Bickford	1973	43
Jacob Efta	1975	26
Andrea Mackey	1979	107
Josiah Hoagland, Sr.	1986	133
Peter Donald Gravdahl	1993	67
Kathleen Anderson	Unknown	252
Richard Bullock	Unknown	97
Heidi Lamb Castle	Unknown	112
Darlene Davidson	Unknown	155
Catherine Fieldseth	Unknown	223
Constance Hinnenkamp	Unknown	235
Elizabeth Anderson Lindsay	Unknown	57
Virginia Wilcowski Long	Unknown	103
Roger H. Majesk	Unknown	179
Doug Maki	Unknown	101
Clifton Melby	Unknown	158
Eileen Olson	Unknown	85
David Steinhorst	Unknown	79